FROM JACOBITE TO CONSERVATIVE

What did it mean to be a "conservative" in Britain before such terminology was even used? Is it possible or even desirable to encapsulate such diverse individuals as George III, Samuel Johnson, Edmund Burke, J. W. Croker and the Younger Pitt within one political nomenclature? What is the relationship between the Jacobitism or Toryism of the early eighteenth century and the ideology of loyalist Englishmen of the latter Georgian period? James Sack confronts these questions in discussing an evolving right-wing *mentalité*, expressed in attitudes towards the past, the monarchy, humanitarianism, reform, and religion.

Although Professor Sack has consulted a wide range of unpublished and printed correspondence, pamphlets, and sermons, his chief sources have been numerous "Church and King" newspapers, journals, and magazines. From this right-wing press, Sack has uncovered a novel way of looking at political, social, and religious issues in the age of the American, French, and Industrial Revolutions. His central contention is that the defense of the Church of England, rather than nationalistic impulses, monarchical sentiment, or even economic self-interest, was the abiding concern of pre-1832 British conservatism.

FROM JACOBITE TO CONSERVATIVE

*Reaction and orthodoxy
in Britain, c. 1760–1832*

JAMES J. SACK

The University of Illinois at Chicago

CAMBRIDGE
UNIVERSITY PRESS

Published by the Press Syndicate of the University of Cambridge
The Pitt Building, Trumpington Street, Cambridge CB2 1RP
40 West 20th Street, New York, NY 10011–4211, USA
10 Stamford Road, Oakleigh, Victoria 3166, Australia

First published 1993

Printed in Great Britain at the University Press, Cambridge

A catalogue record for this book is available from the British Library

Library of Congress cataloguing in publication data applied for

ISBN 0 521 43266 9 hardback

To the memory of two bibliophiles:

James R. Carroll
(1913–1982)
and
Richard Millman
(1932–1983)

Contents

Acknowledgments

Over the past decade, so many archivists, librarians, colleagues, and friends have aided me in one way or another on the research and writing of this book, that to mention some and omit others risks a charge of caddish neglect. In spite of this, I do wish to express my deep appreciation to the staffs of a number of American institutions who have particularly assisted me. Those institutions are: the William L. Clements Library, the University of Michigan (especially Dr. John Dann); the University of Illinois Library, Urbana-Champaign; the University of Iowa Library, Iowa City; the Newberry Library, Chicago; the libraries of Northwestern University, the Garrett-Evangelical Theological Seminary, and the Seabury-Western Theological Seminary, Evanston, Illinois; and the Regenstein Library, the University of Chicago. Most especially, I owe a debt of gratitude to the staff of the University of Illinois Library, Chicago, and to Kathy Kilian of its Inter-Library Loan department. In the United Kingdom, the staffs of the following establishments were unfailingly kind and helpful: The Bodleian Library, Oxford; the main British Library (especially Ian Fletcher) and its Newspaper Library, Colindale; the East Sussex Record Office, Lewes; the Historical Manuscripts Commission, the National Register of Archives, London; the Institute of Historical Research, London; the National Library of Scotland, Edinburgh; the Public Record Office, London; the Victoria & Albert Museum (particularly Bill Pidduck), London; and the West Yorkshire Archives, Leeds. I would also like to express my gratitude to the Librarians of the Sheffield City Libraries, Sheffield, and the Pierpont Morgan Library, New York, for sending me transcripts of selected letters of Edmund Burke and Robert Southey.

The Travel-to-Collections program of the National Endowment for the Humanities and the Campus Research Board of the University of Illinois at Chicago both made available funding which facilitated my research and I would like to thank them.

The British History Association at the University of Illinois at Urbana-Champaign invited me to discuss my research with them on two occasions and I thank the participants (especially Professor Walter Arnstein) for their always good-humored criticism and comments. Two of my departmental colleagues, Bentley B. Gilbert and Richard M. Fried, read my manuscript at various stages of its development and, whatever the final result, it is a far better piece of work because of their comments. Ms. Katharine Stohrer provided me with professional secretarial guidance and, I suspect, caught far more mistakes than she was paid for. I would also like to express my thanks to Professor Gene W. Ruoff, Linda Vavra, Professor Jacob M. Price, Donald E. Geist, Chuck and Jean Kern, Katie and Sarah Kelley, and Robert, Andrew, and Jonathan McCracken.

Abbreviations

Manuscript collections

BL	British Library, Department of Manuscripts, London
Bodl.	The Bodleian Library, Oxford
CL	William L. Clements Library, University of Michigan, Ann Arbor
ESRO	East Susssex Record Office, Lewes
NLS	National Library of Scotland, Edinburgh
PRO	Public Record Office, London
RL	Regenstein Library, University of Chicago, Chicago

Printed books

Aspinall	A. Aspinall, ed., *Later Correspondence of George III* (5 vols., Cambridge, England, 1962–1970)
Burke, *Corr.*	*The Correspondence of Edmund Burke* (10 vols., Cambridge, England, 1958–1978)
Burke, *Works*	*The Works of the Right Honourable Edmund Burke* (12 vols., London, 1887)
DNB	*The Dictionary of National Biography*
Fortescue	Sir John Fortescue, ed., *Correspondence of King George III from 1760 to December 1783* (6 vols., London, 1927–1928)
HMC	Historical Manuscripts Commission
Namier and Brooke	Sir Lewis Namier, John Brooke, eds., *History of Parliament: House of Commons, 1754–1790* (New York, 1964)

Parl. Deb.	T. C. Hansard, ed., *Parliamentary Debates from the Year 1803 to the Present Time* (London, 1812–)
Parl. Hist.	W. Cobbett, ed., *Parliamentary History of England, from the Earliest Period to the Year 1803* (36 vols., London, 1806–1820)
Sedgwick	Romney Sedgwick, ed., *History of Parliament: House of Commons, 1715–1754* (New York, 1970)
Thorne	R. G. Thorne, ed., *History of Parliament: House of Commons, 1790–1820* (London, 1986)

Journals

EHR	*English Historical Review*
HJ	*Historical Journal*
JEH	*Journal of Ecclesiastical History*
PH	*Parliamentary History*
P&P	*Past and Present*
TRHS	*Transactions of the Royal Historical Society*

Introduction

I

This book attempts, as the title emphasizes, to analyze a specific and progressively crucial arena of British political life over the three quarters of a century that saw the gestation of much that is basic to the modern political debate. Between the Seven Years' War and the revolutions of 1830, or in British history between the death of Jacobitism and Toryism in the 1750s and the birth of a Conservative party during the crisis years for the *ancien régime* of 1828 to 1832, the Atlantic world saw the development of modes of political and societal expression which have abided for over two centuries of comment and criticism. As discussed below, the political usage of words such as "conservative" and "liberal," "right" and "left," "ultra" and "utilitarian" originated in Western Europe in these years as terms used to describe philosophical and political tendencies often indeed already in being and hence badly needing some concrete context for discussion. "Right" and "right-wing" (as political expressions) are terms never used extensively, if at all, in England (unlike in France) before 1832. They are used in this book to describe certain political groupings and social and religious attitudes in ways contemporaries might well have found awkward. My only excuse is the horrendous gaucherie which most other terms that did have a contemporary resonance – "Jacobite," "Tory," "conservative," "ultra" – would have if used over the entire 1760–1832 period. "Right" and "right-wing" on the other hand, while they mean something specific to us, would have meant nothing at all in England during the period under discussion and hence as neutral political expressions seem in general an acceptable, if not perfect, nomenclature to use when considering matters high flying.

The usage of "Right" or "right-wing," however, never implies my acceptance of some well-definable, homogeneous "British Right," some early equivalent of Disraelian Conservatism or Chamberlainite Unionism, subsisting in the 1760–1832 period. British political history is not so neat. This study merely posits that one can see operating within discrete political or religious groupings or in the ideological stances of specific individuals (or in the press they sponsored), certain tendencies which a later era might well term "rightist." Such a perspective might help to elucidate vexing problems in British history involving parties, political institutions, religion, the churches, and even reform.

There is an obvious danger of anachronism and special pleading in attempting to tie together for the purpose of this discussion figures as diverse as Samuel Johnson and Lord Mansfield, George III and Edmund Burke, S. L. Giffard and J. W. Croker, or tendencies as disparate as late Jacobitism, High Church Anglicanism, Pittite "Toryism," and ultra Protestantism. These individuals especially disagreed on fundamental issues and might scarcely have appreciated any subsequent attempt to unite them under such a specific nomenclature. This author would argue, however, that there are common threads, if at some times more visible than at others, which justify such a designation. Those common threads are: disposition; a peculiar form of rhetoric; a common historical vision; collective likes and, especially, dislikes; and, most important, a marked insistence, increasing by the early nineteenth century, on the spiritual, Christian, Anglican basis of English political life.

If further excuse is needed, let readers refer to the elegant essay by J. M. Roberts on the "French origins of the 'Right,'" where, in seeming anticipation of my own conundrum, he maintains that the "Right" existed before the word was defined: "There is a moment when a historical reality is coming to birth, is perhaps born, when it is not yet named, but when the awareness that there is something that needs to be named is spreading."[1]

To discover the *mentalité* of this English Right – with forays when appropriate into Boswell and Blackwood's Edinburgh and Giffard and Maginn's Dublin – I have used a variety of sources: parliamentary debates, personal and political correspondence, pamphlets, and sermons. Yet the most important source, the parameters of which are discussed in the first chapter, encompasses newspapers,

---

[1] J. M. Roberts, "French origins of the 'Right,'" *TRHS*, 23, 5th ser. (1973), p. 33.

journals, and magazines, and involves comment from the Jacobite, Tory, Buteite, Northite, Pittite, Burkeian, ultra, Wellingtonian, and high Anglican press. If one wishes to discover the inner core of the British Right in an age of political and economic revolution, a trip to that sometimes shady, often grubby, and now and then uplifting world where politics intersects with the daily leader and where politicians mingle with journalists and editors might be rewarding. The light such a journey might shed on contemporary attitudes ranging from slavery to parliamentary reform, from the apostolic succession to the poor laws might provide the material for a fundamental reassessment of certain aspects of British politics during the mid and late Georgian period.

The burgeoning British press of the late eighteenth and early nineteenth centuries, catering to various philosophical, religious, regional, and political tastes, is a subject much studied for its consequences for modernization or its relationship to political parties and factions, and little read for its actual content. In this study I hope to remedy that unhappy condition for at least a section of that press by revealing a world by no means only political in its inspiration or concerns, where the greatest of the right-wing poets has taught us that the solitary reaper sings both "For old, unhappy, far-off things, / And battles long ago" and for "some more humble lay, / Familiar matters of today."

II

There has always been a semantic problem, producing anachronistic awkwardness, whenever political ideology prior to the French Revolution is under discussion. The terms "right" and "left" or "conservative" and "liberal" are so much a part of our political vocabularies that it is difficult to consider ideological or governmental matters without recourse to them, even though the words were the products of a post-1789 world. Hence, it is common for historians of the sixteenth-century Reformation, for example, to portray Melanchthon or Illyricus Flacius as "conservative" or "right-wing," while the antinomian Anabaptists were on the "Left Wing" of the politico-religious spectrum.[2] Historians of the late seventeenth and early eighteenth centuries are apt to find "right-

---

[2] Clyde Leonard Manschreck, *Melanchthon* (New York, 1958), p. 301. E. Harris Harbison, *Age of Reformation* (Ithaca, 1955), pp. 59–67.

wing" or "left-wing" groupings all over the early Enlightenment.[3] Such linguistic practices reflect the difficulty in attempting any type of meaningful historical discourse without using the language of modern politics. This problem, if indeed it is a problem, becomes even more acute to the student of British history discussing the period from the 1760s through the Reform era of the 1830s, just that epoch when these ordinary terms of modern political discourse were born. The terms traditionally used by contemporaries to describe "Church and King" political groupings – "Jacobite" and "Tory" – (and at any time in the eighteenth century the former is much easier to define than the latter) are for various reasons no longer serviceable. The term "Jacobite" was gone forever when the peculiar loyalty which gave rise to it faded in the aftermath of the Stuart defeat at Culloden. "Tory," however, was to prove much more resilient, though its singular survival needs a more careful discussion and analysis than it has heretofore been given. Nonetheless, between roughly 1760 and 1812, "Tory" is not usually a helpful word.

"Conservative," in a political sense, is a word of the nineteenth century. Some variant of it, however, had been in circulation in England for some time, and the first edition of Samuel Johnson's *Dictionary* defined "conservative" (from the Latin *conservo*) as "having the power of opposing diminution or injury."[4] Edmund Burke in the "Reflections" nudged the word towards a slightly more political connotation when he discussed the necessity of preserving a "rational and manly freedom ... for the great conservatories and magazines of our rights and privileges."[5] Quite possibly the earliest English usage of the word in a starkly political sense occurred in June 1816 in the *Anti-Jacobin Review*, where a contributor lauded the Pitt Clubs as supporting "those conservative principles which all good men ought not passively to foster and cherish, but actually to promote, and sedulously, by combining, to perpetuate."[6] In

---

[3] Such as David Berman's "The Irish counter-Enlightenment," in Richard Kearney, ed., *Irish Mind* (Dublin, 1985), pp. 119ff.

[4] Neither successive pre-1830 editions of Johnson's *Dictionary* nor Noah Webster's 1828 edition of the *American Dictionary of the English Language* gave "conservative" a more political slant.

[5] Burke, *Works*, III, p. 276. In the same work, Burke also proclaimed that the "idea of inheritance furnishes a sure principle of conservation ...," III, pp. 274–5.

[6] *Anti-Jacobin Review*, 50 (June 1816), p. 553. Geoffrey Carnall in his important study of Southey's political views, *Robert Southey and His Age: The Development of a Conservative Mind* (Oxford, 1960), pp. 175–6n, suspected that the poet laureate himself might have been the first to use "conservative" in a modern political context. This would have occurred in a *Quarterly Review* article in July 1816, when Southey acknowledged that "there is a *vis*

Western Europe the *annus mirabilis* of the word was 1818. A Conservative Association was formed at Gloucester.[7] In January 1818, in the *Quarterly Review*, Robert Southey, the poet laureate, was juxtaposing the "struggle between the destructive and conservative principles in society, the evil and the good, the profligate against the respectable."[8] And, perhaps most important, in October 1818, in Paris, Chateaubriand launched a glittering, if short-lived, magazine, *Le Conservateur*, which ultimately secured the aid of notables such as de Bonald and Lamennais.[9] Elie Halévy in the third volume of his *History of the English People in the Nineteenth Century* discussed several additional examples of the political use of the term "conservative" in England between 1819 and 1827.[10] Yet somehow, as an ordinary method of conveying a political message, the word languished in England until suddenly, in January 1830, in one of the most famous *Quarterly Review* essays of the nineteenth century, "Internal policy," by John Miller of Lincoln's Inn, it achieved apotheosis with the suggestion that the Tory party

might with more propriety be called the Conservative party, a party which we believe to compose by far the largest, wealthiest, and most intelligent and respectable portion of the population of this country, and without whose support any administration that can be formed will be found deficient both in character and stability.[11]

conservatrix in the state." See Southey's *Essays, Moral and Political* (Shannon, 1971), I, p. 321. As the *Anti-Jacobin* article, however, came out in June and the *Quarterly* issue bearing the date of July 1816 was postponed in fact until November 1816, Southey might well have seen the *Anti-Jacobin* "conservative" reference before his own article was published. See Hill Shine and Helen Chadwick Shine, *Quarterly Review Under Gifford: Identification of Contributors, 1809–1824*, (Chapel Hill, 1949), pp. 52–3.

[7] Thorne, I, pp. 345–6.

[8] John Rickman was the ostensible author of the *Quarterly* piece, but Southey prepared the article for the press and the wording quoted here is generally attributed to him. Carnall, *Robert Southey*, p. 176. Eight months later, Southey used the word "conservative" again, in a private letter, when he admitted that reading Clarendon had strengthened his hope in "the conservative principles of society." John Wood Warter, ed., *Selections from the Letters of Robert Southey* (London, 1856), Southey to Rickman, September 1, 1818, III, 95.

[9] Strictly speaking, given the above evidence, Karl Mannheim may have been incorrect when he asserted in *Essays on Sociology and Social Psychology* (London, 1953), p. 98, that Chateaubriand first lent "conservatism" its peculiar meaning in *Le Conservateur*. In a grander context, however, Mannheim's point is well taken. Chateaubriand's magazine lasted until March 1820. See Guillaume de Bertier de Sauvigny, *Bourbon Restoration* (Philadelphia, 1966), p. 143, and René Rémond, *The Right Wing in France* (Philadelphia, 1966), p. 67.

[10] *Triumph of Reform, 1830–1841* (London, 1950), pp. 66–7n.

[11] *Quarterly Review*, 42 (January 1830), p. 276. For the solution to the hitherto vexing question of the identity of the author of "Internal policy," see Wilfred S. Dowden, ed., *Journal of Thomas Moore* (Newark, 1986), III, p. 1287.

Yet, like the term "Tory" between 1760 and 1812, because of its specific meaning after 1830, it is awkward to use the term "conservative" in a party context before that date.

It is also difficult, as B. T. Bradfield has perceptively pointed out, to rely too heavily upon that strange word "ultra" as a medium of political discussion before the mid or even late 1820s.[12] In France, but not in Britain, at least by the second Restoration, there was a consensus regarding what it meant to be an "ultra." However, English commentators were as confused regarding an acceptation for "ultra" in, say, 1820, as the French had been in the 1790s. For just as the Jacobins had used the term in a left-wing context against the Hébertists,[13] so, as late as 1823, the Dublin Orangeist daily, the *Warder*, was using the term to apply to left-wing rather than right-wing extremism.[14] To further confuse the picture, a modern historian of the pre-1832 British political discourse, J. C. D. Clark, sees the English ultras, quite correctly, as "conservative Whigs."[15]

To describe the environment about which I am writing, I have, like Jeremy Popkin in his work on the French newspaper press of the 1790s,[16] found "Right" or "right-wing" to be valuable expressions. Apparently[17] dating from the summer of 1789 in the French National Assembly, when the nobles took a position of honor on the President's right and the third estate on his left,[18] one historian of the term "Right," J. M. Roberts, maintains that "Right" and "Left" were used in an ideological sense as early as 1790 or 1791.[19] Perhaps so, though Popkin finds little evidence for this usage in the highly ideologized French press of the 1790s. In fact, he titles his book *The Right-Wing Press in France, 1792–1800* fully conscious that the label "right-wing" is an anachronism which is nonetheless helpful "because it sidesteps the polemical element in terms for the period."[20] In England too, between 1789 and 1832, let alone before that period, unlike "Tory," "conservative," or "ultra," I have

---

[12] B. T. Bradfield, "Sir Richard Vyvyan and the fall of Wellington's government," *University of Birmingham Historical Journal*, 22, no. 2 (1968), p. 141.

[13] Rémond, *Right Wing in France*, p. 37.

[14] *Warder*, March 15, 1823. *John Bull* itself termed the *Warder* "ultra beyond all ultras." March 14, 1830, p. 84.

[15] J. C. D. Clark, *English Society, 1688–1832* (Cambridge, England 1985), p. 400.

[16] Jeremy Popkin, *Right-Wing Press in France, 1792–1800* (Chapel Hill, 1980).

[17] It may, then, be just a fortuitous premonition that the *Morning Herald* on May 22, 1782 discussed the old constitutions of England crucified between two thieves, with Jacobite principles on the right and republican ideas on the left.

[18] See *Oxford English Dictionary* under "centre" and Rémond, *Right Wing in France*, p. 22.

[19] Roberts, "French origins," pp. 33–4.   [20] Popkin, *Right-Wing Press*, p. xv.

found no sustained use of "Right" or "right-wing" as part of any political discourse. The only possible exception to this observation is a remark by William Hazlitt in 1818, when, appropriately, during a discussion of the patriarchalist Sir Robert Filmer and the French Legitimists, he refers to "Right-Liners."[21] Hence, like, Popkin, I have tended to use "Right" or "right-wing" freely, finding the terms both politically meaningful and politically neutral *vis à vis* "Tory" and "conservative."

---

[21] William Hazlitt, *Political Essays* (London, 1819), p. 309. Some Foxites in December 1783, had a limited perception of themselves as the "left wing" of their Coalition. While this probably implies some sense of the Northites as "right wing," I have never seen such a designation actually used. Nor did the notion of "left wing" appear to survive the December crisis. Ian R. Christie, "The anatomy of the opposition in the parliament of 1784," *PH*, 9, pt. 1 (1990) p. 54.

CHAPTER I

The right-wing press from Jacobitism to the Reform crisis: a discussion of sources

It has often been remarked[1] that the early and mid eighteenth century saw the flourishing of a popular, ideologized, hyper-Anglican, xenophobic, humanitarian Jacobite and Tory press. This journalistic genre was not cut up root and branch by the Stuart defeat at Culloden and was, arguably, as important in setting the terms for the political debate in the 1750s (especially in its opposition to Henry Pelham's "Jew Bill" in 1753–1754) as it had been thirty years earlier. Mid-century Jacobite weeklies included John Baptiste Caryll's *True Briton* (1751–1753), and the *Crab-Tree* (1757). A tri-weekly, Richard Nutt's *London Evening Post*, retained a Jacobite orientation until at least 1754 and thereafter exuded a non-dynastic, if high, Toryism. The Jacobite-cum-Tory leanings of the *Post* were echoed by its provincial sympathizers in York (the *Courant*), Oxford (*Jackson's Oxford Journal*), and the West Country (*Felix Farley's Bristol Journal*). The mid-decade saw the birth of two influential non-Jacobite but Tory publications: Richard Beckford's Saturday *Monitor* in 1755[2] and the Smollettian, country-oriented, monthly *Critical Review* in 1756. Some of this Tory press was well subscribed to by contemporary standards. The *London Evening Post*, the most important English newspaper during the period between the administrations of Walpole and North, in its Jacobite period sold over 5,000 copies per issue, more than three times the circulation of the average London daily and almost double that of the average tri-weekly.[3] The *Critical Review*, more than holding its own against its

---

[1] In the works, for example, of Paul Kleber Monod, *Jacobitism and the English People, 1688–1788* (Cambridge, England, 1989); P. M. Chapman, "Jacobite political argument in England, 1714–1766," Ph.D. dissertation (Cambridge University, 1983); H. Erskine-Hill, "Literature and the Jacobite cause," in Eveline Cruickshanks, ed., *Ideology and Conspiracy* (Edinburgh, 1982).

[2] Marie Peters, "Names and cant," *PH*, 3 (1984), pp. 105–6.

[3] Michael Harris, *London Newspapers in the Age of Walpole* (Rutherford, New Jersey, 1987), p. 190.

rival the latitudinarian *Monthly*, sold around 3,000 issues per month.[4]

The Jacobite or Tory spirit which animated this controversial press was largely dead by 1760 or 1761, at least in the newspaper and periodical world. It would not be revived in any meaningful way until 1776. Its last gasp might well be discerned in the *British Magazine*, founded in January 1760, under the influence of two tories-of-sorts, Tobias Smollett and Oliver Goldsmith. This periodical attempted in 1761 to spice up the political and religious discourse of the new reign with favorable articles on the late Jacobite Bishop Atterbury and extreme denunciations of infidelity.[5] But whether from lack of any governmental appreciation or from lack of popular acclaim, the *British Magazine* swiftly turned towards a non-aggressive, even anti-Buteite position,[6] and ceased having much comment on politics or religion.

Other magazines that on the face of it might have been expected to display some sympathy for a "Church and King," neo-Tory, high prerogative world view, for example, the ill-fated Dr. Dodd's *Christian Magazine*, Goldsmith's friend Hugh Kelly's *Court Magazine* of the early 1760s or its putative successor the *Court Miscellany* of the later 1760s, did no such thing. All eschewed much political discussion, though Kelly's reputed journals have difficulty restraining a generally pro-Wilkite outlook.[7] The only continuing support for George III and Bute in the periodical press occurred in Smollett's *Critical Review*. The *Critical* was in fact the one example in the entire English press of a Toryish production of the 1750s shifting to substantial support for George III in all the vicissitudes of the first half of his reign.

Between the accession of George III in 1760 and the Declaration of Independence in 1776, the newspaper press endeavor of those political factions or tendencies peculiarly loyal to the king – Buteite, King's Friends, Northite – was generally pathetic. The Earl of Bute, whose influence with the young king was the direct or indirect cause of much of the ministerial instability of the 1760s, made some feeble attempts to influence the London press in 1761 and 1762. Bute may

---

[4] Marie Peters, *Pitt and Popularity* (Oxford, 1980), p. 17.
[5] *British Magazine*, 2 (June 1761), p. 71; 2 (March 1761), p. 132.
[6] *Ibid.*, 4 (January 1763), p. 32.
[7] See, for example, *Court Magazine*, September 1763, p. 409. Robert R. Bataille, "Hugh Kelly's journalism: facts and conjectures," *Journal of Newspaper and Periodical History*, 1, no. 3 (1985), pp. 3, 7–8.

indeed have known what he needed. In 1762, his undersecretary of state, Charles Jenkinson, approached the furious Tory and indeed Jacobite journalist, John Shebbeare, to aid a fledgling government press effort. Jenkinson was unsuccessful.[8] A historian of the Buteite propaganda effort suspects that except for the *Chronicle*, founded in 1760, almost the entire London press opposed Bute and supported the Pittite or Newcastle opposition.[9] Yet even this purported approval by the *Chronicle* must be highly qualified. From the king's accession in October 1760 until mid-1761, the general tenor of the paper, as reflected in letters to the editor and the position of articles or political comment, did indeed seem to favor the pacific policies of the king and Bute. Yet by the autumn of 1761, the *Chronicle* was as Pittite and pro-war as the rest of the press.[10]

Bute's lack of both independent press support and a reliable government organ no doubt sent him (or his agents) to two distinguished reporters, Arthur Murphy and Tobias Smollett. From mid-1762 to early 1763, Murphy in the weekly *Auditor* and Smollett in the weekly *Briton* defended Bute and the king from their manifold enemies. The ideological intensity of these journals was not very advanced as compared with the Tory or Jacobite journalism of the previous generation. For example, Murphy, who produced the better weekly, concluded a defense of George III's inclusion of Tories in his administration by assuring the public that such men had now abandoned Filmer and adopted Locke![11] The public response to the Buteite press effort was correspondingly pitiful. For example, only 250 copies of the *Briton* were sold per week.[12]

The post-1763 administrations exhibited no more flair than Bute's for obtaining aggressive press support. The historian of the English press in the period in fact admits to an inability to discover any government press effort in the early days of the second Wilkes crisis.[13] Indeed it did exist, but at an extremely low level of vigor. The vast preponderance of the London press was assertively

[8] John Brewer, *Party Ideology and Popular Politics at the Accession of George III* (Cambridge, England, 1976), p. 222.

[9] John Brewer, "The misfortunes of Lord Bute," *HJ*, 16 (1973), p. 16.

[10] For example, see, *London Chronicle*, March 5–7, 1761; April 30–May 2, 1761; December 26–29, 1761.

[11] *Auditor*, December 25, 1762, p. 407.

[12] Robert Donald Spector, *English Literary Periodicals and the Climate of Opinion During the Seven Years' War* (The Hague, 1966), p. 95n.

[13] Robert R. Rea, *The English Press in Politics, 1760–1774* (Lincoln, 1963), p. 122.

Wilkite.[14] Those papers, such as the *General Evening Post*, *Lloyd's Evening Post*, or the *Public Ledger*, which exhibited mildly contrary proclivities[15] were not the commanding forces of contemporary English journalism.

There were no substantial changes in the mild tone of the "government" press in the early or middle 1770s, when the North administration had succeeded the Grafton one. With some exaggeration, Tobias Smollett, ill and dying on the Riviera in 1770, wondered that North and the Cabinet took no pains "even to vindicate their moral Characters from the foulest Imputations."[16] All this altered quite dramatically in 1776 when North inveigled a popular opposition editor into changing his anti-war views and becoming the chief administration supporter in the London newspaper press.

The Rev. Henry Bate (later Dudley) was an eccentric dueling clergyman and poet,[17] a chronic debtor,[18] and, in his old age, a blackmailer of the highest in the land.[19] He was also the father of English aggressive right-wing journalism in the reign of George III. It was Bate in the *Morning Post* (1776–1780) and *Morning Herald* (1781–1782) who resurrected much of the xenophobic, anti-semitic, anti-dissenting, often High Church, quirkily humanitarian, exceedingly invective tone of the pre-1760 Tory and Jacobite newspaper and periodical press. The circulation of the Batean *Post* was high for the period – about 3,000 copies daily.[20] This was over three times the size of that of a normal London daily newspaper.[21]

The highly charged partisan atmosphere of the 1780s, while it saw raw press invective, perhaps, reach a new high water mark, did not, for reasons I discuss in the chapter below on the peculiar nature of Pittite "Toryism," encompass any significant continuation, at least on the government side, of the type of political discourse favored by Nutt in the 1750s or Bate (Dudley) in the 1770s. Oddly, the

---

14 For example, see the following newspapers in 1768 or 1769: *Public Advertiser*, *Westminster Journal*, *Gazetteer*, *St. James's Chronicle*, *Occasionalist*, *Middlesex Journal*, *London Chronicle*, *Independent Chronicle*.

15 See, for example, *Lloyd's Evening Post*, April 10–11, 1769; April 14–17, 1769.

16 BL, Whitefoord Papers, Add. MSS. 36593, Smollett to Caleb Whitefoord, May 18, 1770, fo. 83.

17 John Taylor, *Records of My Life* (London, 1832), I, p. 102.

18 BL, Peel Papers, Add. MSS. 40611, petition of Dudley to George IV, fos. 70–2.

19 *Ibid.*, Add. MSS. 40359, Bate Dudley to Peel, November 8, 1823, fo. 1.

20 Lucyle Werkmeister, *The London Daily Press, 1772–1792* (Lincoln, 1963), p. 46.

21 Lucyle Werkmeister, *A Newspaper History of England, 1792–1793* (Lincoln, 1967), p. 20. Even as late as 1801, *The Times* sold only slightly more than 1,000 copies daily. BL, Windham Papers, Add. MSS. 37853, Cobbett to Windham, n.d., fo. 19.

Fox–North organ of the *Morning Herald*, which remained in Bate Dudley's hands until 1790, and which continued with an anti-French, anti-Dutch, anti-dissenting, even High Church tone, was perhaps the closest approximation in London in that decade to a genuine right-wing press publication in the tradition of the *London Evening Post* or the *Morning Post*. In the 1790s two interrelated, yet distinct, events took place which resulted, for the press at least, in the normalization of such right-wing opinions and attitudes as part of a sustained political discourse: the radicalization of the French Revolution in 1792 and the Irish rebellion in 1798.

During the early period of the French Revolution, Pitt's government spent £5,000 per year on the press. At least nine daily or tri-weekly London newspapers received between £100 and £600 in government subsidies.[22] Although by mid and late 1792, several of these newspapers[23] were becoming aggressively "Church and King" oriented, there was evident dissatisfaction within government circles about the stability and trustworthiness of even this subsidized press. When J. Bland Burges told Lord Auckland the day after the French Republic declared war on Great Britain that the government needed two new and reliable newspapers because almost all of the press "were in the pay of the Jacobins," he was being more than normally perverse. Yet such absurd views probably reflected the opinions of the section of the Pitt administration most concerned with the anti-French propaganda effort.[24] Like the Northites in 1776 with the *Morning Post*, the Pittites in 1792–1793 decided to have absolutely dependable organs to express their views. With the aid of Pitt's friend George Rose, two newspapers were established, the daily *Sun* in October 1792 and the daily *True Briton* in January 1793.[25] John Heriot, a subsidized Treasury writer, edited both.[26] As can be seen from an internal post office memorandum, the *Sun* in the 1790s had the largest circulation throughout the country of any London paper.[27]

[22] A. Aspinall, *Politics and the Press* (London, 1949), pp. 68–9.
[23] Most specifically, *The Times* and Bate Dudley's former organ, the *Morning Herald*.
[24] Bishop of Bath and Wells, ed., *Journal and Correspondence of William, Lord Auckland* (London, 1861), II, pp. 494–5.
[25] Werkmeister, *London Daily Press*, pp. 368–71.
[26] Gayle Truesdale Pendleton, "English conservative propaganda during the French Revolution, 1789–1802," Ph.D. dissertation (Emory University, 1976), p. 54.
[27] Kenneth Ellis, *The Post Office in the Eighteenth Century* (London, 1958), pp. 160–2. The *Sun* itself boasted on January 1, 1800 that it had the largest circulation of any daily paper in the British empire.

If the absolute linkage between Heriot, the Rose and Burges circle, and Pitt is still somewhat obscure, the administration's role in the founding of the Church of England periodical, the *British Critic*, only six months after the start of the *True Briton*, is doubly so. The government may have felt as beleaguered in the realm of the quality monthlies, especially since the defection of that long time supporter of George III's policies, the *Critical Review*, in 1791, as it did in the newspaper press. The idea, even perhaps the prospectus, for the *Critic* seems to have come from the High Church, neo-Tory, Trinitarian apologist, the Rev. William Jones of Nayland.[28] The editors were two clergymen, William Beloe and Robert Nares, and there are hints of initial government involvement and Secret Service funding for the periodical.[29] By the end of the century, the *Critic* had the more than respectable circulation of 3,500 per month.[30]

The appearance between October 1792 and July 1793 of the two resolute Pittite newspapers and the (initially) High Church monthly review midwifed the revival of a right-wing mentality in the English press of the 1790s. Pitt himself (and much of his administration) did not by any means always adhere to a strictly neo-Tory (or Burkeian) political agenda and, after initial bouts of extreme anti-Jacobinism, all three endeavors sometimes reflected the cool rationality which probably inhabited the inner core of Pitt's being. Indeed in the post-1793 years, two newspapers, John Walter's *Times* and John Bell and Peter Stuart's *Oracle*, the one in its extreme pro-monarchicism,[31] the other in its anti-opposition tirades,[32] were sometimes closer to Bate Dudley's example than were the strictly Pittite *Sun* and *True Briton*. What is striking about the founding of the *Sun*, the *True Briton*, and the *British Critic* is that with the backing of sources within or close to government, a press milieu was created, and more importantly sustained, which was in the long haul strikingly similar in its religious, societal, and political appeals, in its rhetoric, and in its overall world view to the Tory–Jacobite press of the 1750s and Northite–Batean press of the 1770s. In the 1790s, however, this type

---

[28] John Freeman, *Life of the Rev. William Kirby, M.A.* (London, 1852), pp. 42–3.
[29] James Hutton, ed., *Selections from the Letters and Correspondence of Sir James Bland Burges, Bart.* (London, 1885), Burges to Nares, January 22, 1794, pp. 243–4. Alvin Sullivan, ed., *British Literary Magazines: The Romantic Age, 1789–1836* (Westport, Conn., 1983), p. 58.
[30] Walter Graham, *English Literary Periodicals* (New York, 1966), p. 189n.
[31] Pendleton, "English conservative propaganda," p. 414.
[32] *Oracle*, January 5, 1797.

of pronounced (what I choose to call) right-wing advocatory journalism, did not disappear with the end of the immediate crisis that had called it into existence. There was no Tory or Jacobite collapse as in 1760 or Yorktown as in 1781 to stifle or at the least modify its impact. Such journalism became a permanent part of the political dialogue. The Irish rebellion of 1798 and the Union of 1801 provided it with the over-riding theme of anti-Catholicism, an issue lacking during the 1750s and 1770s.

After 1793 the growth of a national right-wing press was exponential. It sometimes came from within the bowels of successive "Tory" administrations. William Playfair's weekly *Revolutionary Magazine* in 1795, the tri-weekly *Tomahawk!* in 1796 and Cobbett's *Porcupine* in 1800 were (probably) sponsored by Windhamite or Burkeite elements in Pitt's coalition.[33] Canning in 1798 was primarily responsible for the *Anti-Jacobin* newspaper[34] and, as foreign secretary, in 1808, was proximately responsible (along with his cousin Stratford) for the inspiration (at the least) for the *Quarterly Review*.[35] In 1811 Charles Arbuthnot, Perceval's secretary of the Treasury, and John Charles Herries, Perceval's secretary, helped set up that furious weekly the *Anti-Gallican Monitor* to crusade in a special way against Bonaparte as twenty years before the *Sun* had crusaded against Jacobinism.[36] Two decades later, Herries remained loyal to the outgoing conservative administration and was instrumental in outfitting the new daily *Albion* as a vehicle to present Wellingtonian views during its novel experience of opposition.[37]

Even more active than Windham or Pitt, Herries or Canning in the sustenance of a right-wing press, was the MP and admiralty official, John Wilson Croker. For two decades, as J. G. Lockhart remarked, Croker maintained an "invisible predominance over the

---

[33] BL, Windham Papers, Add. MSS. 37857, Bowles to Windham, October 1, 1795, fo. 227; Playfair to Windham, November 4 and 10, 1795, fos. 247–8, 255; 37876, Miles to Windham, January 1, 1796, fo. 1. Aspinall, *Politics and the Press*, p. 79n.

[34] Emily Lorraine de Montluzin, *The Anti-Jacobin, 1798–1800* (London, 1988), p. 22.

[35] West Yorkshire Archives, Leeds, Harewood Papers, Gifford to Canning, October 12, 1808. BL, Ellis Papers, Add. MSS. 28099, Gifford to Ellis, December 12, 1811, fo. 97. Stanley Lane-Poole, *Life of the Right Honourable Stratford Canning* (London, 1888), I, p. 192.

[36] BL, Liverpool Papers, Add. MSS. 38257, memorandum of L. Goldsmith, May 24, 1814, fos. 355–7.

[37] BL, Herries Papers, Add. MSS. 57404, McEntaggart's view of the newspapers, December 1830, fos. 5–7. A. Aspinall, ed., *Three Early Nineteenth Century Diaries* (London, 1952), p. lxii.

Tory daily press.''[38] He (along with Peel) was responsible for starting the *New Whig Guide* in 1818 and his own paper, the weekly *Guardian* in 1819.[39] More importantly, though the exact state of affairs may always remain murky, Croker appears to have been chiefly responsible for the establishment of *John Bull*, the weekly hammer of Queen Caroline during the crisis of 1820–1821.[40]

Yet most of the abundant London right-wing press of the late eighteenth and early nineteenth centuries, not to speak of its Edinburgh or Dublin counterparts which reached a national audience, was neither started by nor suggested by government moles. It arose from some variety of patriotism or High Church commitment; from a hope (often disappointed) of financial remuneration; from a concern with some specific cause – pro-slavery, anti-radicalism – which editors or publishers felt needed airing. Increasingly, in the second and third decades of the nineteenth century, the Protestant issue became the mainspring of this particular political genre.

The right-wing press of the first three decades (or so) of the nineteenth century, from which a good deal of the content of the following chapters is taken, contained an amalgam of daily, bi-weekly or tri-weekly, and Sunday newspapers; weekly political reviews; monthly or quarterly religious and literary periodicals or reviews; and magazines with some political or religious comment. Unless provincial newspapers, reviews or magazines clearly reached a more than local audience (as did, for example, *Blackwood's Edinburgh Magazine* and some of the other Scottish literary and political reviews) or clearly had a national impact on Tory politics because of their notoriety (as did, for example, the Edinburgh *Beacon* of 1821 or the furious Dublin ultra press of the 1820s) I have tended to confine my discussion to the press which originated in the environs of London.

---

[38] Myron F. Brightfield, *John Wilson Croker* (London, 1940), pp. 91–2. Croker was also the leading Tory contributor to the *Quarterly Review* between its founding and 1854. He helped edit the review during William Gifford's illness in 1823. *Ibid.*, p. 181.

[39] BL, Peel Papers, Add. MSS. 41084, Croker to Peel, July 25 and 27, 1818, fos. 242, 300. NLS, Lockhart Papers, 927, Croker to Lockhart, November 18, 1819, fo. 2.

[40] RL, Hook Papers, Hook to Croker, *c.* 1820, fo. 3. Croker also helped the *Bull's* editor, Theodore Hook, whilst he was in prison in 1824. *Ibid.*, September 1824, fo. 16. Croker's uncharacteristic boasting in 1829 about his "disciples" who in 1820–1821 were his active agents for turning the press around almost completely from opposition to government "which had, I believe, never before happened in the history of English parties," refers, I suspect, to Hook and the astonishing success of the *Bull*. Louis J. Jennings, ed., *Correspondence and Diaries of John Wilson Croker* (London, 1884), Croker to Planta, August 21, 1829, II,

Specific examples of evening daily newspapers which exhibited a rightist ideological hue included the old Pittite *Sun*, until a political turnabout in 1820; Cobbett's *Porcupine* (1800–1802); the *Courier*, at least from the beginning of its subsidization in 1809 until its own liberal political transformation in 1830; the Wellingtonian *Albion* (1830–)*; the Orange-oriented *True Briton* (1820–1822); the ultra *Standard* (1827–); and, for a few years after 1808, the pro-Duke of York *Pilot*. Morning dailies included the Pittite *True Briton*, until its demise in 1803; the fashionable *Morning Post*, dependable in its support of successive Tory ministries after 1807; the *Day*, founded by London auctioneers in 1810 and for a few years thereafter a pro-Perceval newspaper; Dr. Stoddart's *New Times* (1818–1828); John Murray's short-lived *Representative* (1826); and the ultra *Morning Journal* (1828–1830).

Except for the government-subsidized *Courier*, and that only in the closing years of the Napoleonic wars, this daily press was not especially successful. The two great Pittite papers of the 1790s, the *Sun* and the *True Briton*, riven over disputes between two of Pitt's ostensible heirs, Addington and Grenville,[41] rarely flourished in the years after 1801. The *True Briton*, shortly before it was put to sleep in 1803, was apparently selling only 350 copies a day.[42] The *Sun*'s circulation, according to a survey on newspaper dissemination made by the stamp office in 1811, was too small to even be included on its list for comparative purposes.[43] That particular survey also unearthed the information that during the Perceval administration only seventeen out of fifty-three London papers supported the government in any way. These included, besides the *Courier* which at a circulation of 5,800 per day was the most popular newspaper in the kingdom, the *Morning Post*, third in circulation at 3,000 per day, and the *Day*, ninth in circulation at about 1,100 per day.[44] In 1821, of the fifteen leading London daily papers, only four were unequivocally Tory.[45] In 1830, after the Wellington administration's downfall, a survey of the seven leading London dailies which was

---

p. 22.

*Where no second date is supplied the journal in question survived beyond 1832.

[41] Lewis Vernon Harcourt, ed., *Diaries and Correspondence of the Right Hon. George Rose* (London, 1860), II, pp. 111–12. *Sun*, February 24, 1807; March 20 and 28, 1807.

[42] *History of The Times: "The Thunderer" in the Making, 1785–1841* (New York, 1935), I, p. 75.

[43] Denis Gray, *Spencer Perceval* (Manchester, 1963), pp. 132–3. A well-informed observer thought it was only around 300 copies a day in the 1820s. James Grant, *Great Metropolis* (London, 1836), II, pp. 94–6.

[44] Gray, *Perceval*, pp. 132–3.   [45] *Literary Gazette*, June 16, 1821.

commissioned by the outgoing ministers disclosed that only the *Morning Post*, third in circulation at 6,000 copies per day and the *Courier*, fifth in circulation at only 3,500 (and unbeknownst to the surveyor, about to defect to the Whigs), supported the Tories.[46]

The tri-weekly or bi-weekly London press seems not in general to have been especially political in a right-wing direction. Exceptions included the tri-weekly *St. James's Chronicle* which gave an undifferentiated support to the governments of Perceval and Liverpool until its transformation into an ultra organ in the mid-1820s, and W. Hughes' bi-weekly *National Adviser* (1811–1812) which seems to have maintained a peculiarly close relationship with the Perceval administration.[47]

The Sunday weekly newspaper press, as J. W. Croker discovered with his ill-fated *Guardian* (1819–1824), was a difficult order into which to break (perhaps because good "Church and King" supporters were otherwise occupied on the Lord's Day). Besides the *Guardian*, the early nineteenth century is replete with right-wing Sunday papers which failed to survive more than a few issues, a few months, a few years: F. W. Blagdon's *Phoenix* (1808–1810); W. Hughes' *British Commoner* (1812–1813); the *Brunswick or True Blue* (1821); *Common Sense* (1824–1826); *Cooper's John Bull* (1826); the *Tory* (1827); and the *Watchman* (1827–1828). The editors of *John Bull* attempted a Wednesday newspaper, the *British Mercury* (1823–1825) which fared little better than most of the loyalist Sunday crop. When Blagdon surveyed the political views of the Sunday newspaper press in 1810, he discovered that of the fourteen leading papers in circulation (as estimated by the news-sellers), none were significant supporters of the Perceval ministry and most were in decided opposition.[48] Nineteen years later, a well-informed observer estimated that 80 percent of the London Sunday press was "liberal."[49] *John Bull* (1820–) and the *Age* (1825–) were the two extraordinary exceptions to this general tale of Tory woe. These satirical, venomous, and flagrant newspapers were far and away the

---

[46] BL, Herries Papers, Add. MSS. 57404, McEntaggart's view of the newspapers, December 1830, fos. 5–7. Judging from the surviving evidence for 1829 and 1830 at the stamp office, McEntaggart may have greatly overestimated the influence of the *Post*, whose circulation seems to have remained steady at around 2,000 per day. *Irish University Press Series of British Parliamentary Papers: Newspapers*, 2 (Shannon, Ireland, 1971), pp. 84–96.

[47] Aspinall, *Politics and the Press*, pp. 89–90.

[48] *Blagdon's Weekly Political Register*, July 25, 1810.

[49] *Westminster Review*, 10 (April 1829), p. 470.

most successful of all Sunday papers of whatever political stripe in the 1820s.[50]

William Cobbett, in his "Church and King" days, more or less originated the politically committed weekly review. *Cobbett's Political Register*, commencing in 1802, was arguably, in the earliest part of the century, before 1806 and its editor's transformation into a radical, the most energized, ideological, right-wing newspaper in Britain. Cobbett had three major imitators, none of whom could begin to rival the master in investigatory techniques, invective, or prose style: F. W. Blagdon in his *Weekly Political Register* (1809–1811); Henry Redhead Yorke in his *Weekly Political Review* (1805–1811); and Lewis Goldsmith in his *Anti-Gallican Monitor* (1811–1817) and *British Monitor* (1818–1825). Another weekly, William Jerdan's *Literary Gazette* (1817–), attempted, at least until the early 1820s when it ceased political comment, to present a generally Canningite world view to the public.

Besides the *British Critic* (1793–) and the *Anti-Jacobin Review* (1798–1821), which both emerged from the highly charged counter-revolutionary decade of the 1790s, a number of monthly right-wing reviews and magazines appeared in the early nineteenth century. Two, the *Edinburgh Monthly Review* (1819–1821) and the *Monthly Censor* (1822–1823), were unsuccessful. However, by and large, the format proved auspicious, most notably in *Blackwood's Edinburgh Magazine* (1817–), which in the 1820s had the largest circulation of any periodical in the United Kingdom,[51] and *Fraser's Magazine* (1830–), which was the nursery of the Victorian literati. Also important were the especial organ of the Pitt Clubs, the *New Monthly Magazine* (1814–), which changed its politics in a Whig direction in the early 1820s, and the old and liberal *Monthly Magazine*, which between 1826 and 1831 acquired a Tory political coloration. Another significant right-wing monthly, George Manners' *Satirist*, which lasted in a Tory series from 1807 to 1814, was scurrilous, provoking, fearless, and successful. It served as the prototype for the even more weighty *John Bull* and *Age* of the 1820s.

Only one of the specifically right-wing quarterly literary periodicals was extremely successful, John Murray's *Quarterly Review*

---

[50] It was suspected in 1830 that the *Age* had the highest circulation of *any* newspaper, daily or weekly, in the United Kingdom. BL, Herries Papers, Add. MSS. 57404, McEntaggart's view of the newspapers, December 1830, fos. 5–7.

[51] *Blackwood's Edinburgh Magazine*, 8 (October 1820), pp. 80–1.

(1809–). The *Quarterly* followed *Blackwood's* in circulation and far outstripped its *Edinburgh*, *Gentleman's*, or *British* rivals.[52] Others, whether in imitation of the *Quarterly* or not, were much less noteworthy. Dr. Stoddart's *Correspondent* (1817), whose scribblers included such luminaries as Southey, Walter Scott, Chateaubriand, and, possibly, de Bonald,[53] fizzled out after only three numbers. The public seemed equally unimpressed with the *New Edinburgh Review* (1821–1823) and *Knight's Quarterly Magazine* (1823–1825).

The Anglican-oriented right-wing press of the early nineteenth century included: the *British Critic* (1793–), which became increasingly High Church, especially in its several new series after 1813; the *Anti-Jacobin Review* (1798–1821), which in the second decade of the nineteenth century augmented its always substantial religious component and became known formally as the *Anti-Jacobin Review and True Churchman's Magazine*; the Oxford *Orthodox Churchman's Magazine* (1801–1808); Mrs. Trimmer's *Guardian of Education* (1802–1806); the monthly born from within the High Church Hackney Phalanx, the *Christian Remembrancer* (1819–); and the High Church *Quarterly Theological Review* (1824–1826), which merged with the *British Critic* in 1826.

Just as the initial years of the French Revolution had called forth a significant right-wing response in newspapers and magazines (as well as in pamphlet literature), so two crises in the early nineteenth century elicited a similar retort, the revival of a sustained radical challenge after 1816 and the flourishing of political Protestantism after 1812 and even more notably after 1826. None of the specifically anti-radical newspapers, weekly registers, magazines, or digests were particularly successful. None lasted more than a few years; most only for a few issues. They included: John Agg's anti-Cobbettian (but pro-Princess of Wales), satirical monthly *Busy Body* (1816–1817); the *Anti-Cobbett or Weekly Political Register* (1817); Gibbons Merle's weekly *White Dwarf* (1817–1818), and Friday weekly *Aegis* (1818); Croker, Peel, and Palmerston's *New Whig Guide* (1818); the weekly *Anti-Times* (1819); Croker's weekly *Guardian* (1819–1824); two publications geared specifically for the lower classes, Charles Knight's *Plain Englishman* (1820–1822) and the Loyal Association's *Loyalist Magazine* (1821); and W. T. Haley's anti-Carlileian *Bull Dog* (1826).

---

[52] *Ibid.*
[53] NLS, Walter Scott Papers, 3887, Stoddart to Scott: January 1, 1816, fos. 1–2; December 20, 1816, fo. 57.

Of much more moment than the specifically anti-radical press was the Orangeist or ultra press that appeared in London in the years after 1812. An English Orange digest, the *Protestant Advocate* (1812–1816), merged in 1816 with the *Anti-Jacobin Review* and breathed its fierce anti-Catholicism into that venerable publication. Lord Kenyon, the deputy Grand Master of the Orange Order, published a daily London newspaper, the *True Briton* (1820–1822). In Ireland, two ultra, Orangeist newspapers, the daily *Warder* (1823–) and the organ of the Irish Protestant Brunswick Clubs, the Saturday weekly *Star of Brunswick* (1828–1829), had a measurable effect upon not only Irish but also English ultra politics. The real flowering of the English ultra *mentalité* in the press occurred after Canning's controversial accession to the premiership in 1827. Shortly thereafter, the Baldwin newspaper empire gave its full editorial support to the ultra cause, both in its aged tri-weekly *St. James's Chronicle* and in the newly established daily *Standard* (1827–). Other ultra publications included: the Sunday *Watchman* (1827–1828); the *New Anti-Jacobin Review* (1827); the Sunday *Tory* (1827); Robert Alexander's daily *Morning Journal* (1828–1830); and *Fraser's Magazine* (1830–). Two existing right-wing publications, the *Age* and the *Monthly Magazine*, adopted extreme ultra politics in 1828.

The question of the role of successive "Tory" governments in subsidizing this press is a vexing one. The economical reform movement of the early 1780s had in effect limited the amount of Secret Service money available to aid journalists or newspapers.[54] Since, after mid-1793, the Secret Service accounts that were used for press subsidization are lost,[55] the evidence for outright monetary government press aid thereafter is not always clear. But one pattern does emerge. Before the assassination of Spencer Perceval in May 1812, there appears to have been widespread, direct subsidization of the daily press, for example, the *Sun* and the *Courier*, and of the anti-Cobbettian, weekly political registers of F. W. Blagdon and Lewis

---

[54] Probably to around £10,000 per annum: de Montluzin, *Anti-Jacobin*, p. 20. During the Wellington administration, when ministers felt that due to Catholic relief much of the Tory press had deserted them, there were actual Cabinet discussions as to the possibility of foreign ministry and Treasury Secret Service as well as (royal) privy purse funds for influencing newspapers. It was, however, concluded that little was actually available. Lord Colchester, ed., *A Political Diary, 1828–1830* by Edward Law Lord Ellenborough (London, 1881), II, pp. 408–9.

[55] Pendleton, "English conservative propaganda," p. 51.

Goldsmith.[56] As is so often the case when discussing relations between the government and the press the evidence is murky, but it seems that the second Earl of Liverpool, prime minister from 1812 to 1827, was much more resistant than Pitt, Addington, Portland or Perceval had been to this type of direct subsidization.

Though there is no evidence that Liverpool interfered with the normal subsidization of the government's chief propaganda organ, the *Courier*, there is a great deal of evidence that he attempted to rein in other Treasury officials in their normal Pittite expectations of using public money for the press. Lewis Goldsmith, for example, during the Perceval ministry, was more or less promised £1,200 per annum by Charles Arbuthnot of the Treasury, for the pro-Bourbon *Anti-Gallican Monitor*. After Liverpool became prime minister, the enraged Goldsmith saw this sum reduced in 1813 to £300 with the intention of complete elimination after 1814.[57] Liverpool eventually relented and allowed Goldsmith £400 per annum, perhaps because as he said, "He did ... render service by his Bourbon advocacy when that cause seemed lost and forgotten."[58] Liverpool personally tried as hard as possible to sever the tie between government and the *Sun*, even to the point of cancelling his own free subscription.[59] Even J. W. Croker, the government's press manager, evidenced Liverpool's coolness towards direct subsidization. In the aftermath of the Peterloo crisis in 1819, Croker sought to start a weekly anti-radical newspaper, the *Guardian*. He got a subsidy of at least £1,500 from Charles Arbuthnot out of the Secret Service funds.[60] The newspaper was an abject failure. It took Croker over four years, despite repeated requests, pleas of poverty, and perhaps justified anger, to receive the money promised him.[61] Amidst such Treasury foot dragging, Croker understandably came to feel that he held a "distinguished place" in Liverpool's "disesteem, or distaste or dislike."[62]

Yet in his many ruminations about the fate of the *Guardian*, Croker did not necessarily feel that the government subsidization question

[56] Gray, *Perceval*, pp. 87ff, 132–3, 135n. Aspinall, *Politics and the Press*, p. 81. BL, Liverpool Papers, Add. MSS. 38257, claim of L. Goldsmith, May 24, 1814, fos. 355–6.

[57] BL, Liverpool Papers, Add. MSS. 38257, Liverpool to Yorke (copy), May 27, 1814, fo. 358.

[58] *Ibid.* BL, Peel Papers, Add. MSS. 40416, Goldsmith to Peel, March 8, 1835, fos. 280–1.

[59] BL, Liverpool Papers, Add. MSS. 38268, Taylor to Liverpool, October 17, 1817, fo. 271.

[60] CL, Croker Papers, "Personal letter book," Croker to Arbuthnot, September 25, 1819; October 15, 1821.

[61] *Ibid.*, December 3, 1823.

[62] BL, Peel Papers, Add. Mss. 40319, Croker to Peel, August 25, 1822, fo. 62.

(however critical to his own personal exchequer) was the key to the failure of his newspaper. Rather, it was the lack of an indirect form of government subsidization that bothered him. For example, no government officials imparted special, inside information to either of his *Guardian* editors. No government officials bought the newspaper for their offices.[63] By Croker's time, typically, the expectations of newspaper publishers or editors friendly to the Tory administration were of indirect rather than direct subsidization.

The chief means of indirect government influence over the press involved placing (often lucrative) advertisements or official government proclamations in friendly papers; giving sympathetic papers critical foreign or domestic intelligence before their rivals; or the outright purchase of favored papers to circulate.[64] Lord Sidmouth, when home secretary in 1818, took 1,000 copies of the singularly unsuccessful *White Dwarf* for his offices.[65] At the same time, the Treasury allegedly took 300 copies daily of the stripling *New Times* to distribute throughout the country, even to the Highlands of Scotland.[66] Canning, when foreign secretary in the 1820s, fell out with normal government newspapers, and started to favor the somewhat obscure *Star* with choice information and his corrected speeches.[67]

Indirect subsidization may also have involved less sophisticated methods. One manager of the troubled Tory press during the Wellington administration was convinced that the best way to influence daily and weekly London newspapers was neither to buy them outright, an expensive proposition, nor to attempt monetary subsidization, but rather, as the editors were "needy and venal," to have trusted intermediaries flatter, wine, and dine them. After that, it would be "no great difficulty to guide their politics."[68]

The early nineteenth-century right-wing press was, of course, subsidized and aided by sympathetic groups and individuals other than successive Tory ministries. The evidence is fairly strong that the *Courier* was subsidized by Louis XVIII's government and the *New Times* by the French ultras.[69] The virulent Saturday Scottish

[63] CL, Croker Papers, "Personal letter book," Croker to Arbuthnot, October 15, 1821.
[64] See, for example, de Montluzin, *Anti-Jacobin*, p. 48n.
[65] *Fraser's Magazine*, 20 (November 1839), pp. 590–1.
[66] *History of The Times*, I, 464–6.
[67] Harold Temperley, *Foreign Policy of Canning, 1822–1827* (London, 1925), pp. 303–4.
[68] NLS, Gleig Papers, 3870, "Hints for the permanent management of the press," fos. 17–8.
[69] Temperley, *Foreign Policy*, pp. 300–1. *History of The Times*, I, pp. 464–6.

Beacon was started in 1821 by a group of noteworthy local Tories trying to fill a perceived lacuna in the newspaper press of the northern kingdom.[70] Prominent ultra peers and commoners, opposed to the Canning administration, were at least partially responsible for setting up the Protestant press in 1827 and 1828.[71] Just after the conclusion of the Reform crisis of 1832, conservative notables such as the Dukes of Buccleuch and Northumberland and the Marquess of Abercorn, aware that the party was bereft of much substantial press support, started a paper, the *Guardian and Public Ledger*.[72] However, the ostensible head of the party, the Duke of Wellington, made clear that he had nothing to do with the undertaking.[73]

There is not much evidence that the well-subscribed and successful organs of Tory opinion in the period – *Blackwood's*, the *Quarterly*, *John Bull*, and the *Age* – received much, if any, government aid, direct or indirect. John Murray, the publisher of the *Quarterly*, believed in fact that *he* subsidized – and with no favors in return – the government, "paying their undersecretaries of state, secretaries of state, bishops, and prime ministers for articles."[74]

For the government to take heed of the patronage needs of editors and journalists was a matter of a quite different order from subsidization, direct or indirect. North, Pitt, and Pitt's immediate successors assisted friendly newsmen (as well as pamphleteers). The events of 1812 and the commencement of the Liverpool administration, besides marking a change in attitude towards direct subsidization, also pointed the way towards a new dispensation in the patronage relationship between journalists, editors, and government. In the earlier period, James Macpherson, North's press manager,[75] Henry

---

[70] *Parl. Deb.*, VII, n.ser. (June 25, 1822), pp. 1332, 1352.
[71] James Grant, *The Newspaper Press* (London, 1871), II, pp. 102–3. BL, Halsbury Papers, Add. MSS. 56368, Kenyon to Giffard, July 13, 1827, fo. 59. Bodl., S. L. Giffard Papers, MS. ENG. Letters C. 56, Vyvyan to Giffard, January 25, 1828, fos. 512–13.
[72] BL, Aberdeen Papers, Add. MSS. 43243, Mallalieu's petition of 1844, fos. 125–34.
[73] John Brooke and Julia Gandy, *Royal Commission on Historical Manuscripts, The Prime Ministers' Papers: Wellington, Political Correspondence I: 1833–November 1834* (London, 1975), Wellington to Mallalieu, March 5, 1833, p. 106.
[74] Samuel Smiles, *A Publisher and his Friends: Memoir and Correspondence of the late John Murray* (London, 1891), Murray to Hallam, June 27, 1828, II, p. 263.
[75] James Macpherson, in addition to getting £200 per annum for life from Bute, apparently got a pension of £500 per annum from the Secret Service funds when he entered parliament in 1780. The £500, however, may not have been extended into the post-North era. Bailey Saunders, *Life and Letters of James Macpherson* (London, 1894), p. 284. Fortescue, North to the king, March 26, 1782, V, p. 414; reply (?), March 27, 1782, V, p. 418. Rea, *English Press in Politics*, pp. 132–3.

Bate Dudley of the *Morning Post*,[76] William Gifford of the *Anti-Jacobin* newspaper,[77] John Gifford of the *Anti-Jacobin Review*,[78] the Rev. Robert Nares[79] and the Rev. William Beloe[80] of the *British Critic*, John Heriot[81] and R. G. Clarke[82] of the *Sun* and *True Briton*, found themselves well taken care of with government pensions, sinecures, well-placed paid magistracies, and lucrative livings. Following 1812, the situation was less rosy. John Stoddart of the *New Times*, who before his journalistic career had made £2,000 per annum practicing at Doctors' Commons, was granted, upon his retirement from journalism in 1826, a knighthood, the chief justiceship of Malta, and the judgeship of the vice admiralty court at £1,600 per annum.[83] Perhaps, despite the pitiable state of his newspaper, Lord Liverpool felt that he owed Stoddart a position. This, however, was not a general state of affairs. Where Pitt had lavished patronage upon two successive editors of the *Sun* and *True Briton* – Heriot and Clarke – Liverpool refused John Taylor, who was editor after 1817, a vacant commissionership in the lottery or even civil answers to his begging requests.[84]

[76] Bate Dudley's history of government gratuities amidst out and out blackmailing is sometimes difficult to follow. He was getting £200 per annum in the 1770s. The Secret Service account paid him £3,250 in 1781. He told Knighton in 1823 that he had a pension of £300 per annum. Solomon Lutnick, *The American Revolution and the British Press, 1775–1783* (Columbia, Mo. 1967), p. 25. A. Aspinall, ed., *Letters of George IV (1812–1830)* (Cambridge, England, 1938), Bate Dudley to Knighton, December 7, 1823, III, p. 49.

[77] William Gifford in the late 1790s (or shortly thereafter) was comptroller of the lottery office at £600 per annum and paymaster of the band of gentlemen pensioners at £329 per annum. [John Wade], *Black Book* (London, 1820), pp. 43–4. *Cobbett's Political Register*, May 1, 1830, p. 568.

[78] John Gifford received from the home secretary, the Duke of Portland, a police magistracy at Worship St., Shoreditch, at £400 per annum, which he exchanged for a more lucrative one in Great Marlborough St., Westminster. He also had a £300 per annum pension de Montluzin, *Anti-Jacobin*, p. 95. *Cobbett's Political Register*, May 1, 1830, p. 568.

[79] Nares in 1799 became Keeper of Manuscripts at the British Museum. He got the living of St. Mary's, Reading, from Eldon in 1806. He was also Archdeacon of Stafford and Canon of Lichfield at £600 per annum. Aspinall, *Politics and the Press*, p. 176n. *Black Book*, p. 43. *Extraordinary Red Book* (London, 1817), p. 135.

[80] Beloe received a London living, a prebendary at Lincoln cathedral, and the Keepership of Printed Books at the British Museum. Aspinall, *Politics and the Press*, p. 176n.

[81] Heriot was a *paid* justice of the peace for London and its environs. His double commissionership of the lottery came to between £500 and £600 per annum. He was also deputy paymaster-general of the forces in the Windward and Leeward Islands. In 1816, the Duke of York gave him the comptrollership of Chelsea Hospital. PRO, Home Office, 43/12, Portland to Loughborough, August 16, 1800, fo. 72. *Black Book*, p. 43. Aspinall, *Politics and the Press*, p. 176n.

[82] Clarke was made printer and publisher of the *London Gazette*. Aspinall, *Politics and the Press*, p. 176n.

[83] BL, Peel Papers, Add. MSS.: 40525, memorandum of Stoddart, February 23, 1843, fo. 150; 40497, memorandum of Stoddart, December 1841, fo. 284.

[84] BL, Liverpool Papers, Add. MSS.: 38288, Taylor to Liverpool, December 28, 1820, fo. 377; 38278, Taylor to Sidmouth, June 29, 1819, fo. 94.

George Croly (1780–1860), an Irish clergyman and a special protégé of Croker and William Gifford (who both critiqued the young man's work and offered suggestions to improve his writing[85]) had a distinguished career in right-wing journalism. A young theater critic and foreign correspondent for *The Times*, he seceded from that newspaper with Dr. Stoddart, whom he aided on the *New Times*.[86] He edited Croker's ill-fated *Guardian* in 1819 and 1820, and contributed to Jerdan's *Literary Gazette* and *Blackwood's Edinburgh Magazine*.[87] Croly led the venerable *Monthly Magazine* into a new Tory series after 1826. For all this he received nothing from any Tory government. The *St. James's Chronicle*, which thought Croly's services were "not outweighed by those of any Archbishop, Bishop, Dean, or Dignitary now living, and who is nevertheless as independent of the establishment which owes so much to him as he was on the day on which he took orders," found this "disgraceful."[88] It was Lord Brougham and the Whig ministry which first offered Croly a living in 1835.[89]

Eugenius Roche (1786–1829), when very young, became editor of the Percevalian *Day* (1809–1811) and sub-editor of the *Morning Post* (1817–1827), succeeded Stoddart under very difficult circumstances as editor of the *New Times* (1827–1828), and ended as editor of the *Courier* (1828–1829).[90] When he died at forty-three, deep in debt, leaving a widow and nine children, the Wellington administration refused to aid the Roche family in any way.[91]

Some brilliant Tory journalists, such as William Maginn, Theodore Hook, and A. A. Watts, ended up in prison. William Maginn (1793–1842), an Irish Protestant, graduated from Trinity College with a doctorate in laws in 1816 and thereafter devoted much of his time to journalism. As the "Stripling from the West," he wrote the "Noctes Ambrosianae" for *Blackwood's*, contributed to the *Literary Gazette* and the *Quarterly*,[92] edited Hook's Wednesday *British Mercury*

---

[85] CL, Croker Papers, "Private letter book," Croker to Croly, November 26, 1816.
[86] *History of The Times*, I, p. 170.
[87] Maginn thought that Croly was Maga's "staunchest" friend in London. NLS, Blackwood Papers, 4011, Maginn to Blackwood, July 30, 1823, fo. 36.
[88] *St. James's Chronicle*, October 24–27, 1829.
[89] NLS, Blackwood Papers, 4786, 17-page MS. on Croly's life.
[90] BL, Sir R. Owen Papers, Add. MSS. 39954, fo. 14. Eugenius Roche, *London in a Thousand Years; with Other Poems* (London, 1830), pp. ix–xxi.
[91] *Fraser's Magazine*, 2 (August 1830), p. 118.
[92] Michael Sadleir, *Bulwer: A Panorama* (London, 1931), p. 243. Miriam M. H. Thrall, *Rebellious Fraser's* (New York, 1934), p. 127.

(1823–1825), served as John Murray's Parisian and chief domestic political reporter for the *Representative* in 1826,[93] and performed as assistant editor at the *Standard* in the late 1820s. He contributed to the *Age* in the 1830s, and, most importantly, perhaps, (as "Sir Morgan O'Doherty") edited *Fraser's Magazine* from 1830 to 1836.[94] All attempts by Maginn to procure some type of governmental literary patronage were failures.[95] Shortly before his death in 1842, Maginn was thrown into debtors' prison, where he made the acquaintance of another Tory outcast, Richard Oastler. When Maginn left prison in the winter of 1842 he was very ill. In a distant echo of Samuel Johnson's similar predicament in the 1780s, Oastler, hoping to send his new friend to a warm climate, "attempted, from the 'party' which owed so much to Dr. Maginn's pen, to obtain the small sum of thirty pounds, to enable him to cross the channel. The ungrateful, nay the sordid and unfeeling conservatives refused." Maginn died a few weeks later.[96]

Theodore Hook (1788–1841), the editor of the *Bull*, could lay claim to having extricated the Liverpool ministry from the effects of its greatest internal crisis, the Caroline affair. By almost unanimous comment,[97] more than any other organ of opinion, *John Bull*, after its first issue on December 17, 1820, turned around that ephemeral force, public opinion, from a pro-queen to an anti-queen stance. Hook, however, spent over two years in prison between 1823 and 1825 due to £12,000 which he allegedly owed the government stemming from the years he had served as accountant-general and treasurer in Mauritius. Hook thought he was persecuted by a vengeful opposition and not protected by a weak and timid government.[98] Both George IV and Lord Liverpool refused to intervene in the process that kept Hook incarcerated or to give or lend him the

93 Where he was known as "Dr. McGin-and-water." *London Magazine*, 6 (September 1826), p. 115.
94 Sadleir, *Bulwer*, p. 245. R. W. Montagu, ed., *Miscellanies: Prose and Verses by William Maginn* (London, 1885), 1, p. x.
95 BL, Peel Papers, Add. MSS. 40319, Croker to Peel, June 30, 1825, fo. 152. NLS, Lockhart Papers, 928, Croker to Lockhart, January 23, 1835, fo. 20.
96 *Dublin University Magazine*, 23 (January 1844), pp. 95–6.
97 Mrs. Arbuthnot's remark, when the four-month-old *Bull* was already selling 9,000 copies a week, that it "has done more towards putting down the Queen than anything ... " is typical. Francis Bamford and the Duke of Wellington, eds., *Journal of Mrs. Arbuthnot, 1820–1832* (London, 1950), 1, p. 89.
98 NLS, Walter Scott Papers, 3897, Hook to Scott, December 17, 1823, fo. 177.

£12,000 which would have secured his release.[99] This unwillingness to spring Hook from prison is understandable given the political and legal circumstances and constraints of the period. What are perhaps less pardonable are the gaps of five and eight months in the response of Treasury officials to the imprisoned Hook's enquiries about his confinement or its conditions.[100] It was in such an environment that Walter Scott saw a lack of pluck in ministers and *Blackwood's* contrasted patronization by the Whigs of their literary men and the cowardice of the Tory chieftains.[101]

To Alaric Alexander Watts (1797–1864), whom J. G. Lockhart nicknamed Atilla,[102] the Conservative party probably owed more than to any journalist of the first half of the nineteenth century. He was sub-editor of the Pittite *New Monthly Magazine* from 1818 to 1819 and was associated with Jerdan on the *Literary Gazette* from 1819 to 1822.[103] After editing provincial newspapers in Leeds and Manchester in the mid-1820s, Watts returned to London as a sub-editor of the *Standard*. Between 1833 and 1841, he edited the conservative *United Service Gazette*, and from 1839 to 1846, worked again on the *Standard*, and on the newly conservative *Morning Herald*. His leading contribution to the conservative cause, however, was his establishment or renovation, between 1823 and 1843, of twenty-one papers, at a personal cost of £8,000, in London, Manchester, Leeds, Newcastle, Blackburn, Bridgwater, Devonport, Salisbury, Leicester, Dover, Surrey, Sussex, Essex, and Kent.[104] During the second Peel ministry, the prime minister procured Watts' son a clerkship in the Inland Revenue office.[105] Nonetheless, Watts himself spent months in 1848 in debtors' prison with the leaders of neither the Peelites nor the Protectionists making any great effort to procure his release.[106] When Wellington's and Peel's old lieutenant, Aberdeen, was prime minister in 1854, Watts was granted a £100 per annum pension from the Civil List.[107]

---

[99] Aspinall, ed., *Letters of George IV*, Hook to Knighton, February 15, 1824, III, p. 64ff. BL, Liverpool Papers, Add. MSS. 38576, Liverpool to Hook, December 19, 1823, fo. 31 (copy).
[100] RL, Hook Papers, Hook to Croker: December 1824, fo. 23; March 28, 1825, fo. 27.
[101] H. J. C. Grierson, ed., *Letters of Sir Walter Scott* (London, 1971), Scott to Terry, December 22, 1823, VIII, p. 135. *Blackwood's Edinburgh Magazine*, 15 (January 1824), p. 92.
[102] William Bates, ed., *A Gallery of Illustrious Literary Characters (1830–1838)* (London, 1873), pp. 161–2.
[103] Alaric Alfred Watts, *Alaric Watts: A Narrative of his Life* (London, 1884), I, pp. 57, 107.
[104] BL, Peel Papers, Add. MSS. 40524, Watts to Peel, February 1, 1843, fos. 118–20.
[105] *Ibid.*, 40601, Watts to Peel, July 3, 1849, fo. 337.
[106] *Ibid.*, Watts to Peel, June 28, 1848, fos. 334–5.   [107] Watts, *Alaric Watts*, II, p. 275.

The plaintive and melancholy wailings of many of the luminaries of the right-wing press after *c.* 1812 might lead the historian to the conclusion that successive Tory administrations were no longer anxious to subsidize newspapers, directly or indirectly, or to aid the careers of friendly journalists through the judicious dissemination of some type of patronage. No doubt this is partially true. The second Earl of Liverpool did seem temperamentally averse to aiding newspapers and journalists. Yet perhaps disposition has in the end little to do with it. Pitt, who lavished favors on sympathetic pressmen, seemed, from a personal standpoint, equally unfriendly to them. Some politicians – Canning, Brougham, Croker, Windham, and Perceval – appeared drawn to the press, reveled in the attention of journalists, and took great pains to get their ideological and personal views reflected in a sympathetic fashion. Others such as Pitt, Liverpool, Grey, Wellington, and Peel found relations with the press at best a disagreeable necessity. Yet this may be in general of only biographical interest. Liverpool's prime ministership was probably important in press history not because of his evident animosity to the fourth estate but because it coincided with the burgeoning of the ideologically oriented, high Anglican, anti-radical press. The growth of this type of journalism – and the long-lasting prosperity of some of it – meant that successive Tory governments, under any circumstances facing declining sinecurial and Secret Service revenues of the old style, increasingly ceased to play, or indeed needed to play, as formal a role as their predecessors in any intricate system of press rewards and gratuities. But this may not have been the way publishers, editors, and journalists looked at the matter. This is a point to remember in evaluating the increasingly rancid atmosphere within Toryism or conservatism between the 1820s and the 1840s. No doubt genuine ideological differences about religion and economics played the key role in accounting for the turmoil of 1828–1832 and 1844–1846. Nonetheless, the frustrating experiences of right-wing pressmen – and the seeming indifference of Tory governments to their financial plights (so different from the sympathy of Pitt or Perceval) – should not be ignored.

In 1826, William Gifford, editor of the old *Anti-Jacobin* newspaper And of the current *Quarterly Review*, died. An obituary in the *Literary Gazette* suspected that in his importance to government, he should be assigned a rank second only to Burke's. Yet even he, said the memorialist, once asked Lord Chancellor Eldon to aid the son of a dead friend and was refused. Gifford thus had "to digest, as well as he could, the mortification which commonly awaited every political writer, of finding that the favour of a government is self-interested, extorted, and ungrateful."[108] While, admittedly, Tory governments could never do *enough* for friendly journalists, they may have paid in 1830 and 1846 for an excessive indifference.

[108] *Literary Gazette*, June 9, 1827.

CHAPTER 2

The spirit of the English Right in an age of revolution

I

Political theorists, philosophers, sociologists, and historians have often discussed and defined the characteristics germane to the parties and principles of Order. Many, such as Karl Mannheim and Max Weber, have distinguished some dichotomy between a universal traditionalism on the one hand and a conservatism grown out of the dynamic character of modernity on the other.[1] Cecil Driver perhaps had the former in mind when in an essay on radical Toryism in the nineteenth century he extolled the doctrine, with its attraction to rural sentiments, immemorial routines, and organicism, as more a term of social psychology than politics.[2] But most European historians who have reflected on the matter seem convinced that something happened, probably in the course of the eighteenth century, possibly as a result of either the Enlightenment[3] or more specifically the French Revolution,[4] which changed this universal traditionalism into a modern, energetic, and aggressive philosophy which has survived in one form or another, to enlighten (or bedevil) the subsequent political discussion. J. M. Roberts also distinguishes between a status quo conservatism and the doctrinaire "right-wing" world view which emerged in France in the 1780s and 1790s. And he feels that acceptance of this right-wing world view (or its left-wing counterpart) implies the acceptance of politics in general as an either/or business.[5] Almost two centuries ago, Edmund Burke, a man of the Right as opposed to a traditionalist if there ever was one, adopted the notion of the uniqueness of the

[1] Karl Mannheim, *Essays on Sociology and Social Psychology*, (London, 1953), pp. 94-5.
[2] Cecil Driver, *Tory Radical* (New York, 1946), pp. 30-1.
[3] Klaus Epstein, *Genesis of German Conservatism* (Princeton, 1966), pp. 3, 21-4.
[4] J. R. Western, "The Volunteer movement as an anti-revolutionary force, 1793-1801," *EHR*, 71 (October 1956), pp. 603-5.
[5] J. M. Roberts, "The French origins of the 'Right'," *TRHS*, 23, 5th ser. (1973), pp. 28-9.

1790s in terms of political life. He wondered why people of the greatest understanding did not indeed act with a sense of how extraordinary a time it was rather than proceeding as they might have in the 1750s when great errors led merely to slight consequences.[6]

Although I do not question the importance of the 1790s in the formation of a right-wing British agenda – in many ways it was the crucial decade – I would argue that the French Revolution may not have been quite as defining an experience in England as it proved to be in France, Germany, the Low Countries, or even Spain. After all, the chief issues which engaged the English Right in the 1820s and 1830s – Catholic emancipation, the Irish question, parliamentary reform, the role of the monarchy in public affairs – were not as much the consequence of the French Revolution of the eighteenth century as of the Glorious one of the seventeenth. And many of the most characteristic attitudes of a nineteenth-century right-wing English *mentalité* long antedated the French Revolution: fear and loathing of Dissenters or Roman Catholics, (or paradoxically) intense admiration for Roman Catholics, a conspiratorial view of history, Christian humanitarianism, a suspicion of abstract principles, and an identification with prescriptive rights.

If such ideological and political conflict as engulfed France after 1789 was new to much of the continent, England, Ireland, and Scotland had already experienced, if perhaps in less vivid coloring, dethroned and executed kings, a native nobility wandering far from home, revolts of the lower orders inflamed by religious passion, and military government. Out of these seventeenth-century cataclysms, at least as far as the defenders of throne and (Anglican) altar were concerned, arose a set of values, admittedly shaken and torn by the Stuart–Brunswick conflict, which served quite well as their ideological framework both before and after 1789. Consider, for example, the notion of universal conspiracy.[7] American Tories and English loyalists were often convinced that a dissenting intrigue lay behind the critical events leading up to and culminating in the American Revolution. Jonathan Boucher, in letters written in 1776, saw an overweening Presbyterian conspiracy, which by the 1790s he had refined to include both the descendants of the seventeenth-

[6] Burke, *Corr.*, VIII, p. 64.
[7] A notion which as Gordon Wood has pointed out was well established in early modern European life and thought. "Conspiracy and the paranoid style," *William and Mary Quarterly*, 39, 3rd ser. (July 1982), pp. 401–44.

century Puritans and the eighteenth-century latitudinarians.[8] The Rev. John Fletcher, Wesley's High Church friend and fellow Methodist, posited in 1776 that the English Dissenters, restless since the accession of George III, openly tried in the 1760s and 1770s to aid their dissenting brethren in America and to foment divisions in Great Britain. This might have been occasioned, thought Fletcher, to inaugurate an English revolt, overthrow the Church of England, and "raise themselves upon her ruins."[9] Thomas Jones in his *History of New York*, written in the mid-1780s, traced a Presbyterian– republican confluence back to the 1750s in New York City, when the anti-Episcopalian Livingston family and some of their friends founded the Whig Club. There, amid toasts to the memory of the regicide Oliver Cromwell, plans matured to "pull down Church and State," "raise their own Government and religion upon its ruins" and throw all of New York into anarchy and confusion.[10]

Hence in the 1790s, when the Abbé Barruel and Professor John Robison published their influential tomes illustrating the deep-seated conspiracy of the *philosophes*, the Free Masons, the Illuminati, and certain Enlightened sovereigns and their ministers to overthrow the established Churches and states of Europe, they sowed upon seemingly fertile ground. Yet the English Right far preferred its own home-grown conspiracy theories, tried and tested by time, to such exotic flora and fauna from Catholic (or Jacobin) France or Presbyterian Scotland. Seamus Deane, in his otherwise estimable study of the intellectual impact of the French Revolution on Britain, was absolutely in error when he asserted that not until 1802, when Francis Jeffrey reviewed Mounier's refutation of Barruel and Robison in the initial number of the *Edinburgh Review*, was popular belief in this conspiratorial thesis challenged.[11] Jeffrey was merely expressing commonly held opinion. Virtually the entire right-wing press at the end of the eighteenth century condemned such outlandish theories. The *British Critic* thought Barruel had failed in his

[8] "Letters of Rev. Jonathan Boucher," *Maryland Historical Magazine*, 8 (December 1913), Boucher to Eden, January 7, 1776, pp. 338–43. Jonathan Boucher, "View of the causes and consequences of the American Revolution in thirteen discourses" (London, 1797), pp. xxix, 448.

[9] John Fletcher, "A vindication of the Rev. Mr. Wesley's 'Calm address to our American colonies'" (London, 1776), pp. 65–6.

[10] Edward Floyd DeLancey, ed., *History of New York During the Revolutionary War* by Thomas Jones (New York, 1879), 1, pp. 2–5.

[11] Seamus Deane, *French Revolution and Enlightenment in England, 1789–1832* (Cambridge, Mass., 1988), p. 11.

endeavor to convict either the Free Masons and the Illuminati or Voltaire of responsibility for the Revolution *vis à vis* a plot against Christianity.[12] The *Anti-Jacobin* reviewed Barruel twice, in August and in November of 1799. The reviewers felt that the Abbé confounded Jacobinism and philosophism and they ridiculed the notion that Frederick II, Joseph II, or Choiseul had been involved in a plot to overthrow Christianity or indeed religion in general.[13] In 1800 William Cobbett returned from America where he had engaged in many years of pro-British and anti-Jacobin propaganda. He quickly acquired the new daily newspaper, the *Porcupine*. Cobbett's comments on both Barruel and Robison were devastating. Cobbett was convinced that the origins of the French Revolution were in the American conflict. In his own caustic language he remarked that

It is well enough for a man who wants to make money by a book, to attribute the troubles of the world to a conspiracy of a handful of shoe-less German philosophers; such a man may trace Jacobinism up to Cain, and even to Adam ... but for disinterested men to ascribe the French revolution to the fooleries of free-masons, and the lack of Jesuits, is a most incredible abandonment of common sense.[14]

One should never underestimate the extent to which English conservatism was a home-grown product, deriving from a peculiar set of experiences in the seventeenth century, affected, of course, by the French Revolution, but not in all its lineaments molded by it.

When British political theorists of all ideological stripes have come to define in what it was that they believed, they often, even in their traditionally empirical environment, emphasized the role of sentiment. It is noteworthy how frequently those on the Right and those writing about the Right more or less admitted to an inability to define exactly what it was that they were about and, instead, used words like "disposition" and "temperament" to convey their (or their subject's) inner core of beliefs. Johnson's friend Shenstone thought poets were Tories by nature, and hence a fanciful tribe, whereas mathematicians were pragmatic Whigs.[15] The anti-revolutionary Whig, William Windham, in 1793 found that his differences with Charles James Fox over the French Revolution could not easily be reduced to specific points but rather were

---

[12] *British Critic*, 13 (April 1799), pp. 389–91.
[13] *Anti-Jacobin Review*, 3 (August 1799), pp. 497–507; 4 (November 1799), pp. 522–68.
[14] *Porcupine*, November 25, 1800.
[15] P. P. Howe, ed., *Complete Works of William Hazlitt* (New York, 1967), VIII, p. 151n.

differences in feeling.[16] On several occasions, Boswell admitted that whatever his liking for Toryism or Jacobitism he had a difficult time defining either word or even analyzing its attraction for him. For his part, Johnson owned to Boswell that a high Tory made government unintelligible or lost in the clouds.[17] John Galt, the Tory newspaperman, suggested in his memoirs that his temperament made him a Tory and that innate character had more to do with the distinctive marks of Whig and Tory than the bigots on either side would admit.[18] Both Sir Lewis Namier and G. H. Guttridge saw the Whig and Tory divisions of the middle of the eighteenth century as latent in temperament rather than focused on particular political points.[19] Sir Herbert Butterfield, however much he disagreed with Namier on other points, concurred with him that Whiggism and Toryism were difficult to define because they lay in the realm of human thought rather than in any positivistic framework.[20]

Other commentators, of course, attempted slightly more utilitarian definitions of political terminology, though even when they did so non-rationalistic sentiments often intruded. J. W. Croker, for example, saw Toryism as a synonym for stability and Whiggism for experiment and suspected that these two antagonistic principles lay at the root of all government. Yet, the individual hankered for one or the other state on the basis of an ingrained disposition. Thus Burke, thought Croker, was always a Tory as no ministerial or political activities could restrain the original impulse.[21] Macaulay saw Toryism as guarding order and Whiggism as protecting liberty.[22] Coleridge viewed "two great moving Principles of social Humanity – religious adherence to the Past and the Ancient ... and the Passion for increase of Knowledge" operating as a sort of eternal dialectic which formed political life.[23] De Quincey, too, posited

---

[16] Earl of Rosebery, ed., *Windham Papers* (Boston, 1913), I, p. 116.

[17] Frederick A. Pottle, Charles H. Bennett, eds., *Boswell's Journal of a Tour to the Hebrides* (New York, 1936), p. 163. James Boswell, *Life of Johnson* (London, 1953), pp. 1154–5.

[18] John Galt, *Autobiography of John Galt* (London, 1833), II, pp. 196–7.

[19] Sir Lewis Namier, *England in the Age of the American Revolution* (London, 1961), p. 180. G. H. Gutteridge, *English Whiggism and the American Revolution* (Berkeley, 1966), p. 1.

[20] Herbert Butterfield, *George III and the Historians* (New York, 1959), p. 222.

[21] Louis J. Jennings, ed., *Correspondence and Diaries of John Wilson Croker* (London, 1884), II, p. 353.

[22] Lord Macaulay, *Critical, Historical and Miscellaneous Essays* (New York, 1860), VI, p. 2.

[23] Earl Leslie Griggs, ed., *Collected Letters of Samuel Taylor Coleridge* (Oxford, 1971), V, pp. 34–5.

Jacobin and Anti-Jacobin as contrasting principles as old as the human heart.[24]

II

In 1827, a short time after its inauguration as an ultra-Protestant daily newspaper the *Standard* ruminated about the connection between the Tories and the Church of England and concluded that religion stood over all other concerns for that political grouping. This was the "vital principle, from which its other principles are easily deduced as corollaries and this will be found the clue to all the actions of the Tory party ..."[25] This acknowledgment of the close association between the national Church of the sixteenth-century Elizabethan Settlement and a Tory party growing out of the cataclysmic social, political, and religious events of the seventeenth century was not unique. Three quarters of a century before, Samuel Johnson had built such a recognition into his very definition of "Toryism" in the *Dictionary*.[26] Five years after 1827, Richard Oastler put "Altar" before "Throne and Cottage" in his own definition of Toryism.[27] Fox, while admitting that Whigs considered all religion with a view to politics, suspected that Tories referred all politics to religion.[28] In fact, late-seventeenth-century and eighteenth-century Toryism may constitute the normative example for right-wing political groupings throughout Europe and her offshoots beyond the seas in the nineteenth and twentieth centuries: the union (in sentiment if not in law) between some variant of the Christian religion and an organized political party. The Christian political party represented something broader and deeper than the traditional "throne and altar" concept, and was fueled by the

---

[24] Stuart M. Tave, ed., *New Essays by De Quincey* (Princeton, 1966), pp. 49ff. For two interesting discussions of English and European conservatism see Anthony Quinton in *The Politics of Imperfection* (London, 1978), pp. 10ff where he suggests that there are two traditions of conservative thought: one, religious and including Hooker, Clarendon, Johnson, Burke, Coleridge, and Newman; the other secular and including Halifax, Bolingbroke, Hume, Disraeli, and Oakeshott. Robert Nisbet in his foreword to an edition of the works of Joseph de Maistre gives a helpful definition of philosophical conservatism *c.* 1820. Jack Lively, ed., *Works of Joseph De Maistre* (New York, 1971), pp. xiv–xv.

[25] *Standard*, September 24, 1827.

[26] See James Sledd, Gavin Kalb, "Johnson's definitions of Whig and Tory," *PMLA*, 67 (September 1952), p. 882. Johnson, of course, defined "Tory" as "One who adheres to the ancient constitution of the state, and the apostolic hierarchy of the Church of England."

[27] J. T. Ward, *Factory Movement, 1830–1855* (London, 1962), pp. 79–80.

[28] [John Wade] *Extraordinary Black Book* (London, 1832), p. 75.

realization that, as the daily Tory newspaper of the 1830s, the *Albion*, suggested, "Christianity is, in its very essence, *conservative.*"[29]

British historians in the late twentieth century have been rediscovering what their nineteenth-century and early-twentieth-century predecessors – at least through G. M. Trevelyan – seemed to know instinctively: that the political struggles of the eighteenth and even the nineteenth centuries were substantially religious in their character. Without necessarily accepting the full rigor of J. C. D. Clark's argument that pre-1828 Britain was a confessional state, few now, since the extraordinary Clarkite revolution, would agree with John Brooke or Frank O'Gorman on the relative non-religious nature of eighteenth-century British politics;[30] or, as John Brewer did, examine mid-eighteenth-century radicalism without focusing at all on its religious component;[31] or (on the literary side), like Donald J. Greene, so misunderstand Johnson's essential commitment to Anglican Christianity as to classify him with Hume, Gibbon, and Voltaire in a skeptical conservative tradition.[32] John Phillips has now registered his surprise that the late-eighteenth-century partisan alliances he has discovered in assorted English boroughs were largely religious rather than socio-economic in composition, with Dissenters usually Whigs, and Anglicans ministerialists.[33] James E. Bradley, after a judicious examination of addresses and petitions to the crown, views the politics of the 1770s and the American Revolution as based largely on Anglican–Dissenter conflict.[34] Surely the close identification of religion and politics would not have surprised contemporaries. Burke was writing as early as the 1750s that the cause of religion and the cause of government were

---

[29] *Albion*, June 27, 1831.

[30] John Brooke, *Chatham Administration, 1766–1768* (London, 1956), p. 220. Frank O'Gorman, *Emergence of the British Two-Party System, 1760–1832* (London, 1982), p. 8.

[31] John Brewer, *Party Ideology and Popular Politics at the Accession of George III* (Cambridge, England, 1976).

[32] Donald J. Greene, *Politics of Samuel Johnson* (New Haven, 1960), p. 252.

[33] John A. Phillips, *Electoral Behavior in Unreformed England* (Princeton, 1982), pp. xv, 161ff. G. H. Guttridge, of course, suspected this would be the case half a century ago when he saw the difference between Whig and Tory as largely religious with the Dissenters in general as predestined Whigs. *English Whiggism*, p. 5. Norman Gash too suggested that the bases of the Conservative party were religious and constitutional rather than social and economic. *Reaction and Reconstruction in English Politics, 1832–1852* (Oxford, 1965), p. 131.

[34] James E. Bradley, *Popular Politics and the American Revolution in England* (Macon, 1986), pp. 211–2.

similar, and a threat to one was a threat to the other.[35] From his vantage points in Maryland and Virginia, the Anglo-American Tory Jonathan Boucher was convinced that the issue of an Anglican episcopate in the New World aroused almost as much passion as the Stamp Act.[36] Lord Minto told his wife in the 1780s that religious questions before parliament tended to fill the House and arouse excitement and attention.[37] But of course it was the 1790s and the aftermath of the French Revolution that elicited the most noted defense of the importance of religion and its necessity as a bulwark for the status quo. Burke, in one of the most famous passages in the "Reflections," apostrophized religion as "the basis of civil society, and the source of all good, and of all comfort."[38] The Duke of Portland delivered a speech in the Lords proclaiming the cause of the French war to be the maintenance of the Christian religion.[39]

Examining the period from 1750 to 1832 from the vantage point of the right-wing press, we can see that in general religious themes and expressions did dominate its public discussion, cause the most fervent comment and grief, occasion the most expressive flights of exaltation and the most depressing descents into bigotry. The manner in which a right-wing tendency (such as it was) defined itself both self-consciously and in relation to other groups within the society, religious and secular, was largely cast within a spiritual framework. By the 1830s, as Professor Gash has reminded us, the Conservative party was indeed largely a constitutional and religious party,[40]

---

[35] Burke, *Works*, I, pp. 4–5. Croker too in the 1820s thought no political state could exist without a religious component. *Correspondence of Croker*, Croker to Southey, January 3, 1825, I, p. 227.

[36] Boucher, "View of the causes and consequences," pp. 89ff.

[37] Countess of Minto, ed., *Life and Letters of Sir Gilbert Elliot First Earl of Minto From 1751 to 1806* (London, 1874), I, p. 142.

[38] Burke, *Works*, III, pp. 350–1.

[39] David V. Erdman, ed., *Collected Works of Samuel Taylor Coleridge*, III, pt. 1 (Princeton, 1978), p. 127. There is, of course, a different story. Gayle Pendleton shows that in regard to government subsidized pamphlets in the turbulent 1790s a general defense of religion, as opposed to strictures *contra* opposition, the revolution, radicalism or whatever, was by far the smallest topic covered. "English conservative propaganda during the French Revolution, 1789–1802," Ph.D. dissertation (Emory University), 1976. This could be explained on several grounds. Whatever might be said of Burke or Portland, Pitt was no religious crusader and the general spiritual nonchalance of the subsidized Pittite pamphlet might reflect, albeit at some distance, the attitude of the paymaster. Then too, a government by its very nature seeks to be inclusive rather than exclusive. Hence, too much concentration on potentially divisive subjects, pitting Anglicans, and especially Dissenters and Catholics, against each other, might be something to be minimized if not avoided in times of stress.

[40] Gash, *Reaction and Reconstruction*, p. 131.

almost, if not quite, a confessional party in the later nineteenth-century Dutch or German sense.

III

It has often been recognized that the British Right in the eighteenth and nineteenth centuries, as exemplified by Burke and his disciples, though not only by them, mightily distrusted the attempted application of abstract principles[41] and greatly favored the notion of the utility of prescriptive rights.[42] What is perhaps less emphasized in modern discussions of the meaning of early modern conservatism is the role which unalloyed hatred played in defining ideology: hatred for certain forms of dissent, for domestic and foreign radical movements, for Voltaire and the *philosophes*, for atheists and infidels, for Jews, and above all, for the ancient enemy, Whiggery. Macaulay, for example, thought Johnson was a Tory more from passion than from conviction, a passion as strong as that which influenced the Capulets against the Montagues.[43] Mrs. Piozzi, more simply, suspected that her revered mentor loved a man more if he hated a Whig.[44] Hazlitt caught this mood too when he remarked that to be a true Jacobite, a man must be a good hater.[45] The Anglo-American Tory, Jonathan Boucher, loved the English Tory, John Shebbeare, despite his obvious disagreeable qualities, because of his abuse of the Presbyterians.[46]

The ubiquitous right-wing hatred of Dissenters and more equivocal hatred of Roman Catholics will be discussed below. Those on the Right also hated, of course, the main intellectual analysis of the *philosophes*, most pronouncedly when it verged on Deism. Praise of

---

[41] For example, Charles Butler in his "Sketch of Mansfield," suggests that the earl reprobated even the discussion of abstract principles as "the exchange of the well for the better was a dangerous experiment." *Philological and Biographical Works* (London, 1817), II, p. 223.

[42] This was true not only of Burke but of the conservative Whig, Dean Tucker, in his case against Locke in 1783, and of the Tory John Shebbeare in his "Second letter to the people of England" in 1755. Tucker, "Four letters on important national subjects addressed to ... the earl of Shelburne" (London, 1783), p. 110. Shebbeare (London, 1755), pp. 7–8.

[43] Macaulay, *Critical Essays*, VI, p. 182.

[44] S. C. Roberts, ed., *Anecdotes of Samuel Johnson* by Hester Lynch Piozzi (Freeport, New York, 1969), pp. 56–8.

[45] William Hazlitt, *Political Essays* (London, 1819), p. 167.

[46] "Letters of Boucher," IX, p. 66. Of course it may have worked the other way too. Sir Roger Newdigate told the British resident at Vienna in 1776 that the American war would go on for years because the colonials would not yield: "they hate your Government because they hate your religion." BL, Eg. 2001, Strange MSS. Newdigate to Strange, n.d.

both Voltaire and Rousseau, for example, was fairly common in the Tory press of the 1750s and 1760s,[47] but after the outbreak of the French Revolution one can find little save the most vicious attacks upon either individual in "Church and King" circles. Burke's terrible and famous denunciation of Rousseau "as a sort of offal and excrement, [who sends] the spawn of his disgustful amours" to a foundling hospital, is typical.[48] Lord Holland told Tom Moore in 1821 that at the beginning of the revolution, Lord Eldon (as he later became) burned his copy of Voltaire's works and Lord Grenville turned his out of his library.[49] Southey thought Voltaire the "arch-infidel."[50] The *New Times*, a relatively liberal Tory daily, found the Sage of Fernay an "impious, obscene, and traitorous wretch ... [the] everlasting disgrace of his age and country..."[51]

The Right hated Jacobinism and other foreign-sounding European radical movements. It particularly despised female radicals, domestic and foreign, such as Helena Maria Williams, Mary Wollstonecraft, Madame Roland, Mary Ann Carlile and even Madame de Staël, as well as those native male Britons, like Richard Carlile or even Gibbon, whose thinking merged into infidelity and atheism. All such received from the Right in general a sustained and unbending critique often bordering on hysteria. The short-lived Tory Sunday newspaper, *The Brunswick or True Blue* was typical in its assessment, in 1821, when it lumped together the Jacobins of France, the Radicals of England, the Carbonari of Italy, and the Illuminati of Germany as "one and the same kidney" and "bound in common bond of hatred against order, religion, and the best interests of mankind."[52]

One hesitates to state categorically that the English Right in general hated and loathed all forms of radicalism. As will be seen below, significant sections of the Right could adopt singularly advanced positions on subjects ranging from parliamentary reform to anti-slavery to the Irish question. What was difficult or even impossible for it to countenance and what brought all sorts of perfervid emotions to the surface was any suggestion of sexual or religious deviance from accepted familial or spiritual orthodoxies. It

---

[47] *Critical Review*, 7 (January 1759), p. 48; 11 (May 1761), p. 377; 14 (December 1762), pp. 426–39; 23 (May 1767), pp. 374–5.
[48] Burke, *Works*, iv, p. 25.
[49] Wilfred S. Dowden, ed., *Journal of Thomas Moore* (Newark, 1983), ii, p. 464.
[50] Robert Southey, *Life of Wesley and the Rise and Progress of Methodism* (London, 1820), i, p. 2.
[51] *New Times*, July 3, 1819.   [52] *Brunswick or True Blue*, March 18, 1821.

was in opposition to such deviance, rather than from any overwhelming concern for the agricultural interest or opposition to the
land tax, that the uncompromising elements of the early-nineteenth-
century Right in particular came forth. Burke, in his famous letter to
his friend Mrs. Crewe, seeing the temporary explosion of a fledgling
European feminism after 1789, at least paid his opponents the
compliment of taking them seriously in that he thought

> this is no trifling game they are playing. I hope and supplicate that all
> providant and virtuous Wives and Mothers of families will employ all the
> just influence they possess over their husbands and children, to save
> themselves and their families from the ruin [which] ... all that clan of
> desperate, wicked, and mischievously ingenious Women, who have
> brought, or are likely to bring Ruin and shame upon all those that listen to
> them. You ought to make their names odious to your Children.[53]

Canning's highly successful *Anti-Jacobin* newspaper was founded in
1797, partly in order to take on a radical press which ridiculed
chastity and discussed indecency and in which "the *Cross of Christ* is
trampled on with savage exultation."[54] The *Quarterly Review*, a
relatively moderate Tory journal and certainly by no stretch of the
imagination an ultra publication, rejoiced in 1815 at Gibbon's fatal
hydrocele, regarding it as poetic justice for that intellectual debau-
chee.[55]

Surprisingly perhaps, hatred of Jews may have been more prominent on the British Right before than after the French Revolution,
despite Burke's attacks on "Jew brokers" and "Jew Jobbers" in the
1790s.[56] The High Church Tory clique around Jones of Nayland
and Bishop Horne of Norwich, the Tory publicist John Shebbeare,
and the leading Northite newspaper agent of the 1770s, Henry Bate
Dudley, not to speak of the largely Tory-oriented opposition to the
Pelhamite Jew Bill of 1753, gave an anti-semitic tone to eighteenth-
century Toryism or "Church and King" groups that were not
especially sustained in Toryism's nineteenth-century form.[57]
Perhaps part of this decline in right-wing anti-semitism can be

---

[53] Burke, *Corr.*, VIII, pp. 303–4.   [54] *Anti-Jacobin*, April 9, 1798, pp. 119–21.
[55] *Quarterly Review*, 12 (January 1815), pp. 389–91.
[56] Burke, *Works*, III, pp. 294–5, 303.
[57] See, for example, William Jones, *Works of the Right Reverend George Horne, D.D.* (New York,
    1846), I, pp. xvi, 39–42, or John Shebbeare in "A sixth letter to the people of England"
    (London, 1757), p. 18 or *Marriage Act: A Novel* (London, 1754), II, p. 327, in which the
    prominent literary Tory declares the Jews "a Race, whose Lives and Characters are and
    have been, the most infamous and detestable of all the Nations upon Earth, in all places
    where they have resided."

traced to the failure of the leading conspiracy theorists to include specifically Jewish elements in their well-stocked catalogue.[58] Lewis Goldsmith, proprietor and editor of two newspapers highly subsidized by the Perceval and Liverpool administrations, the *Anti-Gallican Monitor* and the *British Monitor*, was an unconverted Jew who made no apologies for his creed or his co-religionists. This may have soured anti-semitic tendencies among his newspaper peers. Even during the Hundred Days, Goldsmith was extolling the French Revolution in his newspaper for the benefit which it conferred on Jews.[59] Much of the right-wing press, both ultra Protestant and Wellingtonian Tory, supported an end to Jewish political disabilities in 1829 and 1830, when the issue came up in the House of Commons. The *Morning Post*, by 1830 probably the leading Tory daily paper loyal to the Duke of Wellington and Robert Peel, supported the Jewish cause as a matter of justice.[60] So did the violently ultra, anti-Wellington, *Monthly Magazine*, edited by the Rev. George Croly.[61] The two leading ultra Protestant dailies of the late 1820s, the *Morning Journal* and the *Standard*, were both sympathetic to the removal of the disabilities, the former enthusiastically so.[62] Reviewers for the *Quarterly* had supported the removal of Jewish disabilities since 1815.[63]

One could encounter some furious anti-semitism in the early nineteenth-century right-wing press. *John Bull* frequently denounced "Jew money-lenders" in the 1820s and in its opposition to emancipation proclaimed Jews "branded with an indelible mark"[64]; *Fraser's Magazine*, too, opposed Jewish emancipation on the religious grounds of their rejection of the true Messiah.[65] However, the *Bull* and *Fraser's* were the exception and not the rule among the Tory publications in their opposition to the removal of Jewish disabilities. The conservative milieu which the young baptized Benjamin Disraeli adopted for his own in that period, while certainly not free of anti-semitism, was remarkably tolerant of Jews given its remarkable intolerance for other non-Anglican social or religious groups.

---

58 For which the Abbé Barruel at least was taken to task by one correspondent in 1806. J. M. Roberts, *Mythology of Secret Societies* (London, 1972), pp. 274–5.
59 *Anti-Gallican Monitor*, April 30, 1815.   60 *Morning Post*, May 18, 1830.
61 *Monthly Magazine*, 9 (March 1830), p. 260.
62 *Morning Journal*, September 4, 1829. *Standard*, May 3 and 18, 1830.
63 *Quarterly Review*, 14 (October 1815), pp. 51–2.
64 *John Bull*, September 10, 1826, p. 293; April 25, 1830, p. 132.
65 *Fraser's Magazine*, 1 (June 1830), p. 541.

English Whiggery (especially in the Foxite version after 1782) served as the perfect foil for anti-Whig groups of a "Church and King" inclination to combine in one bundle opposition to atheism, latitudinarianism, dissent, sexual promiscuity, and advanced radical politics.

Richard Brent has written an insightful monograph on a deeply religious third generation of liberal Whig Anglicans who prepared the way for the age of Gladstone.[66] However, before 1832, insofar as the Tory press had anything to do with it, the image was popularized of what Robert Peel's subsidized magazine, the *Bull Dog*, called "Atheistic Whigs."[67] The Tory attack upon the Whigs as excessively tolerant of latitudinarian, Dissenter, Socinian, infidel, and atheist commenced with the birth of the two parties in the 1670s and 1680s and like most such long-lasting assaults had some element of truth. The current fashion, in the work of J. C. D. Clark and Reed Browning in particular,[68] of viewing early and mid-Georgian Whiggery as possessed of its own version of divine right (rather than contractarian) theory and High Church even non-juring orientation, while no doubt illuminating certain obscure cracks and crevices of the Whig polity, like much revisionism, somewhat obscures the larger picture.

For despite the sound churchmanship of a Newcastle or a Rockingham, there was always plenty of reason to suspect the eternal devotion of crucial elements of Whiggery towards the Church of England or even towards Christianity itself. This was not a foreign idea to the Whigs themselves. In his largely pro-Whig account of George III's reign published in 1803, Robert Bisset, while clearly approving the main thrust of foreign and domestic British policy after 1714, does condemn the Whigs of the reigns of George I and George II for their indifference to religion, their impiety, and their promotion of infidels.[69] Even "A Country Gentleman," the anti-Bute, pro-Rockingham author of the influential 1766 pamphlet "A Parallel," thought that if only the Whigs had taken as good care of the Church as they had of the state in the

[66] Richard Brent, *Liberal Anglican Politics: Whiggery, Religion, and Reform, 1830–1841* (Oxford, 1987).

[67] *Bull Dog*, September 9, 1826.

[68] Reed Browning, *Political and Constitutional Ideas of Court Whigs* (Baton Rouge, 1982), pp. 90–6, 199. J. C. D. Clark, *English Society, 1688–1832* (Cambridge, England, 1985), pp. 182, 276, 408.

[69] Robert Bisset, *History of the Reign of George III* (London, 1803), i, p. 138.

previous reign, all would have been well for them in the 1760s.[70] So when "James III" issued his "Declaration" in 1743, as a prelude to the expected Jacobite–French invasion of Britain, and condemned the Hanoverian regime for "a more than tacit connivance given to all irreligion and immorality,"[71] he was probably touching a nerve common to all vaguely libertarian establishments: in their zest for some type of personal freedom of thought or expression (at least for the higher classes) they would abandon, or ignore, or libel, the traditional and far from libertarian religious orthodoxy.

It goes without saying that the Foxite Whigs, some of their predecessors, and many of their successors, scattered about Holland House, St. Anne's Hill, Chatsworth, Carlton House, Howick, or Woburn Abbey, were sexually and philosophically libertarian. They were also, perhaps most fatally to their political chances, seen to be such and hence open to extraordinary attack by their more strait-laced (or closeted) political enemies and by the Jacobite and Tory press. This sort of attack was a staple of the Tory party before the mid-1760s and was to be a staple of the revived Toryism of the 1790s and beyond. In fact, severe attack on Whig irreligion and impiety is one of the threads, along with dislike of Dissenters and a sort of ersatz humanitarianism which explicitly unites the two ages of Tory philosophical and political agendas. Hence in the 1750s and 1760s, one had, for example, the Tory publicist John Shebbeare asserting that the Whigs were directly responsible for the evil of infidelity, from which terrible sexual debauchery resulted.[72] "Britannicus," the leading political commentator for the Tory *London Evening Post*, echoed this view.[73] During and after the French Revolution, attacks upon Whig individuals on such grounds abound: the *Standard* accused Lady Holland of atheism;[74] the *Tomahawk!* denounced the fifth Duke of Bedford's "sordid propensities" and Sheridan's alcoholism;[75] the *Anti-Jacobin Review*, besides stigmatizing Mrs. Armistead as the partner of Fox's "illicit amours," spent several years in the early nineteenth century dredging up filth

---

[70] "A parallel; drawn between the administration in the four last years of Queen Anne, and the four first of George the Third" (London, 1766), pp. 25, 30–2.
[71] Eveline Cruickshanks, *Political Untouchables: The Tories and the '45* (New York, 1979), p. 48.
[72] John Shebbeare, *History of the Sumatrans* (London, 1763), I, p. 241.
[73] *London Evening Post*, December 20–27, 1757.
[74] *Standard*, January 3, 1828. For a good discussion of skepticism, if not outright atheism, at the *Edinburgh Review*, see Biancamaria Fontana, *Rethinking the Politics of Commercial Society: the Edinburgh Review, 1802–1832* (Cambridge, England, 1985), p. 87.
[75] *Tomahawk!*, November 24 and 27, 1795.

regarding the late Duke of Bedford's irregular sexual and religious life.[76] *John Bull* was, of course, the most egregious hammer of the Whigs, with its slurs on homosexual, premarital, and master–servant sexual relationships within leading Whig families.[77]

How much such incessant criticism and comment hurt the Whig party during the half-century of their political Golgotha is difficult to say. They were ostensibly kept out of power between 1783 and 1830 because no sovereign would call upon them to form a government. But the fact that an anti-Whig or anti-Foxite coalition remained in power for so long, with so little effective public opposition, may well have owed as much to Whig disregard for morality as to the mere wishes of a sovereign. (The one short-lived exception to the long Whig exile was of course the 1806–1807 Grenville–Foxite coalition, led by the highly moral and religious-minded Lord Grenville.) Although conditions were never completely similar, 1742, 1746, 1757, and March 1783 showed that the whims of a king were not enough to sustain a government in power against the wishes of a wider bloc in (or out of) parliament.

Hence, the efforts of George III and George IV to keep the Pittites and Tories in power for so long, despite wartime disasters and peacetime depressions, may have been aided at the least by the utter contempt of the Foxites and Whigs, with their antics amply detailed and commented upon in the right-wing press, for a nascent moral majority. Edward Gibbon, certainly no Christian, but of a Northite disposition, wondered how Fox, who along with Mrs. Armistead had visited him at Lausanne in 1788, could have been so impervious to a scandalized public opinion that he pandered their illicit connection in front of "all Europe."[78] Gibbon was probably correct that such actions took their toll on public opinion. And reinforced by press reports of goings-on at Holland House, Devonshire House, or Woburn Abbey, Whig libertinism should at least be considered (as it usually is not) in any discussion of Whig powerlessness during the later Hanoverian period. When the *Standard*, daily organ of the ultra party, reflected that the Whigs had been unpopular in the country since the time of Walpole, despite their importance in the legislature, it was because "they had notoriously cast off

---

[76] *Anti-Jacobin Review*, 8 (February 1801), p. 198; 12 (August 1802), p. 419.

[77] For example, *John Bull*, December 17, 1820, p. 6; November 25, 1821, p. 396.

[78] J. E. Norton, ed., *Letters of Edward Gibbon* (London, 1956), Gibbon to Sheffield, October 4, 1788, III, pp. 132–3.

all respect for religion; their leaders, indeed, illustrating the sincerity of their infidelity by the profligacy of their lives."[79] Even if stated too simplistically, the *Standard* may have partially explained an unusual phenomenon of British political life: the virtual exclusion of the Whig party from the loaves and fishes of power for nearly half a century.

IV

In the chapters that follow there is a discussion of the political and intellectual underpinnings of right-wing activity in Britain from the 1750s to the 1830s. This discussion involves an examination of the party and factional basis of the various groups of loyalist politicians – Buteites, Northites, Burkeites, Pittites, ultras – who adopted a value system later generations would term conservative, Tory or rightist. The discussion also attempts to focus a peculiar ray upon certain institutions – the monarchy, clubs and pressure groups, the Church of England, the dissenting churches, Roman Catholicism – and upon certain political or social issues – parliamentary reform, "the condition of England question," slavery, the corn laws – which might illuminate their rightist inclination or perspective in a highly charged ideological age of enlightenment and revolution.

[79] *Standard*, April 9, 1832.

CHAPTER 3

Tories and Jacobites in the mid and late eighteenth century

I

Because intellectual and political historians and political theorists are interested in the role of ideas in history and, more specifically, in the institutionalization of those ideas in political groupings, the role (and rise and fall) of political parties has traditionally exerted a fascination for them. This is especially true in England where, seemingly, a nearly continuous institutionalized Whig/Tory dichotomy existed from the last quarter of the seventeenth to the last quarter of the nineteenth century with obvious antecedents stretching back at least to the 1640s. If Whiggery as a fixed idea flourished far better than Toryism in the enlightened optimism of the high eighteenth century, Toryism, with arguably deeper roots in shire and market town, proved more adaptable in the longer haul, and while the Whigs *per se* are little heard of after 1886, Toryism in one form or another lurched forward into the twentieth century and, no doubt, beyond. The one possible disruption in the continuous history of a Tory party occurred between the breakup of the original grouping sometime around the accession of George III in 1760 and the revival of a (or the) Tory party later in the Hanoverian period, dating, depending upon one's historian or one's data base, anywhere from the American crisis of the 1770s, through the reform agitation of the 1830s. Within this context, historians have had two major problems to consider: first, when, why, or even whether, the Tory party ended sometime around 1760; and secondly, when and why that "Tory" revival so obvious by the 1820s and 1830s actually took place.

The preponderant view of modern British historiography, whether Namierite or revisionist (Clarkite or otherwise), is that the old historic Tory party of the seventeenth and eighteenth centuries did indeed cease to exist in any meaningful political sense sometime between 1757 and the late 1760s. Frank O'Gorman, for example, placed the death of the party in the early 1760s;[1] I. R. Christie in 1765;[2] and Paul Langford, with the alleged (and futile) Tory rally to Grenville and Bedford to prevent the repeal of the Stamp Act, in 1766.[3] Whatever their disagreements on the *nature* of the old Tory party, Romney Sedgwick, Eveline Cruickshanks, and J. C. D. Clark, the chief proponents of the "Tories as Jacobite" school, on the one hand, and Linda Colley, more oriented towards viewing the Tories as disgruntled Hanoverians, on the other, all see traditional Toryism as defunct by the early 1760s.[4] While in preparation for the general election of 1768 the Duke of Newcastle and his friends were still discussing Tories amongst themselves, nonetheless, surrounded by such uncommon historical unanimity, there seemed little reason to dispute Namier's contention that to consider a Tory party or compile parliamentary lists of Tories after 1768 is increasingly to employ anachronistic language and methodology.[5]

Recently, however, B. W. Hill, in a second volume of a history of party in Britain between 1689 and 1832, has recanted his former belief that the Tory party lapsed after 1760. Resurrecting the generally held opinion of nineteenth-century historians, Hill surmises that the old Tory party, containing most of its former membership, continued throughout the late eighteenth century, along with the Whigs, as one of the two basic political parties in Britain.[6] Professor Christie, in this case I think speaking for both Namierites and revisionists, has subjected Hill's thesis to a withering – if always good-humored – analysis based on his unrivaled knowledge of the composition of the early parliaments of George III's reign. He found no evidence of any substantial continuity of personnel between the pre-1760 Tory party and the clusters which made up the Northite coalition of the 1770s and 1780s. In fact, the surviving Tories of the age of the American Revolution were as likely or even more likely to be associated with one or another of the Whiggish opponents of

[1] Frank O'Gorman, *Emergence of the British Two-Party System, 1760–1832* (London, 1982), p. 2.
[2] Ian R. Christie, *Stress and Stability in Late Eighteenth-Century Britain* (Oxford, 1984), p. 38.
[3] Paul Langford, *First Rockingham Administration* (Oxford, 1973), p. 172.
[4] For Sedgwick's and Cruickshanks' views, see Sedgwick, I, 77. J. C. D. Clark, "Decline of party, 1740–1760," *EHR*, 93 (July 1978), pp. 526–7. Linda Colley, *In Defiance of Oligarchy* (Cambridge, England, 1982).
[5] Sir Lewis Namier: *England In the Age of the American Revolution* (London, 1961), pp. 212–13; *Personalities and Powers* (New York, 1955), p. 65.
[6] B. W. Hill, *British Parliamentary Parties, 1742–1832* (London, 1985), preface.

George III or Lord North than with king and prime minister.[7] After Christie's seminal critique, it was no longer possible to take Hill's evidence for the survival of Toryism based upon the career patterns of members of parliament any more seriously than Robert Walcott's mid-century argument for the non-viability of Whiggism and Toryism in the parliaments of William III and Anne.[8]

However, if Hill's discussion regarding the survival of the Tory party after 1760 had been translated from the mundane arena of Westminster politics *per se* to the more sublime world of ideological and theoretical considerations, in other words to the question of the survival of basic Tory tendencies as divorced from concrete personalities, he might have had a stronger case.

That there was a Tory revival sometime in the late eighteenth or early nineteenth century, most, though not all, historians admit. On the issue of when this revival occurred or why it happened, there has been little scholarly consensus.[9] J. C. D. Clark, going against the grain on this question as on so many others, dismisses the whole notion of a Tory revival at all, preferring rather to concentrate upon an apotheosis of conservative Whig attitudes, influenced especially by Burke and Eldon.[10] Yet this may be somewhat of a semantic observation and Clark's refusal to use the term "Tory" at all when writing of the years between 1760 and 1832 does not by any means imply that he fails to see a growth in (what I call) right-wing attitudes during the period. Charles R. Ritcheson sees a "seedbed of a new Tory party," encompassing the factions of Grenvillite, Bedfordite, and King's Friends, centered, even before the American Revolution, on George III.[11] John Phillips, too, basing this on his demographic studies of English boroughs, thinks Toryism took on a new meaning in parliament and constituency as early as the 1770s.[12] Lord Blake traces the rise of the new Tory party to the political crisis of the 1782–1784 period, culminating in the emergence of the Younger Pitt as George III's prime ministerial choice.[13] Since the 1782–1784 crisis was chiefly one involving the royal prerogative,

[7] Ian R. Christie, "Party in politics in the age of Lord North's administration," *PH*, vi, pt. 1 (1987), p. 51–7.
[8] Robert Walcott, *English Politics in the Early Eighteenth Century* (Cambridge, Mass., 1956).
[9] J. G. A. Pocock, *Virtue, Commerce, and History* (Cambridge, England, 1985), pp. 284–5.
[10] J. C. D. Clark: "A general theory of party," *HJ*, 23 (June 1980), p. 305; *English Society, 1688–1832* (Cambridge, England, 1985), p. 408.
[11] Charles R. Ritcheson, *British Politics and the American Revolution* (Norman, 1954), pp. x, 31.
[12] J. C. D. Clark, "Eighteenth-century social history," *HJ*, 27 (September 1984), pp. 782–4.
[13] Robert Blake, *Conservative Party from Peel to Churchill* (New York, 1970), p. 8.

and though he does not make specific reference to the period, A. D. Harvey, by implication, seems to have this *crise de la régime* (as well as 1801) in mind when he relates the primary factor of the rise of the new Toryism to the salvation of the royal prerogative.[14] At least three major historians of eighteenth and nineteenth-century party development – Frank O'Gorman, Richard Pares, and Robert Stewart – place the origins of the new conservatism, or the revived Toryism, in the traditions and value system of the Burkeite Portland Whigs and their union, in 1794, under the inspiration of anti-Jacobinism, with Pitt's administration.[15]

J. E. Cookson presents one of the most sophisticated explanations for the revised Toryism. He locates its *fons et origo* in 1787, two years before the storming of the Bastille, when Pitt, once the *beau ideal* of the Dissenters, refused to support the repeal of the Test and Corporation Acts.[16] Cookson thus decoupled a revived Toryism from the reaction against the French Revolution and linked it firmly to religious principles. J. A. W. Gunn, too, was attracted by a religious explanation of the question, though he placed its source twenty years earlier than Cookson, and anchored it on an intellectual rather than on a practical parliamentary footing. And, for Gunn, this Tory revival was largely an expression of traditional High Church beliefs as expressed in tracts, books, and sermons.[17] Clark too, of course, paying generous tribute to Gunn's pioneering efforts in this regard, sees a right-wing revival in precisely these decades – and fueled by religious motifs – though he labels it conservative Whig rather than Tory.[18]

This historian would argue that if Toryism on a national level is to be seen at all in the late eighteenth century, it has to be seen in a largely religious context, in the revival or nurture, often by conservative Whigs, sometimes by avowed Tories who clung to the old name, of right-wing political and especially spiritual attitudes in the press, in pamphlets, and in sermons. These attitudes fueled by the American and French Revolutions, the rise of political dissent, and a general European-wide de-Christianization, would probably have been considered largely Toryish before 1760. My own work has been

[14] A. D. Harvey, *Britain in the Early Nineteenth Century* (London, 1978), pp. 2–4.
[15] O'Gorman, *Two-Party System*, p. 50. Robert Stewart, *Foundation of the Conservative Party, 1830–1867* (London, 1978), pp. xiv, 7.
[16] J. E. Cookson, *Friends of Peace* (Cambridge, England, 1982), pp. 12–16.
[17] J. A. W. Gunn, *Beyond Liberty and Property* (Kingston, 1983), p. 168.
[18] Clark, *English Society*, pp. 275–6.

greatly formed by the conclusions of Cookson, Gunn, and Clark, though my sources, especially the right-wing press, have not, in general, been theirs, nor have I always agreed with their interpretation of various texts. But if there were enduring Tory principles, passed down from the age of Johnson to the age of Peel, they involved far more than commitment to monarchy, a country agenda, or even glorification of or preservation of the social hierarchy. Possibly the key element of Toryism in its post-Jacobite phase involved churchly matters. And however much other temporary issues such as fear of domestic radicalism and dislike of the French (in whatever manifestation), for example, intervened, Toryism as a practical idea and as a philosophy, or even more widely, an emerging right-wing or conservative agenda, involved the preservation of religion and the Church. This is what gave "the Right" its identity and its abiding character.

II

The aged term "Tory" itself by the 1750s and 1760s had become less and less used by those to whom it ostensibly referred. In other words, just as there was a problem applying "Tory" to individuals or groups in the late eighteenth or early nineteenth century, when revived Toryism, so to speak, was coming in, so there had been a similar problem half a century before when the old and well-recognized Toryism was going out. The press reflected this problem. *Jackson's Oxford Journal*, the organ of Midland Toryism in the 1750s, tended to refer to its politics or its allegiance as the "Old Interest."[19] Its counterpart in western England, *Felix Farley's Bristol Journal*, alluded to "the Blues" or "the Blue interest" rather than to the Tories.[20] Of the two historians from the middle years of George III's reign who wrote favourable accounts of the king's general political stance, John Adolphus in his *History of England*, and Robert Bisset, an *Anti-Jacobin* reviewer, in his *History of the Reign of George III*, neither felt comfortable in discussing a "Tory party" or "Toryism" in the 1750s or early 1760s, even when coming to consider George III's ending of proscription in 1760.[21] According to the meticulous

---

[19] For example, *Jackson's Oxford Journal*, June 16, 1753.
[20] *Felix Farley's Bristol Journal*, January 25, 1755.
[21] John Adolphus, *History of England* (London, 1840), I, pp. 117ff, 335. Robert Bisset, *History of the Reign of George III* (London, 1803), I, throughout.

research of the historians on the *History of Parliament* project, only one member of the House of Commons called himself a Tory between 1754 and 1790.[22]

Sir Roger Newdigate, MP for Oxford University between 1750 and 1780, who it seems, epitomized what Namier perceived as the High Church, even Counter-Reformation and Jacobite-oriented Toryism of Midland England, perfectly illustrates the mid-eighteenth-century problem of nomenclature for a politician with right-wing attitudes. By the early 1760s, Newdigate not only admitted the difficulty in deciding upon the exact name of his party in any positive sense but in an unpublished essay on parties termed it ridiculous to refer to his colleagues as Tories and unjust to term them Jacobites; he preferred "a nobler name – the country party." "No other name or distinction as a party will they acknowledge," Newdigate wrote. "They equally disdain the names of Tory and Jacobite; they abhor the principles of both."[23] Whatever Newdigate's personal predicament, it is clear that by 1760, a decided element of the public nation had eschewed the name of "Tory" as at worst something shameful or ridiculous or at best something anachronistic. Where it survived, at least outside of Whig counter-Tory propaganda, it tended to be espoused by literary figures like Johnson or Boswell. One need only compare their views on the seventeenth century or on Catholicism, for example, to see the difficulty of associating Samuel Johnson and Sir Roger Newdigate in the same political grouping. At least by 1760, if not before, Newdigate had a vaguely Whig view of the complicated events in English history between the reigns of Charles I and his grandson, William III.[24] Also, unlike Johnson and his coterie, he was firmly anti-Catholic, despite Namier's identification of him with some sort of Counter-Reformation ideology. Newdigate told the House of Commons in 1772 that Catholicism in its pernicious doctrine might compare with Arianism, Socinianism, and Fifth Monarchism – all seeking "the ruin and confusion of Church and State."[25] Newdigate, indeed, in

---

[22] Thorne, I, pp. 345–6.

[23] J. B. Owen, "Survival of country attitudes in the eighteenth-century House of Commons," in J. S. Bromley, E. H. Kossmann, eds., *Britain and the Netherlands: Metropolis, Dominion and Province* (The Hague, 1971), IV, pp. 68–9.

[24] Peter D. G. Thomas, "Sir Roger Newdigate's essay on party, c. 1760," *EHR*, 102 (April 1987), pp. 396–7.

[25] G. M. Ditchfield, "Subscription issue in British parliamentary politics, 1772–9," *PH*, 7, pt. 1 (1988), p. 50.

both his historical vision and in his anti-Catholicism seems more the ancestor of Croker's Protestant Tories of the 1820s and 1830s or even of Vyvyan's ultras of the anti-Catholic emancipation struggle (who also, incidentally, preferred the use of "country party" to "Tory"[26]) than he seems a colleague of Johnson, Boswell (or, later, Burke), or their High Church coadjutors of Newdigate's own lifetime.

Newdigate's rejection of Toryism in its classical form, though he never quite said so, may have resulted from a weariness with his associations at Oxford University. For as late as the 1750s, however much either Tories or their latterday apologists might deny it, it was difficult to ignore the Jacobite element within, around, and coexisting with Toryism. Were the Tories Jacobites? Linda Colley has argued persuasively, basing this argument on sound and meticulously used material, that they were, in general, not. Eveline Cruickshanks and J. C. D. Clark have equally convincingly argued for the essentially Jacobite quality of eighteenth-century Toryism. In a recent article, Professor Christie, perhaps surprisingly, seems to support the latter viewpoint. Neither side in the controversy had spent much time examining the surviving evidence for purposeful Jacobite links among Tory MPs. Christie, after a careful prosopographical check on the parliament elected in 1741 – and in place, of course, at the time of the Rebellion – concludes that at least 40 percent of the Tory MPs were in some quantifiable way hostile to the Hanoverian monarchy[27] – though a more significant point may have been that *none* rose in arms as the Pretender's son marched into England. Christie's conclusions leave one with the suspicion that Jacobitism was indeed rife if not pervasive within English Toryism at least as late as the middle of the eighteenth century and also that whatever enthusiasm there may have been for Jacobitism among the Tories was exceedingly tempered. Other rebellions in the support of such widespread dynastic or ideological causes achieved some success to balance ultimate failure as the leadership of the Pilgrimage of Grace or even poor Monmouth might attest. But the absence in England, if not in Scotland, of much significant and effective support for Charles Edward Stuart probably witnesses to a

---

[26] *Standard*, July 27, 1830. Two major ultra leaders, the Duke of Newcastle and Sir Richard Vyvyan, preferred "Country party" to other possible designations. B. T. Bradfield, "Sir Richard Vyvyan and the fall of Wellington's government," *University of Birmingham Historical Journal*, 11, no. 2 (1968), p. 156n. *Standard*, August 9, 1830.

[27] Ian R. Christie, "The Tory party, Jacobitism and the 'Forty-five: a note," *HJ*, 30 (December 1987), p. 930.

sentiment shared by Churchman and Dissenter, Whig or Tory, even, oddly, perhaps, by most Jacobites: an aversion to even a remote possibility of a Roman Catholic sovereign.

In some ways the issue of whether the Tories were Jacobites is a moot one. Toryism was so enveloped, historically, ideologically, familially, with an adherence to the Stuarts (though not to the Stuarts' religion) that it could no more escape the Jacobite taint than the French Right in 1871 could ignore the Count of Chambord. Beyond the positive point of Tory affection for the Stuarts were the negative ones of post-1714 proscription, a perceived latitudinarianism in the established Church, and a generations-old Tory hatred as well as envy of Whig success. In the end, the most important ingredient in this complicated stew may have been not so much anti-Catholicism but (not quite the same thing) a dread of a Catholic sovereign. As Newdigate (as well as many other "Tory" MPs) were clearly aware by at least 1760, "Tory" was no longer permissible even for descriptive purposes. Or why else would they have come increasingly to shun the label? There is a sense too of course that Whiggism as well as Toryism went into a decline as a name after 1757, amidst Pittite calls for national unity, or after 1760 and the accession of a new king called into question the whole post-1714 political order. But, even over and above the Rockinghamite claim to represent the true Whig tradition, "Whig" never ceased as a political term of honor and applause as "Tory" so clearly did. And this was probably due to the connection between Toryism and Jacobitism and Toryism and disloyalty to the Brunswick monarchy.

And the anti-Whig, anti-Pelhamite press of the 1750s was not noticeably loyal to the Brunswick succession. The *True Briton*, a Jacobite weekly newspaper of opinion of the early 1750s, was funded by Edward Gibbon, father of the historian; James Edward Oglethorpe, founder of Georgia; and John Caryll, a Roman Catholic gentleman and subsequently secretary of state to the Young Pretender.[28] The historian of Jacobite literary wars found it "if anything more evidently Jacobite than the [Jacobite] journals of the 1720s and 1730s."[29] It contained excessive praise of the Stuart

---

[28] For a discussion of the *True Briton*, see Paul K. Monod, "For the king to come into his own again: Jacobite political culture in England, 1688–1788," Ph.D dissertation (Yale University, 1985), pp. 52, 171, 448.
[29] Howard Erskine-Hill, "Literature and the Jacobite cause," in Eveline Cruickshanks, ed., *Ideology and Conspiracy* (Edinburgh, 1982), p. 59.

monarchs Charles II and James II as well as Jacobite poetry and
denunciation of deistic and republican Hanoverians.[30] One authority on eighteenth-century Jacobitism argues that the *True Briton*
was the "only committed Jacobite journal produced after the '45."[31]
While this statement may be technically correct, a cursory examination of the rest of the Tory press of the 1750s would hardly cause
Hanoverian loyalists to loosen their guard. The short-lived newspaper of 1757, the *Crab-Tree*, bemoaned that the "name and reputation of Farmer *Jacques* and his family ... chiefly by the villainous
stratagems of party was now rendered the most odious that could
possibly be imagined."[32] Much more important than the *Crab-Tree*
was the *London Evening Post*, whose editor Richard Nutt had been
successfully prosecuted by the Duke of Newcastle in 1754 for attributing the evident national malaise to the Glorious Revolution.[33]
This great opponent of the Jew Bill and Hardwicke's Marriage Act
mixed front-page exhortations to the British people to recover the
true faith in Jesus Christ with paeans to James II as a leader who,
like Elizabeth but so unlike William III or the Georges, stood for
England's national interest.[34]

The *London Evening Post* was, in the 1750s, the main supplier of
London and European news and opinion for the provincial Tory
press such as the *York Courant, Felix Farley's Bristol Journal*, and
Jackson's Oxford Journal. Although the same High Church, anti-
German, and anti-Pelhamite influence pervaded them as the
mother paper, they were perhaps less overtly Jacobite. There is,
however, some evidence that the Farleys at least were Jacobites in
the classical sense. A probable scion of the West Country family,
Mark Farley, was given a year in prison in 1754, two years after the
paper's founding, for printing seditious songs on the Old Pretender's
birthday.[35]

The famous and oft-printed Tory journalist and pamphleteer,

---

[30] See, for example, *True Briton*, January 16, 1751, 3, p. 51; February 13, 1751, 7, pp. 154ff;
February 27, 1751, 9, p. 201; March 6, 1751, 10, p. 256.
[31] Paul M. Chapman, "Jacobite political argument in England, 1714–1766," Ph.D dissertation (Cambridge University, 1983), p. 98.
[32] *Crab-Tree*, June 28, 1757, p. 56.
[33] Jeremy Black, *English Press in the Eighteenth Century* (London, 1987), p. 172.
[34] *London Evening Post*, January 1–3, 1754; January 17–19, 1754.
[35] G. A. Cranfield, *Development of the Provincial Newspaper, 1700–1760* (Oxford, 1962),
pp. 57–61. In 1755, the editor of the paper indignantly denied the charge in Edward
Ward's *British Weekly Intelligencer* that the True Blues of Bristol sang Jacobite songs. And a
regular correspondent of Farley's paper avowed his allegiance to the Brunswick line, if not
to their ministers. *Felix Farley's Bristol Journal*, January 11 and 25, 1755.

John Shebbeare, who like young Farley, suffered for his political beliefs, and who throughout the 1750s in his myriad "Letters to the people of England" was as near as any journalist to the forefront of the consciousness of the political nation, certainly helped in the Tory/Jacobite identification. Shebbeare found James II's reign a more favorable period to live in than George II's, regularly denounced *"German* Concubinage" and "Harlotry," and broadly hinted at the illegitimacy of George II and the Queen of Prussia.[36] He was also wont to reflect upon how felicitous the nation would be under so peaceable and religious a man as "James III."[37] Yet when it came to be time not many years later to request a pension from George Grenville (and George II's grandson) for Shebbeare, the *crème de la crème* of Tory politics in the persons of Bagots, Hynde Cottons, Dudley and Wards, Phillipses, Wodehouses. St. Johns, Glynnes, Lowndeses, and Kynestones, all signed the requisition.[38]

Examples of other links between Toryism and Jacobitism abound. The famous example of Gibbon at Magdalen in the 1750s, part of that "little kingdom of Jacobitism" identified by Walpole,[39] observing the fellows toasting the Stuarts, comes to mind.[40] Lord Charlemont in his memoirs thought that Toryism, with Jacobite principles, predominated at Trinity College, Dublin.[41] When George III lifted proscription in 1760, the titular head of the Whig party, the fourth Duke of Devonshire, suggested in his diary that Tories were now magistrates in Derbyshire who had been avowed Jacobites as late as 1758 and 1759.[42] Arthur Murphy's *Auditor*, pro-Buteite and hence a paper sympathetic to the end of Tory proscription and in a qualified way to Toryism in general, considered the new Tories visiting George III to be former Jacobites who had had the mist lifted from their eyes, seen their former errors, and were now loyal subjects of the new king.[43] Well and good for the new king, but even the *Auditor* made no attempt to deny that the Tories were in general Jacobites in

---

[36] John Shebbeare, "Sixth letter to the people of England" (London, 1757), p. 91.
[37] John Shebbeare, "Seventh letter to the people of England" (London, 1758), p. 54.
[38] William James Smith, ed., *Grenville Papers* (London, 1852), II, pp. 271–2.
[39] John Brooke, ed., *Memoirs of King George II* by Horace Walpole (New Haven, 1985), II, p. 23.
[40] Georges A. Bonnard, ed., *Memoirs of My Life* by Edward Gibbon (New York, 1966), pp. 52–3.
[41] Francis Hardy, *Memoirs of the Political and Private Life of Charlemont* (London, 1810), p. 75.
[42] Peter D. Brown, Karl W. Schweizer, eds., *Devonshire Diary*, Camden, 4th ser., 27 (London, 1982), p. 165.
[43] *Auditor*, August 5, 1762.

the late reign. Hence when Wilkes' *North Briton* proclaimed in 1763, "Shew me tory, I'll shew you Jacobite,"[44] he had at least some justification for his charge. Writing of the 1760s, J. C. D. Clark calls Jacobitism "a harmless Oxford mannerism"[45] and he was certainly correct. Jacobitism may indeed have been such by the late 1740s or even earlier, given the alternative of a Roman Catholic sovereign. But Toryism, fairly or not, was stuck with its Jacobite label (and not entirely from Toryism's enemies) and like the famous tar baby, it could not easily pull back from the embrace.

Hence, the evidence is quite clear that during the early 1760s, Toryism as anything but a constricted ideological expression used by a few High Church divines and devotees and their hangers-on was interred.

The Elder Pitt, both by his apparent opposition to the Pelhamite (and even Georgian) political machine and by his war-induced, almost Elizabethan rhetoric of national reconciliation, did a great deal in the 1757–1760 period, even before the death of George II, to reconcile Tories to the Hanoverian dispensation. J. C. D. Clark seems to argue that Toryism *per se* ended during the political crisis of March–June 1757, which concluded in Pitt's consolidation of power.[46] Pitt in the late 1750s gave Tories posts on the county commissions and officerships in the militia, which Gibbon, for one, thought eradicated "the relicks" of Tory or Jacobite prejudice.[47] The Pittite press (as early as 1756 in the *Con-test*)[48] widely proclaimed the end of not only Tory but also Whig distinctions and, as the *Monitor* put it, "the whole body of the nation seems to be inflamed with one common spirit."[49] A poem on the Tories in the formerly Tory but now Pittite *Jackson's Oxford Journal* in 1759 caught this spirit:

> Their old fashion'd tenets quit,
> And step by step at last submit
> To reason, Eloquence, and *Pitt*.[50]

The accession of a new king in October 1760 merely solidified what had become increasingly common practice during the pre-

44 *North Briton*, January 15, 1763, p. 108.
45 J. C. D. Clark, *Dynamics of Change* (Cambridge, England, 1982), p. 10.
46 Clark, "Decline of party," pp. 526–7.   47 *Memoirs of My Life*, p. 111.
48 *Con-Test*, December 25, 1756, p. 31.
49 *Monitor*, June 17, 1758, p. 919.
50 W. R. Ward, *Georgian Oxford: University Politics in the Eighteenth Century* (Oxford, 1958), p. 212.

ceding three years. Proscription came officially to an end. With the support of Bute and Pitt, the Bedchamber was open to Tories.[51] Dr. King from St. Mary's Hall, Oxford, who as late as 1750 had greeted Charles Edward Stuart on his secret London jaunt,[52] was welcomed to Court with his Oxford coadjutors and became a supporter of Bute's peace and Grenville's administration.[53] Portsmouth dockers were informed they could vote as they pleased. And with perhaps some exaggeration, the horrified Duke of Newcastle worried that "Whigs were given up in many parts of England."[54] Paul Langford, who had examined this process, discovered that the Tories rarely competed for Cabinet office but, rather, chiefly concerned themselves with that local patronage of Church and state denied them since Anne's reign.[55] The new parliament met in November 1761. When government supporters appeared at the cockpit to hear the king's speech read, Edwin Lascelles found a huge crowd, Tory as well as Whig, half of whom, he suspected, had never seen the room before.[56] Gibbon, visiting that old Tory London haunt, the Cocoa Tree Club, found it "full of Privy Councellors and Lords of the Bedchamber."[57] George Grenville too, when he became prime minister in 1763, kept in close communication with Tories favorable to his ministry; making sure they got to Westminster and granting them local and electoral patronage.[58] But even by Grenville's time it was becoming difficult to perceive the Tories as a body particularly distinct from the evolving personal factions of the early reign of George III.

Even before 1760, at least one Tory club, in Calne, in that most Tory of counties, Wiltshire, was dissolved.[59] A month after the accession of George III, with some tongue in cheek, *Jackson's Oxford Journal* proclaimed the death "in the Arms of a *few* Friends, the *Old Interest* of Oxfordshire. She was a Lady too well known and esteem'd

---

[51] *Devonshire Diary*, pp. 63–9.

[52] James Lees-Milne, *Last Stuarts* (New York, 1983), p. 89.

[53] BL, EG. 2136, King to Despenser, September 7, 1763, fo. 67.

[54] Lord John Russell, ed., *Correspondence of John, Fourth Duke of Bedford* (London, 1843), II, pp. 424–5.

[55] Paul Langford, "Old Whigs, old Tories, and the American Revolution," *Journal of Imperial and Commonwealth History* (January 1980), p. 126.

[56] George Thomas, Earl of Albermarle, *Memoirs of the Marquis of Rockingham* (London, 1852), I, pp. 68–9.

[57] D. M. Low, ed., *Gibbon's Journal to January 28th, 1763* (London, 1929), p. 185.

[58] John R. G. Tomlinson, ed., *Additional Grenville Papers* (Manchester, 1962), pp. 47–8, 50–3, 123–36, 186–7.

[59] "A second letter from Wiltshire to the *Monitor*" (London, 1759), p. 2.

to need a particular Encomium on her Virtue."[60] In 1761, with Bamber Gascoigne, a Tory, declaring in the House of Commons that Toryism was destroyed,[61] the Red Herring Club, which Dr. King had attended and which contained Jacobite members from Oxford, ceased meeting.[62] In 1762, the editor found the last reference in Sir John Philipp's diary to the Tory and possibly Jacobite Welsh Society of Sea Serjeants[63] and, at Oxford, the Old Interest Club was abolished – though as *Jackson's Oxford Journal* would have it, students still had rowing clubs to occupy themselves.[64] Hence, by the election of 1768, a historian of Georgian Oxford states that even at that politically charged university, the dons had difficulty attributing political labels or even motives to their opponents.[65] The age of Jacobitism as a "harmless Oxford mannerism" had clearly arrived.

III

The historian can almost draw a graph with intersecting lines showing that as the legal paraphernalia constraining Jacobitism declined in importance at the end of the eighteenth century, so the emotional currents of the movement increased in retrospective fondness. One does not have to take seriously either Johnson's absurd statement that as late as the 1770s there was a twenty-to-one Jacobite majority in England[66] or even the somewhat more probable observation of the young Viscount Fitzmaurice that practically everyone he met on a 1756 tour of Scotland, drunk or sober, was a Jacobite sympathizer,[67] to suspect that an emotional attachment to the exiled family was always an important – if not decisive – element on the British Right. If Hume is correct, and he may well be, that the Tories were attached to the Stuart family more by affection than by a love of indefeasible right,[68] the well-known sexual libertinism and alcoholism of Charles Stuart may help explain the travail of the

[60] *Jackson's Oxford Journal*, November 29, 1760.   [61] *Devonshire Diary*, p. 152.

[62] David Greenwood, *William King, Tory and Jacobite* (Oxford, 1969), p. 77.

[63] Francis Jones, "Society of Sea Serjeants," *Transactions of the Honourable Society of Cymmrodorion* (1967), p. 60.

[64] *Jackson's Oxford Journal*, May 22, 1762.   [65] Ward, *Georgian Oxford*, p. 236.

[66] Charles McC. Weis, Frederick A. Pottle, eds., *Boswell in Extremes, 1776–1778* (New York, 1970), pp. 156–7.

[67] Lord Fitzmaurice, *Life of William, Earl of Shelburne* (London, 1912), i, p. 38.

[68] T. H. Green, T. H. Grose, eds., *Essays, Moral, Political, and Literary* by David Hume (London, 1875), i, p. 142.

family after the 1740s. Hence, Dr. King may not have been the only one turning towards George III as a worthier mentor and more deserving of emulation than his Stuart cousin.[69] Only after the death of "Charles III" and the lack of any credible Jacobite alternative could the memories of the dissipation in the Palazzo Muti be forgotten and the brave prince of the 'Forty-five take his place in the imagination of Royalists.

Even before 1760, the Earl Marshal was pardoned and allowed to inherit property.[70] In 1766, after the Old Pretender's death, and perhaps emboldened by "Charles III's" own precarious Catholicism, the Irish Roman Church refused any longer to allow the Stuart Court to nominate bishops for that island.[71] The early 1770s saw a slue of important Jacobites returned to Britain, pardoned, and even received at Court, including the "Earl of Westminster" and the Old Pretender's secretary.[72] In 1784, the forfeited Scottish Jacobite estates were disannexed.[73] Two months after the Young Pretender's death, in 1788, the episcopal bishops of Scotland addressed the home secretary with a submission to the Hanoverian monarchy. When, as the price of their relief, the Scottish episcopalians were legally required to take that oath of abjuration that had once so bothered the young Bentham at Oxford and was later to agitate the middle-aged Scott at Abbotsford, a complacent government tended to look the other way if they refused.[74] In 1793, one of the last of the disaffected pillars of resistance to the Glorious Revolution collapsed, amidst fears of a greater commotion. "Bishop" Cartwright of Shrewsbury, breaking with the policies of other late non-juring bishops such as Gordon and Forbes,[75] admitted to his charges that George III was the rightful sovereign of his country.[76]

---

[69] William King, *Political and Literary Anecdotes of His Own Times* (London, 1818), pp. 200ff.

[70] Bruce Lenman, *Jacobite Risings in Britain, 1689–1746* (London, 1980), p. 268.

[71] R. B. McDowell, *Ireland in the Age of Imperialism and Revolution, 1760–1801* (Oxford, 1979), p. 183.

[72] William Wimsatt, et al., eds., *Boswell for the Defense, 1769–1774* (New York, 1959), pp. 79n., 191. Frank Brady, Frederick A. Pottle, eds., *Boswell on the Grand Tour, Italy, Corsica and France, 1765–1766* (New York, 1955), p. 268n.

[73] Lenman, *Jacobite Risings*, p. 290.

[74] Rev. John Skinner, *Annals of Scottish Episcopacy* (Edinburgh, 1818), pp. 74–9. *Edinburgh Monthly Review*, 1 (January 1819), pp. 75–8. For Bentham's qualms, see Clark, *English Society*, pp. 50–1. For Scott's, see H. J. C. Grierson, ed., *Letters of Sir Walter Scott* (London, 1971), Scott to Miss Claphane, July 13, III, p. 302.

[75] Henry Broxap, *Later Non-Jurors* (Cambridge, England, 1924).

[76] William Phillips, ed., "William Cartwright, non-juror, and his chronological history of Shrewsbury," *Transactions of the Shropshire Archaeological and Natural History Society*, 4, 4th ser. (1914), pp. 23–6.

The survival of some popular Jacobitism after 1760, while present here and there, was hardly momentous. Gibbon thought the Mayor of Southampton in 1762 was a Jacobite.[77] The following year, the Bishop of Gloucester blamed the anti-cider tax riots in his county on local Jacobite interference.[78] Several Jacobite pamphlets appeared during the crisis years of George III's reign: one by the eccentric Joseph Ritson in 1778 avowed "Charles III" as his king;[79] another, anonymously, in 1784, denounced the Dissenters and praised James II.[80] Another political eccentric (if a genius), Robert Burns, seriously showed interest in the claims to the throne of "Charles III's" illegitimate daughter.[81] More importantly, Paul K. Monod discovered some popular Jacobite feeling in England, definitely when the Nottingham framework knitters rioted on "James III's" birthday in 1779, and, in a fascinating if somewhat less convincing aside, in the Pentridge uprising of the second decade of the nineteenth century.[82] Yet, in general, by the 1760s and 1770s, Jacobitism was a pose rather than a threat or even a serious intellectual movement. No doubt Francis Burdett's grandfather did still toast Prince Charles at the Cocoa Tree as did John Gibson Lockhart at Balliol.[83] It was, however, merely an exercise in nostalgia for the *Anti-Jacobin Review* in 1802 to compare a Jacobite favorably to a Dissenter[84] or for an antiquarian MP in 1831 to oppose the repeal of the oath of abjuration because it alone stood between the house of Sardinia and the throne.[85]

The attitude of the Hanoverian royal family towards Jacobitism equally illustrates the politics of nostalgia for their predecessors and a sneaking admiration for those upholding the monarchical ideal. The editors of Bubb Dodington's *Journal* make a convincing case that George III's father, Frederick, Prince of Wales, prefigured his grandson, George IV, and his great-granddaughter, Victoria, in his

---

[77] *Gibbon's Journal*, p. 141.
[78] W. S. Taylor, J. H. Pringle, eds., *Correspondence of William Pitt, Earl of Chatham* (London, 1838), II, p. 255.
[79] Monod, "Jacobite political culture," p. 472.
[80] "Collection of letters on the thirtieth of January and twenty-ninth of May" (London, 1784), pp. iii–ix.
[81] Monod, "Jacobite political culture," p. 11.   [82] *Ibid.*, pp. 291–3.
[83] M. W. Patterson, *Sir Francis Burdett and His Times (1770–1844)* (London, 1931), I, pp. 4–5. Andrew Lang, *Life and Letters of John Gibson Lockhart* (New York, 1970), p. 46.
[84] *Anti-Jacobin Review*, 13 (October 1802), pp. 134–5.
[85] *Parl. Deb.*, II, 3rd ser. (February 4, 1831), p. 141.

emotional, if not political, attachment to things Stuart.[86] George III not only pardoned Jacobites, he also honored them[87] and pensioned them.[88] He also denounced the "warming pan" fiction to his foreign secretary.[89] Queen Charlotte had at least some connection with Jacobites in her entourage when she arrived in England in 1761. This was through no fault of her own and probably reflected an aping of *his* father's policy by George III.[90] Yet thereafter, Charlotte was pursued by radical journalists trying to ferret out her Jacobite loyalties, and more surprisingly, by sober and religious Whigs, like Fitzwilliam's son, Lord Milton, who in 1817 made an extraordinary and even vicious attack in the House of Commons on the – by then – aged queen's Jacobite proclivities.[91] George and Charlotte's children exhibited Jacobite sympathies at times: the Duke of Sussex in his courtesies to Cardinal York in Italy;[92] Augusta in her well-known remark, related by Croker, that only after Cardinal York's death, could she seriously regard herself as *Princess* Augusta;[93] and, most importantly, George IV, in the respect he paid to the surviving Stuart family and to the body of James II.[94]

In the end it was a matter of faithfulness, as Archibald Cameron, the Scottish episcopalian Jacobite executed in 1753, understood only too well when he proclaimed that he died in "the principles of Christian loyalty."[95] Johnson and Boswell understood it too, though they realized that their sort of hankering for the Stuarts, while not properly Jacobite, was "something that is not easy to define."[96] For a party or movement of the Right (even the inchoate Right of the eighteenth century) such loyalty could have fractured their ideology and weakened their impact. It could also have been dangerous, if not critically so, for the Hanoverian dispensation, even after Cul-

---

[86] John Carswell, Lewis Arnold Dralle, eds., *Political Journal of George Bubb Dodington* (Oxford, 1965), p. xix.

[87] Lees-Milne, *Last Stuarts*, p. 187, where it is related that when the Countess of Albany visited London, she was allowed to use the royal box at the opera.

[88] As in the case of the Countess of Albany and Cardinal York, "Henry IX." Aspinall, III, p. 299n.; IV, p. 33n.

[89] *Ibid.*, George III to Grenville, November 24, 1799, III, pp. 299–300.

[90] Namier and Brooke, p. 524.

[91] Lawrence Huston Houtchens, Carolyn Washburn Houtchens, eds., *Political and Occasional Essays* by Leigh Hunt (New York, 1962), pp. 218–19. *Parl. Deb.*, XXXVI (June 23, 1817), p. 1130.

[92] Lees-Milne, *Last Stuarts*, p. 170.   [93] Clark, *English Society*, p. 161.

[94] *John Bull*, September 26, 1824, p. 316.

[95] Lenman, *Jacobite Risings*, p. 27.

[96] Frederick A. Pottle, Charles H. Bennett, eds., *Boswell's Journal of a Tour to the Hebrides* (New York, 1936), pp. 162–3.

loden. What if the Young Pretender's conversion to the Church of England had been convincing? Or if he had married young and begotten an impressive family? Such actions could conceivably have divided English royalism later in the century as much as French royalism was later divided (and weakened) by Legitimism and Orleanism. The house of Hanover may have owed almost as much to those dissipations in the Palazzo Muti as it did to Butcher Cumberland at Culloden.

IV

As to the Tory press of the 1750s, the evidence is overwhelming that it ceased to have any Tory (much less Jacobite) affiliation by the early 1760s. The Saturday weekly newspaper of opinion, the *Monitor*, was founded in 1755 by Richard Beckford, who had ties to Tory City radicalism. Initially at least under the influence of the Tories John Shebbeare and the Rev. John Entick, although it was consistently and unequivocally anti-Jacobite both in a historical and in a contemporary sense, it exhibited a strong Tory bias on religious, foreign policy, and parliamentary reform questions.[97] If there was an organ of Hanoverian Toryism in the 1750s, the *Monitor* exemplified it. But by 1759, it was perceived as having shed any Tory predilections and in the 1760s it consistently followed an extremely anti-Buteist oppositionist line until its demise in 1765.[98]

As to the Tory *London Evening Post* and its provincial commercial off-shoots, *Felix Farley's Bristol Journal*, the *York Courant*, and *Jackson's Oxford Journal*, all four were recognizably Tory, albeit with a Pittite and country tinge through 1760. Calls for the restoration of Convocation, parliamentary reform, a battle against infidelity, and a Bolingbrokian domestic polity abounded.[99] Thereafter, adding fuel to Linda Colley's and Paul Monod's arguments for Tory–radical

---

[97] For the origin of the *Monitor*, see Marie Peters, *Pitt and Popularity* (Oxford, 1980), p. 13n., where she makes clear that Shebbeare, more or less Jacobite-oriented, did not long remain connected with it. For its early anti-Jacobitism, see *Monitor*, August 16, 1755, p. 12. For its Tory program, see *ibid.*, pp. 15–17.

[98] "Honest grief of a Tory" (London, 1759), pp. 3–4, wonders how the *Monitor* could have abandoned its creed.

[99] For the Toryism of the *London Evening Post*, see January 1–3, 1754 or July 18–20, 1754; for that of *Jackson's Oxford Journal*, see June 9, 1753; for that of the *York Courant*, see September 25, 1753; for that of *Felix Farley's Bristol Journal*, see January 18, 1755.

confluence in the middle of the eighteenth century,[100] all four newspapers, with varying degrees of enthusiasm, slid into an anti-Buteite and pro-Wilkite world view, with few, if any, Tory characteristics.[101]

The highly successful monthly, the *Critical Review*, founded in 1756, has nearly always been described in its first series, through 1791, as a Tory periodical[102] to which, among others, Goldsmith, Johnson, Smollett, and Hume were connected.[103] However, the claim that the *Critical Review* is Tory needs a great deal of qualification. On religious matters it consistently betrayed a rather refined Humeian, or, better yet, Smollettian skepticism far removed from the spirit of High Church sentiment that infected the rest of the Tory press. It regularly denounced the absurdity of Hutchinsonianism,[104] called for a revision of the Thirty-Nine Articles to eliminate the need for young collegians to subscribe to Trinitarian doctrines,[105] praised David Hume's views on natural religion,[106] acclaimed Rousseau and Voltaire,[107] and denounced Archbishop Laud.[108] On the other hand, on issues involving parliamentary reform, national politics, and, in general, the historical vision of the seventeenth and eighteenth centuries, it supported views considered country or Tory in the 1750s,[109] and it adhered to Buteite or Northite authoritarianism in the 1760s and 1770s.[110] However, unlike the rest of the Tory press, the *Critical Review* never specifically proclaimed itself Tory or devoted to the Old Interest or the Blues, and hence necessarily invoked a lesser commitment to principles associated in contemporary minds with Toryism.

[100] Linda Colley, "Eighteenth-century English radicalism before Wilkes," *TRHS*, 31, 5th ser. (1981), pp. 4–5. Monod, "Jacobite political culture," p. 310.
[101] See all four newspapers throughout the 1760s.
[102] See, for example, Hill, *Parliamentary Parties*, p. 88n. Walter Graham, *English Literary Periodicals* (New York, 1966), pp. 212ff. Alvin Sullivan, ed., *British Literary Magazines: Augustan Age and the Age of Johnson* (Westport, Conn., 1983), p. 74.
[103] For a discussion of the *Critical Review*, see Claude E. Jones, *Smollett Studies* (Berkeley, 1942), p. 98.
[104] *Critical Review*, 1 (March 1756), pp. 175–6.   [105] *Ibid.*, 1 (May 1756), pp. 365–9.
[106] *Ibid.*, 6 (November 1758), p. 411.
[107] *Ibid.*, 7 (January 1759), pp. 48–9; 11 (May 1761), p. 377.
[108] *Ibid.*, 19 (January 1765), pp. 13–14.
[109] *Ibid.*, 2 (December 1756), p. 471, supporting annual parliaments. Or, 15 (January 1763), pp. 82–90, for a very Toryish view of the reign of Anne and the peace of Utrecht.
[110] For the *Critical Review*'s support of Grafton and North, see 27 (April 1769), p. 320 and 51 (June 1781), pp. 464–5.

CHAPTER 4

Toryism redivivus

I

Between 1768 and 1812 the contemporary use of the term "Tory" was spotty and uneven. Yet any attempt to quantify clearly or unambiguously either "the going out or the coming in" of the word is bound to cause frustration. There is no magical date in the 1760s on which the term "Tory" ceased to apply to a particular group of parliamentarians or country squires – much less to an ideological attitude about society, politics, or religion. Likewise, at any time before 1832, and in some circles as late as the 1860s, "Tory," however rehabilitated the word might have been by the events of 1793–1794 or 1807 or 1812, sat uneasily upon the shoulders of even those who allowed or encouraged themselves to be called thus.

As Namier long ago discussed, the followers of North, George III or the Younger Pitt were frequently termed "Tories" by their Whiggish or radical political opponents. Examples of such nomenclature, whether used by the obscure wife of a Southwark MP[1] or by the leaders of the Whig party,[2] are not difficult to come by. It is much more difficult to discover examples of the victims of this presumed abuse applying this term to themselves or to their political colleagues. One hereditary Tory politician, Sir William Bagot, MP for Staffordshire, defended his ancient creed by name in the House of Commons in 1770 as "the body who disinterestedly supported Government ... who were friends of the Monarchy limited by law, to the Church as it was established by Law," and, perhaps not

---

[1] Charles Ryskamp, ed., *Boswell: The Ominous Years, 1774–1776* (New York, 1963), p. 80.
[2] Rockingham in 1775 thought the King's Friends were Tories. Frank O'Gorman, *The Rise of Party in England: Rockingham Whigs, 1760–1782* (London, 1975), p. 341. Fox in 1793 thought the torrent of Pitt-induced Toryism threatened to overwhelm the constitution. Sir William R. Anson, ed., *Autobiography and Political Correspondence of Augustus Henry Third Duke of Grafton, K.G.* (London, 1898), Fox to Grafton, September 19, 1793, p. 403. Holland in 1793 wrote of Burke in "Toryland." Leslie Mitchell, *Holland House* (London 1980), p. 72.

surprisingly, elicited a waggish query as to whether, then, the whole House was Tory.[3] The Pittite MP George Canning, who had close ties with a literary "Church and King" tradition, on several occasions in private letters wrote of his colleagues as Tories: in 1797 regarding Pitt's supporters and in 1805 regarding Pitt himself as well as his followers.[4] Sylvester Douglas, Lord Glenbervie, Lord North's son-in-law, in 1802 considered the new prime minister Addington and the late North as Tories.[5] Perhaps the most important public utterance on Toryism by a leading Pittite politician – standing out for its uniqueness as well as for the occasion which prompted it – occurred during the 1805 debates in parliament on Catholic emancipation. Lord Hawkesbury, formerly Addington's foreign secretary, currently Pitt's home secretary, the son of George III's leading Friend, and, as second Earl of Liverpool, prime minister himself from 1812 to 1827, urged the defeat of Catholic relief in the House of Lords. During his peroration, in sentiments not heard in parliament since the time of the Elder Pitt a half-century before, Hawkesbury said that to support the established Church and to reject the bill, he will "call upon the tories, the firm, steady, and persevering supporters of the monarchy and the established church."[6]

Literary figures, who in their loyalist state of mind often veered towards royal, Northite, and Pittite political associations, and who frequently possessed greater ideological sensibilities than members of the working political class *per se*, sometimes described themselves or their circle as "Tory." Hence, Mrs. Thrale told her diary in 1780 that Samuel Johnson "calls himself a Tory, & glories in it," or the young Walter Scott in 1805 owned to his "Tory principles."[7] But the unrivaled practitioner of such emotions in terms of his innate comprehension of things right-wing, was the Laird of Auchinleck. James Boswell not only identified himself and his mentor Samuel Johnson as Tories[8] but he also included under that nomenclature

[3] Burke, *Corr.*, Burke to Dennis, April 1770, II, pp. 126–7.
[4] Josceline Bagot, ed., *George Canning and His Friends* (London, 1909), Canning to Wilbraham, June 7, 1797, I, p. 148. Aspinall, IV, p. xvii.
[5] Francis Bickley, ed., *Diaries of Sylvester Douglas, Lord Glenbervie* (London, 1928), I, p. 332.
[6] *Parl. Deb.*, IV, (May 10, 1805), p. 691.
[7] H. J. C. Grierson, ed., *Letters of Sir Walter Scott* (London, 1971), Scott to Ellis, May 26, 1805, I, pp. 253–4. Katharine C. Balderston, ed., *Thraliana: Diary of Mrs. Hester Lynch Thrale (Later Mrs. Piozzi), 1776–1809* (Oxford, 1951), I, p. 448.
[8] Frederick A. Pottle, Charles H. Bennett, eds., *Boswell's Journal of a Tour to the Hebrides* (New York, 1936), pp. 162–3.

Dr. Nowell of St. Mary's Hall, Oxford,[9] George III,[10] the Younger Pitt,[11] and, most presciently, the better part of a decade before the publication of the "Reflections," Edmund Burke.[12] Indeed, one of the guiding motifs of Boswell's relationship with Burke was his early and continued recognition of the Tory qualities in that great Whig philosopher. As Boswell told the perhaps uncomfortable Burke, "You are one of us. We will not part with you."[13]

Churchly figures, too, sometimes expressed a Tory self-awareness, though when John Wesley informed the editor of the *Gentlemen's Magazine* in 1785 that he, his brother Charles, and their late father were Tories in the sense that they held God, not the people, as the origin of all civil power, it is doubtful that the expression was very meaningful in contemporary politics.[14] Lord Mansfield's protégé, and Burke and Johnson's friend from The Club, Thomas Barnard, Bishop of Killaloe, described himself to Boswell as a Tory in 1783.[15] The High Church coterie around George Horne, Bishop of Norwich, also comprised a continuing Tory intellectual tradition from the 1760s through the early nineteenth century. It included, among others, such individuals as William Jones of Nayland, the noted Trinitarian apologist, William Stevens, Treasurer of Queen Anne's Bounty, and the Rev. Jonathan Boucher, the Anglo-American loyalist. If indeed the positive usage of the expression "Tory" survived the party and intellectual shuffles of the 1750s and early 1760s, it was this cluster of High Church, Laudian, and neo-Hutchinsonian friends, along with Samuel Johnson, who most kept the word haltingly alive before its nineteenth-century revival.[16]

Before 1819, few among the right-wing newspapers, journals and periodicals openly avowed themselves "Tory." When the leading

[9] Irma S. Lustig, Frederick A. Pottle, eds., *Boswell: Applause of the Jury, 1782–1785* (New York, 1981), p. 236.

[10] *Boswell: Ominous Years*, p. 80.   [11] *Boswell: Applause of Jury*, p. 175.

[12] *Ibid.*, p. 86.

[13] Geoffrey Scott, Frederick A. Pottle, eds., *Private Papers of James Boswell from Malahide Castle in the Collection of Lt. Colonel Ralph Heyward Isham* (Privately printed, 1932), XVIII, p. 24. Burke himself in the 1790s seemed to approach the "Toryland" to which Lord Holland assigned him with a resigned air. He wrote in a private letter that he did not greatly care if his principles were thought to be Whig or not. "If they are Tory principles, I should always wish to be thought a Tory." Burke, *Corr.*, Burke to Dr. Richard Brocklesby, n.d., IX, p. 446.

[14] John Telford, ed., *Letters of the Rev. John Wesley* (London, 1931), VII, pp. 305–6.

[15] Charles N. Fifer, ed., *Correspondence of James Boswell with Certain Members of The Club* (New York, 1976), Barnard to Boswell, March 2, 1783, III, p. 133.

[16] For Stevens' view of himself as a Tory in 1777, see ESRO, Boucher papers, BOU/B/3, Stevens to Boucher, September 12, 1777. For Horne's view in 1789, see BL Berkeley Papers, Add. MSS. 39312, Horne to Berkeley, July 17, 1789, fo. 100.

London government-oriented newspaper of the period of the American war, the *Morning Post*, tended, at least in some constituencies, to describe the 1780 general election in Whig/Tory terms,[17] this description was not ideologically revealing. As far as I know, there were no other eighteenth-century exceptions in the Northite (before 1783) or Pittite (after 1783) press where the term is employed either (self) descriptively or ideologically. During the first twelve years of the nineteenth century, no London newspaper and only two periodicals seem to have adopted the Tory label. In 1806, the editor of the Pittite *Weekly Political Review*, the nativistic and eccentric Henry Redhead Yorke, declared himself, albeit in passing, a Tory.[18] The *Anti-Jacobin Review*, edited by the Pitt biographer and (later) permanent secretary of the Pitt Club, John Gifford, possessed more sustained and avowed Tory-orientation. Time and time again the periodical expressed a non-juring, neo-Jacobite, Tory allegiance very much out-of-tune with most other elements in the general nineteenth-century right-wing press.[19] Not until the period of Peterloo and the Caroline affair (1819–1821) were government supporters in the daily press (for example, Dr. Stoddart's *New Times*) often grudgingly coming to describe themselves as Tories.[20]

Most of the new enthusiasm for the use of "Tory" came from the Murray press in general and from its leading spokesman, John Wilson Croker, in particular. As early as 1809, a reviewer in the *Quarterly* (not Croker himself) had proclaimed the nation Whig in 1688 and Tory in 1793.[21] In an 1819 private letter to the young Scottish literary man, John Gibson Lockhart, Croker defined Toryism as "morality, legality, [and] respect for constituted authorities."[22] Five years later, he told the prime minister that Pitt's successors, presumably including Liverpool himself, were Tories and that they proceeded on party as opposed to factional principles.[23] The *Representative*, a short-lived daily newspaper of the Murray empire, founded in 1826, happily accepted the appellation "Tory" as defined as "attachment to the King and Constitution, to Church and State."[24]

[17] *Morning Post*, July 12, 1780.
[18] *Redhead Yorke's Weekly Political Review*, February 22, 1806.
[19] *Anti-Jacobin Review*, 5 (March 1800), p. 290; 22 (September 1805), p. 95; 38 (February 1811), pp. 116–7.
[20] *New Times*, November 16, 1821.   [21] *Quarterly Review*, 2 (November 1809), pp. 247–9.
[22] NLS, Lockhart Papers, 927, Croker to Lockhart, November 18, 1819, fo. 2.
[23] BL, Liverpool Papers, Add. MSS. 38299, Croker to Liverpool, October 13, 1824, fos. 141–2.
[24] *Representative*, January 31, 1826, p. 22.

Croker and the *Quarterly* were entirely successful in legitimizing and domesticating "Toryism" and then retrospectively applying it to all sorts of historical figures and situations where it had no contemporary resonance. The Younger Pitt was proclaimed a "stone-blind Tory" in 1827;[25] Addington as well as (in their Canningite days) Melbourne and Palmerston in 1835;[26] George III himself in 1849;[27] and the young Fox in 1851.[28] The *Quarterly* in 1830 also generalized about the Tory party operating in English politics, as opposed to the Whigs, in the 1780s.[29] So even before the passage of the first Reform Bill in 1832, the notion of a Tory party as defining loyalist politics throughout George III's reign was well advanced.

There were some caveats to these *Quarterly* descriptions. A reviewer in *Blackwood's Edinburgh Magazine* in 1832 wondered with what precision Lord North and the early ministers of George III were now designated as Tories.[30] And Southey a year earlier, in the *Quarterly* itself, from which Croker had momentarily resigned, admitted that Pitt, Lord Grenville, and the Portland Whigs "were not professed Tories"; a welcome piece of historical truth somewhat marred by his follow-up assertion that they rather "formed the conservative party."[31] But the return of Croker to the *Quarterly* in 1831 generally stifled such doubts.[32] When in 1836, Sir Robert Peel commissioned from Miss Howarth a memoir of his family, and she remarked that in 1790, when the elder Robert Peel entered parliament, that Pitt led the Tory party,[33] she was repeating what was fast becoming received wisdom. Hence, J. C. D. Clark's assertion that Lord John Russell and the Earl of Albemarle strove in the middle of the nineteenth century to invent, for domestic Whig political reasons, a late-eighteenth-century Tory party, needs some qualification.[34] Croker and his coadjutors on the *Quarterly* had long since accomplished that dubious historical task.

---

[25] *Quarterly Review*, 36 (June 1827), p. 66.

[26] *Ibid.*, 53 (February 1835), p. 270; 54 (July 1835), p. 264.

[27] *Ibid.*, 79 (March 1849), p. 517.   [28] *Ibid.*, 88 (March 1851), p. 497.

[29] *Ibid.*, 42 (March 1830), p. 306.

[30] *Blackwood's Edinburgh Magazine*, 31 (May 1832), pp. 772–5.

[31] *Quarterly Review*, 45 (July 1831), p. 518.

[32] Lord Mahon, the fifth Earl Stanhope, in the 1840s criticized applying the label "Tory" to the King's Friends of the early 1760s. J. C. D. Clark, ed., *Memoirs and Speeches of James 2nd Earl Waldegrave, 1742–1763* (Cambridge, England, 1988), p. 119.

[33] Charles Stuart Parker, ed., *Sir Robert Peel From His Private Papers* (London, 1899), I, p. 7.

[34] J. C. D. Clark. "A general theory of party, opposition and government, 1688–1832," *HJ*, 23 (June 1980), pp. 298–9.

Yet relative acceptance and even ubiquity of "Tory" as the main descriptive term for the party of the Right – always far more popular than "Pittite" or even "conservative" – was not won without qualms and hesitations. Several politicians of high rank were seemingly resistant to the term. Wellington, an upholder of the Clarendonian and Northite traditions of the importance of royal service, could never get a clear idea of what Tory principles meant.[35] Norman Gash found only one occasion, in an 1827 speech, when Robert Peel called himself a Tory.[36] During the late 1820s, some of Wellington's ultra enemies in the struggle to preserve the Protestant Constitution blanched at the use of "Tory." Lord Mansfield wanted to resurrect the old party name of "King's Friends."[37] The Duke of Newcastle preferred almost any designation save Tory.[38] At the other end of the loyalist spectrum, so to speak, Wilberforce, at least according to the *Edinburgh Review*, refused to answer to the name of Tory.[39] And the heir-presumptive to the throne, HRH the Duke of Clarence, found such a word as Tory "mere nonsense ... nowadays."[40]

Some of the right-wing press, too, questioned the resurrection of "Tory" from its eighteenth-century tomb. As early as 1797, the *British Critic*, then the only "Church and King" periodical in London, wanted the term dropped.[41]

The most important press attack upon the word occurred between 1819 and 1821, just at the time that the daily right-wing newspapers were beginning, awkwardly or not, to apply "Tory" to themselves. The *Anti-Jacobin Review*, which in a different series a decade earlier had been the leading exponent of avowing and reviving the explicit Tory ideal, but which in 1816 subsumed the Orange-oriented *Protestant Advocate*, led the assault in 1819. It reminded its readers that "the circumstances which gave rise to the epithet have long ceased to exist; and a *Tory* is now, like many other vulgar errors, a political

---

[35] Duke of Wellington, ed., *Despatches, Correspondence, and Memoranda of Field Marshal Arthur, Duke of Wellington* (London, 1868), III, p. 453.

[36] Norman Gash, *Reaction and Reconstruction in English Politics, 1832–1852* (Oxford, 1965), p. 119.

[37] D. G. S. Simes, "Ultra Tories in British politics, 1824–1834," D.Phil. thesis (Oxford University, 1974), p. 305.

[38] Charles, Lord Colchester, ed., *Diary and Correspondence of Charles Abbot, Lord Colchester* (London, 1861), Newcastle to Colchester, January 24, 1828, III, p. 542.

[39] *Edinburgh Review*, 46 (June 1827), p. 432.

[40] Louis J. Jennings, *Correspondence and Diaries of John Wilson Croker* (London, 1884), I, p. 405.

[41] *British Critic*, 14 (July 1799), p. 96.

non-entity existing only in the imaginations of the ignorant ..."[42]
William Jerdan's *Literary Gazette* in 1820 found "Tory" an inapplica-
ble term in current circumstances.[43] The most successful and interesting of the right-wing monthlies, *Blackwood's Edinburgh Magazine*,
also in 1820, denounced "Tory" as "that foolish name ... this long
extinguished superstition ... [which] had passed away with the
barbarism and stupidity in which alone it could have breathed" and
pronounced it ridiculous to brand the late king a Tory.[44] A year
later, the Scottish *Beacon* found it "absurd" to label government
advocates or the Younger Pitt, "a true English whig," as "tories."
The *Beacon* felt that "a more foolish, odious appellation cannot
present itself to the mind of any man who is competently instructed
in British history."[45] But this was a losing war.

The chief reason for the reluctance in some, though not all,
right-wing quarters to accept the Tory nomenclature had to do, as
J. C. D. Clark has perceptively pointed out,[46] with their continued
adherence to the glamour and ideology of the orthodox Whig vision
of the Glorious Revolution and its ensuing "Protestant Constitution" – an adherence that historical Toryism, with its closet full of
Jacobites, crypto-Catholics, non-jurors, Laudians, and Hutchinsonians, could never quite celebrate with the same élan. Also, in the
1820s, as opposition to Catholic emancipation increasingly became
the *ne plus ultra* of right-wing expectations, a creed that commemo-
rated in varying degrees Henrietta Maria or James II, and understood even if it did not quite coronate "James III" and "Charles
III," would have a difficult time giving its aged name to those new
devotees of the Protestant Constitution, the ultras.

Hence, somehow the term "Tory" had to be grafted onto a vision
of the past which encompassed a generally non-Tory view of certain
events of the seventeenth and eighteenth centuries. This was done
essentially by repudiating the historical pre-1760 "Tory party"
while at the same time, fervently or grudgingly, accepting a "Tory"
appellation for the nineteenth century. Interestingly, those most
concerned with such a repudiation were Scottish and Orange Irish
loyalists to whom Toryism represented a quite different sentiment
than it did in its English manifestation. As early in the debate as

[42] *Anti-Jacobin Review*, 55 (January 1819), p. 453.
[43] *Literary Gazette*, November 11, 1820.
[44] *Blackwood's Edinburgh Magazine*, 6 (February 1820), p. 576.
[45] *Beacon*, January 20, 1821, April 21, 1821.
[46] J. C. D. Clark, *English Society 1688–1832* (Cambridge, England, 1985), pp. 275–6.

1812, the *Edinburgh Annual Register*, patronized by Walter Scott and John Gibson Lockhart, compared the revolution Whigs with the Perceval ministry.[47] And during the early and mid-1820s, both the Scottish *Beacon* and *Blackwood's* glorified in both the 1688 and, more surprisingly, perhaps, the American Revolutions, the latter asserting explicitly that the Whiggism of 1688, 1776 and even the 1780s was now Toryism.[48] The Irish Protestant loyalists, with their Orange tradition, were even more emphatic on these points. The Orange-oriented Dublin weekly, the *Warder*, which *John Bull* called the "ultra of all ultras,"[49] meditated upon the virtues of temporal liberty as against the tyranny of kings and denounced Elizabeth and the Stuart sovereigns who for their elevation of monarchical over parliamentary power became the "scourge of the people." It praised the seventeenth-century Whigs "who dared to rise from the attitude of the slave to that of the freeman, and worship liberty in that spot [Westminster], which, thanks to the Third William and to British virtue, is now her chosen temple."[50]

The London daily *Standard*, edited by a second-generation Orangeist Irish newspaperman, S. L. Giffard, regularly denounced in the 1820s and 1830s such Tory icons as Charles I,[51] Archbishop Laud,[52] the Earl of Bute,[53] and George III (for his role in the American war),[54] while maintaining with the same regularity that the "truth is that Locke's doctrines are the doctrines of modern Toryism ..."[55] George Croly, the Irish Protestant clergyman who edited Croker's *Guardian* in 1819 and the ultra *Monthly Magazine* a decade later, wrote a pamphlet in 1828 condemning Charles I and praising not only William III but also Oliver Cromwell, Newton, Locke, and, most surprisingly, Benjamin Franklin.[56] Indeed, the charter of the Orange society contained the sentence that "Orange principles ... are the Old Whig principles."[57] Croker himself, an Irish Protestant though no Orangeman and, indeed, a lukewarm supporter of Catholic emancipation, was prepared to forward the

---

[47] *Edinburgh Annual Register*, 5 (1812), pp. 119–20.
[48] *Beacon*, March 24, 1821. *Blackwood's Edinburgh Magazine*, 14 (July 1823), p. 76; 17 (January 1825), p. 12.
[49] *John Bull*, March 14, 1830, p. 84.　　[50] *Warder*, April 26, 1823.
[51] *Standard*, August 1, 1827.
[52] BL, Halsbury Papers, Add. MSS. 56369, Rose to Giffard, n.d. fos. 109–10.
[53] *Standard*, December 8, 1827.
[54] *Ibid.*, November 25, 1827.　　[55] *Ibid.*, April 2, 1831.
[56] George Croly, "Englishman's polar star" (Preston, 1828), pp. 13–15.
[57] *Orange Institution: A Slight Sketch* (London, 1813), pp. 16–17.

vision of modern "Toryism" only as long as that word was understood as a historical evolution from ancient Whiggism. He made
crystal clear in his *Quarterly* articles that he and indeed the Tory
party in general resembled the Whigs of Walpole's time, and had no
sympathy with any Jacobite tradition.[58] In the House of Commons
during the Reform debates, Croker claimed the Tories as the real
heirs of Somers "and the other great men of the revolution for I am
not aware of any doctrine held by them which are not now held by
the Tories."[59]

The Scottish and Irish Tories were by no means the only elements
in British political life which qualified their modern Toryism with
Whig antecedents. The former literary radicals whom age and
experience as well as opportunity and inclination had beckoned on
that well-trod path from left to right, perhaps salvaged some of their
youthful opinions by continuing to identify with the historical tradition – if not on matters of immediate politics – in which they had
matured politically; rather as American neo-conservatives supported Ronald Reagan or George Bush while claiming to still
adhere, historically, to the tradition of Franklin D. Roosevelt or
Harry S. Truman. Thus, for example, both Coleridge and Southey
denounced the Jacobite–Tory tradition and heaped praise, in the
latter's words, on William, Lord Russell as "one of our state-
martyrs."[60] It was also in this spirit that in 1830 in the House of
Commons the former Whig Sir James Scarlett – now Wellington's
repressive attorney general – accused the extreme Tory Robert
Alexander of the *Morning Journal* of libelling the Glorious Revolution. This must have been one of the last echoes of what had once
been standard political practice.[61]

The extent to which early nineteenth-century English Toryism in
general identified with historical English Whiggism is more difficult
to gauge. The young Disraeli certainly did not.[62] But Disraeli's was

[58] *Quarterly Review*, 54 (September 1835), pp. 370–1; 84 (March 1849), p. 549.
[59] *Parl. Deb.*, IX, 3rd ser. (December 17, 1831), p. 435.
[60] Earl Leslie Griggs, ed., *Collected Letters of Samuel Taylor Coleridge* (Oxford, 1971), Coleridge
to Cary, April 22, 1832, VI, pp. 901–2. *Quarterly Review*, 16 (January 1817), pp. 520–1.
[61] *Parl. Deb.*, XXII, n.ser. (March, 2, 1830), p. 1207.
[62] Disraeli, of course, denied the whole notion that Whigs and Tories of the seventeenth and
eighteenth centuries had, so to speak, exchanged positions. To him, a Whig of the age of
Walpole resembled in his attitude towards the monarchy, local government, and the
Church hierarchy, a Whig of the age of Grey and Melbourne. J. A. W. Gunn, et al., eds.,
Benjamin Disraeli Letters, 1835–1837, II (Toronto, 1982), Disraeli to Peel, July 27, 1836, II,
p. 342. Such eccentric English radical Tories as Burdett or Cobbett failed to identify with
the "Whig as Tory" historical tradition as well.

probably a minority viewpoint on this as on other issues at least until after mid-century and his increasing intellectual dominance over his party's vision of itself. When that happened, Sir Richard Vyvyan, ultra Tory leader in the 1820s and 1830s, who in 1828 had drunk to "the memory of my attachment to the Constitution Kg. William constituted & established, in 1688 ...,"[63] disavowed the name of Tory and lamented in an 1847 election address that "there were gentlemen now to be found who affected to regard with disfavour the great revolution of 1688."[64]

The orthodox religious periodical the *British Critic* in 1825,[65] the *Anti-Jacobin Review* in 1818 (reversing a pro-Jacobite stand which it had adopted a decade earlier),[66] and the satirical weekly *John Bull* in 1823,[67] proclaimed modern Toryism the equivalent of 1688–1714 Whiggism, though the *Critic* added the very important qualification, "with the exception of the great tendency to infidelity and irreligion" of the Whigs. Hence, this may have been a majority sentiment especially as the Catholic emancipation struggle heated up. Lord Skelmersdale, the chairman of the London Pitt Club, was greeted with enormous cheering when he proclaimed himself at an 1828 meeting of the club an "old Tory," like his father, but not "a primitive Tory"; and he defined the former as a "moderate Whig of 1688."[68]

The Tories' opponents were mindful of the force of the "Whig as Tory" argument but in general unimpressed by its conclusions. In a slightly different political context, the young Burke had addressed this question in "Cause of the present discontents" and concluded: "Few are the partisans of departed tyranny; and to be a Whig on the business of an hundred years ago, is very consistent with every advantage of present servility."[69] A discussion of this conundrum elicited from Macaulay in the *Edinburgh* perhaps his clearest statement on the Whig theory of history.[70] Hazlitt, of course, considered that the old Whigs resembled the modern Jacobins![71]

---

63 Bodl., MS. ENG. Letters C. 56, Giffard Letters, c. 1820–1840, Vyvyan to Giffard, January 25, 1828, fo. 572.

64 B. T. Bradford, "Sir Richard Vyvyan and Tory politics with special reference to the period 1825–46" Ph.D. dissertation (University of London, 1965), pp. 337–9.

65 *British Critic*, 23 n.s. (February 1825), p. 119.

66 *Anti-Jacobin Review*, 54 (July 1818), p. 389.

67 *John Bull*, September 14, 1823, p. 292.   68 *Ibid.*, June 1, 1828, p. 174.

69 Burke, *Works*, I, p. 442.

70 Lord Macaulay, *Critical, Historical and Miscellaneous Essays* (New York, 1860), VIII, pp. 302–4.

71 William Hazlitt, *Political Essays* (London, 1819), pp. xxx–xxxi.

In fairness to their political acumen, both the two leading practitioners of the use of "Tory," Boswell in the late eighteenth and
Croker in the early nineteenth century, were aware of the utilitarian
or even necessitarian function which "Tory" performed for the
political nation. Boswell, who often had discerning things to say
about politics, put it best in 1764 in a disquisition on Whigs and
Tories.

> I use these ludicrous terms because the fact is that they have been in use so
> long that they give us instantly the ideas of these different parties and give
> it even with a particular force which explanation does not give ... We have
> been accustomed to hear those words from our earliest youth in a particular
> sense. Consequently they make a more lively impression on us than a long
> argument.[72]

Using much less elevated reasoning, Croker privately defended his
use of "Tory" in the 1820s simply on the grounds that there was a
marked and distinct party in the country "which might for brevity"
be given the name.[73] Of course, there were always those who found
in "Tory" (or "Whig" for all that) an altogether deeper matter than
mere necessitarianism. When Sir Francis Burdett denied in the
House of Commons in 1827 that he was either Whig or Tory and
denied further that the words had any contemporary meaning, Sir
Thomas Lethbridge, first elected an MP for Somerset in 1806,
begged to differ.

> The hon. baronet, the member for Westminster had said, that he was
> neither Whig, nor Tory and that there were no such distinctions. He would
> not talk of it, if the House did not like those terms; but as he understood it,
> there were two different parties in the country professing opposite prin-
> ciples, and he thought it useful for the country. The people knew where to
> find them when they were wanted.[74]

II

The whole question of the survival of orthodox Toryism after 1760
has somewhat obscured the very real post-1760 authoritarian, anti-
Enlightenment, right-wing patronage and factional networks which
grew up about ostensibly Whig politicians and which in many cases
directly intersected with important constituents of the so-called

[72] Frederick A. Pottle, ed., *Boswell in Holland, 1763–1764* (New York, 1952), pp. 129–30.
[73] *Correspondence of Croker*, I, p. 405.
[74] *Parl. Deb.*, XVII, n.ser.: (May 3, 1827), p. 529; (May 4, 1827), p. 558.

Tory revival of the 1790s and beyond. Lord Bute's is an interesting case in point, even though the earl's political career was effectively terminated by the mid-1760s. Bute was ideologically, and perhaps spiritually, more adventuresome than the now celebrated high court Whiggery discussed by, among others, Reed Browning, and exemplified by Archbishop Herring, Bishop Squire, and Lord Hardwicke.[75] When Governor Hutchinson reported that the second Earl of Hardwicke said of his father the Lord Chancellor, that while he was a Churchman, he opposed sending Church of England bishops to America, the response of the exiled loyalist was that he must have been a "very moderate" Churchman indeed![76] Similarly, it is difficult to see figures like Herring of York and (then) Canterbury, with what F. C. Mather has called his "Advanced Latitudinarian" views, his anti-Catholicism, his high view of reason and his horror of superstition,[77] as quite receptive to all the nuances of style and tone which permeated the atmosphere of Bute's (or Jenkinson's or Mansfield's) coterie. When George III, in 1762, still very much under Bute's influence, confided to his prime minister his desire to "attack the irreligious,"[78] he was not necessarily continuing in any Court Whig tradition of Queen Caroline, George I or George II, or even of his own father. And Bute himself told George Grenville in that same year that he prized ecclesiastical patronage above all other kinds for the good he could do for his king and country.[79] After the fall of Bute in 1763, Sir John Dalrymple, the historian and a Buteist apologist, advanced an interesting rationale for his patron's political collapse: some of the political nation viewed Bute's religiosity and his (and his family's) frequent reception of the Sacrament with either fits of laughter or cool contempt.[80] However, if not of immediate political resonance, such High Church attitudes were harbingers of ideological views which would flourish after 1793.

Bute was admired by his own political family, his circle of secre-

---

75 Reed Browning, *Political and Constitutional Ideas of Court Whigs* (Baton Rouge, 1982), pp. 90–6, 132, 199. See also Stephen Taylor, "Sir Robert Walpole, the Church of England, and the Quaker tithe bill of 1736," *HJ*, 28 (March, 1985), pp. 51–2.
76 Peter Orlando Hutchinson, *Diary and Letters of ... Thomas Hutchinson* (London, 1886), II, p. 131.
77 F. C. Mather, "Georgian churchmanship reconsidered: some variations in Anglican public worship, 1714–1830," *JEH*, 36 (April 1985), p. 275. Browning, *Court Whigs*, pp. 90–6.
78 Romney Sedgwick, ed., *Letters from George III to Lord Bute, 1756–1766* (Westport, Conn., 1981), p. 166.
79 William James Smith, ed., *Grenville Papers* (London, 1852), I, p. 419.
80 Sir John Dalrymple, "Appeal to the facts" (London, 1763), p. 19.

taries and professional men: Wedderburne, who helped procure
Johnson his pension;[81] the elder Sir Gilbert Elliot, the apparently
happy recipient of Hume's denunciation of those "plaguy Prejudices
of Whiggism;"[82] and Charles Jenkinson, who told Grenville in 1761,
"I am absolutely in love with Lord Bute."[83] Bute was also the
patron, during his short ministry, of the prominent Trinitarian
apologist and moderate Hutchinsonian Jones of Nayland.[84] The line
connecting Bute and his circle to later developments, to the Portland
Whigs and the Loyal Association, to the Club of Nobody's Friends
and the *Scholar Armed*, to Mrs. Trimmer and the Society for the
Reformation of Principles, to Johnson and the later Burke, while not
always the straightest, is nonetheless usually visible enough for us to
draw certain conclusions. Much time has been spent linking
pre-1760 Tories with their post-1760 political positions as Northites,
Rockinghamites or whatever and finding very little of use. It might
repay the effort to examine as keenly the religious and political
networks of Bute, Jenkinson, Mansfield, and their cohorts.

Charles Jenkinson, father of the prime minister, raised by Pitt to
the Earldom of Liverpool in 1796, of an old Tory Oxfordshire
family, had become reconciled to the Whig establishment by 1754.[85]
If he had earlier and different principles, an examination of his
patronage network might suggest that he never quite shed them. As
a (and eventually *the*) political counsellor of George III after his
master Bute lost office, Jenkinson was regarded by Horace Walpole
as both the king's "tool" and (with his cohort Mansfield) "the
suggester of all arbitrary measures."[86] A friend of the Tory Jones of
Nayland at Charterhouse, the two had a long association; Jones
dedicated a book to Jenkinson; Jenkinson procured Jones and his
family patronage.[87] He also looked after his and Jones' friend the
Tory academic and priest George Horne's successful search for
preferment and a bishopric.[88] In the House of Commons in the

[81] James Boswell, *Life of Johnson* (London, 1953), p. 264.
[82] J. Y. T. Greig, ed., *Letters of David Hume* (Oxford, 1932), Hume to Elliot, March 12, 1763,
    I, p. 379.
[83] *Grenville Papers*, Jenkinson to Grenville, March 24, 1761, I, p. 359.
[84] *Short Account of the Life and Writings of the Rev. William Jones* (London, 1801), p. ix.
[85] N. S. Jucker, ed., *Jenkinson Papers, 1760–1766* (London, 1949), p. vi.
[86] G. F. Russell Barker, ed., *Memoirs of the Reign of King George III* by Horace Walpole
    (London, 1894), IV, p. 56. A. F. Steuart, *Last Journals of Horace Walpole* (London, 1910), II,
    p. 222.
[87] BL, Liverpool Papers, Add. MSS. 38308, Jenkinson to Jones, March 31, 1781 (copy),
    fo. 102; 38307, Jenkinson to Jones, December 25, 1779.
[88] *Ibid.*, Add. MSS. 38310, Hawkesbury to Horne, October 22, 1788, fo. 27G.

1770s, Jenkinson defended Laud's reputation as well as the uniqueness of the Church of England, and denounced Rousseau and Hume as members of "that despicable tribe of sceptics and infidels."[89] He was John Reeves' greatest patron.[90]

Like Jenkinson, the former Jacobite William Murray made his peace with Pelhamite orthodoxy, despite a youthful pledge of loyalty to "James III."[91] Murray, elevated in 1756 to the Lords as Baron Mansfield, and then made Lord Chief Justice of King's Bench, was, of course, one of the noted judges of modern English history. During the Bute period he too encouraged high prerogative views in George III[92] and was suspected by the Whigs, certainly unjustly, after Bute's fall, of unwarrantable influence over national affairs.[93] He was originally closely connected with both Pope and Bolingbroke,[94] and this relationship coupled with his hereditary, if disposable, Jacobitism no doubt influenced his later politics which were not classically Whig. Hence, Mansfield once praised Dean Tucker in the Lords for his confutation of Locke's theories on civil government.[95] Mansfield did favor some Tories. He supported his great Tory friend William Blackstone for the Regius Professorship of Civil Law at Oxford in 1753.[96] He had attended Westminster School with William Markham in the 1720s and Shelburne accused the two of them in later years of consistently "pursuing a Machiavellian line of policy."[97] Mansfield recommended Markham to George III as the Prince of Wales' tutor, hence facilitating that orthodox Churchman's rise to the archbishopric of York.[98] Markham was for a time a special friend to Burke, edited "The sublime and the beautiful," assisted on the *Annual Register*, and served as godfather to Richard.[99]

Mansfield also oversaw the patronage needs of that avowed Tory clergyman Thomas Barnard. Barnard's father was Newcastle's chaplain and his uncle, Andrew Stone, was Newcastle's secretary and George III's controversial tutor, accused of inculcating him

[89] *PH*, 17: (February 6, 1772), pp. 269–70; (February 23, 1773), pp. 752–3.
[90] See, for example, BL, Liverpool Papers, Add. MSS. 38222, Reeves to Liverpool, December 12, 1787; 38293, Reeves to Liverpool, 1823, fos. 97–8.
[91] Clark, *English Society*, p. 154n.
[92] *Letters from George III to Bute*, George III to Bute, April 7, 1763, pp. 211–12.
[93] *Last Journals of Walpole*, p. 222. [94] *Letters from George III to Bute*, p. xxviii.
[95] Paul Leicester Ford, *Josiah Tucker and His Writings* (Chicago, n.d.), p. 14.
[96] David A. Lockmiller, *Sir William Blackstone* (Chapel Hill, 1938), p. 39.
[97] Lord Fitzmaurice, *Life of William Earl of Shelburne* (London, 1912), I, pp. 238–9.
[98] Sir Clements Markham, *Memoir of Archbishop Markham (1719–1807)* (Oxford, 1906), p. 40.
[99] *Ibid.*, p. 12.

with Jacobite principles. Mansfield had also known the Stones at
Westminster School, so the Murray–Barnard connection was a
natural one. In 1769 Mansfield got Barnard (the friend of Burke,
Johnson, and Boswell) the deanship of Derry, as a prelude to a series
of Irish bishoprics culminating in Limerick.[100]

In men like Markham, Blackstone, and Barnard, the melding of
traditions can be seen which makes party nomenclature difficult but
which points the way towards the reaction of 1792–1794 and
beyond. The first was a High Churchman who bemoaned in public
that liberty had no English definition save "one which goes to every
thing that is wild and lawless."[101] The second was a Tory who
became something of the "high-priest of orthodox Whiggery."[102]
The third passed from a kind of hereditary Pelhamitism to Johnsonian Toryism. Mansfield's patronage support of J. A. Park[103] (like
the relationship of Jenkinson with Jones of Nayland) connected him,
too, if at one remove, with High Church circles like the Hackney
Phalanx. Park wrote the biography of the prominent Tory, William
Stevens, Treasurer of Queen Anne's Bounty, and a lay leader of the
High Church movement.

Taking the above names – Bute, Jones of Nayland, Bishop
Barnard, Charles Jenkinson, Reeves, Wedderburne (Lord Loughborough), Bishop Horne, Blackstone, Archbishop Markham, Burke,
J. A. Park, Samuel Johnson, Gilbert Elliot, William Stevens, Lord
Mansfield – all connected in patronage or friendship networks of the
first or second degree to the Bute or Mansfield circles (Burke, of
course, at first as their abiding critic), one sees something beyond
Court or high Whiggery, something leading to the creation of a new
ethos involving Church, state, liberty and obligation, which a later
generation would term Tory or conservative. Some of their contemporaries, partially for immediate party gratification perhaps,
recognized that there was something ideologically distinct about
some or all of these individuals or networks. And these critics had
little doubt what it was. Shelburne thought the Stones, Mansfield,
and Archbishop Markham were "Whig connections with Tory

---

[100] *Boswell Correspondence with Members of The Club*, pp. xxix–xxxi.

[101] William Markham, "Sermon preached before the society for the propagation of the gospel
in foreign parts, February 2, 1777" (London, 1777), pp. xviii–xix.

[102] Margaret E. Avery, "Toryism in the age of the American revolution: John Lind and John
Shebbeare," *Historical Studies: Australia and New Zealand*, 18 (April 1978), p. 30.

[103] BL, Liverpool Papers, Add. MSS. 38226, Park to Liverpool, March 6, 1791, fo. 76.

principles."[104] Junius thought Mansfield was a Whig with Jacobite principles.[105] Lord Charlemont thought that Burke "was a Whig upon Tory principles."[106] These musings may all reflect the paucity of political vocabulary before the French Revolution or indeed before the 1830s. It no doubt reflects too what Jonathan Boucher, the Anglo-American Whig of the 1760s who turned Tory loyalist of the 1770s, remarked upon when he met the Tory episcopalian William Stevens, that they experienced an "instinctive congeniality of temper and principles."[107]

Lord North is another case in point where political ideology and commitments, as well as networks, produced a political stance that seemed to verge on what his contemporaries – and by no means all of these were enemies – defined somewhat awkwardly as Toryism. North as prime minister cultivated what remained of the old Tories in parliament, for example Newdigate, MP for Oxford University,[108] or William Bagot, the Staffordshire Tory whom the malignant Horace Walpole called North's "particular friend."[109] Chatham in 1770 thought North the head of the Bute faction in the Commons;[110] Lord John Russell thought him a scion of a Tory family, with Tory principles, who inaugurated a Tory government;[111] Newdigate thought him a good man who tried to do right.[112] His son-in-law described him as a friend to prerogative and the Church of England, and as opposed to parliamentary reform, a Tory.[113] But even more than in his attitude towards the American war, or, until 1783, his marked reverence for the throne, it was religious matters that most distinguished his aggressive right-wing attitudes. In 1772, North told the House of Commons during the debate on the clerical petition against subscription to the Thirty-Nine Articles that the petitioners wanted to bring back the days of the Fifth Monarchy Men and overthrow the Church of England.[114] In 1773, during the debate on the removal of University subscription to the Thirty-Nine

---

[104] Fitzmaurice, *Life of Shelburne*, pp. 238–9.
[105] John Cannon, ed., *Letters of Junius* (Oxford, 1978), p. 208.
[106] Wilfred S. Dowden, ed., *Journal of Thomas Moore* (Newark, 1983), II, p. 796.
[107] Jonathan Bouchier, *Reminiscences of an American Loyalist, 1738–1789* (Boston, 1925), p. 146.
[108] G. M. Ditchfield, "Subscription issue in British parliamentary politics, 1772–79," *PH*, 7, pt. 1 (1988), p. 50.
[109] Namier and Brooke, II, p. 38.
[110] W. S. Taylor, J. H. Pringle, eds., *Correspondence of William Pitt, Earl of Chatham* (London, 1839), Chatham to Calcraft, April 10, 1770, III, p. 443.
[111] Alan Valentine, *Lord North* (Norman, 1967), I, p. 54.
[112] BL, Strange Papers, EG. 2001, Newdigate to Strange, 1776, fo. 131.
[113] Bickley, *Diaries of Sylvester Douglas*, I, p. 332. [114] *Parl. Hist.*, 17 (February 6, 1772), p. 274.

Articles, North as Chancellor at Oxford joined the two University MPs, Newdigate and Dolben, as well as Charles Jenkinson, to oppose the motion on the grounds that, "The reforming notions of this age are dangerous in their tendency; something more than reformation is intended; something that deserves an harsher appellation; and to which if we give way, adieu to religion, adieu to everything dear to us as men and as Christians."[115] Fourteen years later, prematurely aged and blind, North told the House of Commons, debating Beaufoy's motion for the repeal of the Test and Corporation Acts, that the Test Act was "the cornerstone of the constitution, which should have every preservation."[116]

The Northite press, small as it was, most notably the *Morning Post* in the 1770s and the *Morning Herald* in the 1780s, reflected (or perhaps far exceeded, though the prime minister was the paymaster) North's religious views on both current and (presumably) past issues. Hence, Charles I was a martyr for the cause of the Church of England, and the *Post*, in 1779, pointedly wondered why only eight bishops attended the January 30 memorial service for him.[117] The *Post* further suggested that those bishops who in 1779 supported a mild extension of Dissenters' rights were vipers in the bosom of the Church.[118] In the end, by 1783–1784 and North's adherence to the coalition with the Foxites, the Church may have come well before the monarchy in his scale of values. Perhaps in a sense he was one of the first on the Right to reach that confessional point of view so common by the late 1820s and 1830s. Although by the time of the Regency crisis the *Morning Herald* tended to support Pitt rather than Fox and North, and Bate Dudley himself left as editor in 1790, during the initial period of the French Revolution that journal, with perhaps some Northite vestiges remaining, had the most critical attitude of the entire national press toward French policy against the Church of Rome. A historian of the London press during the French Revolution in fact found the *Herald* more pro-Church than pro-monarchical. Perhaps this is also a correct description of Lord North's final disposition.[119]

In some ways North exemplifies the difficulty, once the American war had ended, of categorizing English politicians and their ideo-

---

[115] *Ibid.*, 17 (February 23, 1773), p. 757.   [116] *Ibid.*, 26 (March, 28, 1787), pp. 818–21.
[117] *Morning Post*, February 2, 1779.   [118] *Ibid.*, March 23, 1779.
[119] Rosemary Edith Begemann, "English press and the French Revolution, 1789–1793," Ph.D. dissertation (Emory University, 1973), pp. 86–8, 116.

logical commitments. The historian Klaus Epstein suggested that *German* conservatives were bewildered as they faced the world in the 1780s, as they were "unable to isolate their enemies, identify them clearly, and confront them efficiently."[120] Perhaps this was true in England as well as in the German states. A number of well-informed contemporaries were convinced that the party structure in Britain after 1783, in essence Pittite versus Foxite, had little to do with fundamentals. Thus Horace Walpole in mid-decade found parties so jumbled that "Whig" and "Tory," his favorite political usages, were virtually meaningless words and "no shadow of principle remained in any party."[121] Gibbon at the end of the decade thought "Whig" and "Tory" odious designations that might have had some meaning during the American war but were now obsolete. For since 1783, he wrote, "all general principles have been confounded and if there ever was an opposition to men not measures it is the present."[122] Bishop Thomas Barnard, a self-proclaimed Tory, suggested to the seemingly quintessential Whig, Edmund Burke, that while they differed in *party*, they had never differed in *principles*.[123] Boswell too, when he visited Sir Francis Basset, and heard the "high Tory talk" from this buff and blue Foxite, who had had three grand-uncles killed in battle for Charles I, concluded that during the current reign, party had little to do with principle.[124]

Oxford "Church and King" sentiment, perhaps the purest replica in the kingdom of the Old Interest and the True Blue, was strangely equivocal about politics in the 1780s. Dr. Thomas Nowell of St. Mary's Hall, the preacher of the controversial January 30 Remembrance sermon in 1772, and whom indeed Boswell regarded along with himself and Johnson as the "very perfection of Toryism," refused to sign a loyal address to George III in 1784 endorsing, in essence, the Pitt administration.[125] Francis Page, MP for Oxford University from 1768 to 1801 and a strong supporter of the Church of England and the American war, also opposed the Younger Pitt after 1784.[126] His colleague Sir William Dolben favored Fox's East

120 Klaus Epstein, *Genesis of German Conservatism* (Princeton, 1966), p. 100.
121 *Last Journals of Walpole*, II, p. 518.
122 J. E. Norton, ed., *Letters of Edward Gibbon* (London, 1956), Gibbon to Sheffield, August 7, 1790, III, p. 195.
123 Sheffield City Libraries, Burke Papers, BK1/2219, Barnard to Burke, May 31, 1790.
124 *Private Papers of Boswell from Malahide Castle*, XVIII, p. 152.
125 *Whitehall Evening Post*, March 13–16, 1784.
126 Namier and Brooke, III, p. 242.

India Bill in 1783.[127] And Samuel Johnson, certainly a spiritual if not always a physical Oxonian, in the last year of his life, made clear his backing for Fox against Pitt, if not always for Fox against George III.[128]

Fox (or North) also retained in the 1780s the political commitment of former Tory MPs like Edward Bouverie,[129] the Tory Foleys of Herefordshire and Worcestershire,[130] and Henry Dawkins, a Tory of the 1760s and brother of a Jacobite,[131] as well as of the Jacobite theoretician Joseph Ritson.[132] Wraxall claims that the aged Lord Mansfield in the House of Lords, in 1784, supported the opposition to Pitt.[133]

The London press, too, seemed ideologically confused in the 1780s. Two historians of the press during this decade see newspaper loyalties to politicians and principles as inconsistent when compared with their greater integrity during the American war years.[134] Hence, besides the notorious and incessant switching of party allegiance that characterized most newspapers between 1781 and 1789, one has, in 1784, Foxite papers reporting censoriously on how republican Presbyterians were rushing to support the crown,[135] and the Pittite press confirming the late existence of a noxious Bute–North coalition.[136] Three years later, when the Test and Corporation Act repeal was a major issue, such unusual political transfigurations were still present in the press. The Northite *Morning Herald* denounced repeal as a "dangerous project" and the motion's sponsor Henry Beaufoy as a "sanctimonious son of a quaker."[137] The Pittite press, while opposing (though very mildly) the repeal motion, as did the prime minister, tended to be much less opinionated and ran pro-dissenting letters in strategically important areas of the papers.[138]

---

[127] *Ibid.*, II, pp. 328–9.
[128] Earl of Ilchester, ed., *Journal of the Hon. Henry Edward Fox, 1818–1830* (London, 1923), p. 34.
[129] Linda Colley, *In Defiance of Oligarchy* (Cambridge, England, 1982), pp. 141–2.
[130] Namier and Brooke, III, pp. 444–6.
[131] *Ibid.*, II, p. 304.
[132] Paul K. Monod, "For the king to come into his own again: Jacobite political culture in England, 1688–1788," Ph.D. dissertation (Yale University, 1985), p. 472.
[133] Sir N. William Wraxall, *Historical Memoirs of My Own Time* (Philadelphia, 1837), pp. 440–1.
[134] K. Schweizer, R. Klein, "French Revolution and developments in the London daily press to 1793," *Publishing History*, 18 (1985), p. 89.
[135] *Morning Post*, January 28, 1784.   [136] *St. James's Chronicle*, February 5–7, 1784.
[137] *Morning Herald*, March, 19, 1787.
[138] *Morning Chronicle*, March 28, 1787.

The Whiggish Gilbert Elliot, Lord Minto, the son of Bute's friend, wrote to his wife that the division that occasioned Beaufoy's defeat "had nothing to do with party."[139] Minto may indeed be accurate in his assessment but it points to a general confusion on the opposition as well as the government side, confusion on what might later be termed the party of the Left and the party of the Right, which was not present in the 1770s and would not be present in the 1790s. The *True Briton*, one of the two leading Pittite newspapers of the 1790s, even accused the Fox of 1783 of being a Tory![140]

Politics were highly personalized (and not, in general, ideologized) in the 1780s in a manner peculiar if not unique in modern English history. Sir John Macpherson told the Prince of Wales in 1789 that "the appellations of *Whig* and *Tory* are not mentioned – the descriptive title of *King's Friend* is now seldom made use of ... but *Pittite* and *Foxite* are resounded in every quarter ..."[141] The personal viciousness of national politics in the 1780s, as exemplified by *The Rolliad*, probably stemmed from this non-typical political environment which necessarily spread confusion and vindictiveness in the absence of easily recognizable political or ideological divisions. If one ignores for a moment the prerogative issue, the Foxites, long before the term "Portland Whig" became a defined entity, contained a substantial bloc of past and future Rightists. Fox himself put it well in the 1790s when, bemused over the fate of the Whig party and the defection to Pitt of some of his followers, he remarked that "Our old Whig friends are many of them more Tories than those whom they have joined."[142]

Much of the ideological muddle of the 1780s can, of course, be traced directly to the Younger Pitt, started by George III in 1783 on the longest prime ministerial career since Walpole's. Unlike Bute's or North's propensities earlier in the reign or Addington's, Portland's, or Perceval's at its conclusion, it is difficult to discover the "Church and King" adherent or the Rightist or even the Christian, embryonic or fully formed, in Chatham's son. A case can be made that as the crisis engendered by the French Revolution continued on its course, Pitt, reluctantly, adopted "Toryish" principles, yet one

---

139 Countess of Minto, ed., *Life and Letters of Sir Gilbert Elliot First Earl of Minto from 1751 to 1806* (London, 1874), I, p. 143.
140 *True Briton*, October 11, 1793.
141 A. Aspinall, ed., *Correspondence of George, Prince of Wales 1770–1812* (New York, 1964), II, p. 25.
142 "The Crewe Papers," *Miscellanies of the Philobiblon Society*, 9 (London, 1865–1866), p. 4.

always retains the impression that he was led kicking and screaming to embrace them. Thanks to the efforts of his modern biographer, John Ehrman, the outlines of Pitt's intellectual makeup are now as complete as we are likely to possess from evidence left by that undemonstrative statesman. Ehrman skillfully develops Pitt's Whig philosophy with its additions in theology and history as rooted in Cambridge and derived largely from Isaac Newton and John Locke rather than from Plato and Aristotle.[143] When the distant Tory apologist Jonathan Boucher admitted that he could never bring himself to like Pitt[144] or the closer Edmund Burke described Pitt's ministry as "Cold as ice ... [It] never could kindle in our breasts a spark of that zeal which is necessary to a conflict with adverse zeal,"[145] it should be remembered that Pitt's favorite author was William Paley!

Above all, Pitt was in no established sense of that term a Christian. If not unique, Pitt was unusual among the many prime ministers of George III (or George IV) in his lack of spiritual feeling. Not for him the High Church religiosity of a Bute or North, the solid Churchmanship of the Grenvilles, Addington, Portland, or Rockingham, or the evangelical piety of a Perceval.[146] Pitt would scarcely have understood the tortuous spiritual path of a Grafton towards the final serenity of the Unitarian chapel in Essex Street. In a way, among George III's premiers, his religious position most resembled, superficially, the cool rationalism, tinged with dissenting sympathies, of his old Chathamite colleague, Lord Shelburne. Yet Shelburne at least was *interested* in matters clerical and (Paley or no Paley) there is little evidence that Pitt was. After Pitt's death his Tory successors strove to Christianize his memory, even to the extent of repeatedly publishing and maintaining that he had received the Sacrament on his deathbed.[147] That this was a lie was well known among Pitt's intimate circle, from Canning to Wilberforce, and at least one of his coterie during his lifetime, William Eden, Lord Auckland, had the courage to remind the prime minister that purity of mind and strictness of morality would not alone suffice on the final

---

[143] John Ehrman, *The Younger Pitt* (New York, 1969), p. 16.
[144] ESRO, Boucher Papers, BOU/A/3/6, Boucher to Eden, January 8, 1794.
[145] Burke, *Works*, v, p. 292.
[146] Lord Grenville, ed., "Letters written by the late earl of Chatham to his nephew Thomas Pitt ..." (London, 1821).
[147] James J. Sack, "The memory of Burke and the memory of Pitt," *HJ*, 30 (September 1987), pp. 623–40.

day.[148] The Pittite Christianization campaign came to a gradual
end in the 1830s, along with the general conclusion of the Tory
attempt to memorialize the late statesman through clubs and
monuments, by which time with the embarrassing accumulation of
memoirs and reminiscences, Croker was reduced to writing that Pitt
was a *secret* Christian.[149] The proverbial nail in the coffin, however,
was delivered by Pitt's niece, the Lady Hester Stanhope, in her
memoirs, published in 1843. The motherless Lady Hester had lived
with her uncle for long periods of her young life and she stated, with
no doubt some pardonable exaggeration, that Mr. Pitt never went
to church in his life. "Nothing prevented his going to church when
he was at Walmer; but he never even talked about religion, and
never brought it upon the carpet."[150]

Hence, Pitt, with his support for parliamentary reform, his early
cordiality with the dissenting interest, his hostility to the American
war, and his refusal to attend church or to avow religious sentiments
which he did not feel, was an unusual individual, even for the high
enlightenment of the eighteenth century, to be leading a party of the
Right; and, in fact, Pitt at least in the 1780s may not have been
leading such a party at all. This has led to some historiographical
disorder. For example, Karl Schweizer and R. Klein appear
bemused that Henry Sampson Woodfall, the radical-oriented
printer of the *Public Advertiser*, made an about-face between 1784
and 1793 from his "earlier liberal position" to support Pitt as a
"proponent of Tory principles."[151] In fact, of course, Woodfall was
not doing anything of the sort and only in retrospect does such a
statement make any sense. The French Revolution changed a great
deal in the development of British party politics but even here the
role of chance may have been more important than any deeply laid
political commitment. Lord Brougham, upon reflection, felt that the
sides which Pitt and Fox took upon the Revolution and its manifes-
tations were not predetermined and depended mainly on the acci-
dent of one being in office and the other in opposition. Had a
Regency been formed in 1789 and Fox found himself minister, it
might well have been Pitt who led the forces of Reform rather than

---

[148] Bishop of Bath and Wells, ed., *Journal and Correspondence of William, Lord Auckland* (London, 1861), Auckland to Pitt, May 10, 1800, IV, p. 108.
[149] *Quarterly Review*, 62 (June 1838), p. 246.
[150] Robert Rouiere Pearce, *Memoirs and Correspondence of the Most Noble Richard Marquess Wellesley* (London, 1846), II, p. 406.
[151] Schweizer, Klein, "French Revolution," p. 93.

the forces of Order.[152] Yet whatever his own hesitations or whatever the disdain felt for him by the Burkes or Windhams or Reeveses of loyalism, by the end of his first ministry Pitt was indubitably leading an anti-Reform party which took much of its spiritual inspiration from seventeenth and eighteenth-century forces with which before 1793 the Younger Pitt (or his father) would certainly not have chosen to associate himself.

Insofar as Pitt thought about such matters at all, which given his busy, even exhausting, schedule, was perhaps not a great deal, the January 30, 1789 Charles I memorial sermon of his former tutor and close friend, Pretyman, Bishop of Lincoln, was probably reflective of his own views. At a time of high drama, in the midst of the Regency crisis, it is doubtful that the Bishop of Lincoln would have embarrassed Pitt with a controversial anathema upon the prime minister's own views. And Pretyman delivered at Westminster Abbey one of the most anti-Charles I sermons of the eighteenth century. The Stuart monarch, said Lincoln, showed contempt for the rights of the English people. The bishop praised those who had resisted Charles in the 1630s and 1640s as worthies who saved England from absolutism and popery.[153] As late as January 1793, in one of the first issues of the new, government-inspired daily newspaper, the *True Briton*, and at a time when the evidence is fairly clear that the Pittite leadership was quite concerned with the content of both it and its sister publication, the *Sun*, a fairly negative assessment of Charles I's reign appeared. Charles enforced "hateful" prerogatives on his subjects. While Louis XVI, lately executed, "might have been suffered to live, without danger to the people; ... *Charles* left the *English* no other option than to make him their victim ..."[154]

Such views from within Pitt's inner circle of the late 1780s and from his leading newspaper of the early 1790s were quite distinct from those of a slightly later period and illustrate the extent to which the Pittite tradition changed its tune after the Terror. Pitt's subsidized hacks of the 1790s like John Bowles, the Rev. John Ireland, John Gifford or William Cobbett had quite different views of English history from those of the Bishop of Lincoln or the early *True Briton*. John Bowles, one of the leading English anti-revolutionary

---

[152] Henry Lord Brougham, *Historical Sketches of Statesmen Who Flourished in the Time of George III* (London, 1839), III, pp. 304–5.

[153] George, Lord Bishop of Lincoln, "A sermon preached before the Lords ... on ... January 30, 1789" (London, 1789), pp. 12–14.

[154] *True Briton*, January 28, 1793.

propagandists of the 1790s, put forth the view that Charles I made too many (not too few) concessions to the malcontents of the 1630s and early 1640s. Hence, he "laid the foundations of his own ruin, and of all the calamities which afterwards afflicted his country." The lesson Charles I thereby left to his successors was never to "*begin* to concede their just and lawful rights." Bowles praised the king for going to war in 1642 and for his firmness then, even though things turned out badly "*in consequence* of the delay which had *attended the adoption of vigorous measures.*"[155] Another of Pitt's stable of pamphlet writers, the Rev. John Ireland, in "Vindiciae Regiae," in a most un-Chathamlike fashion, compared seventeenth-century Puritans with eighteenth-century Jacobins and accused the Long Parliament of the 1640s and the French Assembly of the 1790s of legislating upon "certain imaginary wrongs."[156] John Gifford, the recipient of much Pittite largess founded the *Anti-Jacobin Review* on the principles of Charles Leslie and Jones of Nayland and "We profess ourselves to be *Tories* and *High Churchmen.*"[157] When Cobbett returned from America in 1800, he was offered the editorship of one of the two chief Pittite newspapers, the *True Briton*, which he declined.[158] He also dined at Windham's house, with the prime minister and George Canning – a singular, even unique, honor for a journalist as far as Pitt's presence was concerned.[159] He then became editor of a new daily, the *Porcupine*, which John Heriot, editor of the traditional Pittite papers, the *Sun* and the *True Briton*, suspected was now favored by the public offices "in points of confidential communication," over his own papers.[160] This new "Tyrtaeus of newspapers," as Sir Frederick Morton Eden called it,[161] quickly achieved a Cobbettian slant on history which in the absence of any refutation and in view of the personal and financial honors heaped on Cobbett in the year before Pitt's resignation as prime minister, probably approximates to what passed for Pittite Toryism in the last hours of the eighteenth century. Cobbett questioned the propriety and even the naturalness of rejoicing at the Revolution of 1688, as placing a foreigner on the throne could only be justified by

---

[155] John Bowles, "French aggression praised from Mr. Erskine's 'View of the causes of the war'" (London, 1797), pp. 123–4.
[156] [Rev. John Ireland], "Vindiciae Regiae" (London, 1797), pp. 69–70.
[157] *Anti-Jacobin Review*, v (March 1800), p. 290.
[158] *Cobbett's Political Register*, October 12, 1805.   [159] *Ibid.*, 69 (April 10, 1830), p. 456.
[160] BL, Windham Papers, Add. MSS. 37880, Heriot to Windham, November 16, 1800, fo. 12.
[161] Sir Frederick Morton Eden, "Eight letters on the peace" (London, 1802), pp. 1–2.

a dire necessity.[162] He also blamed the French Revolution on the American model: "*the example of America* has ... been the principal foundation of that poisonous stream of republicanism, which has watered but too great a part of this island."[163] Such sentiments are after all difficult to reconcile with whatever was known by educated readers of the views of the youthful Younger Pitt. So, by the time of his death in 1806, while there is scant evidence that Pitt himself changed his relatively liberal views on issues ranging from parliamentary reform to abolition, from the need for eventual Catholic emancipation to a Whiggish outlook on history, philosophy, and theology, nonetheless, much of the propaganda which his pamphlet and newspaper hacks sent forth to the British people told a quite different story. Even before the obscenity of the attempt to transform him into an extreme (and finally ultra) Protestant Tory had gained steam, Pitt's private and public personas were perhaps more dichotomized than those of most politicians.

I have written elsewhere of the attempt by his followers to Christianize and Protestantize Pitt after 1806, and the split, broadly, between the pro-Catholic and anti-Catholic Pittites which ensued.[164] For almost a generation after his death, Pitt's followers could much more enthusiastically embrace the name of "Pittite," and far more efficaciously embrace the often spurious legacy of their master, than ever they did the name or principles of "Tory" or "Toryism." Some of this was almost comical. Lord Malmesbury resolved to conduct his political career and hang his principles "on what I supposed would be his [Pitt's], were he still in existence, whether in or out of office."[165] Other Pittites quarreled over who were the pure and who were the not-so-pure Pittites.[166] The term and the memory were made elastic enough that all sorts of disparate figures could accept it. Thus, within the royal family, the Duke of Cumberland kept a bust of Pitt in his library,[167] while his wayward sister-in-law, the Princess of Wales, was proud to "name herself a Pittite" and hoped that the "Pittites may reign for ever and ever

---

[162] *Porcupine*, November 10, 1800.   [163] *Ibid.*, November 25, 1800.

[164] Sack, "Memory of Burke," pp. 623–40.

[165] Third Earl of Malmesbury, ed., *Diaries and Correspondence of James Harris, First Earl of Malmesbury* (London, 1844), IV, p. 350.

[166] For example, Lord Fitzharris, Earl of Malmesbury, ed., *Series of Letters of the First Earl of Malmesbury, His Family and Friends from 1745 to 1820* (London, 1870), Fitzharris to Malmesbury, November 20, 1809, II, p. 191, and reply, November 23, 1809, p. 195.

[167] *Correspondence of Prince of Wales*, VII, pp. 275–6.

..."[168] But there is no need to doubt the sincerity of those like Lord Liverpool who as prime minister himself "endeavoured to make the Principles of Mr. Pitt the chief guide of our Political conduct ..."[169] or of J. C. Herries who sought to establish an apostolic succession between Pitt and his successors Portland, Perceval, Liverpool, Canning, and Goderich.[170]

Some within literary loyalism wished to ditch Toryism altogether as a proper descriptive name for the party of the Right. The *Anti-Jacobin Review*, in a series later than the one which trumpeted its Tory identity, decried the usage of "Tory" in 1819 as anachronistic and suggested that "the only real English party [is made up of] the supporters of the *Pitt System*."[171] In 1822, the *New European Magazine* disavowed the "invidious distinctions of Whig and Tory" and declared itself Pittite.[172] But with the controversy surrounding the Protestantization of the Pitt Club and the increasing popularity of "Tory'" and eventually "conservative," the term gradually died out save in a few peculiar circumstances. Croker kept the name up: in 1838, he described himself in a private letter in almost funereal terms as a "humble and far distant follower of Mr. Pitt";[173] in one of the last articles he wrote for the *Quarterly*, in 1852, he repeated the usage.[174] Charles Newdigate Newdegate, MP for Warwickshire, reflecting, consciously or not, his distant relative's dislike of the Tory name, also preferred Pittite to Tory as late as mid-century.[175]

A major problem with the Pittite usage was, of course, the mere lapse of time. As first the years, then the decades, passed since Pitt's death, a new generation of politicians grew up who had not placed their hands in his wounds and who were thus much less influenced by his personality or presence.

Then, too, the artificiality of the William Pitt of the Pitt Clubs was so blatant as to cause Pitt and his principles to be almost as controversial in death as they were in life. For example, on Catholic

---

[168] *Ibid.*, Caroline to Dundas, April 11, 1807, VI, p. 164n.
[169] BL, Liverpool Papers, Add. MSS. 38255, Liverpool to John Gifford, January 8, 1814 (draft), fo. 315.
[170] BL, Herries Papers, Add. MSS. 57403, Herries to Bexley, December 28, 1827, fo. 168.
[171] *Anti-Jacobin Review*, 55 (January 1819), pp. 453–6.
[172] *New European Magazine*, 1 (September 1822), p. 255; 1 (October 1822), p. 296.
[173] [Earl of Rosebery], *Wellesley Papers* (London, 1914), Croker to Wellesley, April 5, 1838, II, p. 329.
[174] *Quarterly Review*, 91 (June 1852), p. 254.
[175] Walter L. Arnstein, *Protestant Versus Catholic in Mid-Victorian England* (Columbia, Mo., 1982), p. 15.

relief, Canning asserted in the House of Commons in April 1812 that had Pitt been living he would have voted for a motion which Canning sponsored.[176] A year later, another of Pitt's old chums, George Rose, asserted with equal vehemence that Pitt would have voted against Grattan's motion for a committee on the Catholic claims.[177] This Canning then denied.[178] A few weeks later, on the second reading of the Catholic Relief Bill, the eccentric and possibly insane Dr. Duigenan, asserted that Pitt would never have supported the bill at all.[179]

A similar quarrel took place on Pitt's mature attitude towards the cause he had espoused as a young politician, parliamentary reform. In 1817, on Francis Burdett's motion for a reform of parliament, Sir John Nicholl, on flimsy evidence, stated that Pitt had changed his mind since the 1780s. Burdett chose to interpret this as a "slander upon his [Pitt's] memory."[180] As late as 1831, Lord Harewood told a Pitt Club meeting that the late prime minister would never have supported the Reform Bill![181] Such assertions and counter-assertions went on and on until, most probably, the political nation tired of them as later generations tired of the debate over Canning's or Peel's principles.

If Pitt's life and legacy, however artificial they might prove to be, were a, arguably in fact the, main element in a developing early nineteenth-century British conservative tradition, another constituent was the ideological legacy of Edmund Burke. In retrospect, of course, Burke appears as by far the leading European conservative figure of the eighteenth or nineteenth centuries, more than justifying Gilbert Elliot's description of him as "the new and better Aristotle,"[182] whose impact on French, German, and Anglo-American philosophical and political thought is obvious. I have argued elsewhere, however, that in the short run of the early nineteenth century, Burke's legacy to an emerging British conservative movement was so controversial, especially in its Irish Catholic and Indian aspects, as to leave him sometimes reviled and often ignored by many of his "Church and King" confrères. It was much easier to construct an artificial Pitt to celebrate rather than to

[176] *Parl. Deb.*, xxii, (April 23, 1812), pp. 1038–9.
[177] *Ibid.*, xxiv, (March 2, 1813), p. 1028.
[178] *Ibid.*, p. 1071.   [179] *Ibid.*, xxvi (May 13, 1813), p. 119.
[180] *Ibid.*, xxxvi (May, 20, 1817), p. 746.
[181] *Standard*, May 30, 1831.
[182] Burke, *Corr.*, Elliot to Burke, November 6, 1790, vi, p. 156.

wave incense before a Burke who incessantly denounced *even in the last decade of his life* racism in India or injustice in Ireland.[183] But there was a Burkeian tradition in British politics of the late eighteenth and early nineteenth centuries, in most ways in implicit rivalry with the Pittite tradition, and often fitting the British Right as uncomfortably as the Pittite one (however bogus the cloth) fitted most of it easily.

There is a sense, of course, even despite the obvious political differences of the protagonists, that the Burkeite tradition grew out of the older Johnsonian one. Johnson and Burke were intimate from the 1750s and admired each other; indeed, Arthur Murphy recalled that the two men spent Christmas Day together in 1758 and observed that "Johnson would from Edmund hear contradiction, which he would *tolerate* from no other person."[184] Despite their intense disagreement on *factional* political issues, on crucial questions involving royalism, Ireland, Catholicism, the state of the Church of England, a humanitarian quality to life, even in a wider sense, on their skeptical attitudes towards the Enlightenment, they shared strikingly similar views: one might say that they both had Counter-Reformation minds. They were each loyal members of The Club and E. C. Mossner thought Johnson greatly influenced prejudices there.[185] The Johnson inveighing against Rousseau as one who "ought to be hunted out of society" and transported,[186] resembles even in cadence the aged Burke at Beaconsfield telling his Christmastide guest James Mackintosh that as regards the new school of philosophers, "They deserve no refutation, but those of the common hangman."[187]

This Johnsonian quality to Burke's mind did not go unnoticed by his contemporaries. Horace Walpole thought in the early 1770s that Burke was no moderate man and on non-Rockinghamite issues leaned to the arbitrary side;[188] Sheridan questioned his true reformist tendencies in the early 1780s;[189] Jane Burke told Boswell in 1778 that her husband was a monarchist;[190] Boswell

[183] Sack, "Memory of Burke," pp. 623–40.
[184] John Pike Emery, *Arthur Murphy* (Philadelphia, 1946), p. 46.
[185] Ernest Campbell Mossner, *Forgotten Hume: Le Bon David* (New York, 1943), pp. 195–6.
[186] Boswell, *Life*, p. 359.
[187] Robert James Mackintosh, ed., *Memoirs of the Life of the Right Honourable Sir James Mackintosh* (London, 1836), I, pp. 93–4.
[188] *Last Journals of Walpole*, I, p. 81.   [189] Namier and Brooke, II, p. 152.
[190] Charles McC. Weis, Frederick A. Pottle, eds., *Boswell: In Extremes, 1776–1778* (New York, 1970), p. 270.

told Johnson at the time of the Coalition that Burke was a Tory.[191]

Johnson and Burke shared many friends: Boswell of course, Bishop Barnard, Windham. Both men made some attempt to use their dominating intellectual positions (and their drawn-out death-bed scenes) to attract and influence promising young men who would carry principles dear to them into another time. Hence, Lord Eldon many years later reflected how the dying lexicographer sent him, young John Scott, a pleading message to attend public worship every Sunday in the Church of England.[192] On that same deathbed Johnson placed a New Testament in Windham's hands.[193] Windham and Burke were among Johnson's pallbearers and Windham performed the same rite a decade and a half later for Burke.

It is also interesting how terms like "idol" or "incense" or "god" are used so frequently when Johnson and Burke and their circles are discussed. Lord Holland thought Johnson was the "living idol" of The Club and that after his death Windham and Sir William Scott (Eldon's brother) worshipped and "officiated as High Priests," offering incense before his shrine.[194] As far as Windham's relations with Burke were concerned, Holland thought he was "the great god of his idolatry."[195] And Wilberforce, observing the attention which Windham, French Laurence and others of that group paid to Burke on *his* deathbed was reminded of "the treatment of Ahitophel of old. It was as if one went to inquire of the oracle of the Lord."[196] Windham indeed told Mackintosh that Burke's words were simply "the source of all good."[197]

It was the glamorous young Windham, of course, despite concupiscence and despite Glasgow University, who was chosen to carry the pure spirit of Johnsonian Tory Anglicanism and Burkeite counter-revolutionary ideology into the realms of practical politics. It is clear from his published *Diary*, despite an early radical disposition, that Windham took religion seriously. Even as a young man he attended

---

[191] *Boswell: Applause of Jury*, p. 86.
[192] Horace Twiss, *Public and Private Life of Lord Chancellor Eldon* (London, 1844), I, p. 168.
[193] Mrs. Henry Baring, ed., *Diary of the Right Hon. William Windham, 1784 to 1810* (London, 1866), p. 28.
[194] Lord Stavordale, ed., *Further Memoirs of the Whig Party, 1807–1821* by Henry Richard Vassall, Third Lord Holland (New York, 1905), p. 361.
[195] Henry Edward Lord Holland, ed., *Memoirs of the Whig Party During My Time* by Henry Richard Lord Holland (London, 1854), II, p. 207.
[196] Burke, *Corr.*, IX, p. xxiv.   [197] *Memoirs of Mackintosh*, I, p. 127.

church and read sermons.[198] Before ascending into the heavens on his famous balloon ride, he left behind an affirmation of his faith in Christ's divine commission.[199] He took some trouble in 1809, before his fatal operation, to receive the Sacrament.[200] His politics too had an ideological edge to them quite consonant with Johnson and Burke's principles but foreign to Pitt's. It was to the Portland Whig Windham that John Reeves came for patronage,[201] that John Bowles and William Playfair saw as the mentor for their *Revolutionary Magazine*,[202] who aided Cobbett with enthusiasm when he returned from America,[203] who supported (nearly alone) Reeves in his trauma over the high prerogative pamphlet of 1795,[204] who received from John Robison the dedication to *Proofs of a Conspiracy* in 1797,[205] and who took up the cause of the Royalists in the Vendée and elsewhere; as he told Dundas in 1796, "I would, from the beginning, have made this the principal object of the war . . ."[206]

If Windham was to be the principal bearer of the Johnsonian–Burkeite legacy, as Canning in his own mind (if in the minds of few others) was to be that of Pitt's, the choice may have been a flawed one. Windham lacked that generosity of spirit which marked out both Johnson and Burke (and, at times, Canning), and, again, unlike Canning or Perceval, on the Pittite side, was unable to attract more than a few devoted followers to his cause. The term "hatred" often crops up when Windham is discussed. Hazlitt had it on fairly good authority that Pitt, not an excessively retributive politician, hated Windham.[207] Wilberforce came as close as a saint could to such a sentiment.[208] Windham himself, odd for a politician at any time, refused to attend Pitt's funeral in the Abbey.[209] He was, I

[198] *Diary of Windham*, pp. 8–10.
[199] Earl of Rosebery, ed., *Windham Papers* (Boston, 1913), I, p. 79.
[200] *Diary of Windham*, p. 505.
[201] For example, BL, Windham Papers, Add. MSS. 37874, Reeves to Windham, August 1, 1794, fo. 37.
[202] *Ibid.*, Add. MSS. 37875: Bowles to Windham, October 1, 1795, fos. 219–27; Playfair to Windham, November 4, 1795, fos. 247–8.
[203] For example, *Ibid.*, Add. MSS. 37853, Cobbett to Windham, August 4, 1800, fo. 1.
[204] *Ibid.*, Add. MSS. 37876, Reeves to Windham, May 21, 1796, fo. 118.
[205] See the dedication to John Robison's *Proofs of a Conspiracy Against All the Religions and Governments of Europe* (Edinburgh, 1797).
[206] BL Windham Papers, Add. MSS. 37876, Windham to Dundas (copy), May 1, 1796, fo. 89.
[207] *New Monthly Magazine*, 17 (April 1826), p. 175.
[208] Robert Isaac Wilberforce, Samuel Wilberforce, eds., *Correspondence of William Wilberforce* (London, 1840), Wilberforce to Hannah More, November 15, 1804, I, p. 340.
[209] *Life of Minto*, Minto to his wife, February 22, 1806, III, p. 379.

suspect, the ideological politician par excellence, unable to take criticism, constructive or not, of his (or Burke's) ideas, lacking, especially as he grew older, the talent for good fellowship on any sustained basis; in a way, as Brougham recognized, the perfect follower, but unable to transform himself in any creditable way into a lead actor.[210]

Orthodox Burkeianism was already somewhat diluted before the master's death from its pure canon of 1793 and 1794, when it was the leading intellectual current in the decision of the Portland Whigs to adhere to Pitt's ministry. The same fissure, Ireland and Catholicism, this time in the form of the Fitzwilliam viceroyalty, that plagued the British Right throughout the nineteenth century, had caused irreparable damage to the Portlandites by 1795. Burke by that point decided that his old friend the Duke of Portland, Pitt's home secretary, was "the very man who destroyed the Catholicks, and his own friend [Fitzwilliam], and himself, for ever."[211] Burke and Portland were never really reconciled. Burke rarely saw or communicated with him thereafter, and he was only asked to carry the pall at Burke's funeral because he had performed the same function for Richard Burke in 1794.[212] Burke's other special followers, Lord Fitzwilliam, French Laurence, William Elliot, and Windham, scarcely four years after Burke's death, found themselves in opposition to one of Burke's other pallbearers, Henry Addington, and, shortly thereafter, in alliance with the Foxite Whigs. Though in the case of Windham, the alliance was an uneasy one, there they stayed, in opposition to the living and dead Pittites.

As in the case of the Pittite succession, there were public quarrels in the House of Commons over the exact nature of the Burkeite legacy, especially over Catholicism and slavery. From an ideological perspective, Whigs or not, the surviving Burkeites were probably at the extreme Right of the political spectrum. But as the years passed and circumstances changed, it became difficult to see anything particularly Burkeian in their activities. French Laurence, whom Burke once tipped as one who would "by degrees ... become a central point to which Men of talents might be aggregated,"[213] by

---

[210] Brougham, *Historical Sketches*, I, pp. 219–20.
[211] Burke, *Corr.*, Burke to Bishop Hussey, November 27, 1795, VIII, p. 352.
[212] *Ibid.*, Burke to Mrs. Crewe, December 27, 1796, IX, p. 207; Laurence to Fitzwilliam, July 9, 1797, IX, p. 374.
[213] *Ibid.*, Burke to Laurence, December 23, 1796, IX, pp. 196–7.

the nineteenth century enrolled Burke in the pro-slavery cause,[214] and, in a commentary on *Revelation*, suggested that the Bishop of Rome just might be Anti-Christ after all.[215] The Duke of Portland told the king in 1807 that the Grenvilles and Foxites (with their Burkeian allies), with their paltry attempt to allow Roman Catholics into the higher positions in the army and navy, were striving to "subvert the Constitution of the country in Church and State."[216] Windham, with his nineteenth-century volte-face on the abolition of the slave trade,[217] his suspicions of the Spanish rebels as too democratically oriented,[218] his antagonism towards Curwen's bill against selling and buying parliamentary seats,[219] and his extreme aversion to a cruelty-to-animals bill,[220] became a simple out-and-out reactionary of a more settled variety than virtually anyone else in the political nation. Fitzwilliam, besides his anti-government activities during the Peterloo crisis, set up a British and Foreign Bible Society at Sheffield.[221]

All of these views, save perhaps the opposition to Curwen's bill, were a far cry from Burke's beliefs. Hence, in a way, and despite all the fuss, Burke may have had no successor. Perhaps, even somewhat unwittingly, his purported disciples all tried in varying degrees to wiggle out of his admittedly unpopular legacy. That legacy, a stern opposition to British imperialism in India and Ireland, no less than French imperialism and radicalism in Europe, was difficult to graft onto the body of any British political party or faction whether of his native Whiggery or of Pittite Toryism.[222]

Jonathan Clark was only the latest historian or political theorist to argue that Burke "departed from his early radicalism to emerge, after the French Revolution, as a champion of the Anglican-aristocratic-monarchical regime."[223] Yet I doubt that Burke was ever very radical or, if Ireland was included, and few of his loyalist contemporaries would have been prepared to exclude it – very much of a champion of the Anglican-aristocratic-monarchical regime. Or if he were such a champion it was on his own anti-imperialist and pro-Catholic terms – terms which few of his friends in the party of

---

[214] *Parl. Deb.*, II (January 7, 1804), pp. 552–7.
[215] *British Critic*, 41 (February 1813), pp. 147–52.
[216] Aspinall, IV, p. 550.   [217] *Parl. Deb.*, II, (June 7, 1804), pp. 552–7.
[218] *Further Memoirs of Whig Party*, p. 15.
[219] Aspinall, V, p. 269.   [220] *Parl. Deb.*, XIV (June 13, 1809), pp. 1029ff.
[221] A. D. Harvey, *Britain in the Early Nineteenth Century* (London, 1978), p. 77.
[222] Sack, "Memory of Burke," pp. 639–40.   [223] Clark, *English Society*, p. 250.

Order could really accept. On abiding issues, Burke was remarkably consistent through all the stages of his life.

Hence by the second and third decades of the nineteenth century, in many ways, Burke's political legacy was remarkably battered and had experienced in the short run, a near fatal encounter with that of Pitt. Pitt and Burke, while hardly soulmates, were not on the opposing sides, necessarily, of the issues which Burke regarded as the most important ones of his life: opposition to the French Revolution, the Hastings affair, and the wrongs done to the Irish Catholics. But the seeming lack of personal passion of Pitt and his immediate coterie on these questions hardly melded well with the consuming ardor of the Burkeians.

The Pittite–Burkeite quarrels about the conduct of the war, about the priority of Ireland, and in a grander sense, about the purpose of life in general, forged in the crucible of the Cabinet during the years after the accession of the Portland Whigs to the Pitt administration, were reflected in the press as well as in high politics. The leading Pittite organs, the *Sun* and the *True Briton*, rarely gave Burke the benefit of the doubt. The *Sun* had no qualms in twitting Burke as much as the opposition press did about his famous pension. It suggested in 1796, that he cease to meddle in the politics of the day and in 1797, that his war-like opinions were no longer practicable.[224] The *True Briton* in 1802 supposed that the Burke school lacked common sense and was too quick to push its ideas to extremes.[225] John Taylor, editor of the *Sun* in the early nineteenth century, always remained extremely loyal to Pitt's memory, adored Lord Eldon, and had nothing but praise for other right-wing epistolary luminaries like John Bowles, John Reeves, and John Gifford.[226] But, as he admitted in his memoirs, he found Burke an "irritable man" with a "vulgar mind" and expressed surprise that "Dr. Johnson should have held him in such high admiration ..."[227]

Along with Burke's "Reflections," the contemporary work which most defined the nineteenth-century British Right was Sir Richard Musgrave's *Memoirs of the Different Rebellions in Ireland*, published in 1801. Musgrave's account, from the preface to the conclusion, was a long critique of Burke's baneful influence on Irish and English life

[224] *Sun*, October 7 and 12, 1796; November 10, 1797.
[225] Quoted by *Cobbett's Political Register*, August 21–28, 1802.
[226] John Taylor, *Records of My Life* (London, 1982), II, pp. 216, 279, 356–9.
[227] *Ibid.*, I, pp. 124–5; II, pp. 194, 259.

and politics. Musgrave's Burke was a hypocrite who "always shewed a decided attachment to popery." Indeed, he almost converted to Catholicism in the 1750s while studying law in London at a time when he was a "slave ... to the passion of love" for the Romanist Jane Nugent.[228] On a personal level, Burke raised up his only child, that "over-weaning, petulant young man," Richard, with a "predilection for popery."[229] On a wider political stage, Burke "sedulously and successfully" from his very first entrance into the Rockinghamite party in the mid-1760s, attempted to enroll the Whigs into a pro-Catholic stance and hence they "departed from those wise lessons which the history and experiences of past ages uniformly afford, and adopted a visionary system of concession, which shook the pillars of the throne."[230] Then in a rather crude attempt to link Burke, who after all died in 1797, with the horrors of the rebellion of 1798, Musgrave discussed the "enormities" of the Jacobite Whiteboys of the 1750s and 1760s in ways in which the reader might well confuse Jacobite with Jacobin. Musgrave accused Burke of raising money from the Irish Catholics for the use of these "exclusively papist" marauders.[231] Thus was Burke presented to the loyalist reading public only four years after his death.

George III too, while he learned to appreciate Windham's war views, was always able to restrain his admiration for his ancient enemy, Edmund Burke, suddenly transmogrified into the supporter of all kings. Especially in regard to Ireland, the king, certainly no Pittite despite 1783, but probably more representative than his prime minister of a right-wing strain in the political nation, in 1795 denounced the "desire of paying implicit obedience to the heated imagination of Mr. Burke";[232] and in 1804, bemoaned the "wild ideas" of Burke which had ensnared even the pragmatic Dundas in the resignations of 1801.[233] If George III, the Duke of Portland, or Sir Richard Musgrave attacked the Burkeites from the Right in regard, especially, to Ireland, the Tory loyalist Jonathan Boucher, showing that not all Tories had forgotten or forgiven 1776–1781, did as well with regard to America. In his influential "View of the causes and consequences of the American revolution," published in

---

[228] Sir Richard Musgrave, *Memoirs of the Different Rebellions in Ireland*, (Dublin, 1802), I, pp. 40–1.

[229] *Ibid.*, I, p. 108.   [230] *Ibid.*, I, pp. vii–ix.   [231] *Ibid.*, I, p. 43.

[232] Earl Stanhope, *Life of the Right Honourable William Pitt* (London, 1861), George III to Pitt, February 6, 1795, II, p. xxv.

[233] *Ibid.*, George III to Pitt, May 5, 1804, IV, p. ix.

1797, Boucher remarked that "Had Mr. Burke prefaced his Reflections ... with an acknowledgement of his having been in error
respecting that of America, ages to some, as well as the present,
would have blessed his memory." Yet, as it was, Burke's "fair fame"
was "tarnished" as the "abettor of the American revolt."[234]

Therefore whether the reaction was Pittite, or in the case of the
king, Musgrave or Boucher, somewhere to Pitt's right, one must
never overestimate the extent to which Burke and his legacy were
integrated into an emerging Tory dogma in the decades after the
French Revolution. The nadir of formal relations between the
Pittites and Burkeites occurred in 1806 surrounding the fuss
Windham made in the House of Commons over the motion to grant
the deceased Pitt a public funeral. A good deal of the Windhamite
opposition to this motion came from an admitted jealousy that
Burke in 1797 had not received such (or any) public honors on his
death.[235] By this time, of course, the Burkeites were in a firm alliance
with the Grenvillites and Foxites in opposition, first to Pitt himself,
and then to his heirs. This schism turned a fledgling Tory party into
something quite different than it would have been had Burke and his
principles triumphed or at least coexisted with those of Pitt's heirs.

In his famous letter to Sir Hercules Langrishe in 1795, Burke had
written that "I think I can hardly overrate the malignity of the
principles of Protestant ascendancy, as they affect Ireland; or of
Indianism, as they affect ... Asia; or of Jacobinism, as they affect all
Europe, and the state of human society itself. The last is the greatest
evil."[236] But, upon reflection, shortly before his death, Burke
decided that Indianism was of the three evils, "the worst by far."[237]
These were hardly sound Tory notions to edify the age of Peel and
Wellington. Burke, of course, had his admirers on the Right. J. W.
Croker was one. But his comments on Burke in the *Quarterly Review*
at mid-century show the problems for a committed conservative
having to grapple with Burke's legacy. Croker thought it strange
that Burke, in the midst of the wars of the French Revolution,
thought the matter of Warren Hastings was "the most important
labour of his life." Try as he might, Croker wrote, the "enthusiasm
of hostility" which Burke felt for Hastings was something "we have

[234] Jonathan Boucher, "View of the causes and consequences of the American revolution in
thirteen discourses" (London, 1797), pp. xv–xviin.
[235] *Parl. Deb.*, VI (January 27, 1806), pp. 50–1.
[236] Burke, *Corr.*, Burke to Langrishe, May 26, 1795, VIII, p. 179.
[237] *Ibid.*, Burke to Loughborough, *c.* March 17, 1796, p. 432.

always felt ourselves unable satisfactorily to account [for] ..."[238]
Samuel Johnson, however, whose *Life* by Boswell Croker edited for
John Murray in 1831, would have understood perfectly.

III

Norman Gash has emphasized in his research on the fortunes of the
Conservative party in the 1830s and 1840s the importance of the
Carlton Club, founded in 1831, as a meeting place and party
headquarters in the capital and how by the election of 1841 Con-
servative Associations and Constitutional Associations dotted the
English counties.[239] Although the crucial role which a club like the
Carlton played in Conservative party successes was new, the local
Conservative Associations were not. From at least the 1790s, the
decade of domestic agitation surrounding the French Revolution,
they had grown swiftly throughout England. Before 1790, the evidence for the existence or importance of loyalist clubs is more spotty.
John Brewer has noted how remarkable it was in the 1760s that

existing clubs and associations ... rapidly pledged themselves to the radical
cause, and how few (I know of none) came out in opposition to reformist
politics. The Albion, the Antigallican, the Brethren of the Cheshire
Cheeses, the Bucks ... all seem to have deliberately chosen to align
themselves with the forces of reform.[240]

Hence, just as it was difficult to find many pro-royalist newspapers
during the Wilkite crisis, so it was also difficult to find an openly
pro-royalist club. There is some evidence that this changed during
the American war. Bristol, for example, had a Loyal and Constitutional Club, replete with "Church and King" toasts, in 1779.[241]
Westminster had a Constitutional Club in the 1780s to oppose the
Foxite Whig Club. At Nottingham, the Old Tory Interest formed
the White Lion in 1774, a Northite organization which gave way to
a series of loyalist clubs at the end of the eighteenth century and to a
Pitt Club in the nineteenth.[242] In 1790, 300 Manchester gentlemen,
influenced by the Dissenters' assault on the Test and Corporation

---

[238] *Quarterly Review*, 79 (March 1847), p. 490.
[239] Norman Gash, *Aristocracy and People* (Cambridge, Mass., 1979), p. 163.
[240] John Brewer, "English radicalism in the age of George III," in J. G. A. Pocock, ed., *Three British Revolutions: 1641, 1688, 1776* (Princeton, 1980), p. 358.
[241] *Morning Post*, July 10, 1779.
[242] Frank O'Gorman, *Voters, Patrons, and Parties: The Unreformed Electoral System of Hanoverian England, 1743–1832* (Oxford, 1989), pp. 330–1,

Acts, formed an association for the support of the Church.[243] A historian of the Reevesian Association movement, suggests that in 1792 and 1793, former Constitutional Societies in places as diverse as Manchester, Penzance, Wednesbury, and Rotherham merely changed their names to Loyal Associations.[244] Since by February 1793, there were over 1,000 Loyal Associations throughout Britain, it is possible once the Jacobin internal danger seemed less severe, that these were the origins of many of the loyal clubs and associations that proliferated in the late Hanoverian period.

By the early nineteenth century, besides the Pitt Clubs, the two chief local loyalist organizations appear to have been True Blue Clubs and King and Constitution Clubs. Maldon,[245] Derby,[246] Colchester (established in 1806),[247] Leeds,[248] Nottingham,[249] and Gloucester[250] had True Blue Clubs or as the Derby organization called itself, a Loyal True Blue Club. York (with 300 gentlemen members, established in 1819),[251] Norwich,[252] and Sutherland (with 100 members),[253] had King and Constitution Clubs. Doubtless there were many more of both varieties. Other such clubs were established to commemorate particular individuals or events. In Ipswich, the True Blue Club turned itself into a Wellington Club in 1825.[254] Stockport also had a Loyal Wellington Club, with 300 members, which met four times a year.[255] In addition to its King and Constitution Club, Norwich had a Waterloo Club,[256] a Brunswick Club (formed in 1816),[257] and an Eldon Society (established by tradesmen in 1831).[258] Liverpool had a Canning Club, formed in commemoration of the famous victory of 1812, and Gladstone senior served as president of it in the 1820s.[259] Most of these clubs, associations, or organizations were probably rather unfocused and, however important they may have been in their own communities as

---

[243] *St. James's Chronicle*, February 25–27, 1790.
[244] Robert R. Dozier, *For King, Constitution, and Country* (Lexington, 1983), p. 59.
[245] *Morning Journal*, November 12, 1829.   [246] *New Times*, April 24, 1821.
[247] *Ibid.*, November 26, 1821.
[248] *Standard*, June 10, 1831.   [249] *New Monthly Magazine*, 1 (July 1, 1814), p. 505.
[250] A. Aspinall, ed., *Three Early Nineteenth Century Diaries* (London, 1952), p. 174.
[251] *New Times*, February 26, 1819.   [252] *Ibid.*, June 1, 1820.
[253] *Ibid.*, October 30, 1821.
[254] O'Gorman, *Voters*, p. 332.   [255] *Standard*, October 6, 1827.
[256] *New Times*, March 5, 1821.
[257] PRO, Home Office 43/125, John Becket to Fayerman, December 30, 1816, fo. 333.
[258] R. L. Hill, *Toryism and the People, 1832–1846* (London, 1929), p. 44.
[259] Lewis Melville, ed., *Huskisson Papers* (London, 1931), pp. 400–1.

a medium of social control or as a focal point for local politics, they probably had little wider impact.

The unfocused aspect of the local loyal clubs changed at least somewhat with the superior position which the Pitt Clubs took over them after 1812.[260] The first local Pitt Club with significant ties to the London parent body was the North Staffordshire organization, founded in May 1813. It differed from previous local Pitt Clubs in that its members were not just London Pitt Club members associating together whilst in the country. Rather, it had a local president, secretary, treasurer, and committee of correspondence. Its members wore special dress, a Pitt commemorative medal, and adopted the same toasts as the London club. In January 1814, the parent body approved the Staffordshire organization and sent its constitution as a model into every county with a recommendation for general adoption.[261] Numerous local loyalist clubs that previously had sustained no special connection with Pitt's memory submerged themselves into this national organization. These included the Norwich King and Constitution Club,[262] the Colchester[263] and Leeds True Blue Club,[264] and, in a more qualified sense, as it retained its original name and identity, the Stockport Loyal Wellington Club.[265]

There were two abiding criticisms leveled at the Pitt Clubs: one, that they lacked a valid historicity and two, that they were elitist. The first criticism, based on the charge that some Tories through the medium of the Pitt Club (and its notorious Protestant Ascendancy toast), sought to transform the image of the Younger Pitt from the supporter of Catholic emancipation into its opponent, I have discussed elsewhere.[266] Its flavor can be ascertained by a scene in the House of Commons in 1827 when W. C. Plunket, Liverpool's attorney general for Ireland, told the House that the Pitt Club was "the most audacious forgery of modern times,"[267] and when Canning protested "against making use in any way of the authority of Mr. Pitt in order to disparage the cause which I profess to inherit from that great man."[268]

---

[260] There were around fifty local Pitt Clubs by the 1820s. Sack, "Memory of Burke," p. 635.
[261] *New Monthly Magazine*, 6 (August 1, 1816), p. 25.   [262] *New Times*, June 1, 1820.
[263] *Ibid.*, November 26, 1821.   [264] *Standard*, June 10, 1831.
[265] *New Times*, June 26, 1820.
[266] Sack, "Memory of Burke," pp. 635–8.
[267] *Parl. Deb.*, xvi, n.ser. (March 6, 1827), pp. 930–1.
[268] *Ibid.*, p. 1006.

The second criticism of the Pitt Club, that is was elitist, reflected on the situation in which the governing party or coalition in Britain found itself during the first three decades of the nineteenth century. To put it as simply as possible, as long as the king supported his Pittite or Tory ministers, a political change in direction was unlikely. Only three brief times after all (or, arguably, four if one considers 1827–1828) during the reigns of George III and George IV, and then only in extraordinary political circumstances, did the main body of the Whig opposition come to power. Only after Wellington's "loss" of the 1830 general election, the resultant reform of parliament, and the decline in the political power of the crown, all of which heralded a more "normally" functioning party system, did an alternating Whig–Tory political structure in Westminster require a more formal appeal for sustenance to the governing classes and beyond at general elections. Before 1830, relatively secure in the possession of office, ministers in particular and the governing elite in general, did not overly concern themselves with appeals to the people or any other such quasi-democratic stirrings.

The Pitt Club reflected this lack of a popular concern. Interestingly it was most felt by those elements of the Right most excluded from the magic circle of wealth and privilege. As early as 1809, the former convict, and habitué of the London Corresponding Society, Henry Redhead Yorke, editor of the Pittite *Weekly Political Review*, criticized the London Pitt Club for not giving the slightest public notice of their meetings.[269] The Jewish Lewis Goldsmith wondered in his *British Monitor* in 1818 why the Pitt Club members appeared as "nothing else than a meeting of Gentlemen, who sit down to a good dinner." Why, he asked, are they not meeting more often, printing and distributing loyalist pamphlets, giving energetic speeches, and providing the poor with free loyal newspapers?[270] The *Standard* too, edited by an Irish Protestant, S. L. Giffard, almost neurotically unsure of his own social status,[271] besought the Tories in 1832 to "root out of their minds the nonsense that to collect a club of rich men is to make a national party ..."[272] Giffard was no doubt accurate in his assessment, and the passage of the Reform Bill would

---

[269] *Redhead Yorke's Weekly Political Review*, June 3, 1809, pp. 423–4.
[270] *British Monitor*, May 24, 1818.
[271] BL, Bliss Papers, Add. MSS. 34572, Giffard to Bliss, October 17, 1837, fo. 266, where Giffard maintains that Merton College, Oxford is prejudiced against his relatively poor son.
[272] *Standard*, March 31, 1832.

immediately change matters, but underlying the failure of the Pitt Clubs to promote aggressively any far-flung right-wing agenda (however their ubiquitous Protestant Ascendancy toast might get on Catholic or liberal nerves) was an emotion deeper than nonchalance or disdain for the non-elite: there was also dread of the lower orders.

There is little doubt that the Jacobin disturbances of the 1790s had engendered a healthy fear within the English governing class of clubs and associations. One almost ubiquitous characteristic of the English Right in the early nineteenth century was its conviction that a revolution was imminent. No Marxist in Geneva in 1910 could have been more certain of this simple fact. Southey in 1816 foresaw a revolution in three years;[273] Peel in 1824 thought it at no great distance;[274] Charles Arbuthnot in 1825 that Huskisson's liberal Toryism was leading Britain towards it.[275] *Blackwood's Edinburgh Magazine* in 1827 concluded that Britain resembled France in 1788.[276] Wellington was convinced in 1831 that a rotten people would soon annihilate all property.[277] Wordsworth a year later contemplated leaving the country due to the imminence of revolution.[278] Queen Adelaide in 1834 took the fate of Marie Antoinette as her own probable destiny.[279] Given such all-encompassing views, the mistrust of the loyalist politicians and sections of the Tory press for popular right-wing organizations (not to speak of Hampden Clubs) becomes more explicable.

Even in the decade of the greatest ostensible danger from an incipient radical movement, the 1790s, the government was always able to contain its enthusiasm for both the "Church and King" mob violence in Birmingham against Dr. Priestley as well as for John Reeves and his Loyal Association.[280] There is a whole literature on the relationship (or lack thereof) between Pitt's administration and

---

273 Thomas Sadler, ed., *Diary, Reminiscences, and Correspondence of Henry Crabb Robinson* (London, 1869), II, pp. 21–2.
274 *Three Early Nineteenth Century Diaries*, p. 118.
275 A. Aspinall, ed., *Correspondence of Charles Arbuthnot*, Camden, 3rd ser., LXV (London, 1941), p. 74.
276 *Blackwood's Edinburgh Magazine*, 21 (June, 1827), p. 762.
277 Seventh Duke of Wellington, ed., *Wellington and His Friends* (London, 1965), Duke to Mrs. Arbuthnot, May 11, 1831, p. 95.
278 *Diary of Robinson*, III, p. 3.
279 Sir Herbert Maxwell, ed., *Creevey Papers* (New York, 1904), Creevey to Miss Ord, November 25, 1834, p. 642.
280 R. B. Rose, "The Priestley riots of 1791," *P&P*, 28 (November 1960), pp. 68–88. Bruce Coleman, *Conservatism and the Conservative Party in Nineteenth-Century Britain* (London, 1988), p. 31.

the Loyal Association which John Reeves called into being in
November and December of 1792 and which mushroomed
throughout the country printing and circulating loyalist propa-
ganda, and serving as the inspiration for the equally important
Volunteer movement.[281] All in all, the Association was, as Marilyn
Butler perceptively called it, a sort of counter *levée en masse*.[282]
Although in 1799 Reeves received the very lucrative position of
King's Printer, with its oversight of the printing of all Bibles and
Prayer Books in England, before this he was mortified by the
administration's evident lack of interest in his welfare. He told
Windham that during 1793 and 1794, he received "not one single
mark of civility" from the government. Pitt had never even thanked
him for his loyal activities. Why, wondered Reeves, are others made
marquesses or knights? Was not the peace of England worth more
than the taking of a French frigate?[283] When Reeves informed Pitt
in 1795 that he was preparing new Loyal Association activities, the
silence from Downing Street was deafening.[284] Robert Dozier suspects, probably correctly, that the brouhaha in late 1795 over
Reeves' high prerogative pamphlet, with Pitt and his party in
general denunciation of it, had as much to do with the potential fear
of a revived Loyal Association as it did with horror of the pamphlet
per se.[285] Reeves himself, despite his £4,000 per annum as King's
Printer, never forgave Pitt and was a solid supporter of Addington in
the early nineteenth century.[286] Cobbett asserted thirty years later
that a disappointed Reeves told him that he hated the Pitt government and its principles. He had learned from his bitter experiences
that one must either kiss government's ass or kick it.[287] Reeves
evidently preferred the latter but executed the former.

The experience of A. Thomas Fayerman, a Norwich surgeon, is
probably typical of governmental nonchalance regarding lower-
class loyalist political organizations even when faced with the threat
of radical Hampden Clubs. Fayerman, who was a nephew of John

---

[281] See especially, Dozier, *For King*; E. C. Black, *The Association* (Cambridge, Mass., 1963);
Austin Mitchell, "The Association movement of 1792–3," *HJ*, IV (1961); D. E. Ginter,
"Loyalist Association movement of 1792–3 and British public opinion," *HJ*, IX (1966).
This by no means exhausts the literature.
[282] Marilyn Butler, *Romantics, Rebels, and Reactionaries* (Oxford, 1981), p. 55.
[283] BL, Windham Papers, Add. MSS. 37874, Reeves to Windham, August 1, 1794, fos. 36–9.
[284] PRO, Chatham Papers, 30/8/170/261, Reeves to Pitt, November 10, 1795.
[285] Dozier, *For King*, p. 170.
[286] BL, Hardwicke Papers, Add. MSS. 45038, Reeves to Yorke, December 29, 1804, fos. 71–2.
[287] *Cobbett's Political Register*, 69 (May, 1, 1830), pp. 568–9.

Thomas, a late-eighteenth-century Bishop of Rochester, first established a Norwich Brunswick Club in 1816. When as a courtesy he informed the home secretary of his actions, an undersecretary responded that "Lord Sidmouth's opinion is, in general, unfavourable to Political Clubs of any Description."[288] In 1817, calling themselves the Brunswick Knights, members of the club put out a formal declaration opposing reform of parliament, calling for aid to the indigent, and declaring John Hampden a traitor. They published 500 copies per week of an unstamped paper, *The Brunswick Weekly Political Register*, given at no cost to the poor, presented a loyal address to the regent at his levee, signed by 258 poor freemen of Norwich, and, in general, followed the organizational lead of the more radical left-wing clubs.[289] When Fayerman, however, expressed a desire for the British consulship at Nice, Sidmouth refused even to forward his petition to higher authorities. As Lewis Goldsmith remarked of the Fayerman case in the *British Monitor*: "Such conduct on the part of ministers will paralyse the efforts and damp the zeal of their firmest supporters."[290] The message, however, was clear. Government preferred to handle radical organizations by themselves, without recourse to the aid of the lower orders, however friendly to the cause of king and constitution.

The famed Constitutional Association, founded in December 1820, in the wake of the government defeat over the Caroline affair, was another case in point. It was established in essence as a private organization to ferret out and then prevent by prosecution, if necessary, the publishing and circulation of objectionable books, pamphlets, and newspapers. Hence, it functioned as a sort of unofficial *Index prohibitorum librorum*.

While the initial response to the Constitutional Association by the governmental establishment, the right-wing press, and loyalist literary figures was generally positive, second thoughts were often more equivocal. By 1822, of the right-wing London daily press, only the Association's original sponsor, Dr. Stoddart's *New Times*, viewed it with any enthusiasm,[291] and of the weekly London press, Goldsmith's *British Monitor*,[292] Hook's *John Bull*,[293] and Croker's *Guardian*[294] had long opposed it. Shortly thereafter the home secretary,

[288] PRO, Home Office, 43/25, John Becket to Fayerman, December 30, 1816, fo. 333.
[289] *Anti-Gallican Monitor*, July 20, 1817, August 3, 1817.
[290] *British Monitor*, November 8, 1818.   [291] *British Monitor*, December 22, 1822.
[292] *Ibid.*, May 20, 1821.
[293] *John Bull*, February 13, 1825, p. 52.   [294] *Guardian*, May 27, 1821.

Robert Peel, as well as the attorney general, Sir John Copley, turned against it.[295] Some of this growing Tory opposition to the Constitutional Association had to do, no doubt, with tactical politics; other objections were legal. But running through the literature of opposition was also simple fear of the existence of such a organization, however highly motivated its purpose. Both Wordsworth and Lewis Goldsmith worried about the precedent of private clubs or associations usurping powers properly belonging to government, and Goldsmith in the government-subsidized *British Monitor* thought parliament should formally suppress it.[296] Robert Southey, the poet laureate, also agreed that the Constitutional Association was dangerous because it reversed the natural order of things; a government should not rely on ordinary citizens to undertake its functions. He wrote to a close friend that the Constitutional Association and indeed all "political associations in turbulant times are very dangerous things. Clubs may be met by clubs, anti-Jacobins by Jacobins – till we come to club law."[297]

The two right-wing organizations most important in terms of membership in early-nineteenth-century Britain were the Orange society and the Protestant Brunswick Club of 1828–1829. When in the second and third decades of the nineteenth century, opposition to Catholic emancipation grew on the English Right, criticism of the Orange Order became more and more difficult to find in the Tory press. *John Bull* was the exception. Long a critic of the exclusivity of the Orangeists, by 1825, the *Bull* was applauding their quelling in Ireland and hoping for their suppression in Great Britain as well.[298] But the *Bull*'s critique was very much against the common grain. Professor Aspinall thought that by 1827, there were between 300,000 and 500,000 members of Orange lodges in the United Kingdom, of which the great bulk resided in Ireland: [299] indeed the well-informed Mrs. Arbuthnot thought the Orange party "the Gentry of Ireland."[300] The modern historian of early Orangeism thinks that there were about 6,000 in British lodges, most of them

[295] *Parl. Deb.*, XII, n.ser. (February 15, 1825), p. 579. *British Monitor*, February 27, 1825.
[296] Alan G. Hill, ed., *Letters of William and Dorothy Wordsworth* (Oxford, 1978), Wordsworth to Lonsdale, c. January 12, 1821, IV, pp. 10–11. *British Monitor*, June 11 and 17, 1821.
[297] John Wood Warter, ed., *Selections from Letters of Robert Southey* (London, 1856), Southey to Wynn, January 11, 1821, III, p. 227.
[298] *John Bull*, February 20, 1825, p. 60.
[299] A. Aspinall, *Politics and the Press* (London, 1949), p. 345.
[300] Francis Bamford, Duke of Wellington, eds., *Journal of Mrs. Arbuthnot, 1820–1832* (London, 1950), I, p. 218.

urban laborers, with an aristocratic leadership in the persons of the royal Dukes of York (albeit briefly) and Cumberland and the second Baron Kenyon.[301] Like the radical London Corresponding Society of 1792, and perhaps in imitation of it, one of the first ordinances of the Orange Institution was that it "consist of an unlimited number of Brethren."[302]

Closely associated with the Orangeists were members of the Protestant Brunswick Club, established in the summer and autumn of 1828 amid defections, actual and rumored, of supporters of the Wellington administration from the anti-Catholic cause. By November 1828, almost all the principal towns in England and Ireland had Brunswick associations and by December the *Standard* could proclaim, "the whole country is fast cementing into one great Brunswick Club."[303]

It is difficult to know how seriously to take either the early-nineteenth-century Orange movement, dissolved in the 1830s amidst rumors of rebellion and coup d'état, or the much more fleeting Protestant Brunswick cause. Both might repay the type of close local study often given to radical associations and unions. But all the evidence collected so far suggests that the Protestant Brunswick Club was far more effective in Ireland than in England[304] and for perhaps the same reason as the failure or marginalization of other English clubs and associations. The fourth Duke of Newcastle, as much as anyone the father of the English ultra movement, distrusted Orangeism as tainted with democracy and freemasonry. He also acted as a brake on his colleagues who desired the incipient English Brunswick Clubs to include committees of correspondence, declarations of principles, and a permanent national committee; in other words to form an effective organization. To the duke, such tactics smacked of Jacobin clubs.[305] Such sentiments motivated other Protestants like Viscount Sidmouth who was no more enamored of the Brunswick Clubs of 1828 than he had been of the Norwich Brunswick Knights of a decade earlier.[306] Lord Eldon, the icon of the ultras, distrusted the Brunswick Clubs and saw traditional petitioning, futile as it generally was, as the desired means of

---

[301] Hareward Senior, *Orangeism in Ireland and Britain, 1795–1836* (London, 1966), pp. 155–8, 270.
[302] *Laws and Ordinances of the Orange Institution* (London, 1822), p. 7.
[303] *Standard*, December 15, 1828.
[304] Simes, "Ultra tories," p. 201.   [305] *Ibid.*, pp. 347–8.   [306] *Ibid.*, p. 362.

anti-Catholic action.[307] Even some of the ultra supporters of the highly charged Kent county meeting on Pennenden Heath on September 24, 1828, like Sir Edward Knatchbull and Lord Bexley, were lukewarm in their espousal of the Brunswick cause.[308] A historian of this phase of the ultra movement thinks that, partially because of this timidity, and despite the impressive number of signatures collected on the English Protestant petitions in 1829, there were only around twenty important Protestant Brunswick Clubs in England.[309] And, in 1828, only one borough, Leeds, with a turnout of around 25,000 people, had a large Protestant meeting to rival the Kent county assemblage.[310] The Leeds exception was no doubt due to the influence of Michael Thomas Sadler.

In one way at least, a close examination of both the Orange Order and the Protestant Brunswick clubs might surprise a reviewer. The *Age* remarked of the Orangeists in 1827 that "a more liberal set of men never constituted the bulwark of any constitution."[311] Oddly, to a large extent, the *Age* did not exaggerate. For the ties which linked together the Orange Order and its deputy Grand Master Lord Kenyon with the cause of the factory children in Manchester or the Protestant Brunswick Clubs with the Fixby Hall compact of Sadler and Oastler are strong if not always acknowledged. Lord Kenyon, whom F. K. Brown has called the Wilberforce of the High Church group,[312] emerged from the Tory circle of his preceptor Jones of Nayland,[313] joined the Orange Order in 1808,[314] and thereafter propagated, in fair weather and foul, its anti-Catholic principles. Yet, the Liverpool manuscripts in the British Library are dotted with his pleas to the prime minister on behalf of humanitarian factory legislation.[315] His concern for the "poor children" was as long-lived as his anti-Catholicism. His evening newspaper the *True Briton* (1820–1822), on which he allegedly lost around £7,000,[316] besides lending back-handed support on religious grounds for Queen Caroline, crusaded against the death penalty for forgers,

[307] *Life of Eldon*, III, pp. 58–61.   [308] Simes, "Ultra tories," pp. 366–7.
[309] *Ibid.*, p. 201.
[310] *Ibid.*, pp. 369–70.   [311] *Age*, March 18, 1827, p. 84.
[312] Ford K. Brown, *Fathers of the Victorians* (Cambridge, England, 1961), p. 352.
[313] W. J. Hardy, ed., *HMC*, 14th report, Appendix, pt. IV, *Manuscripts of Lord Kenyon* (London, 1894), Jones to Kenyon, November 13, 1790, p. 532.
[314] Senior, *Orangeism*, p. 166.
[315] For example, BL, Liverpool Papers, Add. MSS. 38277, Kenyon to Liverpool, May 24, 1819, fo. 126.
[316] *Westminster Review*, 10 (January 1829), pp. 221–2.

supported an extension of the poor laws, and denounced ministers and the landed interest for their selfishness over the corn laws.[317] The *True Briton* also espoused the cause of Spanish, Neapolitan, and Greek liberals in their battles for freedom against despotic rulers.[318] Kenyon's superior in the Orange society, the Duke of Cumberland, who has one of the worst reputations in British history, at least had the moral responsibility to support successive Factory Acts.[319] It was out of this milieu too, where royal and urban Orangeism met Irish and British Brunswick emotion that one can find that mixture of Tory humanitarianism and anti-Catholic enthusiasm which characterized the *Standard* under the Dubliner S. L. Giffard or the *Morning Journal* under the Scot Robert Alexander, and from which Michael Thomas Sadler emerged in the late 1820s for his brief sojourn in national politics.

Nothing shows more clearly the fundamental role which distinctions of social class played in the political structure of nineteenth-century Toryism than the attitude towards the now largely forgotten national political career of Michael Thomas Sadler, a not very successful linen manufacturer from Leeds, with a background replete with the juxtaposition of Methodism with Anglicanism and Wilberforcian humanitarianism with anti-Catholicism. Sadler came from a middling Tory social milieu similar to many a Brunswick or Orange journalist or editor and they adored him in their newspapers and magazines. On the other hand, the aristocratic and gentry elite which really ran Tory affairs disparaged him. A noted and self-educated economist of a cheap money school which Harold Perkin identified as proto-Keynesian,[320] Sadler praised population growth, not population stability, as a key to national wealth.[321] He thus fit in both intellectually and morally with ultra Toryism. His maiden speech in parliament, at the height of the Catholic emancipation crisis in March 1829, was virtually unequalled in its brilliance as far as the ultra press was concerned. *Blackwood's* found him ready to take the place of the apostate Peel;[322] the Dublin *Star of Brunswick* thought it the greatest maiden speech since the Younger

317 See *True Briton*, July 29, 1820; January 1, 1821; January 28, 1822.
318 *Ibid.*, July 11, 1820; May 2, 1821.
319 Anthony Bird, *Damnable Duke of Cumberland* (London, 1966), p. 296.
320 Harold Perkin, *Origins of Modern English Society, 1780–1880* (London, 1969), pp. 242ff.
321 [Robert Benton Seeley], *Memoirs of the Life and Writings of Michael Thomas Sadler* (London, 1842), p. 187.
322 *Blackwood's Edinburgh Magazine* 26 (August 1829), p. 234.

Pitt's;[323] the *Age* delivered a panegyric;[324] the *Standard* attempted day after day in 1829 to build him up as the spiritual and able hope of the waning Protestant cause.[325] The journalists and ultra leaders saw to it that 500,000 copies of Sadler's anti-Catholic speech were circulated round the country.[326]

But if there was one thing on which the Wellingtonians and the ultra leadership concurred, it was that this scion of the Brunswick Club of Leeds would not achieve any party authority. Part of the problem may have been Sadler's own, inevitable, fault. His biographer surmises that his speeches were dissertations on economics and religion and overly long for an impatient House of Commons.[327] Southey thought that Sadler was addicted "to the sin of committing rhetoric in his speeches." As a self-educated man he used certain "flowers of speech" which betrayed his living with men inferior to him in natural powers.[328] Upon hearing the much-vaunted maiden speech, Ellenborough, from within the Wellington Cabinet, was immediately certain that Sadler would "never have power."[329] Sadler's ostensible ally, the Kent ultra leader Sir Edward Knatchbull, mentioned to the Cornish ultra leader Sir Richard Vyvyan that Sadler would never be a minister.[330] And, indeed, when delicate ministerial negotiations went on between the Huskissonians and the ultra Protestants in the late summer and autumn of 1829, despite Sadler's endeavor to join a projected government,[331] no offer to him was in contemplation.[332] He left parliament, defeated by Macaulay at Leeds in 1832, and spent the remainder of his short life, appropriately, in Belfast.[333] He may indeed have been as Richard Oastler said of him, "that heaven-born man of whom this age has not had the like,"[334] but his aborted career points to the difficulty, among other things, of reaching high national position, however talented one may be, from a provincial clubbist background.

[323] *Star of Brunswick*, March 21, 1829.   [324] *Age*, September 20, 1829, p. 300.
[325] See for example, *Standard*, September 23, 1829.
[326] *Memoirs of Sadler*, p. 115.   [327] *Ibid.*, pp. 92–3.
[328] *Selections from Letters of Southey*, Southey to Rickman, September 29, 1829, IV, pp. 150–1.
[329] Lord Colchester, ed., *A Political Diary, 1828–1830* by Edward Law, Lord Ellenborough (London, 1881), I, p. 397.
[330] Sir Hughe Knatchbull-Hugessen, *Kentish Family* (London, 1960), p. 184.
[331] Bradfield, "Sir Richard Vyvyan," Sadler to Vyvyan, August 25, 1829, p. 74.
[332] Kenneth Bourne, ed., *Letters of the Third Viscount Palmerston to Laurence and Elizabeth Sulivan, 1804–1863*, Camden 4th ser., XXIII (London, 1979), pp. 232–6.
[333] *Memoirs of Sadler*, p. 2.
[334] Cecil Driver, *Tory Radical: Life of Richard Oastler* (New York, 1946), p. 305.

To return to the former query of how seriously to take the Orange movement and the Brunswick Clubs in the 1820s, the evidence might suggest a minimalist interpretation. The former was certainly taken seriously in 1797 and 1798 in Ireland when the Marquis of Buckingham found them a *"loyal association upon Jacobin principles."*[335] But whereas rebellion inspired by both Catholics and Jacobins might well animate Protestant Ireland with its own *levée en masse*, confident of English support, the situation in 1828–1829 was quite different with the first soldier in Europe as prime minister of a United Kingdom dedicated to the removal of Catholic political grievances. And the duke knew his quarry in the Orange and Brunswick movements. Will the Duke of Newcastle, Lord Kenyon, or Lord Winchelsea, he asked Mrs. Arbuthnot, go over to Ireland and risk their throats in support of the Protestants? Would Lords Aldborough, Longford or Farnham stay in Ireland if there was civil war in consequence of their clubs? The answer for the Duke of Wellington was obviously a resounding "No."[336]

The Brunswickers themselves, as we have seen, were divided on the utility of their clubs as a pressure group against a strong loyalist government. The leading historian of the 1829 crisis, G. I. T. Machin, suggests that the Brunswickers "were defeated not so much by pro-Catholic opposition as by their own inherent conservatism, which prevented them from taking measures that might appear unconstitutional."[337] In this wariness of any club activity, even their own, so typical of a revolution-obsessed generation, the ultra and Orange-oriented Protestants were quite different from their predecessors in the 1790s or their successors after 1885. Was this perhaps, because even to themselves, their cause in the 1820s was less defensible?

---

[335] *HMC, Manuscripts of J. B. Fortescue, Esq., Preserved at Dropmore*, (London, 1905), Bukkingham to Grenville, July 23, 1798, IV, p. 265.

[336] *Wellington and His Friends*, Wellington to Mrs. Arbuthnot, September 23, 1828, p. 84.

[337] G. I. T. Machin, *Catholic Question in English Politics, 1820 to 1830* (Oxford, 1964), p. 155.

CHAPTER 5

The British monarchy and the Right, 1760–1832

Linda Colley recently bemoaned the lack of a serious study on the British monarchy between 1688 and 1837.[1] Colley herself has contributed, however, not a little to the theoretical outlines of this subject in positing that late-eighteenth-century Britain experienced a conservative, state-sponsored nationalism that was every bit as potent as the more commented-upon liberal nationalism flowing from the French Revolution. Institutions like the British monarchy were the chief beneficiaries.[2]

Other historians have also tackled aspects of the political importance or the public perception of the monarchy in the Hanoverian period. A. D. Harvey echoed Lord Brougham's nineteenth-century thesis in suggesting that the issue of royal prerogative was the single most divisive issue in British politics before the first Reform Bill and more than any other antagonism defined the differences between Foxite Whiggery and Pittite Toryism.[3] Reed Browning and J. C. D. Clark portrayed the mid and late Georgian monarchy as exemplifying the conservative, Anglican (even sometimes High Church) aspects of seventeenth-century Whiggery, or "Court Whiggery" as Browning terms it, made perhaps even more conservative after its post-1760 absorption of its Tory rival.[4] Hence, such mid-eighteenth-century Georgian Churchmen as Archbishop Herring of York and Canterbury, Samuel Squire of St. Davids, Bishop Gibson of London,[5] Bishop Potter of Oxford as well as devout Anglican lay

---

[1] *Times Literary Supplement*, June 23–29, 1989, p. 701.

[2] Linda Colley, "The Apotheosis of George III," *P&P*, 102 (1984), p. 106.

[3] A. D. Harvey, *Britain in the Early Nineteenth Century* (London, 1978), pp. 2–4. Henry Lord Brougham, *Historical Sketches of Statesmen Who Flourished in the Time of George III* (London, 1839), I, pp. 301–2.

[4] Reed Browning, *Political and Constitutional Ideas of Court Whigs* (Baton Rouge, 1982), p. 90. J. C. D. Clark, *English Society, 1688–1832* (Cambridge, England, 1985), pp. 275–6.

[5] Whom Stephen Taylor portrays as virtually Laud's heir. "Sir Robert Walpole, the Church of England, and the Quaker tithe bill of 1736," *HJ*, 28 (March 1985), pp. 52–3.

statesmen such as the Duke of Newcastle and Lord Hardwicke were the real ideological forerunners of George III, North, and Burke later in the century.[6] While Clark, of course, in line with his general refusal to use "Toryism" as an expression between 1760 and 1832, perceived this monarchical revival as Whig or even Whig–Jacobite induced,[7] other historians, such as J. A. W. Gunn and J. E. Bradley, were more inclined to suspect traditional Toryism lurking about its foundation. Gunn saw the resiliency of Tory claims of the divine right of kings in the neo-Tory pamphlet and sermon literature of George III's reign.[8] Bradley imagined that the traditionalist view in Whig historiography of George III-as-Tory had a good deal of merit.[9]

What all these historians have in common, however they might disagree about labels, is a renewed emphasis upon the importance of the monarchy in the development of an intellectual or political consensus in Britain in opposition to Whiggish libertarianism, utilitarianism, or radical Jacobinism. Basing this view largely though not exclusively on a reading of the right-wing press in the age of George III and George IV, I am somewhat less convinced than most of them that the monarchy played the major role as the rallying point for the higher levels of patriotism or in validating a conservative consensus, whether within a Court Whig or Tory or a neo-Jacobite atmosphere.

I would also be less inclined than Clark and Browning (and to an extent Namier[10]) to emphasize the continuity between the high Whig tradition of the 1740s and 1750s and whatever it was that George III and his advisers were trying to accomplish after 1760. In other words, as Bradley and the nineteenth-century Whig historians have suggested, from a certain perspective, there were extraordinary differences in the way monarchy was perceived before and after 1760. There were also very good reasons why the Old Corps of Whigs (even Browning and Clark's Court Anglican Whigs) were nervous and uncertain about the future after 1760, over and above fear of personal disadvantages. From the perspective of 1820 and the reign's conclusion, it is clear that the fear of the Old Corps was

---

[6] Browning, *Court Whigs*, pp. 90, 132, 199, 235. Clark, *English Society*, p. 408.

[7] Clark, *English Society*, p. 182.

[8] J. A. W. Gunn, *Beyond Liberty and Property* (Kingston, 1983), p. 136.

[9] James E. Bradley, *Popular Politics and the American Revolution in England* (Macon, 1986), pp. 211–12.

[10] Sir Lewis Namier, *England in the Age of the American Revolution* (London, 1961), p. 53.

groundless except indeed on that personal level which led to such events as the Massacre of the Pelhamite Innocents. For whatever it was that George III (or Bute) stood for, they were singularly unsuccessful in achieving it, and possibly uncertain and halting in even attempting anything significant. George III was certainly no Tory, did not perceive himself as a Tory, and, in fact, like Newdigate, the term probably held little meaning for him save in some neo-Jacobite sense. It may indeed have implied to George a commitment to Convocation, which he never exhibited, parliamentary reform and a radical city tradition, which he abhorred, and a general tolerance for Stuarts, in which he could hardly join. Other aspects of Toryism as it existed in the 1750s no doubt did appeal to him: hatred of the Old Corps of Walpoleian and Pelhamite Whiggery and a distrust of continental commitments, in which he along with Bute participated; a desire for an end to proscription, which he achieved; and an intense devotion to the Anglican Church, which he shared. And some of these later elements of 1750s Toryism were quite compatible with (or of no concern to) the Court Whiggery of Archbishop Herring.

But it was on the issue of monarchical prerogative almost in its pure intellectual sense rather than in any overt power grab by George that most irritated and perhaps frightened his contemporaries and that caused a schism in the establishment and between the monarchy and the main body of the Whigs which was not healed until 1831. All this may not have been entirely George's fault. He grew up with the Jacobite threat – which represented high monarchical prerogative and willy-nilly forced the Hanoverian dynasty into an aggressively constitutional atmosphere – visibly receding and thus, theoretically at least, was given the opportunity to reassert the traditional prerogatives of the crown. George also grew up with his European royal contemporaries affirming enlightened despotic nostrums signifying the importance of royal power in the amelioration of grievances. Given that George did little or nothing about increasing his own powers in any manner more offensive than his Whiggish predecessors, he may be posthumously congratulated if not for his tact then for his adherence to the 1688 and 1714 settlements. However, we who know the end of the story are in a better position to offer such felicitations. His contemporaries, obviously, had no such assurances.

Much has been written about the Earl of Bute's influence on the youthful Prince of Wales and king. Most are agreed that George had every right to appoint Bute his chief minister, even if the Scottish earl clearly was not physically, emotionally, or practically up to the job. No doubt much of the Whig opposition to Bute (and Grenville too) was based on anger by Pitt, Newcastle, or their followers on losing valued and accustomed places. But certain odd aspects of the new reign, as exemplified in the press, in sermons, and in pamphlet literature, have perhaps not received the attention they deserve. Immediately upon George's accession, the old Tory press, which despite the statesman–philosopher's religious views, was still predominantly pro-Bolingbrokian, began to print copious extracts from the "Patriot King," "their great Master's"[11] call for a revived and non-partisan monarch; whom they clearly identified with George. While George or his friends probably had no influence over, for example, the *York Courant*,[12] the one London newspaper that supported Bute in 1760 and early 1761, the new tri-weekly *London Chronicle*, took up this call as well.[13] The more or less Tory journal, the *Critical Review*, provided the only significant and sustained support which George III or Bute received in the entire London press after the parameters of their pro-peace, anti-Pittite, and anti-Old Corps activities became clear. The *Critical* since its inception in 1756 had loathed the Duke of Newcastle and the Old Corps and had adopted Smollettian rhetoric replete with endless anti-war, anti-standing army, and anti-Hanover comment.[14] Hence, it took no substantial ideological jump for the popular *Critical* to adopt Bute's pro-peace and anti-Spanish-war stance in 1761.[15] It also generally praised Bolingbroke and thought his purported moral blemishes "exaggerated."[16] The *Critical* adopted a very Toryish view of the events of Anne's reign and the peace of Utrecht,[17] the latter serving, save for the activities of James II, as the most significant event in modern English history to inhabit a prominent place in Whig demonology.

In 1761, at the time of George's coronation, George Horne, who had no qualms calling himself a Tory,[18] published a sermon on the

---

[11] As the most important contributor to the *London Evening Post* in the 1750s, Britannicus, called Bolingbroke, August 23–25, 1757.
[12] *York Courant*, December 30, 1760.
[13] *London Chronicle*, November 6–8, 1760; November 8–11, 1760; November 13–15, 1760.
[14] See, for example, *Critical Review*, 1 (April 1756), pp. 258–60.
[15] *Ibid.*, 12 (October 1761), p. 264.
[16] *Ibid.*, 30 (August 1770), pp. 82–8.   [17] *Ibid.*, 15 (January 1763), p. 90.
[18] BL, Berkeley Papers, Add. MSS. 39312, Horne to Berkeley, July 17, 1789, fo. 100.

"Christian King," stating that it must be eradicated out of the minds of men that diabolical principles of resistance to government in Church and state are allowed.[19] Horne, partially through Lord North's favor, rapidly ascended the ladder of Oxford patronage, was Chaplain in Ordinary to the King from 1771 to 1781, and in the 1780s was made, under North, Dean of Canterbury, and under Pitt, Bishop of Norwich. In 1762, at least one pro-Buteite pamphlet appeared, "The true whig displaced," advocating absolute passive obedience on the grounds that an evil sovereign should be punished by God not his subjects.[20]

With most of the British press closed to his views, Bute, in 1762 and 1763, increasingly turned to weekly, Saturday, papers of opinion, the *Auditor*, edited by Arthur Murphy, a Jesuit-educated former Roman Catholic who had been prominent in the press opposition to the Jew Bill,[21] and the *Briton*, edited by Tobias Smollett, one of the conductors of the *Critical* and the author of the famous denunciatory paragraph on William III in his *Complete History of England*.[22] Both the *Auditor* and the *Briton*, Bute's (and perhaps by extension George III's) chief means of communication with a literate public, were understanding of Tories as might be expected of papers supporting a government which had just ended proscription, irritating though this might be to some Whigs. Thus, for example, the *Auditor* reminded its readers that Tories too had been prominent in 1688.[23] The *Briton* defended the Utrecht settlement and denied that Great Britain was any longer under a Whig administration in any generic sense.[24]

But among the Tory, or Jacobite, or anti-Whig talent available to Bute even as well-known a writer and journalist as Smollett was dwarfed in public notoriety by John Shebbeare, who had spent his

[19] William Jones, *Works of the Right Rev. George Horne D.D.* (New York, 1846), II, p. 315.
[20] "True Whig displaced" (London, 1762), pp. 8–9.
[21] For Murphy's religious background and ideological viewpoint, see, John Pike Emery, *Arthur Murphy* (Philadelphia, 1946), p. 2 and Thomas W. Perry, *Public Opinion, Propaganda, and Politics in Eighteenth-Century England: A Study of the Jew Bill of 1753* (Cambridge, Mass., 1962), p. 105.
[22] For Smollett's views on William III, see *Complete History of England ... to the Treaty of Aix la Chapelle* (London, 1757), IV, p. 235.
[23] *Political Controversy, Auditor*, 2 (November 25, 1762), pp. 233–4; 2 (December 25, 1762), p. 407.
[24] *Briton*, October 9, 1762; January 22, 1763. I do not agree with Marie Peters that both Buteite papers in 1762 "seemed to be prepared to accept the Tory label" and then drew back. I do not think that the evidence, odd enough as it is, supports such an interpretation. "'Names and cant,'" *PH*, 3 (1984), p. 119.

time in the pillory for his attacks on the reigning dispensation of the 1750s. John Brewer said that Charles Jenkinson approached Shebbeare in 1762 with a request to aid the government journalistic effort (such as it was) but met with a refusal.[25] Shebbeare, unlike Smollett, was a high Tory in a religious sense. In his famous Tory preface to Clarendon's *History of the Reign of Charles II*, written around 1757 but not immediately published due to opposition from a Hyde heiress, he advocated that Dissenters should wear by law a green stocking or yellow cap.[26] In his notorious "Fifth letter to the English people," he libeled the Glorious Revolution[27] and in his "Sixth letter" he favorably compared James II's reign with the 1750s and broadly hinted that George II was illegitimate.[28] It is interesting that Bute approached *him* for journalistic aid and even more interesting that the Grenville administration bestowed upon him a £200 per annum pension.[29] Just one year before George III granted this pension, Shebbeare had published one of those allegories on current affairs so popular in the eighteenth century, *The History of the Sumatrans*, in which he praised passive obedience, and exhibited a quite favorable view of James II ("Abdullah") and negative view of his son-in-law, William III ("Ibraheim").[30] In regard to this pension, as Shebbeare informed the no doubt enthralled British public, in the midst of a pamphlet full of innuendoes on William III and his homosexuality, "his majesty was pleased to speak of me in terms too favourable for me to repeat ... "[31] Needless to say, this pensioning of Shebbeare caused some comment in Whig circles, and was regularly denounced in the press and the House of Commons.[32]

Johnson himself, a well-known apologist for the Tories[33] and for

---

[25] John Brewer, *Party Ideology and Popular Politics at the Accession of George III* (Cambridge, England, 1976), p. 222.

[26] John Shebbeare, ed., *History of the Reign of King Charles the Second from the Revolution to the end of the Year 1667*, by Edward Hyde, first Earl of Clarendon (London, 1757?), p. xxvi.

[27] John Shebbeare, "Fifth letter to the people of England on the subversion of the *constitution*" (London, 1757), pp. 11, 14, 15.

[28] John Shebbeare, "Sixth letter to the people of England on the progress of national ruin" (London, 1757), pp. 9–10, 121.

[29] William James Smith, ed., *Grenville Papers* (London, 1852), II, pp. 270–1. James R. Foster, "Smollett's pamphleteering foe Shebbeare," *PMLA*, 57, no. 4, pt. 1 (December 1942), p. 1091. See, *DNB* under "John Shebbeare."

[30] John Shebbeare, *History of the Sumatrans* (London, 1763), I, pp. 149–50, 156 ff.

[31] John Shebbeare, "An answer to the queries" (London, 1775), pp. 29, 83–5.

[32] *Parl. Hist.*, XVII (February 16, 1774), pp. 1057–8.

[33] Whom J. C. D. Clark suggests could well have been out in 1745. It is not clear whether this is meant as a joke. *English Society*, p. 186.

Archbishop Sancroft and the non-jurors,[34] was also given a £300 per annum pension by George III.[35] His first biographer and friend, Sir John Hawkins, said that Johnson never spoke of "King William but in terms of reproach, and, in his opinion of him, seemed to adopt all the prejudices of jacobite bigotry and rancour."[36] Shortly after Johnson was pensioned, Boswell told Rousseau, perhaps unfairly, though no doubt reflecting public consensus, during their famous interview at Môtiers, that Johnson "is a Jacobite."[37] Two Bolingrokians, both Deists, were given pensions or otherwise employed by Bute: David Mallet, apologist and memoirist of Bolingbroke, received a £300 per annum sinecure from Bute in 1763;[38] and John Cleland, like Shebbeare arrested by Newcastle (for *Fanny Hill*), who continued his long career as a political journalist defending Bute and the government in the newspapers.[39]

Timothy Brecknock, a lawyer and pro-Newcastle newspaper journalist of the 1750s,[40] was disappointed in the duke's evident lack of concern for his advancement in life.[41] Hence, with the elimination of the Old Corps of Whigs from office in 1762, he may have been casting about for new patrons. He wrote "Droit le Roy" in 1764 during the Grenville administration. In his pamphlet Brecknock explicitly denied any validity to mixed monarchy or any coordination in the supremacy among king, Lords, and Commons. The king was, quite simply, the supreme governor in temporal and spiritual matters.[42] Brecknock stood for the absolute principle of passive resistance: even to think, much less speak, of the overthrow of a king was a grievous sin.[43] He stood also for the dispensing power of the sovereign.[44] One of the most controversial aspects of the pamphlet was Brecknock's assertion that neither king nor parlia-

---

[34] *Literary Magazine*, 2 (May 15 – June 15, 1757).
[35] James Boswell, *Life of Johnson* (London, 1953), p. 264.
[36] Sir John Hawkins, *Works of Samuel Johnson* (London, 1787), I, pp. 504–5.
[37] Frederick A. Pottle, ed., *Boswell on the Grand Tour, Germany and Switzerland, 1764* (New York, 1953), pp. 262–5.
[38] See *DNB* under "David Mallet." As secretary to the late Prince of Wales, Mallet may have had other claims on the king. Mallet dedicated works to both Mansfield and Bute. *Poetical Works* (Edinburgh, 1780), p. vii.
[39] William H. Epstein, *John Cleland: Images of a Life* (New York, 1974), pp. 23, 115–16, 140, 144–50.
[40] BL, Newcastle Papers, Add. MSS. 32866, Brecknock to Newcastle, July 8 and 28, 1756.
[41] *Ibid.*, Add. MSS. 32929, Brecknock to Newcastle, October 19, 1761, fo. 379.
[42] [Timothy Brecknock], "Droit le Roy" (London, 1764), pp. 12–14.
[43] *Ibid.*, p. 29.   [44] *Ibid.*, p. 63.

ment had any right to "dispose of this kingdom in prejudice to the next heir in blood ... no not though the parties interested in the succession should commit treason."[45] In regard to George III's lawful right to the throne, Brecknock stressed James II's voluntary abdication and, in what must have been the last time the story was used to justify the exclusion of the male Stuart line, the warming pan thesis.[46] The historian of the English press in the 1760s doubts, though he does not completely dismiss, the theory that Brecknock's controversial pamphlet – burned by the common hangman on the order of both Houses of Parliament – was written at ministerial instigation.[47] Certainly the views expressed by Brecknock are not echoed in George Grenville's previous or subsequent career. No doubt, Brecknock was a restless, ambitious, and disappointed man, on the fringes of both journalism and the law, whose cutting of corners eventually led him to the gallows in the 1780s.[48] The interesting thing is not the unanimous denunciation of the pamphlet by parliament but rather the evident expectation by Brecknock that such high prerogative views would somehow serve his ambitious purposes. Indeed, perhaps they did. J. C. D. Clark takes Brecknock quite seriously, regarding him as "the forerunner" in his espousal of doctrines which would later be echoed in Blackstone and Reeves. I suspect this is unfair to Blackstone and even Reeves, but Clark did discover that a "Mr. Brecknock" by the early 1780s was in receipt of Secret Service funds from George III[49] – an intriguing, though ultimately inconclusive, disclosure.

George III in the 1760s also clearly approved of David Hume's controversial *History of England* with its measured, academic, and non-polemical understanding of the monarchical authority of the Tudor and early Stuart sovereigns as opposed to parliamentary claims, its negative view of puritanism, and its famous passage denouncing Locke's theory of the right of revolution.[50] Hume was pensioned through Bute's influence and was careful to write letters to Bute's secretary, Gilbert Elliot, denouncing not, for example, the usurped power of the Old Corps of Whigs but Whiggism in gen-

---

[45] *Ibid.*, pp. 17ff.   [46] *Ibid.*, p. 24.
[47] Robert R. Rea, *The English Press in Politics, 1760–1774* (Lincoln, 1963), p. 104.
[48] See "An authentic account of the trials at large of George Robert Fitzgerald, esq., Timothy Brecknock ... " (London, 1786), pp. 166, 178–9.
[49] Clark, *English Society*, pp. 202–4.
[50] David Hume, *History of England* (New York, 1879), IV, pp. 271–4; V, p. 296.

eral.[51] Despite his anti-Christian views, Hume was openly favored by the king. George during the mid and late 1760s, in hopes Hume would continue his *History* into the eighteenth century, considerably augmented Hume's pension, opened all the public records and offices to him, and sent him papers from Hanoverian archives.[52]

George III in addition gave sensitive positions about the Court to former Tories and Jacobites. It was one thing after all to give Tories Bedchamber positions and place them at Court (what else would the end of proscription mean?); it was quite another to send a former Jacobite, David Graeme, to fetch his young and politically inexperienced future queen from Mecklenburg as well as establishing him as her secretary.[53] In 1762, the queen told the Duke of Devonshire, who reported in his diary and no doubt elsewhere, that Col. Graeme defended Jacobitism in an argument with one of her ladies.[54] Then George appointed a Tory MP, Sewallis Shirley, comptroller of Charlotte's household.[55] At the same time, George's letters to Bute sound like Tory press leaders from the *London Evening Post* of the previous decade. For example, the king wants Bute's aid to "attack the irreligious, the covetous ... purg[e] out corruption ... "[56] And Lord Mansfield was sending the king the high prerogative advice to allow fewer Cabinet meetings and to get extra-ministerial advice regarding Church patronage so that the "great engine of power" could be kept in George's own hands.[57]

During his tour of Italy in 1764 and 1765, the voluble Boswell, only a little more than a year after Bute's resignation as prime minister, met Bute's son and heir, Lord Mountstuart, whom he introduced to a level of dissipation not approved of by his straitlaced father. But in the course of their conversations, the indiscreet Mountstuart told Boswell that he never would have taken the oath of abjuration to the Stuarts during the late reign but would do so

[51] J. Y. T. Greig, ed., *Letters of David Hume* (Oxford, 1932), Hume to Elliot, March 12, 1763, I, p. 379.
[52] *Ibid.*, Hume to Comtesse de Bouffleurs, November 27, 1767, II, p. 172; Hume to Marquise de Barbentane, May 24, 1768, II, p. 177.
[53] Namier and Brooke, II, p. 524.
[54] Peter D. Brown, Karl W. Schweizer, eds., *Devonshire Diary*, Camden 4th ser., XXVII (London, 1982), p. 171.
[55] Namier and Brooke, III, p. 436.
[56] Romney Sedgwick, ed., *Letters from George III to Lord Bute, 1756–1766* (Westport, Conn., 1981), p. 166.
[57] *Letters from George III to Bute*, King to Bute, April 7, 1763, pp. 211–12.

now that George III exercised authority.[58] One doubts that the gossipy Boswell kept this piece of political poison very secret when he dined out in London or Edinburgh a few months later.

It is within such contexts that one must evaluate Dr. King's jokes that the Court was now Jacobite[59] or Leslie Mitchell's perceptive explanation for Oxford University's evolving stance from opposition before 1760 to a Northite bulwark in the 1770s; indeed, Oxford was one of the few places in England to address the crown *supporting* government during the 1769–1770 Wilkes' embroglio.[60] Indeed was J. A. W. Gunn wrong when he decided that claims by Whigs of a post-1760 Tory revival were "perhaps not without foundation?"[61] It is within such a context too that one must evaluate the Whig critique of George III's monarchy, almost received wisdom in the nineteenth century, only to be re-examined and discarded by the Namierite revisionists of the twentieth, who, no doubt accurately in the long haul, perceived a king responsible to precedent and to parliament. For the Whigs, however defined or grouped, seemed convinced, as the *North Briton* observed in 1762, that passive obedience and non-resistance were "preached up by every pamphleteer"[62] or as the *Morning Post* declared during its own short-lived oppositionist period, in 1775, that passive obedience, non-resistance, and the divine right of kings "again echo from every corner."[63] Horace Walpole, self-proclaimed heir to his father's Whig tradition, remarked in his *Memoirs* of George's reign that "*Prerogative* became a fashionable word, and the language of the time was altered before the Favourite dared to make any variation in the Ministry."[64] John Butler (later Bishop of Hereford) thought Bute's system depended upon Tories and Tory maxims.[65] Dodington thought Bute and his friends a "Tory engraftment."[66] And the author of the influential Whig pamphlet, the "History of the late minority," in 1765 accused Bute of attempting to form a high prerogative, neo-Jacobite, and

[58] Frank Brady, Frederick A. Pottle, eds., *Boswell on the Grand Tour, Italy, Corsica, and France, 1765–1766* (New York, 1955), p. 84.

[59] BL, Berkeley Papers, Add. MSS. 39311, Horne to Berkeley, October 6, 1762, fos. 121–2.

[60] L. S. Sutherland, L. G. Mitchell, eds., *History of University of Oxford*, v, *Eighteenth Century* (Oxford, 1986), pp. 160–1.

[61] Gunn, *Beyond Liberty*, p. 168.　　[62] *North Briton*, December 25, 1762, p. 97.

[63] *Morning Post*, March 10, 1775.

[64] G. F. Russell Barker, ed., *Memoirs of the Reign of King George III* by Horace Walpole (London, 1894), I, p. 13.

[65] [John Butler], "Address to Cocoa-Tree from a Whig" (London, 1763), p. 9.

[66] John Carswell, Lewis Arnold Dralle, eds., *Political Journal of George Bubb Dodington* (Oxford, 1965), Dodington to Thomson, March 27, 1762, p. 434.

anti-revolutionary Tory ministry.[67] A more famous pamphlet, Edmund Burke's "Thoughts on the cause of the present discontents," simply found the alleged Bute system of government by King's Friends "undermining all the foundations of our freedom."[68]

Sir Lewis Namier, John Brooke, and Ian R. Christie are no doubt correct in their assessments of George III as a constitutional sovereign who, as when choosing ministers in 1761, 1783, 1801 or 1807, merely used the power immanent in his kingship and who certainly did not in any substantial way increase the power of that throne left to him by his ancestors. Some circumstances in the 1760s, however, for example, the lack of a reversionary interest in the person of a mature heir to the throne, altered the traditional political environment. Indeed, some of the critique of George's kingship came from the traditional upholders of a strong (or stronger) monarchy as well as from Whiggish sources. Oliver Goldsmith, who like Smollett, emerged from a non-religious but somewhat high prerogative Tory tradition, in the preface to his 1771 *History of England from the Earliest Times to the Death of George II*, argued on a utilitarian rather than on a divine right level for a stronger monarchy in England.[69] And David Hume in the same year bemoaned the *loss* not the *growth* of government power during George's reign: giving up the right of displacing judges; giving up general warrants; lessening the coercive power of the House of Commons; annihilating libel laws; and diminishing the revenue of the civil list.[70]

However, the fact that the Namierites are generally accurate in their overall negative assessment of the "George as Tory" myth, does not necessarily mean that the Whigs, in Namier's celebrated term, were merely mouthing "cant" when they fretted and worried about George's innovations. Simply observing the trend in the government-inspired press or in the odd choices turning up in the pension list, or just listening to well-founded gossip, provided plenty of cause for concern for a political community that had still failed, on the evidence of Clark, Cruickshanks, and even Christie, fully to integrate the results of 1688 or 1714 into its system. Judged from those standpoints, there was indeed evidence that George III (or the Earl of Bute) was attempting to change the 1688–1714 settlement in a profound way.

---

[67] "History of the late minority" (London, 1765), p. 23.   [68] Burke, *Works* I, p. 535.
[69] Arthur Friedman, ed., *Collected Works of Oliver Goldsmith* (Oxford, 1966), v, pp. 338–9.
[70] *Letters of Hume*, Hume to Mrs. Strahan, June 25, 1771, II, pp. 244–5.

It is difficult to measure the impact which the intellectual high prerogative rhetoric from his own friends on one hand or the resultant Whig criticism on the other had on George III or in a wider sense on the development of the British monarchy. George seemed to go out of his way thereafter to reassert his fundamental Whiggism and his adherence to the Glorious Revolution. He told the old scion of the Hardwicke connection, Sir Joseph Yorke, in 1771, that "my political creed is formed on the system of King William"[71] and thirty years later told the Duke of Portland that he was "an old Whig; that he considered the statesmen who made the barrier treaties, and conducted the last years of the succession war, the most able ones we ever had."[72]

Beyond the attempt to define his essential Whiggism and his identification with the policies of William III, the evidence that George III was stung to the quick by his critic's charges and his supporter's high prerogative rhetoric is circumstantial but worthy of consideration. Bute may indeed have been, as Samuel Johnson described him, "a man who had his blood full of prerogative ... a theoretical statesman."[73] If so, he rarely if ever saw the summit of his desires after 1765. Bute's daughter, seventy-five years after her father's resignation as prime minister, lamented that all through the 1770s and 1780s there were "the most manifest signs of *dis*favour" by the king to the Stuart family. None of the family or their wider connections "could obtain anything from King or Minister" in Church, state, or military, until her father's death in 1792.[74] Thus did the Fountain of Honour break with his high prerogative mentor.

There are other, admittedly less concrete and more fluid examples that might signify George's chagrin for the overstatement and excesses of his early reign. He never, unlike George II, attended the January 30 memorial services for Charles I, where high prerogative ideas could potentially receive their widest audience.[75] He cold-shouldered John Reeves, the exemplar of high prerogative notions in the 1790s,[76] as much as he failed to prefer Dr. Nowell, Reeves'

---

[71] Fortescue, II, p. 204.
[72] Third Earl of Malmesbury, ed., *Diaries and Correspondence of James Harris, First Earl of Malmesbury* (London, 1844), IV, p. 44.
[73] Boswell, *Life of Johnson*, p. 619.
[74] Mrs. E. Stuart Wortley, ed., *A Prime Minister and His Son* (London, 1925), p. 240.
[75] A. Francis Steuart, ed., *Last Journals of Horace Walpole* (London, 1910), I, p. 40n.
[76] BL, Dropmore (Grenville) Papers, Add. MSS. 58986, Reeves to Grenville, June 5, 1806, fos. 120–1.

intellectual predecessor in the 1770s. Samuel Johnson received no augmentation of his pension during the last year of his life to allow the dying lexicographer to regain his health in a Mediterranean clime.[77]

The high prerogative overstatement of the early 1760s may explain too the coolness of the government propaganda response to the Wilkes crisis later in the decade. John Wesley was surprised in 1768 that the newspaper writers "are mostly on one side" and that the anti-government one.[78] This shocked Smollett in 1770 as well.[79] The pro-government pamphleteer "Verus," writing in *Lloyd's* in July 1769, even tried to make a virtue of this governmental nonchalance regarding the press.[80] There may have been other reasons than George III's fear of being thought a Tory or Jacobite or unconstitutional for this royal and governmental understatement in the face of what really was a major crisis of confidence in the regime beginning in 1768. But I would suggest it may have played a role.

J. C. D. Clark takes Timothy Brecknock quite seriously as "the forerunner" to Blackstone or Reeves' high prerogative views.[81] And indeed Brecknock did have his intellectual successors, though I would argue that neither Blackstone nor Reeves were among them. It is rare, though not impossible, to find an unqualified assertion of passive obedience and non-resistance in later Georgian England in line with Brecknock or with the Jacobite *True Briton*'s statement in 1751 that resistance is unlawful under any circumstances.[82] Two High Church protégés of Bishop Horne (as he became) seemed wedded to virtually unqualified passive obedience: the High Church lay leader William Stevens, Horne's first cousin, and the Rev. Jonathan Boucher, the American loyalist. Stevens in 1776 and 1777 was reprinting both long extracts from Mary of Modena's attorney general, Roger North, defending passive obedience and non-resistance,[83] as well as obscure sermons of George Horne from the decades of the 1750s and 1760s asserting that wicked rulers are God's revenge for sin. Stevens evoked a Cranmerian view of society, affirming that passive obedience is a "principle of liberty," and that governments, even of evil Roman emperors, must always be

---

[77] John Wain, *Samuel Johnson* (New York, 1974), p. 371.
[78] John Telford, ed., *Letters of the Rev. John Wesley, A.M.* (London, 1931), v, p. 371.
[79] BL, Whitefoord Papers, Add. MSS. 36593, Smollett to Whitefoord, May 18, 1770, fo. 83.
[80] *Lloyd's Evening Post*, July 3–5, 1769.   [81] Clark, *English Society*, pp. 202–4.
[82] *True Briton*, May 8, 1751, pp. 434–6.
[83] [William Stevens], "A discourse on the English constitution" (London, 1776).

obeyed.[84] In a slightly less aggressive manner, Boucher in his collection of American sermons, published and obviously edited in the 1790s, also seemed to defend absolute passive obedience and non-resistance.[85] Horne, Stevens, and Boucher were all avowed Tories, even after 1760.

There was, however, another, much more important, level of discussion of passive obedience and non-resistance to the established authorities which merely asserted the Pauline doctrine of Christian obedience to the magistrate as a holy thing or which exalted the normal functioning of the monarchical power on utilitarian grounds. Such reasoning ought not to be confused with the high Tory doctrine of Brecknock, Horne, Shebbeare, Stevens, and Boucher. For example, in his *Commentaries*, while certainly arguing that in the exercise of his *lawful* prerogatives the king is absolute, Blackstone allowed that resistance to princes was justifiable if the state was endangered. Yet he cautioned against carrying the resistance doctrine to republican or anarchical lengths.[86] John Reeves, thirty years later, in his controversial "Thoughts on English government," condemned by the House of Commons, was merely writing a historical tract, generally sound at that, though perhaps impolitic. He maintained that the Lords and Commons had sprung from the king, branches on a tree on which the throne is the trunk. Parliament could not survive without the throne, though the throne could survive without parliament, as it clearly did during the reigns of Henry I or Henry II or John.[87] Edmund Burke and French Laurence, among others, argued that Reeves' view was historically valid.[88] John Gifford, editor of the *Anti-Jacobin Review* made the sound point that the actions of the House of Commons *contra* Reeves set it up as "literary inquisitor" seeking to exercise a Napoleonic tyranny over the minds of historians.[89]

In general, the other high prerogative voices of George III's reign followed this qualified Christian-submission (or utilitarian) path rather than the unqualified neo-Jacobite one. David Hume, of

[84] [William Stevens], "The revolution vindicated and constitutional liberty asserted ... " (London, 1777), pp. 13ff, 31–3, 49.

[85] Jonathan Boucher, "A view of the causes and consequences of the American revolution in thirteen discourses" (London, 1797), pp. 528–9, 544–5.

[86] Sir William Blackstone, *Commentaries on the Laws of England* (Philadelphia, 1862), I, p. 250.

[87] John Reeves, "Thoughts on the English government" (London, 1795), pp. 12–13.

[88] Burke, *Corr.*, Burke to Windham, November 25, 1795, VIII, p. 347; Burke to Dundas, December 6, 1795, VIII, p. 354.

[89] John Gifford, "A letter to the Earl of Lauderdale" (London, 1800), pp. xvi–xvii.

course, in his often revised and republished *History of England*, admitted at his most high prerogative moments the necessity of exceptions to his doctrine of obedience.[90] Samuel Johnson, says his first biographer, was not a Filmerian and did not agree that resistance to government oppression was always wrong.[91] Robert Nares, editor of the *British Critic*, defended a qualified and necessary right of resistance in his "Principles of government" in 1792;[92] as did John Bowles in a riposte to Paine.[93] Even the deputy Grand Master of the Orange Institution in 1832 argued that non-resistance and passive obedience must always be qualified.[94]

Yet the Whigs had become, perhaps understandably after their experiences of the 1760s, thin-skinned to high prerogative notions of any stripe. For example, Myles Cooper, President of King's College, New York, preached a Fast Day sermon at Oxford in December 1776, in which he merely attacked the historicity of the Lockeian notion of an original compact and the resultant popular commotion which extreme Lockeianism could cause.[95] He found himself assaulted in the press,[96] and by Walpole in his memoirs,[97] as having libeled the Glorious Revolution. Lord Shelburne, a leader of the Chathamite opposition in 1777, attacked the Archbishop of York, William Markham, former tutor to the Prince of Wales, for a reasonably harmless sermon, accusing him of upholding non-resistance and passive obedience.[98] Rockingham and Stanhope took similar umbrage when Leonard Smelt, a sub-governor to the prince, and one of the few who defended the king at the giant Yorkshire meeting in 1779, opposed Dunning's resolution and described the monarch as "the life and soul of the constitution."[99]

One of the few normal and uniform events that could perhaps take the temperature of the governing class as to its attitude towards high prerogative notions at least on a theoretical level would be the

---

[90] Hume, *History of England*, v, p. 296.   [91] Hawkins, *Works of Johnson*, i, pp. 504–5.
[92] Robert Nares, "Principles of government" (London, 1792), p. 141.
[93] [John Bowles], "A protest against T. Paine's 'Rights of man'" (Edinburgh, 1792), p. 19.
[94] *Westminster Review*, 30 (January 1836), pp. 494–5.
[95] Myles Cooper, "A sermon preached before the university of Oxford ... Dec. 13, 1776" (Oxford, 1777), p. 22. Also, see unmarked press insert in the British Library's copy of the sermon.
[96] Even the *Critical Review* (January 1777), p. 74, was critical.
[97] *Last Journals of Walpole*, i, pp. 594–5.
[98] William Markham, "A sermon preached before the society for the propagation of the gospel in foreign parts, February 2, 1777" (London, 1777). For Shelburne's reaction see, Lord Fitzmaurice, *Life of William Earl of Shelburne* (London, 1912), II, pp. 6–7.
[99] Burke, *Corr.* Rockingham to Burke, January 6, 1780, IV, p. 184.

annual January Remembrance sermons for Charles I's execution, preached at Westminster Abbey for the Lords and at St. Margaret's, Westminster for the Commons. Between the accession of George III and 1795 and again between 1807 and 1811 the sermons were annual. The British Library contains a collection of many of the sermons from the Lords, though fewer from the Commons. Of the thirty-nine sermons which were preached to the Lords, twenty-five survive in that collection; of the thirty-nine preached to the Commons, only ten survive there. Of the twenty-five surviving Lords' sermons, chiefly from 1762–1784 and 1807–1810, six (in 1762, 1763, 1765, 1772, 1784, and 1789) were extremely critical of Charles I and his policies; twelve (in 1764, 1769, 1770, 1771, 1773, 1776, 1777, 1778, 1779, 1780, 1782, and 1808) were generally neutral on the constitutional issues agitating the seventeenth, eighteenth and early nineteenth centuries; and only seven (in 1774, 1775, 1781, 1783, 1807, 1809, and 1810) were unconditionally high prerogative defenses of Charles I. Of the surviving ten preached to the Commons, only one (in 1766) was extremely critical of Charles; seven (in 1763, 1767, 1768, 1769, 1770, 1771, and 1811) were neutral; and only two (in 1764, and Dr. Nowell's famous sermon in 1772) were enthusiastic endorsements of Charles and his policies.

Some of the episcopal denunciations of Charles I before the Lords were quite brutal: the Bishop of Peterborough in 1758 proclaimed Charles a tyrant and questioned the utility of the sermons at all;[100] the Bishop of St. Davids, Samuel Squire, whom Reed Browning has identified as a leading Court Whig, at the height of the Bute-oriented high prerogative campaign, denounced those who magnified or deified the sovereign or his prerogatives and suggested "the royal head ... be an admonition to all succeeding princes ... ";[101] a sentiment echoed by the Bishop of Llandaff in 1772.[102] Laud and his High Church clergy were censured by name in 1763,[103] 1765,[104] and

---

[100] Bishop of Peterborough, "Sermon preached before the House of Lords ... on ... January 30, 1758" (London, 1758), pp. 1–11.

[101] Bishop of St. David's, "Sermon preached before the Lords ... on ... January 30, 1762" (London, 1762), pp. 9–13.

[102] Bishop of Llandaff, "Sermon preached before the Lords ... on ... January 30, 1772" (London, 1772), pp. 12–13.

[103] Bishop of Lincoln, "Sermon preached before the Lords ... on ... January 31, 1763" (London, 1763), pp. 9–10.

[104] Bishop of Carlisle, "Sermon preached before the Lords ... on ... January 30, 1765" (London, 1765), pp. 6, 18.

1772.[105] In 1784, the Bishop of Llandaff delivered a pro-American sermon.[106] In 1789, Pitt's friend, the Bishop of Lincoln, arraigned Charles as preparing England for absolutism and popery.[107]

J. A. W. Gunn, finding the claims of the divine right of kings to be "extremely resilient" during George III's reign, wrote that "the survival of [these] sermons was one strand that tied the eighteenth century to the seventeenth."[108] But none of the exhortations, even those most defensive of Charles, came anywhere near to defending the divine right of kings or were especially oriented towards high prerogative notions. The one possible exception was a sermon delivered to the House of Commons by the Master of Emmanuel College, Cambridge (of all places), William Richardson, Chaplain in Ordinary to the King, in January 1764, only a few months after Bute's resignation. Richardson, in a very anti-parliamentary speech, wanted obedience to the king "without murmuring or repining" to whatever "Injunctions ... he shall lay upon us."[109]

In some ways the famous 1772 sermon by Thomas Nowell before the House of Commons on January 30, was less high prerogative oriented than Richardson's eight years before.[110] Nowell, an Oriel College man, was a Glamorgan client of the Tory Dukes of Beaufort.[111] In 1764, as the Tory Dr. King's successor, he became principal of St. Mary's Hall, Oxford, and by 1772 was Professor of Modern History, Public Orator, and secretary to the Chancellor of

---

[105] Bishop of Llandaff, "Sermon preached before the Lords ... on ... January 30, 1772" (London, 1772), pp. 12–13.

[106] Bishop of Llandaff, "Sermon preached before the Lords ... on ... January 30, 1784" (London, 1784).

[107] Bishop of Lincoln, "Sermon preached before the Lords ... on ... January 30, 1789" (London, 1789), pp. 12–14.

[108] Gunn, *Beyond Liberty*, pp. 136, 150. Robert Hole suspects that the 1783 and 1787 Remembrance sermons preached to the Lords were unique up to that point in the reign for their royalist sentiment. Furthermore, he argues that they "were in line with the general change in ideological tone of the sermons from 1782 onward, which reflected both the political crises in Britain and the empire and an increased concern with the growth of Enlightenment irreligion in Europe." I doubt that these sermons reflect anything other than the personal likes or dislikes of the episcopal preachers. Certainly, in 1784 and 1789, two of the most anti-Charles I sermons of the century were preached, by the Bishops of Llandaff and Lincoln. *Pulpits, Politics and Public Order in England, 1760–1832* (Cambridge, England, 1989), pp. 52–3.

[109] William Richardson, "Sermon preached before the ... House of Commons ... on ... January 30, 1764" (London, 1764), pp. 8–18.

[110] Thomas Nowell, "Sermon preached before the ... House of Commons ... on ... January 30, 1772" (London, 1772).

[111] J. P. Jenkins, "Jacobites and Freemasons in eighteenth-century Wales," *Welsh History Review*, 9 (December 1979), p. 403.

the University. His notorious sermon to commemorate Charles' death had first been given before the University of Oxford in 1766, and Nowell had had it published that same year without causing comment.[112] The sermon was largely a tirade against the seventeenth-century Puritans but contained the perhaps too contemporary thought that "the sword of the Magistrate is drawn to execute wrath upon the children of disobedience; to be a terror to evil works; to repress the violence, and stop the fury of the oppressor."[113] Only the Speaker of the House of Commons and four members were present at this exhortation. Routine thanks were offered to the good doctor. When the thanks were expunged a few weeks later, no warning was ever given of the debate, and a thin House in essence censured Nowell.[114]

This light attendance at Charles I Remembrance sermons was normal. In 1764, only the Speaker and five members were present for Richardson's high prerogative sermon, and in the Lords, only one temporal peer – Mansfield – bestirred himself to attend that year.[115] In 1788 and again in 1791, only one temporal peer frequented the service.[116] J. C. D. Clark, who along with Gunn, is convinced of the high seriousness of the divine right of kings and passive obedience traditions in the late Georgian period, suggested that the American and then the French Revolutions "reinvigorated" the January 30 sermon.[117] If so, at the first such ceremony at St. Margaret's after the signing of the Anglo-American peace treaty, only the Speaker and no other MP appeared at the sermon.[118] The one sermon of the entire period in which I have found any parliamentary interest occurred ten days after the execution of Louis XVI, when, not surprisingly, Pitt, Dundas, most of the Cabinet, the Speaker, and one hundred MPs attended St. Margaret's. The Abbey was also "thronged" with peers.[119] Thereafter, the normal pattern ensued. In 1794, in the midst of the Terror, only two lay lords attended[120] and in 1795, only the Lord Chancellor and a few

[112] *Jackson's Oxford Journal*, February 1, 1766. *History of Oxford*, v, pp. 168–9.
[113] Nowell, "Sermon," pp. 7–8, 14.
[114] John Adolphus, *History of England* (London, 1840), i, pp. 509–11. *History of Oxford*, v, pp. 168–9.
[115] *Jackson's Oxford Journal*, February 4, 1764.
[116] *The Times*, January 31, 1788; February 1, 1791.
[117] Clark, *English Society*, p. 160.   [118] *Morning Post*, January 31, 1784.
[119] *Morning Herald*, January 31, 1793.
[120] *The Times*, January 31, 1794.

bishops went.[121] After 1795 the embarrassing ceremonies were stopped altogether.

During the last years of the Pitt ministry and during the Addington administration, no special services were held at St. Margaret's or the Abbey. Perhaps to score a point with the Grenville–Grey administration, in 1807, at the request of George III, the services were resumed, and three MPs attended.[122] In 1810, an embarrassed Perceval again wanted to stop the services; as in the previous year only three or four MPs and three or four lords had gone to church on the stated day. The king, in the year of his Jubilee, refused.[123] The regent, more pliable after only two MPs attended in 1811, agreed to the permanent suspension of the formal service.[124] When Newdigate, defending the memory of Charles I in the House of Commons in 1772 called the king "the only canonized saint" of the English Church, he "occasioned an universal laughter throughout the House."[125] If one wishes to find support for or sympathy with high prerogative notions or extraordinary veneration for royalty in the late Georgian period, one will have to look elsewhere than parliament.

Since the most sustained sources on which this book is based are right-wing newspapers, magazines, and journals, it is possible that I have partially overlooked pamphlets as a telling source in which to gauge public and elite opinions. Gayle Pendleton suggests that thirty-seven pamphlets of the 1790s in forty-five editions urged non-resistance principles and thirty-five pamphlets in forty-nine editions argued submission to magistrates as a Christian duty.[126] Part of this may of course reflect the temporary fright which revolutionary Jacobinism put into the English literate classes. Part of it may reflect Paul Langford's argument that by the late eighteenth century divine right and non-resistance were applied more and more to the entire governmental apparatus of king in parliament and not just the throne as in former times[127] – though in that sense

[121] *Ibid.*, January 31, 1795.
[122] Arthur Aspinall, ed., *Correspondence of George, Prince of Wales, 1770–1812* (London, 1971), Perceval to McMahon, January 24, 1812, VIII, pp. 349–50.
[123] Aspinall, Perceval to the king, January 20, 1810, V, pp. 489–90; king to Perceval, January 20, 1810, V, p. 490.
[124] See footnote 122.   [125] *Parl. Hist.*, XVII (April 3, 1772), pp. 435–8.
[126] Gayle Trusdale Pendleton, "English conservative propaganda during the French Revolution, 1789–1802," Ph.D. dissertation (Emory University, 1976), p. 22.
[127] Paul Langford, "Old Whigs, old Tories, and the American Revolution," *Journal of Imperial and Commonwealth History*, 8 (January 1980), p. 124.

the concept somewhat loses its peculiar bite. Certainly there was an attempt by the Younger Pitt's propaganda machine to glorify the monarchy as long as the monarchy did not in any way interfere with the politics of Mr. Pitt. Hence, one of his leading pamphlet hacks, the Rev. John Ireland, Vicar of Croydon, said of the king in the "Vindiciae Regiae" that in his quality of civil ruler he "is to us what the Deity was to the Hebrews."[128]

Then too there may have been a diminution in the importance of pamphlet literature as a gauge of public or elite opinion in the second half of the eighteenth century. However they may otherwise disagree on the importance of the eighteenth-century media, Jeremy Black, Marie Peters, and John Brewer[129] all perceive during that period a movement away from pamphlets to newspapers or magazines as *the* important vehicles of communication by print. William Playfair too, perhaps Pitt's leading pamphleteer in the 1790s, in a memoir written in 1813, waxed eloquent on the decline during his lifetime of the importance of pamphlet literature as opposed to those other means of communication.[130] Still, taking the right-wing press as a whole between the American Revolution and the passage of the 1832 Reform Bill, certain conclusions can be drawn regarding its attitude towards the throne and towards the royal family in general.

There is very little evidence of any cult of royalty or cult of George III in the eighteenth-century right-wing British press. The one periodical which in its loyalism extends from the commencement of the reign to its transfiguration into an opposition, mildly pro-French journal in the early 1790s, the *Critical Review*, while politically supportive of the ministerial side of controversial matters such as the Stamp Act,[131] the conduct of the American war,[132] and the regency crisis,[133] was not, even in the 1750s, an example of high prerogative or orthodox religious aspects of the Tory vision. Hence, for example, it was extremely caustic regarding Dr. Nowell's high prerogative sermon in 1772.[134] So while the *Critical* defended the king from imputations that Jenkinson was a representative of an

---

128 [John Ireland], "Vindiciae Regiae" (London, 1797), p. 25.
129 Jeremy Black, *English Press in the Eighteenth Century* (London, 1987), p. 145. Marie Peters, *Pitt and Popularity* (Oxford, 1980), p. 17. Brewer, *Party Ideology*, pp. 146–7.
130 William Playfair, *Political Portraits in This New Area* (London, 1813), I, pp. iv–vi.
131 *Critical Review*, 19 (March 1765), p. 225.
132 *Ibid.*, 40 (October 1775), pp. 305ff.   133 *Ibid.*, 46 (December 1788), pp. 492ff.
134 *Ibid.*, 33 (March 1772), p. 258.

interior Cabinet[135] or that George had acted unconstitutionally in the crisis of December 1783,[136] the defense tended to be rather mundane.

The pro-government tri-weekly press during the American Revolution, *Lloyd's Evening Post* and the *General Evening Post*, also tended to be rather matter-of-fact when it came to discussing the king or the royal family, with the latter paper in 1779 mildly critical of George for seeming to absorb too much power into his own hands.[137] A more effective government supporter, Bate Dudley's *Morning Post*, was highly ideological and opinionated in its coverage of all sorts of issues: the war, Roman Catholics, Ireland, Dissenters, the opposition leadership. But it was somewhat circumspect regarding the throne. There were exceptions. In 1778, George III was termed "the Augustus of the age"[138] and in 1780, it was announced that "the memory of him who now fills the throne of England, and the ministers who act under his royal direction, will be held in veneration for the noble stand they have made ... "[139] Yet, in general, whatever excessive praise there was of George was neither sustained nor particularly noteworthy. In 1780, when Bate Dudley started the *Morning Herald*, the same pattern of high ideological content coupled with a questionable attitude towards too close a connection with the monarchy prevailed. The *Herald* even printed an absurd assertion in 1781 that the queen's German female servants might have too much control over public affairs.[140]

The Pittite press of the 1780s and 1790s likewise treated the king or the royal image gingerly. The Pittite press too had a problem with the royal family with which the Northite press of a decade or so before had not been burdened. This involved the children of George III and Queen Charlotte and their increasingly discreditable conduct as they reached adulthood. During the 1783–1784 crisis, when George III dismissed the Fox–North coalition which had the support of the House of Commons and replaced it with a ministry headed by the Younger Pitt, the pro-administration press was anything but subservient to the king. The *Public Advertiser*, while comparing Fox with Cromwell, told the public that Charles Jenkinson was playing an unconstitutional role in his relations with the

---

[135] *Ibid.*, 53 (February 1782), p. 146.   [136] *Ibid.*, 57 (January 1784).
[137] *General Evening Post*, November 6–9, 1779.
[138] *Morning Post*, June 30, 1778.   [139] *Ibid.*, February 4, 1780.
[140] *Morning Herald*, December 6, 1781.

king.[141] The somewhat unimaginative but pro-Pittite *St. James's Chronicle* besought the new prime minister to "drive from behind the Throne all that secret Influence which has been productive of so much Mischief."[142] The *General Evening Post*, which asserted its Pittite credentials early in the crisis, nonetheless berated George for the secret non-ministerial influence he allowed in his closet.[143]

The French Revolution in general did not greatly change matters. The two special Pittite daily newspapers, the *Sun* and the *True Briton*,[144] while obviously royalist and counter-revolutionary, were not above criticism of the senior members of the royal family when they seemed in any way about to embark on policies inimical to those of the prime minister. For example, for obvious reasons the Pittite press always printed negative comments on the Prince of Wales, tied as he was socially and politically to the Whig opposition. This led them, necessarily, to champion the cause of Caroline, Princess of Wales, when her husband deserted her in 1796.[145] With the king often ill, Caroline, in her own right and as mother to the second-in-line to the throne, was obviously seen between 1796 and 1811, when the regency was inaugurated and her usefulness to the Pittites abruptly terminated, as a powerful weapon for use against a potential Foxite Whig–Carlton house administration. However, when Queen Charlotte, always the fond mother to her disreputable eldest son, seemed prepared to support the prince against the princess, a torrent of criticism against Charlotte poured forth from the *Sun* and the *True Briton*.[146]

The right-wing press in the early nineteenth century idealized the late William Pitt almost to the point of idolatry.[147] The same was true of the living prime minister in the 1790s – though this could not be said of the general attitude of *his* subsidized press towards Lord North in the 1770s and 1780s. Hence the *True Briton* remarked in 1797 that "To the wisdom, firmness, fortitude, and caution of Mr. Pitt, the British nation is indebted for its escape from the miseries and horrors of Revolution. To him and his friends do we owe the

---

[141] *Public Advertiser*, January 2, 1784; January 5, 1784.
[142] *St. James's Chronicle*, February 5–7, 1784.
[143] *General Evening Post*, January 8–10, 1784; February 5–7, 1784.
[144] Werkmeister, *London Daily Press*, pp. 368–71.
[145] For example, *Sun*, June 4, 1796.
[146] See, for example, *Sun*, June 4, 1796; September 9, 1796. *True Briton*, May 28, 1796; June 2, 1796.
[147] James J. Sack, "Memory of Burke and memory of Pitt," *HJ*, 30 (September 1987), pp. 623–40.

very existence of that happy system of Government, our glorious Constitution ... "[148] Or consider the views of the scurrilous *Tomahawk! or Censor General*, a highly-charged daily paper of 1795–1796. Here Pitt was the *"Patriot Guardian*, if not very *Saviour* of the *British Constitution*,"[149] while George III was merely noticed for his firmness, as contrasted with Louis XVI's temporizing.[150] Presumably the *Tomahawk!* meant the king's firmness in calling to and sustaining William Pitt in power. The cult of Pitt was always more prominent in the right-wing press in the late eighteenth and early nineteenth centuries than the cult of George III.

In the nineteenth century, as Linda Colley has pointed out in her important article on the apotheosis of George III, where she combines sources as diverse as loyal addresses, newspapers, accounts of parades, and thanksgiving services, the king became an important font in the nationalistic stream which she is studying.[151] I do not doubt that this thesis is generally sound, especially in its emphasis upon the middle-class rally to the throne which occurred after 1793 or even 1783. The termination of Grenville's ministry in 1807, the Jubilee of 1809, the wide-spread recognition of George III as one of the national symbols in the long struggle against Napoleonic despotism, the death of the queen in 1818, or of the king himself, long shut away from the active world, in 1820 – all such events allowed the loyalist press to pour forth praise of the king in his role as protector of the Church or as national icon. The tribute of the Dean of Winchester, published in the *New Times* on George's death, is typical of the genre. The dean at the Temple Church called the late king "the champion of Christianity. Who but remembered, about thirty years ago, when the civilised world was threatened to be deluged with infidelity, anarchy, and confusion ... our venerable King fearlessly stood alone, and, at the head of his people, braved the pestilential storm ... "[152]

But ignoring seminal moments such as royal jubilees or funerals, the glorification of George III or that of the rest of his family by the loyalist press, seems to me tinged with qualification and unease. The whole Pittite tradition after all, had opposed the American revolutionary war, so identified with the king, and much of the Protestant right-wing press was quite sympathetic to the Glorious Revo-

[148] *True Briton*, April 14, 1797.   [149] *Tomahawk!*, November 4, 1795.
[150] *Ibid.*, November 25, 1795.
[151] Colley, "Apotheosis of George III."   [152] *New Times*, February 19, 1820.

lution and William III and as late as the 1820s clearly resented the Buteian, neo-Jacobite atmosphere in which the reign had begun. George's much vaunted middle-class virtues, his obedience to the seventh commandment, his protection of a Church in Danger, were much appreciated on the Right but inevitably ran up against the most assailable activity of the later Hanoverian monarchy, whose very existence was in some ways a reproach to George's own obvious role as *pater familias*, perhaps the most scandalous royal family in British history.

If one were to look chiefly at royal accessions, jubilees, or funerals for the image of the monarch or the royal family, one might well conclude that the right-wing press indeed was uncritically attached to its kings. The *Morning Post* in 1820 even discovered that "the moral virtues" of George III were perpetuated "in his illustrious son," George IV.[153] And ten years later, as if to answer the more liberal *Times*' famous query as to what eyes ever wept for him, the *Post* proclaimed the dying king "the most precious treasure of the Empire he so wisely rules."[154] The scurrilous weekly, the *Age*, found the late regent and king "the first of men and the best of Monarchs."[155] George Croly, the furious Protestant editor of the *Monthly Magazine* produced a sanitized version of the *Life and Times of George IV* with the sex left out,[156] as he later produced a sanitized *Life of Burke* (1840) with Roman Catholics left out. But a closer inspection of the way the royal family in general was treated in what after all in the loyalist press was their most favorable turf might suggest that the pre-Victorian monarchy was at best an equivocal source of inspiration to emerging English conservative nationalism.

Some of the criticism of king or monarchy in the loyalist press was starkly political, even if tinged with moralistic or religious overtones. The Pittite press kept up a sustained attack upon the licentious and politically unreliable Prince of Wales until he became its master in 1811. The *Sun*, the leading Pittite daily, said of the prince in 1796 that it had "long looked upon his conduct as favouring the cause of Jacobinism and Democracy in the Country, more than all the speeches of *Horne Tooke*, or all the labours of the

---

153 *Morning Post*, February 2, 1820.
154 Wilfrid Hindle, *Morning Post, 1772–1937* (London, 1937), pp. 106–8.
155 *Age*, July 11, 1830, p. 220.
156 George Croly, *Life and Times of His Late Majesty George the Fourth* (London, 1830).

Corresponding Society."[157] Another Pittite daily, the *Tomahawk!*, in 1795, reminded the prince of the fate of Marie Antoinette.[158]

Not surprisingly other members of the royal family who had the slightest proclivity for the Whig party or even distant Whig sympathies could expect little fellow-feeling from the right-wing press.[159] *John Bull* attacked the Duke of Sussex in 1822 as "a wretch who marries a woman under false pretences, begats children which are legally illegitimate, and then takes advantage of the law to cast her off and abandon her."[160] The ultra *Star of Brunswick* in 1829 made a furious assault upon the admittedly dim intelligence and (by that year, long respectable) morals of the Duke of Clarence.[161] In 1830 *Blackwood's Edinburgh Magazine* made an equally ungracious censure of the prospect of a regency under the Duchess of Kent, who had imbibed some of the Whig sympathies of her late husband.[162] Certainly unpopular with the Right was the Duchess of Kent's brother, the widower of Princess Charlotte of Wales, the Prince Leopold. All through the 1820s, for example, *John Bull* kept up a constant stream of jokes and allusive double entendres against the pensions, stinginess, and mistresses of the future founder of the Belgian royal family.[163] Equally prominent, though more cruel, as perhaps less deserved, were the "Silly Billy" jokes directed by *John Bull* and the equally popular Tory weekly, the *Age* against the dim-witted Duke of Gloucester.[164] Gloucester had married quite late in life for both of them, George III's daughter, and his first cousin, the Princess Mary. The Tory press contained cruel animadversions on her inevitable childlessness and the *Age* even suggested that she sing, in public, "For unto us a child is born" at London's next performance of Handel's *Messiah*![165]

I have suggested elsewhere that Wellington and Peel were subject to a ferocious Tory and Protestant press attack when they turned tail and endorsed Catholic emancipation in 1829.[166] The king, however reluctantly, as was well-known, he went along with his prime minister, was by no means immune from an equally spirited assault.

[157] *Sun*, June 2, 1796.   [158] *Tomahawk!*, December 3, 1795.
[159] *Morning Chronicle*, January 2, 1784.
[160] *John Bull*, January 17, 1822, p. 468.   [161] *Star of Brunswick*, February 28, 1829.
[162] *Blackwood's Edinburgh Magazine*, 28 (August 1830), p. 291.
[163] For example, *John Bull*, August 10, 1821, p. 285; September 6, 1829, p. 286.
[164] *Ibid.*, October 10, 1824. *Age*, March 5, 1826.
[165] *Age*, March 5, 1826, p. 341.
[166] James J. Sack, "Wellington and the Tory press, 1828–1830," in Norman Gash, ed., *Wellington* (Manchester, 1990), pp. 159–69.

With the exception of his own marital embroglio in 1820 and 1821, the king had received reasonably good press coverage from the Right since he became regent in 1811. His press Golgotha began in 1827, when, against the wishes of the Protestant Tories, he appointed a supporter of Catholic emancipation, George Canning, to succeed the ailing Lord Liverpool. Shortly thereafter, slurs not only against the king but against his mistress, Lady Conyngham, became standard features in the Tory press. The *Age* reminded the king that in *foro constientiae* he was still married to Mrs. Fitzherbert.[167] The *Standard* compared Lady Conyngham's nefarious influence with that of the Earl of Bute;[168] the *Watchman* compared her with Queen Anne's "Mrs. Masham";[169] the *Star of Brunswick* found her a "venal woman;"[170] the *Morning Journal* accused her of taking money in return for political favors;[171] and *Fraser's Magazine* attacked her as a concubine who amassed riches, and first accumulated and then dispensed places under the crown.[172] Both the monthly *Blackwood's Edinburgh Magazine* and the *Morning Journal* accused George IV of destroying that constitution of 1688 which had been bequeathed to him by his father.[173]

Attacks upon the lack of moral seriousness of the royal family were not uncommon when the political slant was not so evident. Perhaps the leading critic of the entire Hanoverian royal family was the extreme right-wing, avowed Tory *Anti-Jacobin Review*. In one of its earliest numbers the monthly expressed deep concern that five of the royal princes openly in the House of Lords opposed the bill criminalizing adultery.[174] That journal thereafter, rather fearlessly, took on most important members of the royal family. It wondered again and again how George III, "the *Head* of the *Church* himself," and Charlotte could support with their considerable patronage the "Anti-Christian system" of Joseph Lancaster,[175] in whose educational scheme Dissenters and Anglicans were equally serviced by non-denominational religious material. They severely criticized the queen for allowing her (then) only legitimate grandchild, Princess

---

[167] *Age*, November 4, 1827, p. 173.   [168] *Standard*, December 8, 1827.
[169] *Watchman*, May 6, 1827.
[170] *Star of Brunswick*, April 25, 1829.   [171] *Morning Journal*, February 5, 1829.
[172] *Fraser's Magazine*, 2 (August 1830), pp. 92ff.
[173] *Blackwood's Edinburgh Magazine*, 28 (August 1830), p. 231. *Morning Journal*, April 4, 1829.
[174] *Anti-Jacobin Review*, 6 (June 1800), p. 203.
[175] See, for example, *Ibid.*, 23 (January 1806), pp. 85–6; 29 (January 1808), p. 45; 39 (June 1811), p. 209.

Charlotte of Wales, to socialize at Frogmore with her other, illegitimate, grandchildren, the Fitzclarence brood.[176] Of Princess Charlotte's father, while the editors of the *Anti-Jacobin* would show him
Christian obedience should he become king, they

> most seriously assure him, that, to judge from the unanimous declaration of
> every Company into which we enter, and from the sentiments of every class
> of people which we have heard upon the subject, there is not, at this
> moment, so unpopular a character in his Majesty's dominions.[177]

George III's second son, the Duke of York, who in 1809 was in the
midst of the scandal which ultimately drove him, temporarily, from
the command of the army, was "a determined and systematic votary
of vice," and the *Anti-Jacobin* vigorously disagreed with the vote in
the House of Commons that more or less acquitted him.[178] Following the York affair, the *Anti-Jacobin* hoped never again to see a
member of the royal family placed in a position of responsibility.[179]
Having attacked the moral surroundings of the first three in line to
the throne, the *Anti-Jacobin* also took on the fourth by an open
stigmatization of the Duke of Clarence's alliance with the actress
Mrs. Jordan.[180]

Other loyalist newspapers and magazines laid siege to the royal
family. F. W. Blagdon's *Phoenix*, in 1808 one of the few Pittite
Sunday papers, found the childless Duchess of York's pandering to
her dogs disgusting and suggested that she spend her money on "the
widows and orphans of brave men who have fallen in defence of
their country, and of her august family."[181] The *Courier*, in 1809 fast
becoming the chief government organ in the entire press, was
extremely unforgiving of the scandal involving the Duke of York
and Mrs. Clarke, calling it a "filthy brothel story" and wondering
how people could with much credibility any longer pray in church
for the royal family.[182] In the second decade of the nineteenth
century, John Agg, Cobbett's "Humphrey Hedgehog" and coadjutor from the loyalist days of the 1790s, published an anti-radical
magazine, the *Busy Body*, replete with both severe denunciations of
radicals such as Orator Hunt and William Cobbett and monstrous
colored illustrations of the Brunswick family in grotesque poses. Agg

[176] *Ibid.*, 39 (July 1811), p. 331.   [177] *Ibid.*, 24 (August 1806), p. 437.
[178] *Ibid.*, 32 (February 1809), pp. 210–12; 32 (March 1809), pp. 317–18.
[179] *Ibid.*, 32 (March 1809), p. 322.   [180] *Ibid.*, 24 (August 1806), pp. 509ff.
[181] *Phoenix*, October 2, 1808.
[182] *Courier*, February 9, 1809.

accused the Duke of Cumberland of murdering his valet and attacked the Princess Charlotte of Wales for her décolletage.[183] The oft-repeated story of Cumberland sodomizing and then murdering his *valet de chambre* was long a staple of left-wing propaganda in Britain. The right wing, however, made use of it too. Even the scandalous *Age*, which ideologically was quite close to Cumberland's own ultra-Protestant position, frequently brought up the valet story, spicing it up with charges that Cumberland had committed incest with his own royal sister.[184] The editor of the *Age*, the notorious Charles Molloy Westmacott, was deeply involved in the blackmail surrounding the Captain Garth affair and the alleged relationship between young Garth and his putative mother the Princess Amelia.[185]

The ambivalent attitude of the right-wing press (and perhaps to an extent the reading public) towards the Hanoverian monarchy can best be shown by an examination of its collective attitude towards the two greatest public scandals of the entire 1714–1832 period: the affair of the Duke of York and Mrs. Clarke in 1809 and, more importantly, the trial of the queen in 1820. Of the London loyalist press which commented on the York scandal, the monthly *Anti-Jacobin Review* and two dailies, the *Courier* and the *Day*, were vehemently opposed to the duke; three dailies supported the duke, the *Sun*, the *Morning Post*, and the *Pilot*; while Lewis Goldsmith's weekly paper, the *Anti-Gallican Monitor*, though not founded until early 1811, vigorously espoused his reinstatement as commander-in-chief of the army.[186] The *Pilot* was a rather undifferentiated ministerial supporter, mildly oriented towards Canning. It was taken over by an army man, Col. James Willoughby Gordon, in 1809, specifically to defend the Duke of York. It did not do well in circulation.[187] The *Sun* had been the great Pittite newspaper of the 1790s, yet its circulation was pitiable in 1809.[188] The *Morning Post*, which had fallen in circulation from 4,500 in 1803 to 3,000 in 1811,[189] lost much of this number in 1809 (its leader writer admitted in his memoirs) over its editorial support of the Duke of

---

[183] *Busy Body*, June 1, 1816, pp. 145ff, 177.   [184] *Age*, February 26, 1826.
[185] See, for example, *St. James's Chronicle*, November 14–17, 1829.
[186] *Anti-Gallican Monitor*, May 26, 1811.
[187] See, *Pilot*, March 15, 1809. Arthur Aspinall, ed., *Letters of George IV (1812–1830)* (Cambridge, England, 1938), Willoughby Gordon to McMahon, February 25, 1813, I, p. 224.
[188] William Jerdan, *Autobiography* (London, 1852), II, pp. 69–70.
[189] *Ibid. Gentleman's Magazine*, 9, n.s. (June 1838), p. 579.

York.[190] Of the anti-York press, the *Day*, though supportive of both Portland and Perceval, was never a very ideologically-oriented newspaper. It nonetheless had a much greater daily circulation in its anti-York period than either the *Pilot* or the more established *Sun*.[191] The editors of the *Courier*, which soundly supported Portland and Perceval, one can only surmise, had no intention of letting the unpopularity of the Duke of York and his general support by the administration interfere with their growing circulation. In 1809, they vigorously attacked York and their editors got an enormous subsidy too.[192]

The Caroline case differed from the York case of a decade earlier not because the right-wing press was any less divided but because a strong aggressive ministry was in place, unlike in 1809, dedicated to aiding the king who, after all, had put them in their places, and from all indications putting pressure on any subsidized or favored part of the press to toe the party line. Such a policy may have gone against the grain of a significant portion of the loyalist community. Among literary Tories, for example, both Coleridge and Wordsworth had considerable sympathy for the queen's cause or at least her case.[193] The tendency of High Church religious periodicals like the *British Critic* or the *Christian Remembrancer* to ignore or downplay the affair probably reflected a religious bias against divorce or perhaps disgust at the then Prince of Wales' conduct in the 1790s. The *Quarterly Review*, too, ignored the queen's trial as much as possible, easier of course for a publication appearing only four times a year than for one that appeared monthly, tri-weekly, or daily. Dr. Stoddart's daily *New Times*, which throughout most of its more than ten years of existence always maintained an uneasy amalgam of liberal Toryism as associated with Stoddart's university friend, George Canning, and excessive anti-radicalism as befitted the chief literary prop of the Constitutional Association, initially, in 1820, like Canning's own position from within the Cabinet, was vaguely sympathetic towards Caroline. As late as the middle of June, the *New Times* favored the controversial policy of placing Caroline's name as queen

---

[190] Jerdan, *Autobiography*, I, pp. 111–12.
[191] Denis Gray, *Spencer Perceval* (Manchester, 1963), pp. 132–3.
[192] *Courier*, February 9, 1809; March 20, 1809. Gray, *Perceval*, pp. 132–3.
[193] David V. Erdman, ed., *Collected Works of Samuel Taylor Coleridge* (Princeton, 1978), III, pp. 275ff. Ernest de Selincourt, ed., *Letters of William and Dorothy Wordsworth* (Oxford, 1970), III, p. 643n.

in the liturgy of the Church.[194] But by August, possibly under pressure from other more anti-Caroline ministers, the *New Times* shifted towards the view that those who sustained the queen supported revolution.[195]

The chief champion of Caroline's cause on the Right was, perhaps surprisingly, the Orange Order, both in its chief active representative in the House of Lords, the deputy Grand Master of Great Britain, Lord Kenyon, and in its daily London evening paper, the *True Briton*. The *True Briton* stated in November 1820 that it could find not one Orangeman in the Lords who supported the Bill of Pains and Penalties against the queen.[196] This remark was surely an exaggeration as the soon-to-be Grand Master in Great Britain, the Duke of York, supported his royal brother, though others may have tactfully absented themselves from the trial. Yet one wonders if the rather hasty resignation of the heir to the throne, the Duke of York, from the Grand Mastership in June 1821, ostensibly due to doubts about the validity of the Orange oath,[197] might not have had as much to do with the Orange rally for the queen. While there was no ultra-Tory group *per se* in parliament as early as 1820, the presence of such later ultra leaders as Charles Wetherell, MP for Oxford City, on the queen's side should at least be noted.[198]

There is no reason to doubt that the Orange rally to Caroline was largely on religious grounds. Kenyon in a speech on November 9, 1820 dubbed the Bill of Pains and Penalties "odious, unjust and unchristian." He wondered how the king, of all people, could apply for relief from his wife when Christ had said that whosoever puts away his wife save for adultery causes her to commit adultery. How, Kenyon wondered, could the bishops contravene Christ's own law? He charged the bishops with lowering the public estimate of the Church of England by asserting, essentially, a different role of Christian morality for king and subject.[199] In a way Kenyon's speech against a Church leadership prepared to bend the rules of Christian morality curiously prefigures his own and other ultra leaders' perorations nine years later against a Church leadership prepared to uproot the constitutional settlement of 1688. The *True Briton*, of which Kenyon was the proprietor, led a long campaign in

---

[194] *New Times*, June 21, 1820.   [195] *Ibid.*, August 26, 1820.
[196] *True Briton*, November 14, 1820.
[197] Hareward Senior, *Orangeism in Ireland and Britain, 1795–1836* (London, 1966), pp. 172–5.
[198] *New Times*, March 26, 1821.   [199] *Parl. Deb.*, III. n.s. (November 9, 1820), p. 1731.

favor of restoring the queen's name to the liturgy, withdrawing the Bill of Pains and Penalties against her, and ultimately allowing her to participate as queen consort in the coronation ceremony of George IV.[200] Kenyon winced at some of the radical associations his path crossed while supporting Caroline but this did not deter him.[201] The tri-weekly *St. James's Chronicle*, a general supporter of the Liverpool administration, was decidedly neutral on the queen's case in 1820.[202] Possibly this was due to the Orange sympathies of its editor, S. L. Giffard, a second generation Orange newspaperman, and to emerge in the late 1820s as the leading ultra-Tory press spokesman in the United Kingdom.

But the preponderance of the right-wing press supported George IV in his attempt to deprive his wife of her marriage and her dignities. T. B. Macaulay saw the Caroline affair as involving a union in support of the queen between the middling orders and the unruly lower orders, an irresistible union ultimately overseeing the capitulation of the Liverpool government and the withdrawal of the Bill of Pains and Penalties.[203] Although the evidence is largely circumstantial, a cursory examination of the right-wing press that opposed Caroline seems to indicate a possible withdrawal of public support from such loyalist supporters of a corrupt and unpopular king. *Blackwood's Edinburgh Magazine*, then at its most scintillating and outrageous, and perhaps for those very reasons, seems not to have been hurt by its support of George.[204] Nor was the daily *Morning Post*, whose offices were attacked by a mob on November 10, 1820.[205] But the *Post* had a small but select and aristocratic circulation which led to higher prices charged for advertisements.[206] This may have helped it weather the Caroline storm. *The* government daily newspaper, the *Courier*, with the largest circulation in the United Kingdom in 1815 – at least 8,000 per issue[207] – was also attacked by a mob in early November 1820.[208] A loss of circulation

[200] *True Briton*, August 12 and 24, 1820; September 19, 1820; January 16, 1821; July 12, 1821.
[201] Edmund Phipps, *Memoirs of the Political and Literary Life of Robert Plumer Ward* (London, 1850), II, pp. 98–9.
[202] *St. James's Chronicle*, September 21–23, 1820.
[203] Lord Macaulay, *Historical and Miscellaneous Essays* (New York, 1860), VI, p. 425.
[204] *Blackwood's Edinburgh Magazine*, 8 (November 1820), pp. 212ff.
[205] *St. James's Chronicle*, November 11–14, 1820.
[206] *Tait's Edinburgh Magazine*, 1, n.s. (December 1834), p. 791.
[207] Ian R. Christie, *Myth and Reality in Late Eighteenth-Century British Politics and Other Essays* (London, 1970), p. 324.
[208] *St. James's Chronicle*, November 11–14, 1820.

from that height was probably inevitable under any circumstances due to the fall-off of interest in the press after the end of the absorbing Napoleonic wars.[209] But the circulation decline seems to have been precipitous in the early 1820s – down to 5,000 in 1821.[210] By 1822, according to Professor Gash, Peel and Palmerston were reduced to personally writing articles for the *Courier* to revive its sinking sales.[211] Yet it never really recovered. In a way, the *Courier*'s great days as a leading newspaper began with its vitriolic attacks on the Duke of York in 1809 and ended with its cringing espousal of George IV in 1820. The old Pittite daily *Sun*, in minor ways subsidized by the ministry,[212] whose circulation had dipped to around 500 issues per day anyway before 1820,[213] had in line with the rest of the administration press violently attacked Caroline in 1820.[214] Under new ownership it suddenly switched to a pro-Caroline, though, oddly, not necessarily to an anti-ministerial stance in 1821.[215]

John Wilson Croker organized a new Sunday newspaper, the *Guardian*, in late 1819, just in time, in other words, for the new reign. In 1820, while considering itself the "Guardian of national morals," it defended the propriety of the classic "double standard" when discussing the queen's case.[216] The *Guardian* was poorly written and conceived, and probably not fated for a long life under any circumstances.[217] The Caroline case obviously did not help it. Also violently against the queen was Lewis Goldsmith's subsidized weekly *British Monitor*.[218] There is no particular evidence that it was hurt by its opposition to the queen, and it had a circulation problem anyway, as Goldsmith himself admitted, "confined to the *higher classes* only."[219]

As to the periodical press, at least three anti-Caroline journals could probably trace negative connotations to their espousal of George IV's cause. The *Anti-Jacobin Review*, never sycophantic to royalty, wanted Caroline executed like Catherine Howard.[220] After nearly a quarter century as a leading right-wing journal, it ceased

[209] Christie, *Myth and Reality*, p. 324.   [210] *Ibid.*

[211] Norman Gash, *Pillars of Government and Other Essays on State and Society, c. 1770–c. 1880* (London, 1986), p. 26.

[212] BL, Liverpool Papers, Add. MSS. 38277, Taylor to Liverpool, June 1, 1819, fo. 266.

[213] James Grant, *Great Metropolis* (London, 1836), II, pp. 94–6.

[214] See, *Sun*, throughout 1820.

[215] *Sun*, November 2, 1821.   [216] *Guardian*, July 2, 1820, November 12, 1820.

[217] CL, Croker Papers, "Private letter book," Croker to Croly, January 10, 1820.

[218] For example, *British Monitor*, May 28, 1820.

[219] PRO, Foreign Office, 97/169, Goldsmith to Canning, December 6, 1824.

[220] *Anti-Jacobin Review*, 59 (September 1820), p. 44.

publication in 1821. William Jerdan's Saturday weekly, the *Literary Gazette*, was mildly supportive of the king in 1820, and such was the outcry that, commencing in 1821, it ceased to comment on political affairs at all.[221] Charles Knight, editor of a new loyalist and anti-Caroline monthly geared especially for the working classes, the *Plain Englishman*, admitted in his memoirs that the endeavor failed because of the competition of the queen's trial as news for the lower orders.[222] The one definite exception to the above litany of failure, partially at least associated with the aggressive espousal of George IV's cause, was the extraordinary success of the new "Loyalist and Royalist" Sunday paper, *John Bull*, edited by the noted wit and raconteur, Theodore Hook. The *Bull* never gave an inch in its denunciation of the queen. She was a "sickening woman," the "paramour of Bergami"; it even attacked her unmercifully when she was on her deathbed.[223] But others did this as well. What made the *Bull* stand out was its adherence to the principle that the best defense is a good offense. Hence, the public was entertained with scandalous and libel-inducing stories of the queen's male and female Whig-supporters along the lines of the pre-nuptial pregnancy of Mrs. Henry Brougham or the lesbianism of the Hon. Mrs. Damer.[224] The *Bull*'s outrageousness sickened some of its own side[225] but it also showed the length to which ministerial supporters were forced to go to restore some handle on the popular press in the wake of the Caroline fiasco.

The Lake poets and their friends were less than enthusiastic about the monarchy. Whatever demons (or angels) drew them in a Tory direction, it was not their veneration of royalty. De Quincey was shocked in November 1807 when he first met Southey and heard his and Wordsworth's conversational disrespect for the royal family and especially for George III.[226] The following year, Coleridge in a private letter termed the king and the Dukes of York, Kent, and Cambridge as "State-Agents – and not a shadow of responsibility in them or their tools."[227] Twelve years later, as an apostle of British

[221] *Literary Gazette*, July 1, 1820; June 16, 1821.
[222] *Plain Englishman*, August 1820, p. 412. Charles Knight, *Passages of a Working Life During Half a Century* (London, 1864), I, p. 246.
[223] *John Bull*, December 17, 1820, p. 4; August 12, 1821, p. 276; May 6, 1821, p. 164.
[224] *Ibid.*, December 17, 1820, p. 6.
[225] Southey, for example, refused to subscribe to it. John Wood Warter, ed., *Selections from the Letters of Robert Southey* (London, 1856), Southey to Bedford, August 31, 1821, III, p. 267.
[226] Geoffrey Carnall, *Robert Southey and His Age* (Oxford, 1960), pp. 82–3.
[227] Earl Leslie Griggs, ed., *Collected Letters of Samuel Taylor Coleridge* (Oxford, 1956), Coleridge to Poole, December 4, 1808, III, p. 132.

loyalist political thought, Coleridge failed to make public his sympathies for Queen Caroline only for fear it would hurt the careers of his two sons.[228]

Hence there may have been a less significant or sustained cult of royalty in late Hanoverian Britain than first meets the eye. Perhaps Hume in the end was correct in his assessment that what bound the people of Britain to the Stuarts, even in the years of their adversity in the eighteenth century, was not the love of high prerogative but the ties of affection. Few such affectionate ties were present in the later Hanoverian period, except perhaps in a residual way to George III and (if only briefly) to Princess Charlotte. The attitude of the loyalist and Tory press towards the Brunswick house resembled more the harrying of Louis XVIII and Decazes by the ultra press in France than anything remotely like the cult of royalty Novalis and others helped sustain around Frederick William III and Queen Louisa or even of Louis XV after Metz. By 1820, and even more by 1830, the British monarchy was no longer, if it ever had been, the salvation of the Right on a level, for example, with the Church of England. Indeed the right wing disregarded and at times disdained it as much as Fox had in his day. When J. C. D. Clark asserted that both Whigs and Tories "largely shared similar attitudes to monarchy,"[229] he was not, I suspect, thinking in negative terms of that *ancien régime* institution. But he may have been accurate nonetheless.

[228] *Ibid.*, Coleridge to Allsop, October 25, 1820, v, p. 119.
[229] Clark, *English Society*, p. 52.

CHAPTER 6

Parliamentary reform and the Right, 1750–1832

If in the middle of the eighteenth century there was one issue which united the Oxford, religious-oriented, High Church sector of the Tory (or country) party with the City, radical, more libertarian wing, it was the perceived necessity for a thorough regeneration of the electoral system. Tory support for parliamentary reform was both natural and pragmatic. Members of what was, arguably, the national governing party of England, winners, as Linda Colley has pointed out, of 50 percent of English and Welsh county seats as late as 1761, and, in terms of votes cast, of the 1722, 1734, and 1741 general elections,[1] paralyzed not only by a continued proscription from shire, judicial, Church, and military offices under the crown, but also by a Whig-originated Septennial Act that lessened the necessity of consulting an at least spasmodically sympathetic electorate with any sustained frequency, the Tories had no particular reason to revel in the established form of electoral institution. Hence arose their commitment to a rather complete overhaul of a system which had victimized and marginalized their contribution to the national experience. The Tory leadership and press vigorously pressed the issue, if with no discernible result, and, unlike the Whigs in 1831, with no recognized panacea. Some parliamentary chiefs such as Sir William Wyndham, Sir John Hynde Cotton, and Sir Roger Newdigate advocated annually elected parliaments.[2] Publicists such as Tobias Smollett in the Tory monthly, the *Critical Review*,[3] "Britannicus," the most important columnist in the Tory *London Evening Post*,[4] and the neo-Jacobite, John Shebbeare,[5] agreed. Wyndham, Cotton, and Shebbeare also promoted universal

[1] Linda Colley, *In Defiance of Oligarchy* (Cambridge, England, 1982), pp. 122–5.
[2] Helen M. Swartz, Marvin Swartz, *Disraeli's Reminiscences* (New York, 1976), pp. 36–7. Namier and Brooke, III, p. 198.
[3] *Critical Review*, 2 (December 1756), p. 471.   [4] *London Evening Post*, March 17–20, 1759.
[5] John Shebbeare, *History of the Sumatrans* (London, 1763), I, p. 185.

male suffrage.[6] Other mid-century Tory commentators advocated less dramatic measures. *Jackson's Oxford Journal* proposed triennial parliaments.[7] The *York Courant* and the *Crab-Tree* seemed chiefly concerned with the intricacies of personal electoral corruption.[8] Alderman William Beckford wanted equal electoral districts.[9]

Historians have tended either to ignore or belittle this eighteenth-century Tory effusion for reform. John Cannon in his otherwise thorough account of parliamentary reform between the summoning of the Long Parliament and the passage of the first Reform Bill has little or nothing on Tory parliamentary reform attitudes.[10] J. C. D. Clark suspects that the Tories supported parliamentary reform not for its own sake but rather in the hope that a majority of the newly empowered would favor a Stuart restoration. Hence, to Clark, the Tory vision was "doctrinally superficial, so that no intellectual tradition sustained the issue as a vital and immediate one after the party was no more."[11] Yet both Cannon by his omission and Clark by his dismissal may have underplayed a major component of the Tory political tradition. I remarked in chapter 3 on the post-Tory, reformist orientation of much of the Tory national and local press, for example, the *Monitor*, the *London Evening Post, Felix Farley's Bristol Journal, Jackson's Oxford Journal*, and the *York Courant*. Might this not bespeak an intellectual commitment to parliamentary reform that was more than superficial and certainly more than Stuart-oriented? Then, too, B. W. Hill has discovered the interesting fact that the former Tories still in parliament after the mid-1760s who supported the more authoritarian factions, were inclined to desert the Court and support opposition on parliamentary reform divisions.[12] Probably the most notable examples in late-eighteenth-century parliaments of the pre-1760 High Church Tory (however Newdigate came to dislike the name) tradition were the MPs elected from Oxford University. Newdigate in 1768 supported annual parliaments and

---

[6] Swartz, *Disraeli's Reminiscences*, pp. 36–7. John Shebbeare, "Fifth letter to the people of England" (London, 1757), p. 17.

[7] *Jackson's Oxford Journal*, October 27, 1764.

[8] *York Courant*, November 6, 1753; February 5, 1754; April 30, 1754. *Crab-Tree*, July 5, 1757, p. 63. *Felix Farley's Bristol Journal* also favoured some sort of undefined reform of parliament, February 2, 1755.

[9] *London Evening Post*, April 4–7, 1761.

[10] John Cannon, *Parliamentary Reform, 1640–1832* (Cambridge, England, 1973).

[11] J. C. D. Clark, *English Society, 1688–1832* (Cambridge, England, 1985), pp. 291n, 308.

[12] B. W. Hill, *British Parliamentary Parties, 1742–1832* (London, 1985), p. 39.

payment of MPs.[13] In 1772, both Newdigate and his colleague Francis Page favored the Wilkite radical John Sawbridge's motion for shorter parliaments.[14] Their High Church heir, Sir William Dolben, representing Oxford during the quarter century between Lord North's ministry and Lord Grenville's, upheld parliamentary reform both in its Pittite heyday in 1783 and 1785 as well as in a darker age in 1797, when Charles Grey introduced his controversial motion on the matter.[15]

But then the late-eighteenth-century press supportive of George III was not inevitably against parliamentary reform either. One of the few major pro-government organs in London during the Wilkite embroglio, *Lloyd's Evening Post*, praised triennial parliaments in a strategic section of the paper.[16] During the 1783–1784 political crisis, Pittite newspapers like the *Public Advertiser* (which compared Fox to Cromwell) and the *Whitehall Evening Post* wanted universal male suffrage and annual parliaments.[17] The *General Evening Post* and the *Morning Post*, both suporters of the Fox–North coalition, on the other hand, were strongly opposed to any parliamentary reform.[18] Then suddenly, as was common in those days, on January 6–8, 1784, the *General Evening Post* switched allegiance to the royal and Pittite side and proclaimed its support for a scot and lot electorate and annual parliaments.

Running through much of the literature of the history of parliamentary reform is the assumption that, in general, the forces of the Right tended to oppose any substantial reform of parliament or the electoral system until, angered in 1829 by the Wellington administration's capitulation on the Catholic issue, and convinced that Catholic emancipation was passed despite a lack of public support, a certain portion of the so-called ultra Tory movement, what D. C. Moore called "the other face of reform," suddenly embraced reform in a spirit of revenge and redress of grievance. Actually, whether its origin lay in pragmatism or in a Tory or Pittite nostalgia, a significant section of the loyalist press at least had long supported parliamentary reform. From the perspective of the Tory press, 1829

[13] Namier and Brooke, III, p. 198.   [14] *Ibid.*, III, p. 198; III, p. 242.
[15] *Ibid.*, II, pp. 328–9. Thorne, III, p. 603.
[16] *Lloyd's Evening Post*, June 30–July 3, 1769.
[17] *Public Advertiser*, January 2 and 10, 1784. *Whitehall Evening Post*. March 13–16, 1784.
[18] *General Evening Post*, January 3–6, 1784. *Morning Post*, January 28, 1784.

was less a quirky leap in the dark than the culmination of decades of reflection and discussion.[19]

There was an intellectual and political tradition in Britain that was unambiguous in its failure to countenance any reform of parliament. It was to this tradition that the Duke of Wellington appealed in his famous speech on November 2, 1830 extolling the current system of representation and discountenancing even the possibility of any reform.[20] But the predecessors of such Wellingtonian (and before it, perhaps even Canningite) intransigence tended to be more the somewhat politically marginal Northite, Burkeian, and Windhamite traditions of orthodox Whiggery rather than the neo-Tory or Pittite traditions dominant on the Right in the early nineteenth century. The former school was unequivocal and firm: the constitution created between the Glorious Revolution and the Septennial Act was perfect and ought to be retained. Lord North, in the second year of his coalition with the Foxite Whigs, and supported by Edmund Burke, opposed Pitt's motion in 1785 for the non-compulsory purchase of thirty-six small boroughs, the extension in number of county MPs, and the enlargement of the electorate by 40s. copyholders, on the grounds that the constitution was "the most beautiful fabric that, perhaps, had ever existed from the beginning of time. He never would consent to any attempt to tamper with such a fabric."[21] A quarter century later, the anti-Pittite William Windham, as much as any figure of the period Burke's political heir, termed John Christian Curwen's motion to limit the purchase of parliamentary boroughs "dangerous and mad" on the grounds of the reforming precdeent it would create. On a more historical level, Windham bade his colleagues in the House of Commons remember the American war and the French Revolution: in its capacity to disturb, "Parliamentary Reform was of the same cast and character."[22]

---

[19] Frank O'Gorman in his study of the unreformed electorate agrees that the "overwhelming success of the reformers at the election of 1831 ... was not due to influence, to violence, or to mobbery, but to the immense popularity of the bill and the years of persuasion which had preceded it" in regards the press etc. However, he seems not to realize that much of the persuasion came from the right-wing press. See, for example, his comments that before the early 1820s to advocate the reform of parliament was to argue "a disreputable opinion" or "shocking." Such was certainly *not* the case. *Voters, Patrons, and Parties: The Unreformed Electoral System of Hanoverian England, 1734–1832* (Oxford, 1989), pp. 309–10.

[20] Elizabeth Longford, *Wellington: Pillar of State* (New York, 1972), pp. 226–8.

[21] *Parl. Hist.*, xxv (April 18, 1785), p. 456. John Ehrman, *The Younger Pitt: The Years of Acclaim* (New York, 1969), pp. 226–7.

[22] *Parl. Deb.*, xiv, (May 4, 1809), pp. 368–70. A. D. Harvey, *Britain in the Early Nineteenth Century* (London, 1978), p. 249.

Such Northite and Windhamite absolutist views were seldom reflected in the contemporary loyalist press.[23] Most right-wing newspapers and journals tended either to ignore parliamentary reform or, gingerly, to endorse it, albeit often for some tantalizingly distant age. In the 1790s, both the Pittite *Times* and the *British Critic* supported eventual parliamentary reform.[24] In 1792 even John Reeves' Loyal Association admitted the ultimate need for such action.[25] During the first decade of the nineteenth century, reform was not a leading matter on the national agenda until 1809, when the scandalous affairs of the Duke of York led to a revived radical and (to a lesser extent) Whig call for serious electoral amelioration. As the radical movement gathered steam, the increasingly Toryish poet Wordsworth was by no means the only voice on the Right suporting a thorough reform of parliament.[26] *Blagdon's Weekly Political Register*, subsidized by the Perceval ministry,[27] called for a uniform £10 urban franchise as well as the possibility of further reform.[28] The *Courier*, by 1810 fast becoming the leading, even almost the official, voice of the Perceval ministry, while it realized the prudence of awaiting the war's conclusion, favored the disenfranchisement of rotten boroughs and the transference of their members to populous towns; a scot and lot borough and a copyhold county franchise; and triennial parliaments.[29] Another daily loyal to the Portland and then the Perceval administrations, the *Day*, also wanted reform of parliament.[30]

Thereafter, with the waning of political radicalism after 1812, and although parliamentary reform *per se* never became a political issue of the first magnitude until the late 1820s, various sections of the government-oriented press seemed supportive of it. During another post-war radical resurgence in 1817, Lord Sidmouth's indirectly subsidized *White Dwarf*[31] stated its agreement with its otherwise radical Cobbettite adversaries on the corruption of the

---

[23] One exception was *Redhead Yorke's Weekly Political Register* on May 20, 1809.

[24] Gayle Trusdale Pendleton, "English conservative propaganda during the French Revolution, 1789–1802," Ph.D. dissertation (Emory University, 1976), p. 278. *British Critic*, 13 (January 1799), p. 14.

[25] Donald E. Ginter, "Loyalist association movement of 1792–93 and British public opinion," *HJ*, 9 (1966), pp. 181–8.

[26] Ernest de Selincourt, ed., *Letters of William and Dorothy Wordsworth* (Oxford, 1970), Wordsworth to Daniel Stuart, March 26, 1809, II, p. 296.

[27] Denis Gray, *Spencer Perceval* (Manchester, 1963), p. 87.

[28] *Blagdon's Weekly Political Register*, January 24, 1810; February 14, 1810.

[29] *Courier*, May 2 and 23, 1810.   [30] *Day*, May 4, 1809.

[31] *Fraser's Magazine*, 20 (November 1839), pp. 590–1.

current representative system and the need for reform.[32] The most important Tory journal, the very well-subscribed *Quarterly Review*, decided in 1812 to take a neutral position on parliamentary reform as it had done on Catholic emancipation.[33] Its neutrality on Catholic relief lasted for almost two decades. That on reform did not. In 1816, Robert Southey, in a *Quarterly* article, decided that moderate parliamentary reform might be conceded in a future time of civil peace.[34]

The proto-ultra, Orange-leaning press also supported reform. S. L. Giffard became editor in 1819 of the *St. James's Chronicle*, the mildly pro-Liverpool tri-weekly flagship of the Baldwin newspaper chain. A furious Protestant, he began the process of moving the *Chronicle* to the Right on most issues, though not on parliamentary reform. Starting in 1819, the *Chronicle* and, after its founding in 1827, its daily sister newspaper the *Standard* (also edited by Giffard), favored a parliamentary reform divorced, as the *Chronicle* put it, from the ideals of Robespierre, Napoleon, or Madison.[35] The Orangeist *True Briton* in 1822 was tolerant at the least of Lord John Russell's motion for the House to take the state of the representation under "the most serious consideration."[36] This is not to assert that all or even most of the Tory press was seriously supporting parliamentary reform before 1829 – only to point out that some of it did and that there was no sudden ultra-Tory lurch in 1829 into unrecognizable climes. That "other face of reform" of 1829–1831 had been significantly prefigured at least since the French Revolution.

In fact, before 1819 it is quite difficult to find any Tory newspaper or journal which explicitly denounced parliamentary reform or adopted an uncompromisingly Northite or Windhamite (or what afterwards could be called Wellingtonian) attitude towards it. After 1819, with the radical movement associated with Peterloo succeeded in quick order by the radical movement associated with Queen Caroline, definite opposition to parliamentary reform became much more common. The *Morning Post* and the *New Times*, announced their opposition in 1819;[37] *Blackwood's Edinburgh Magazine* in 1821;[38]

---

[32] *White Dwarf*, December 13, 1817.   [33] *Quarterly Review*, 7 (June 1812), p. 280.
[34] *Ibid.*, 16 (October 1816), p. 255.
[35] *St. James's Chronicle*, January 26–28, 1830. *Standard*, January 28, 1830.
[36] *True Briton*, April 27, 1822. J. E. Cookson, *Lord Liverpool's Administration, 1815–1822* (Hamden, Conn., 1975), p. 361.
[37] *Morning Post*, July 2, 1819. *New Times*, February 16, 1819.
[38] *Blackwood's Edinburgh Magazine*, 8 (February 1821), p. 496.

and *John Bull*, in 1828.[39] Nonetheless, when the *crise de régime*
commenced in 1828, there were certainly no orthodox Tory or
Pittite attitudes towards parliamentary reform, at least insofar as
those attitudes were expressed in the press. Any reader, casual or
committed, of the right-wing press during the previous quarter
century might well have assumed that parliamentary reform was as
much (or perhaps even more of) an "open question" for loyalist
Englishmen as was Catholic emancipation.

With the breakup of Tory unity in the late 1820s, after the
adoption of the Catholic cause by the main body of Wellingtonian
Toryism, parliamentary reform, at least in the anti-Catholic, ultra-
Tory press, became a *cause célèbre*. The ultra politicians in parliament, however, were not nearly as enthusiastic about parliamentary
reform as their ostensible representatives in the press. Only a few
supported their fellow ultra, the Marquess of Blandford, in his
rather extensive parliamentary reform motion of 1830, calling for
the repeal of the Septennial Act; a general scot and lot urban and a
copyhold rural franchise; the abolition of rotten boroughs and the
transference of their seats to populous towns and shires; the payment
of MPs; and a general reform of the Scottish representative system.[40]
Indeed, one of the reasons for the weakness of ultra-Protestant Tory
sentiment during the entire 1827–1832 period was its evident inability to coalesce effectively around any positive program beyond
inchoate opposition to the repeal of Catholic disabilities. This lack of
coherence was partially responsible for their debacle in the general
election of 1831. Sir Edward Knatchbull, for example, the leader of
Kentish ultraism, had no problem supporting Blandford's attempt
to disenfranchise corrupt boroughs and transfer their privileges to
large towns but he opposed the rest of the motion.[41] He likewise
opposed the ultra *Morning Journal's* crusade for an extensive parliamentary reform, even though he sympathized with it over its prosecution for libel in 1829 by its Wellingtonian enemies.[42] Other
leaders of the ultra party in the Commons, such as Henry Bankes

---

[39] *John Bull*, March 30, 1828, p. 100. Two less important organs, both short-lived – a
monthly, the *New Edinburgh Review* (July, 1821), p. 163ff, and a Sunday paper, the *Tory*
(June 17, 1827) – opposed it as well.

[40] Cannon, *Parliamentary Reform*, pp. 193–4.

[41] Sir Hughe Knatchbull-Hugessen, *Kentish Family* (London, 1960), pp. 198–204. *Parl. Deb.*,
XXII, n.s. (February 18, 1830), pp. 724–6.

[42] B. T. Bradfield, "Sir Richard Vyvyan and Tory politics, with special reference to the
period 1825–46," Ph.D. dissertation, (University of London, 1965), p. 70.

and Sir Richard Vyvyan also opposed Blandford's motion.[43] Another ultra chieftain, Sir Charles Wetherell, suspected that Jacobinism was at the bottom of the entire parliamentary reform movement.[44] In the House of Lords, a major ultra figure and rotten borough holder, the Duke of Newcastle, of course opposed the abolition of small boroughs though by 1832 he had no objection to the enfranchising of large towns. In general, however, he opposed parliamentary reform and all who advised it.[45] On the other hand, in addition to the generous views of Lord Blandford, Michael Thomas Sadler, the Leeds ultra Tory leader, wanted a scot and lot urban franchise,[46] the Duke of Richmond supported Grey's bill as a member of the Reform Cabinet, and the Earl of Winchelsea, whom Wellingon as prime minister challenged to a duel, favored triennial parliaments, the removal of bishops from the House of Lords, and supported Grey for the first seven months of his administration.[47] When finally, in June of 1831, Winchelsea returned to his Tory brethren, he made it clear in the House of Lords that he acted not in opposition to the Reform Bill but over churchly matters.[48]

In general, the ultra Tory press did not reflect the ambivalence of its parliamentary leadership. Its attitude can best be summarized in the admonition of the *Standard* three weeks *after* the introduction of the first Reform Bill to two skeptical ultra leaders, Charles Wetherell and Sir Robert Harry Inglis, that they should realize that the "*whole people desire reform.*"[49] Virtually the entire ultra press (pace the Duke of Newcastle) supported the abolition of rotten boroughs and the transference of their seats to populous shires and unrepresented towns.[50] On the other hand, there was virtually no support for the Ballot, annual parliaments, or, with some qualifications, universal suffrage. The ultra press, however, in its call for reform often did go much further than the Whig bill. The Baldwin newspapers and the *Age* supported triennial parliaments.[51] *Blackwood's Edinburgh Maga-*

---

[43] *Parl. Deb.*, xxii, n.ser. (February 18, 1830), pp. 724–6.
[44] *Ibid.*, ix, 3rd ser. (December 17, 1831), p. 512.
[45] BL, Halsbury Papers, Add. MSS. 56368, Newcastle to Giffard, January 5, 1831, fos. 149–50. *Parl. Deb.*, XII, 3rd ser. (May 7 1832), p. 709.
[46] J. T. Ward, *Factory Movement, 1830–1855* (London, 1962), p. 70.
[47] *Parl. Deb.*, xxi, n.ser. (April 6, 1829), pp. 424–5.
[48] *Ibid.*, iv, 3rd ser. (June 21, 1831), pp. 108–9.   [49] *Standard*, March 19, 1831.
[50] See, for example: *St. James's Chronicle*, March 1–3, 1831; *Morning Journal*, March 16, 1830; *Fraser's Magazine*, 2 (September 1830), p. 195; *Age*, January 30, 1831, p. 36. The one exception to this rule was *Blackwood's Edinburgh Magazine*, 29 (February 1831), pp. 235–54.
[51] *St. James's Chronicle*, January 26–28, 1830. *Standard*, July 30, 1830. *Age*, February 14, 1830, p. 52.

zine at least tolerated the idea of a Quinquennial Bill.[52] William Maginn, one of the editors of *Fraser's Magazine*, favored universal male suffrage,[53] and was certainly responsible for *Fraser's* initial position in favor of a £5 urban rent scale for the franchise, low enough so that in Sheffield and Paisley, for example, the "Honest and industrious operatives" and "poor weavers" should have the vote.[54] By August 1831, *Fraser's* was gingerly suggesting the preferability of both universal male *and* female suffrage to the £10 franchise component of the Whig's bill which, it felt, would greatly favor the manufacturing over the aristocratic interest. *Fraser's* then issued a call for Tories in parliament to move for universal suffrage.[55] *Fraser's* suffrage viewpoint, however, represented the outer fringe of ultra opinion. It was not endorsed elsewhere. The very influential Baldwin newspapers advocated, with Blandford, a wide scot and lot urban franchise. The *Age*, *Blackwoods*, and George Croley's *Monthly Magazine*, however, preferred a much more limited, if uniform, urban franchise.[56]

Beyond their general call for – in some cases – substantial parliamentary reform, the ultra press also endorsed sometimes quirky, sometimes creative solutions to perceived electoral or representational anomalies. The *St. James's Chronicle* suggested ambulatory parliaments meeting regularly in Dublin and Edinburgh as well as in London.[57] The ultra but democratic *Morning Journal* favored restoring the Irish 40s. (and largely Catholic) freehold franchise.[58] *Fraser's* wanted the complete assimilation of the English and Scottish political systems.[59] *Blackwood's* favored the legal elimination of canvassing for votes; single-day elections throughout the country; MPs resident in the boroughs they represented; and MPs sitting in Westminster from India, Canada, and the West Indies.[60]

---

[52] *Blackwood's Edinburgh Magazine*, 29 (February 1831), pp. 235–54.
[53] *Dublin University Magazine*, 23, (January 1844), p. 97.
[54] *Fraser's Magazine*, 3 (April 1831), pp. 276–8.
[55] *Ibid.*, 3 (April 1831), pp. 276–8; pp. 4–5.
[56] *St. James's Chronicle*, January 26–28, 1830. *Age*, January 30, 1831, p. 36. *Blackwood's Edinburgh Magazine*, 29 (February 1831), pp. 235–54. *Monthly Magazine*, April 1831, p. 353.
[57] *St. James's Chronicle*, September 3–5, 1827.   [58] *Morning Journal*, September 25, 1829.
[59] *Fraser's Magazine*, 3 (April 1831), pp. 276–8.
[60] *Blackwood's Edinburgh Magazine*, 27 (April 1830), pp. 652ff; 29 (February 1831), pp. 235–54; 30 (July 1831), pp. 33. The ultra Tories in Britain would and did blanch when any observer compared them with their fellow ultras in France (or elsewhere in Catholic Europe). Yet when the Baldwin newspapers and the *Morning Journal* gave vociferous support to the Birmingham Political Union (*St. James's Chronicle*, January 26–28, 1830 and *Morning Journal*, January 27, 1830), when Coleridge suggested that he wanted the franchise

The Wellingtonian press, which experienced bleak days after 1829,[61] naturally followed their leadership in parliament in opposition to Blandford's resolutions in 1830 and to Lord Grey's Reform Bill a year later. They managed to keep up a relatively united front as a small enclave of reaction surrounded by reformers – presumably supported by the vast bulk of the political and the non-political nation – to their right and their left. The only major daily London newspaper remaining to the Wellingtonians after the *Courier* defected in 1830 to the Whigs, the *Morning Post*, steadily maintained that parliamentary reform was "strictly equivalent to" revolution.[62] *John Bull* supported virtual representation and on those grounds even opposed the franchise transference from Penryn to Manchester.[63] The *Quarterly* actually proposed *raising* the electoral franchise and eliminating both scot and lot votes in the boroughs and, even more revolutionary, the traditional English 40s. freehold rural franchise as well.[64] Only the new, non-ultra but Tory, London daily, the *Albion*, founded at the same time that the Duke of Wellington's ministry fell, and supportive of the duke, made a minor pitch, in the spirit of Chatham and Pitt, for some parliamentary reform such as the transference of the franchise from small boroughs to large unrepresented towns.[65]

extended in the early 1830s due to fears of the shopkeeper class (T. Ashe, ed., *Table Talk and Omniana of Samual Taylor Coleridge* [London, 1909], pp. 149–50), when Maginn called for universal male suffrage (see footnote no. 53), when Southey wanted William IV on his own authority to issue electoral writs for Birmingham, Manchester, Leeds, and Sheffield (Charles Cuthbert Southey, ed. *Life and Correspondence of Robert Southey* [London, 1850], Southey to Rickman, September 11, 1830, VI, pp. 117–18), and when Disraeli called for the Ballot and triennial parliaments (J. A. W. Gunn, et al., eds., *Benjamin Disraeli Letters, 1835–1837* [Toronto, 1982], II, p. 47) one wonders whether the ideals, if unacknowledged, of Abbé Duvoisin and the French Catholic ultras were not as potent a force as the remembrance of Wyndham or Hynde Cotton.

[61] James J. Sack, "Wellington and the Tory press, 1828–1830," in Norman Gash, ed., *Wellington* (Manchester, 1990), pp. 159–69.

[62] *Morning Post*, March 3, 1831.   [63] *John Bull*, March 30, 1828, p. 100.

[64] *Quarterly Review*, 40 (January 1830), p. 273.

[65] *Albion*, November 15, 1830.

CHAPTER 7

Tory humanitarianism and political economy, 1760–1832

I

Prince Albert once said of Benjamin Disraeli that the arriviste politician was "a dangerous radical, even a revolutionary . . . not in his heart favourable to the existing order of things . . . with democratic tendencies . . . he may become one of the most dangerous men in Europe."[1] That the Prince Consort could consider one of the great conservative forces in nineteenth-century Europe a dangerous radical or even worse points to a curious paradox (by no means only observed in this case) of the interrelationship or intertwining of forms of radicalism and forms of conservativism in early-modern and modern European societies. "Radicalism" is as elusive in definition in an eighteenth and nineteenth-century context as is the vocabulary of the Right, but it generally implies some sort of commitment to popular participatory politics, an enlarged suffrage, and an opening to various and sundry reforming impulses relating to Church and state, employers and employees, rich and poor, free men and slaves, and dominant and deviant sexual connections. Obviously, not all radicals embraced all reforming impulses. The Whiggish or Benthamite devotees of the political economists might well emphasize reform in Church and state or anti-slavery, while preferring to ignore (or even exacerbate) the plight of the employee or the poor. Likewise, the so-called Tory radical might weep copiously over the woes of the Manchester or Sheffield labouring poor and ignore or even applaud the state of the Jamaican black slave or Irish Catholic tithe payer, not to speak of the rebel against conventional marital or sexual norms.

Tory radicalism, such as it was, was based on normal Christian

[1] Sarah Bradford, *Disraeli* (New York, 1983), pp. 213–14.

humanitarianism, on noblesse oblige ideals endemic to the traditions of powerful monarchies, and on simple hatred of modernizing (and hence faintly anti-monarchical and anti-clerical) classes and individuals. Historians such as E. P. Thompson and R. L. Hill have recognized the Jacobite or neo-Jacobite nature of such radicalism stretching from the eighteenth-century Blacks of Hampshire and Berkshire protesting the rigors of the law of 9 George I c.22[2] to the Tory (or country) magistrate implicitly countenancing riots to prevent notorious forestalling of grain[3] to the ideological origins of the Young England movement of the early Victorian age.[4] Other historians, looking merely at a Tory as opposed to a Tory–Jacobite tradition, have also addressed this question. The most non-ideological of British historians of the eighteenth century, Sir Lewis Namier, without entering into much detail, recognized affinities between radical and Tory viewpoints as opposed to Whig centrism.[5] Linda Colley described a mid-eighteenth-century Tory party tempted into alliance with the politically excluded, hence resulting in the City radicalism of William Beckford and his associates and prefiguring the Wilkite radicalism of the 1760s and 1770s.[6] J. G. A. Pocock, too, suggests that even in the early nineteenth century, some kinds of Toryism retained radical strains – a fact, he believes, too often neglected by historians.[7]

Contemporaries, too, were aware of what Namier and Colley regarded as Tory-radical or Tory-lower class affinities. Charles Jenkinson worried in 1763 that a parliamentary attempt then being mooted to abolish the yearly memorial services to commemorate Charles I's execution, might lead to "disturbances among the lower kind of people."[8] The highly ideologically oriented Pittite daily, the *Oracle*, in its quite suggestive obituary of Edmund Burke, accused

[2] E. P. Thompson, *Whigs and Hunters* (New York, 1975), pp. 163–6.

[3] E. P. Thompson, "Moral economy of the English crowd in the eighteenth century," *P&P*, (1971). For a good discussion of the Christian view of the "moral economy" from Apostolic times, see Gregory Claeys, *Machinery, Money and the Millennium* (Princeton, 1987), pp. 2ff.

[4] R. L. Hill, *Toryism and the People, 1832–1846* (London, 1929), p. 16.

[5] Sir Lewis Namier, *England in the Age of the American Revolution* (London, 1961), pp. 180–4.

[6] Linda Colley, "Eighteenth-century English radicalism before Wilkes," *TRHS*, 5th ser., 31 (London, 1981), pp. 4–6.

[7] J. G. A. Pocock, *Virtue, Commerce, and History* (Cambridge, England, 1985), p. 297. Frank O'Gorman on the other hand regards Tory Radicalism as one of the "might-have-beens of British history." *Voters, Patrons, and Parties: The Unreformed Electoral System of Hanoverian England, 1743–1832* (Oxford, 1989), p. 301.

[8] Ninetta Jucker, ed., *Jenkinson Papers, 1760–1766* (London, 1949), Jenkinson to Lowther, February 2, 1763, p. 131.

the late statesman of Jacobinism with regard to Ireland on the grounds that his vociferous support for the claims of the Irish Catholics were "such as in our opinion, justified ... the change in the form of Government in that kingdom, which admitted the great body of the people to the enjoyment of political rights and a share in the legislature."[9] The leading political correspondent of the *Morning Post*, organ of main stream Wellingtonian Toryism, viewed the ultra *Standard*, in 1830, and with some justification, as a "Protestant Radical" newspaper. "They have lost their *caste*, and we now associate them with all the low reformers of the day" such as the Hunts, the Carliles, Cobbett, and Burdett.[10]

Yet, despite the *Morning Post*'s identification of Burdett with the "low reformers," Namier's Tory-radical affinities can indeed be found in the general Tory press treatment of Sir Francis Burdett, scion of a Jacobite family, and with the self-proclaimed views of an Anneian Tory.[11] During at least the first three decades of his long political life, the radicalism of "Westminster's pride and England's hope" was far more pronounced than any vestigial Toryism. Nonetheless there were some atmospherics about Burdett, difficult to define or even locate exactly, yet which keen observers immediately recognized, and which set him off from his normal Whig and radical supporters. Lord Holland suspected that Burdett "hated the Whigs and the Revolution as much as the abuses in our representation."[12] Joseph Hume, a good political economist, disapproved of Burdett's sponsorship in the 1820s of attempts to mitigate the exploitation of child labor by cotton manufacturers.[13] The Tory press, ultra and Orangeist, anti-Catholic and pro-Wellingtonian, had a pronounced soft spot in its collective heart for the baronet.[14] Long before his much-heralded official conversion in the 1830s to the cause of conservatism, the Tory press appeared to agree with Tom Moore's observation that nature had written "Tory" on Burdett's brow.[15]

The Tory press treatment of another radical Tory-of-sorts, William Cobbett, whom William Thomas sees as having quite

[9] *Oracle*, July 11, 1797.   [10] *Morning Post*, February 2, 1830.
[11] M. W. Patterson, *Sir Francis Burdett and His Time (1770–1844)* (London, 1931), II, p. 670.
[12] Lord Stavordale, ed., *Further Memoirs of the Whig Party, 1807–1821* by Henry Richard Vassall, third Lord Holland (New York, 1905), pp. 102–3.
[13] Barry Gordon, *Economic Doctrine and Tory Liberalism, 1824–1830* (London, 1979), p. 9.
[14] See, for example, *John Bull*, June 17, 1821, p. 213; June 11, 1826, p. 189. *Watchman*, September 23, 1827, p. 228. *Brunswick or True Blue*, February 18, 1821, p. 58. *Morning Journal*, February 20, 1830. *Representative*, April 18, 1826.
[15] Wilfred S. Dowden, ed., *Journal of Thomas Moore* (Newark, 1986), III, p. 1116.

similar views, despite their frequent political quarrels, to Burdett's,[16] was in no way parallel. Newspapers and magazines were started to counteract Cobbett's influence; successive Pittite governments persecuted and prosecuted him. Why the marked difference in treatment? Part of the answer may lie in the realm of class bias. Cobbett was writing for an often lower-class audience, he himself was of lowly origins, and no one in Britain, before or after, could point a barb so devastatingly at Pitt or Pitt's successors. A more significant reason, however, may have involved a sense of betrayal. Unlike Burdett, Cobbett was an apostate; nurtured by Pittites, he betrayed them in his quest, admittedly of a nostalgic bent, for a Britain free from rapacious borough-mongers, corrupt clergy, and malevolent factory owners. It was only after 1829, when at least a section of the ultra press found itself persecuted and prosecuted in its turn, that at least the *Morning Journal* paid tribute to Cobbett as one who conferred "great benefits on his country." More indeed than any of its more celebrated military or naval heroes, Cobbett's ideas on agricultural improvements, finance, and the currency, thought the *Journal*, "throw into the shade the voluminous and absurd notions of ... Ricardo ... Mac Colloch ... Mill ... Place ... and all the quacks and economists."[17]

In general, however, when Daniel O'Connell maintained that he was a Tory at heart[18] or Feargus O'Connor proclaimed that he preached Tory radicalism,[19] or, even more absurdly, when the reactionary Wordsworth, while avowing his dislike for Whigs, suspected that "I have a great deal of the Chartist in me,"[20] they are announcing a doctrinal interrelationship between two traditions which by the 1830s must have seemed suspiciously dated to many contemporaries. That there was a Tory radicalism, as exemplified most profoundly by the humanitarian tradition of Oastler and Sadler, Wood and Bull, was indisputable. It might indeed be argued that in the eternal scheme of things, 1830 should be more remembered for the anti-factory pact at Horton Hall between Richard Oastler and John Wood on the feast of St. Michael and All Angels than for the advent of the Reform ministry in Westminster. Yet, especially after the rejection of Michael Thomas Sadler, first, in

---

[16] William Thomas, *Philosophical Radicals* (Oxford, 1979), pp. 58–9.
[17] *Morning Journal*, July 13, 1829.
[18] *Hill, Toryism*, pp. 14–15.   [19] *Ibid.*, p. 20.
[20] Keith Feiling, *Sketches in Nineteenth Century Biography* (London, 1930), p. 79.

essence, by his own parliamentary colleagues, then by the voters of Leeds, it was difficult to see this Tory-radical tradition as part of practical politics, however aspects of it might be reflected in the press or in various humanitarian movements. By the mid-1830s, Oastler himself was wondering how the term "Toryism" could subsume both Peel and Sadler.[21] R. L. Hill in his study of this tradition sees Tory radicalism after 1832 as divorced completely from the parliamentary Conservative party.[22] The ultra *Morning Journal*, reflecting on the same theme in 1830, during the Wellington administration, wondered what possible relationship Manchester had to Ministers, or Downing Street to Huddersfield or Apsley House with the mills of Macclesfield.[23] Greville too, in 1837, ridiculed Tory radicals as individuals seeking to agitate the people merely to create popular discontent with the existing Whig government. Hence, he maintained, all the Tory animadversions against the horrors of the New Poor Law of 1834 were cant. Were the Tories themselves in power, they would renew the controversial bill![24] Greville's point, while well-taken, merely gives a modern gloss upon the eternally valid observation that while most governments in power practice pragmatism, most oppositions are radical. Nonetheless, that certain humanitarian and political reforms did occur in nineteenth-century Britain no doubt owes something to their espousal by literary, political and press forces of the Right. While the importance of the Tory-radical and Tory-humanitarian tradition is difficult to gauge, not least because of the divorce between parliamentary politics and literary and local conflict, still, at times at least, words and their frequent reiteration may in the longer run be as important in the amelioration of grievances and the change of age-old ideas as momentary parliamentary majorities.

II

There was a significant right-wing (Jacobite, Tory, Buteite, Northite, Johnsonian) humanitarianism in the eighteenth century. It is perhaps not always recognized how deep and how broad that tradition was. W. Jackson Bate in his magisterial biography of

[21] Cecil Driver, *Tory Radical: Life of Richard Oastler* (New York, 1946), p. 294.
[22] Hill, *Toryism*, pp. 28–9.
[23] *Morning Journal*, January 7, 1830.
[24] Lytton Strachey, Roger Fulford, eds., *Greville Memoirs, 1814–1860* (London, 1938), III, pp. 392–3.

Samuel Johnson regards it as unfortunate that Boswell saw Johnson "through the spectacles of his own romantic Toryism, with the result that Johnson has been – and perhaps will unfortunately always be – viewed as an 'arch-conservative.'"[25] Donald J. Greene also wonders how seriously Johnson took the label of Tory "that his biographers so readily pinned on him." Possibly, suggests Greene, he did not take it very seriously at all.[26] If I understand these two leading Johnsonian scholars correctly, they are bemused that so humanitarian a creature as Johnson could be viewed as a Tory or an arch-conservative. However, in some ways both Bate and Greene may have seriously misunderstood or underestimated the essentially philanthropic nature of the political circles closely or roughly associated with Samuel Johnson and vulgarly labelled "conservative." From such a perspective, Johnson was a typical, albeit more talented, example of an "arch-conservative" even in his humanitarianism.

Johnson's Christian humanitarianism, perhaps derived partially from Jacobite and non-juring moorings as well as from a natural generosity of spirit, is well known and celebrated. At Oxford, he toasted the "next insurrection of the negroes in the West Indies."[27] He thought the severe regime which the Protestants of Ireland exercised over the Roman Catholics worse than the Ten Persecutions and preferred seeing an end to British influence on the island rather than a maintenance of the iniquitous status quo.[28] Johnson's opinion of Clive's Indian conquests were equally harsh.[29] At the beginning of the Seven Years' War, he defended the French enemy as opposed to his own countrymen's treatment of the American Indians. The British, he wrote, had "no other purpose in view than immediate profit, [and therefore] use all the arts of an European counting-house, to defraud the simple hunter of his furs ..."[30] Johnson also opposed, in the *Rambler* and the *Idler*, experimental mutilation of animals, the tyranny of country squires over their tenants, the press gang, imprisonment for debt, and the frequent use of capital punishment,[31] while espousing charity towards prosti-

[25] W. Jackson Bate, *Samuel Johnson* (New York, 1975), p. 365.
[26] Donald J. Greene, *Politics of Samuel Johnson* (New Haven, 1960), p. 18.
[27] James Boswell, *Life of Johnson* (London, 1953), p. 876.   [28] *Ibid.*, pp. 439, 544.
[29] *Ibid.*, p. 993.
[30] Donald J. Greene, ed., *Yale Edition of the Works of Samuel Johnson* x: *Political Writings* (New Haven, 1977), p. 150.
[31] Bertrand J. Bronson, *Johnson Agonistes and Other Essays* (Cambridge, England, 1946), p. 48–50.

tutes.[32] Johnson, says Boswell, told a clerical friend that "a decent provision for the poor is the true test of civilization."[33] Another friend, Mrs. Piozzi, in her memoir of Johnson, said that he felt severity towards the poor was an attribute of Whiggism and she never saw anyone who loved the poor as Dr. Johnson did.[34]

Such views are not unique among Johnson's political and literary coteries. The Tory London Evening Post in the 1750s frequently attacked, in the name of the poor, the forestalling or adulteration of grain. Indeed, it wondered why a rogue who stole a trifle was executed while an adulterator putting alum into bread or berries into beer was merely fined.[35] Bute's propaganda to the British people not only questioned the legitimacy or necessity of the Seven Years' War but also reminded his countrymen that the American Indians were "human creatures like ourselves" and hence worthy of more generous treatment than the Pelhamite regime had meted out to them.[36] In the 1760s, Johnson's friend the Tory Oliver Goldsmith also ridiculed the Seven Years' War in the Public Ledger in Johnsonian or even Voltaireian terms.[37]

The intellectual as well as political leadership of American Toryism proved in some sense more humanitarian than that of their colonial opponents. The biographers of Jonathan Boucher found that the Anglican divine was as libertarian on racial matters as Burke.[38] Governor Hutchinson, says a recent biographer, condemned racial prejudice against negroes and opposed the legal distinction made in colonial courts between killing American Indians and killing Europeans.[39] Another friend of Johnson's, indeed almost a mentor, General Oglethorpe, likewise from a Jacobite family and tradition,[40] used his position as an MP and founder of Georgia to agitate for prison reform in general and the condition of debtor prisoners in particular. He also attempted to

[32] Greene, Politics of Johnson, pp. 50–1.   [33] Boswell, Life of Johnson, p. 446.
[34] S. C. Roberts, ed., Anecdotes of Samuel Johnson by Hester Lynch Piozzi (Freeport, New York, 1969), pp. 56–7.
[35] London Evening Post, January 5–7, 1758; October 7–10, 1758.
[36] Sir John Dalrymple, "Appeal of reason to the people of England on the present state of parties in the nation" (London, 1763), p. 21.
[37] Arthur Friedman, ed., Collected Works of Oliver Goldsmith (Oxford, 1966), II, pp. 72–3.
[38] Anne Young Zimmer, Alfred H. Kelly, "Jonathan Boucher: constitutional conservative," Journal of American History 58 (March 1972), p. 898.
[39] William Pencak, America's Burke: The Mind of Thomas Hutchinson (Washington, 1982), pp. 178–9
[40] Phinizy Spalding, Oglethorpe: A Brief Biography (Macon, 1984), pp. 2–3.

ameliorate the condition of negroes and American Indians in the New World.[41]

Some Tory and High Church MPs were noted for their humanitarian concerns. Namier discovered in Charles Gray, MP for Colchester, a "humanitarian with a real feeling for the poor and for negro slaves and indentured labour, and ill-treatment by white settlers of natives."[42] Sir William Dolben, MP for Oxford University, urged in the 1780s the abolition of press gangs and supported a relief bill for debtors.[43] In short, there were probably many Tories (or Jacobites) who deserved the sobriquet of Sir Walter Blackett, MP for Newcastle-upon-Tyne, of "Father of the Poor."[44]

The leading Northite newspaper of the 1770s, the *Morning Post*, admitted that the British administrations had governed Ireland badly since the Revolution and that reform was in order. The *Post*, in fact, as early as 1780 favored the abolition of Poyning's Law, which tied the Irish parliament in Dublin in a colonial fashion to the English administration.[45] The pro-Northite *Critical Review*, in 1781, advocated a tax on absentee Irish landlords.[46] As to the Asian Indian situation, the *Post* in 1778 remarked that the "tyranny of European Demagogues in the East has thrown the name of Christians into contempt."[47] Philip Lawson recently discovered that Lord Mansfield was more consistently for religious toleration than John Wilkes and bemoaned the fact that Mansfield "has fallen foul of a ... modernist interpretation ... that ... he was the hammer of everything, perceived today as liberal and progressive."[48] The same judgment may in many cases be applied to Mansfield's conservative political confreres.

But it is African slavery in the British colonies, of course, which, quite rightly, most agitates the modern sensibility about the humanity of the men of affairs of eighteenth-century Britain. As far as the rightist disposition is concerned, one may find there hidden strands of anti-slavery or anti-slave trade feelings seldom, if ever, recognized by modern historians who have preferred (save for the well-known

---

[41] *Ibid.*, pp. 15–31, 47. David Brion Davis has a somewhat cynical view of Oglethorpe's purported abolitionist views. *Problem of Slavery in Western Culture* (Ithaca, 1966), pp. 145–6.
[42] Namier and Brooke, II, pp. 534–5.   [43] *Ibid.*, II, pp. 328–9.
[44] *Memoirs of the Public Life of Sir Walter Blackett* (Newcastle, 1819), pp. xiv–xv.
[45] *Morning Post*, October 27, 1779; February 22, 1780.
[46] *Critical Review*, 51 (May 1781), p. 389.
[47] *Morning Post*, April 17, 1778.
[48] Philip Lawson, "Anatomy of a civil war," *PH*, 8 (1989), 146.

views of Johnson and Wesley) to look elsewhere for the origins of this branch of the humanitarian movement. Part of the opposition to slavery undoubtedly came from a neo-Jacobite and High Church milieu, most exemplified by the family background and abolitionist tendencies of the Wesleys. Johnson's friend Oglethorpe, too, named "James Edward" after his king, was responsible for the prohibition of negro slavery in Georgia during the first two decades of its existence – and hence responsible too for its economic retardation.[49] Oxford University had a High Church anti-slavery tradition. Francis Page, MP for the university from 1768 to 1801, was, according to R. G. Thorne, a relic from the days of Jacobite squires. During the last decade of his long parliamentary career, Page, Thorne thinks, was inactive in the Commons save for coming down to vote in 1796 for the abolition of the slave trade.[50] His colleague at Oxford, Sir William Dolben, was effective at Wilberforce's side. Wraxall in his memoirs recounts an anecdote of May 1788, when Pitt wanted to postpone the discussions of the slave trade until the next session. Dolben objected that 10,000 lives could be sacrificed "to our criminal delay."[51] One of Dr. Nowell's colleagues at St. Mary's Hall, Oxford, William Agutter, in that same year, preached before the corporation of the City of Oxford that the traffic in human blood blasphemed the name of Jesus and only the complete abolition of the trade would avert God's wrath from Britain.[52] Other High Church and neo-Tory figures from the late eighteenth century who made public their qualms regarding slavery or the slave trade included the Rev. John Fletcher, Wesley's friend and disciple, who in one of his government-sponsored anti-American pamphlets in 1776 called his countrymen to repent not only for the horrors of the slave trade but for British conduct in India as well;[53] Bishop Horsley of Rochester, who denied in the House of Lords any linkage between abolition and Jacobinism;[54] and, to a lesser extent, Jonathan Boucher, the Anglo-American loyalist, who questioned in his "Causes and consequences of the American Revolution" the utility of slavery.[55]

[49] Spalding, *Oglethorpe*, p. 47. I. R. Christie, *Crisis of Empire*, (New York, 1966), p. 7.
[50] Thorne, IV, p. 703.
[51] Sir N. W. Wraxall, *Posthumous Memoirs of His Own Time* (Philadelphia, 1845), p. 295.
[52] William Agutter, "Abolition of the slave trade considered" (London, 1788), pp. 27–8.
[53] John Fletcher, "American patriotism" (London, 1776), pp. 97, 109–10.
[54] *Speeches in Parliament of Samuel Horsley, Late Bishop of St. Asaph* (Dundee, 1813), pp. 196–7.
[55] Jonathan Boucher, "View of the causes and consequences of the American revolution in thirteen discourses" (London, 1797), p. 39.

One place never examined, I believe, for anti-slavery antecedents is the Northite press, called "Tory" by its political enemies during the 1770s and early 1780s. Condemning slavery under the circumstances of war meant, of course, that there was an ulterior motive: pointing out the yawning gaps in the otherwise mildly libertarian world view of the American colonists. No doubt it was not only Samuel Johnson who wondered "how it is that we hear the loudest yelps for liberty among the drivers of negroes?"[56] Yet such cynicism should not be overdone. The loyal West Indian proprietors would hardly have looked too kindly upon such consistent rhetorical sarcasm. And the loyalist press showed signs of unease over slavery even before the flowering of the American issue. As early as 1769, the anti-Wilkite *Critical Review* suggested that parliament ought to take up the question of Britain's tolerating slavery in the empire, quoting with approval Cicero's remark that "whatever is against humanity and good faith, can never be of utility to the public."[57] And a year after the signing of the Anglo-American peace treaty, the *Critical*, judging the condition of slaves as worse than that of Spartan helots, was still urging parliament to act and finding it "mortifying to humanity" that it had not.[58] Practically the entire Northite newspaper press inveighed against slavery. The *General Evening Post* in 1777 found it "revolting to humanity";[59] *Lloyd's Evening Post* found the slave trade "infamous" and kept up a running barrage against it throughout the war;[60] the *Morning Post* (in its Shelburnite phase in 1783) condemned it.[61] When Henry Bate Dudley transferred his subsidized newspaper editorship from the *Post* to the newly inaugurated Northite *Morning Herald* in 1780, the paper shortly thereafter called for a "happy resolution" in the West Indies by endorsing a parliamentary bill to free all newborn Negroes.[62]

So the eighteenth-century right-wing tradition was a fundamentally humanitarian one. In some ways this was sustained in the nineteenth-century Tory and conservative traditions; in most ways, however, it was not. No doubt there were always some like the curate of Horton who told Oastler he was a "Tory of the old school ... he would destroy all oppression, cruelty, tyranny, and Malthu-

---

[56] *Yale Edition of Works of Johnson*, x, p. 454.
[57] *Critical Review*, 28 (August 1769), pp. 199–222.
[58] *Ibid.*, (May 1784), p. 386.   [59] *General Evening Post*, March 15–18, 1777.
[60] For example, *Lloyd's Evening Post*, May 17–20, 1776; June 17–19, 1776; June 16–19, 1780.
[61] *Morning Post*, July 9, 1783.   [62] *Morning Herald*, November 22, 1781.

sianism and have a sound and Christian legislation based upon that old-fashioned book, the Bible."[63] The curate, however, represented neither the parliamentary party nor the Tory press.

The burgeoning nineteenth-century Tory press, in Oastler and Sadler's generation, exhibited a wide range of humanitarian concerns. It was almost as if each newspaper, magazine, or monthly journal felt obliged to champion one or two worthy causes in order to keep up a certain respectability among its readers. Among the dailies, the *New Times* championed the cause of the boy chimney sweeps.[64] The Orangeist *True Briton* wanted direct government aid to the unemployed.[65] The *Morning Herald*, dependably conservative after 1834, opposed capital punishment.[66] And the ultra *Standard* (and the *St. James's Chronicle*, its sister tri-weekly), whose commitment to Christian humanitarianism may have been deeper and more genuine than that of other organs of Tory opinion, supported the general Sadlerian and Oastlerian crusade for the working poor.[67] As government newspapers, not surprisingly both the *New Times*[68] and the *Courier*[69] supported Peel's Factory Act in 1819 for the relief of children in cotton factories. Among magazines and journals, the *Quarterly Review*, largely under the influence of Robert Southey's pronounced Christian humanitarianism, endorsed the exclusion of children as chimney sweeps, the complete elimination of night hours in factories, the severe limitation of day hours for factory children,[70] as well as a general concurrence in Romilly's enlightened capital punishment views.[71] The *Anti-Jacobin Review* favored the cessation of imprisonment for debt.[72] *John Bull* in 1823 embarked upon a long campaign to persuade the British public of the evil of the treadmill in prisons.[73] Lewis Goldsmith's *British Monitor* favored direct government aid to the suffering Spitalfield weavers.[74]

Perhaps surprisingly, the vexations and omnipresent Irish ques-

[63] J. C. Gill, *Ten Hours Parson* (London, 1959), p. 188.
[64] *New Times*, February 17, 1818.
[65] *True Briton*, December 27, 1820.
[66] James Grant, *Great Metropolis* (London, 1836), II, pp. 35–6.
[67] See, for example, *Standard*, January 14, 1832.   [68] *New Times*, February 17, 1818.
[69] David V. Erdman, ed., *Collected Works of Samuel Taylor Coleridge* (Princeton, 1978), III, pp. 483ff.
[70] *Quarterly Review*, 15 (April 1816), pp. 222–4.   [71] *Ibid.*, 8 (March 1812), pp. 159ff.
[72] *Anti-Jacobin Review*, 48 (April 1815), pp. 374–5.
[73] *John Bull*, August 24, 1823, pp. 268–9. Neither the *British Critic* nor the home secretary, Robert Peel, were convinced by the arguments. *British Critic*, 20, n.ser. (August 1823), p. 133.
[74] *British Monitor*, June 15, 1823, p. 10281.

tion brought out the humanitarianism of the nineteenth-century Tory press at its strongest. Interestingly, this apparent concern for the Irish poor took place at the same time that the Tory press in general was becoming more and more opposed to Catholic emancipation. There was a remarkably uniform viewpoint in the right-wing press that the deteriorating conditions in Ireland were a product of economic oppression. Whether ultra or Wellingtonian Tory, the press denounced absentee Irish (usually Protestant) landlords and their obnoxious middlemen and their ubiquitous land subdivision. *Blackwood's Edinburgh Magazine* thought the Irish middlemen as bad as the common executed robber.[75] The *Anti-Jacobin Review* noticed that the Irish peasants suffered much more wretchedness than the West Indian slaves.[76] The ultra *Standard* and the two leading Tory reviews, *Blackwood's* and the *Quarterly*, suggested that parliament intervene, in the case of the *Quarterly*, anticipating Parnell's demands to stop eviction of peasants by the middlemen, and in the case of *Blackwood's*, anticipating Gladstone's Land Acts, to lower their exorbitant rents.[77] The *Standard* wanted government money given to the poor in the west of Ireland in the name of Christianity.[78]

In general, the right-wing press was far more censorious of the Irish Protestant landlord class than it was of the West Indian proprietor class of slave holders. The latter were seen as victims of historical forces largely outside of their control. The former were, however, agents, after the Glorious Revolution, of their own nefarious situation. The anti-Irish landlord feeling, so obvious in Great Britain at the time of the potato famine of 1845–1849, was fully present in the right-wing press, the Irish Protestants' most fervent supporters on the religious issue, a generation and more earlier.

As well as direct parliamentary action to aid the Irish poor, the almost universal panacea for Ireland's economic doldrums from the viewpoint of the Tory press was the introduction of English-style poor laws into Ireland. One other proposal, advocated for example by *Blackwood's*, which as a Scottish organ was less sensitive than the Tory norm to episcopalian concerns, was the commutation of tithes paid, directly or indirectly, by the (largely Roman Catholic) Irish

[75] *Blackwood's Edinburgh Magazine*, 19 (January 1826), p. 76.
[76] *Anti-Jacobin Review*, 50 (March 1816), p. 278.
[77] *Standard*, April 2, 1828. *Quarterly Review*, 33 (March 1826), pp. 456–62. *Blackwood's Edinburgh Magazine*, 15 (March 1824), pp. 270–4.
[78] *Standard*, June 8, 1831.

poor to organs of the established Church of Ireland.[79] Needless to say, such essential expropriation of Church assets[80] was never seriously considered by a "Church and King" party or press. The only real opposition I have found in the entire Tory press to the introduction of poor laws into Ireland came from the *British Critic*, which also opposed the English poor laws,[81] and the Orange-oriented Dublin ultra newspaper, the *Warder*, which opposed any governmental conciliation policy in Ireland.[82] Such an extreme position brought the *Warder* harsh criticism from its fellow English ultra and Orange-oriented confreres.[83] The forced, if necessary, introduction of largely landlord and gentry financed poor laws into Ireland was not a controversial point in the Rightist press. Wellingtonian Tory papers such as the *Morning Post*[84] or *John Bull*[85] favored it as did the ultra press such as the *Morning Journal*,[86] *Fraser's Magazine*,[87] or the *Age*. The *Age* felt that the Irish landlord class must be compelled to care for the poor.[88] The *Quarterly Review* suggested that if the poor laws were not established immediately, and if the Irish poor in consequence starved, their blood would be on England's hands.[89]

Regarding the treatment of the English poor, the right-wing press was almost, if not quite, as sympathetic as it was towards the poor of Ireland. Of course, unlike Ireland, where the poor had no regularly constituted source of poor relief until the late 1830s, the English had what some regarded as profligate benefits paid to its unemployed, aged, or handicapped. In fact, such were the disallocations of the long years of war, occasional industrial depression and recession, weather problems, demobilization, and, especially, the extraordinary population growth, that the poor rates charged the local rate payers (usually the better off in the population) grew rapidly from *c.* £4,000,000 in 1803 to *c.* £7,000,000 in 1817.[90]

Especially controversial in the general scheme of poor relief in the

[79] *Blackwood's Edinburgh Magazine*, 15 (March 1824), p. 277.
[80] See the critique of tithe-reform in *John Bull*, February 10, 1822, p. 484.
[81] *British Critic*, 23, n.ser. (January 1825), p. 95; 19, n.ser. (June 1823), pp. 615ff.
[82] *Warder*, January 4, 1823.
[83] *Ibid.*; September 13, 1823. The *True Briton*, an English Orange newspaper, also denounced absentee Irish landlords but had no solution to their evil policies. After all, the paper concluded, it is their property. February 11, 1822..
[84] *Morning Post*, May 6, 1829.   [85] *John Bull*, August 11, 1822, p. 692.
[86] *Morning Journal*, May 11, 1829.
[87] *Fraser's Magazine*, 2 (December 1830), p. 581.   [88] *Age*, June 19, 1831, p. 196.
[89] *Quarterly Review*, 44 (February 1831), pp. 515, 554.
[90] E. P. Thompson, *Making of the English Working Class* (New York, 1966), p. 221. Asa Briggs, *Making of Modern England, 1784–1867* (New York, 1959), p. 279.

England of the late eighteenth and early nineteenth centuries, and anathema to the political economists and to the politically progressive, were the Speenhamland experiments, begun in Berkshire by the magistrates in a year of intense famine, 1795, and gradually extended throughout many of the southern and midland shires. The Speenhamland enactments allowed justices of the peace to supplement the income of indigent workers from local parish rates, thereby encourging, said its critics, low wages and a propensity on the part of the lower orders to excessive breeding. There was some though not much right-wing press support for Speenhamland. Croker's *Guardian* found Speenhamland a necessary evil in 1821.[91] The *Anti-Jacobin Review* had condemned Speenhamland in 1803.[92] In a different series, during the last three years of its existence (1818–1821), the *Review* was extremely anti-Malthusian and gloried in the laws.[93] The Orangeist *True Briton*, true to its humanitarian outlook, also saw Speenhamland's value in 1820.[94]

Some forces on the Right opposed the poor laws altogether, Speenhamland or no Speenhamland. In England, the relatively liberal Canningite daily, the *New Times*, in 1818,[95] and the Wellingtonian Tory daily, the *Albion*,[96] in 1831, were frankly Malthusian and against the poor laws. More surprisingly, perhaps, so was the Anglican-oriented *British Critic*, which proclaimed Malthus the "first economist of our time"[97] and endorsed the abolition of poor laws, albeit gradual.[98] Some of the Scottish Tory publications, imbued with the advantages of their own peculiar parochial poor relief system, questioned the utility of the English poor laws. These included the *New Edinburgh Review*[99] and *Blackwood's*, which was Malthusian in its early years and convinced that the nation faced "universal beggary."[100]

---

[91] *Guardian*, October 21, 1821.   [92] *Anti-Jacobin Review*, 14 (January 1803), p. 91.

[93] *Ibid.*, 54 (March 1818), p. 38.

[94] *True Briton*, December 27, 1820.   [95] *New Times*, September 3, 1818.

[96] *Albion*, February 5, 1831.

[97] *British Critic*, 15, n.ser. (March 1821), p. 247. It is in the *British Critic*, more than in most other organs of the English Right, that one can see, at times, the rather odd alliance between the Christian Political Economists or "Cambridge moderates" and the Philosophical Radicals. A. M. C. Waterman, *Revolution, Economics and Religion: Christian Political Economy, 1798–1833* (Cambridge, England, 1991), pp. 153, 179.

[98] *British Critic.*, 19, n.ser. (June 1823), pp. 615ff.

[99] *New Edinburgh Review*, April 1823, pp. 440, 467–8.

[100] *Blackwood's Edinburgh Magazine*, 4 (November 1818), p. 208; 8 (February 1821), pp. 493–5. Walter Scott imagined the poor laws "gnawing into the bowels of England" and produ-

In general, however, the right-wing press opposed Speenhamland but supported the more restrictive yet traditional Elizabethan poor law structure. Some favored certain reforms. Lewis Goldsmith's *British Monitor* preferred the central government as opposed to local agents of the magistrates taking over the collection of the poor rate.[101] Southey, in the *Quarterly Review*, called for the end of the Caroline Settlement Act, which restricted poor relief to the parish of one's birth.[102] But in most cases, without any particular qualification, the right-wing press regarded the English poor laws, in the words of the Orangeist *True Briton*, "glorious to our nation, as a Christian people."[103] In the late 1820s, they were fully prepared to endorse the anti-Malthusian views of Michael Thomas Sadler who favored a vigorous population growth and grounded his energetic support of the poor in a natural law tradition. By 1831, in the Wellingtonian *Quarterly*, Southey was proclaiming that any Malthusian interference by the government in the natural increase of population was the equivalent of procuring abortion.[104]

If, with a few exceptions, the nineteenth-century Tory press followed a Christian humanitarian social line on complicated and controversial subjects like the persistence of Irish poverty or the English poor laws, on the slave question it broke not only with contemporary humanitarianism but with its eighteenth-century forebears as well. The eighteenth-century or pre-1789 anti-slavery views that prevailed so strikingly within certain right-wing groupings and in the right-wing press, partially derived from Christian, Jacobite, and Tory world views, were severely challenged after the advent of the French Revolution and the resulting world war it engendered. The activities of the Burkeites and Windhamites, heirs in many respects of the Christian humanitarianism and anti-slavery opinions of Samuel Johnson's circle, are indicative of the changing pattern. Around 1780 Burke himself drew up a plan, reasonably advanced for the time, for the gradual abolition of slavery. He supported Wilberforce's bills for the total abolition of the trade in 1789 and 1791.[105] After 1792, however, Burke's views become more cloudy. Clearly abolition had never been a particular humanitarian

cing "deep and spreading gangrene." H. J. C. Grierson, ed., *Letters of Sir Walter Scott* (London, 1971), Scott to Southey, March 23, 1818, 5, p. 114.

[101] *British Monitor*, March 29, 1819.   [102] *Quarterly Review*, 15 (April 1816), pp. 219–20.

[103] *True Briton*, January 1, 1821.   [104] *Quarterly Review*, 44 (January 1831), p. 31.

[105] Roger Anstey, *Atlantic Slave Trade and British Abolition, 1760–1810* (Atlantic Highlands, N. J., 1975), p. 108.

cause célèbre for him, on a par with the evils of British imperialism in Ireland or India for example. Burke, though alive, was not in parliament when Wilberforce again brought up the issue in 1796. In 1804, on Wilberforce's bill to abolish the slave trade, one of Burke's principal heirs, French Laurence, stated in the House of Commons that Burke had reprobated the attempt to abolish slavery (by which I assume that Laurence meant the slave trade). Wilberforce defended Burke's memory from Laurence's assertions.[106] Three years later, as the final and successful slave trade abolition measure travelled through the Commons, William Windham, another of Burke's disciples, seemed to argue against the bill on economic grounds. He stated that his opinion on the question had been uniformly guided by Burke's 1780 plan for gradual abolition of both the trade and slavery itself rather than Wilberforce's more aggressive bill. Wilberforce immediately responded that Windham had no right to shelter himself under Burke's authority. He had often unavailingly requested to see Burke's celebrated gradualistic plan. However, Burke had often told him privately, and stated in the House to others, that "he had abandoned his former ideas on the subject and thought exactly as they did."[107] This seemingly concrete statement was not quite the end of the controversy. Almost a generation later, when Burkeians like William Elliot, Windham, or Laurence, were long since dead – as was also another close intellectual defender of Burke, George Canning – Henry Brougham revived the issue. He informed the House of Commons on Wilberforce's authority that Burke "avowed to him that he had once been favourable to the abolition of the Slave Trade, but that he had altered his opinions, and could only consider it to be a shred of the accursed web of Jacobinism," Brougham adding, somewhat unfairly, "Viewing everything as he did, through the distorted medium of one engrossing subject."[108]

The surviving evidence leaves Burke's mature anti-slavery views somewhat in limbo. The best that can be said for him is that anti-slavery became increasingly a marginal subject for him in the 1790s, by no means the moral equivalent of Jacobinism, Indianism, or Irish oppression. Such relative nonchalance regarding slavery can be seen working among the larger Burkeian grouping as well. Windham had been one of Wilberforce's most loyal voters in the

---

[106] *Parl Deb.*, II (June 7, 1804), pp. 552–7.   [107] *Ibid.*, IX (March 16, 1807), pp. 136–9.
[108] *Ibid.*, XVIII, n.ser. (February 26, 1828), pp. 775–6.

early struggle – Roger Anstey lists him in the 1790s as one of the twenty-six hard-core abolitionists in the House of Commons.[109] Certainly after Burke's death, if not before, Windham underwent a major, if perhaps uneasy, change of heart on the issue. In 1796, before Burke's death, the *Tomahawk!*, a Windham-oriented tri-weekly, was vigorously opposing abolition.[110] His protégé of sorts, William Cobbett, announced in the *Political Register* in 1802 that Windham supported the slave trade.[111] In 1804, Windham publicly opposed Wilberforce's abolition bill on the grounds that, as other European nations would continue the trade, it would damage the national prosperity.[112] In 1806, however, when the Grenville–Sidmouth–Foxite coalition was formed after Pitt's death, Windham remarked that he wanted nothing more than the abolition of the slave trade and, in the future, the abolition of slavery itself.[113] In the event, however, in 1807 as in 1804, he opposed the final bill on economic grounds.[114] He was also only one of three in the Cabinet who opposed abolition of the trade.[115] Significantly, perhaps, two others among Burke's pallbearers, Sidmouth and Lord Fitzwilliam, were the other two.[116]

Other right-wing politicians and groupings took a harder stance on the slave trade during the 1790s. George III and the royal family in general had always, even in the enthusiasm of the liberal 1780s, been firm slave traders and their example no doubt influenced others. Lord Loughborough, an old Buteite and Northite, and one of the earliest of the Whigs to endorse the Pitt government after the French Revolution, said at the time of his initial conversations with Pitt that the prime minister admitted he went too far in the 1780s in support of Wilberforce's cause, both because of the king's attitude and because the popular participatory aspects of it set a dangerous precedent.[117] The daily press most loyal to Pitt's political viewpoints, such as the *True Briton*, was solidly anti-abolitionist by 1796 for both commercial and religious reasons.[118] Pitt thus defected for all intents and purposes from the anti-slave trade cause after the

---

[109] Anstey, *Atlantic Slave Trade*, p. 286.   [110] *Tomahawk!*, February 23, 1796.
[111] *Cobbett's Political Register*, August 21–28, 1802.
[112] *Parl. Deb.*, II (June 7, 1804), pp. 552–7.   [113] *Ibid.*, III (June 10, 1806), p. 602.
[114] *Ibid.*, IX (March 16, 1807), pp. 136–7.
[115] Anstey, *Atlantic Slave Trade*, pp. 398–9.   [116] *Ibid.*
[117] Third Earl of Malmesbury, ed., *Diaries and Correspondence of James Harris, First Earl of Malmesbury* (London, 1844), II, pp. 463–4.
[118] *True Briton*, August 20, 1796.

war with France commenced. Sidmouth, like Windham, followed a somewhat tortuous path through the 1790s and 1800s on this issue. In 1792, on Wilberforce's Slave Trade Abolition bill, the then Henry Addington had voted against the bill but had suggested the time for passage might be right in 1796.[119] In the latter year, however, he again voted against Wilberforce.[120] During his premiership, Addington made *The Times*, his leading newspaper organ, a stalwart of the anti-abolition cause.[121] In 1806, when he joined a predominantly Whig government as Lord Privy Seal, the then Lord Sidmouth stated that he now favored the general principles of slave trade abolition but opposed the current measure; an odd position which Lord Stanhope thought "whimsical."[122] He ended up opposing it in Cabinet in 1807.[123] The erstwhile leader of the Portland Whigs, the Duke of Portland, along with the neo-Tory first Earl of Liverpool and the Northite Lord Carlisle were also in the 1790s firmly supportive of the slave trade.[124]

Hence, despite Wilberforce's victory of 1807, and the abolition of the British slave trade, various rightist forces, both among politicians and the press, were clearly moving in an opposite direction (if, indeed, they had ever been sympathetic). Even the *British Critic* founded as an organ of anti-revolutionary Anglican Toryism by the Society for the Reformation of Principles, to its subsequent shame and chagrin, refused in the 1790s to support any abrupt abolition of the slave trade.[125]

By the time of the proliferation of right-wing publications in the first, second, and third decades of the nineteenth century, the Right was coming to be virtually, if not quite, identified with a moderate or extremist pro-slavery position. There were always some ultra Tory politicians, like Henry Bankes or Sir Edward Knatchbull, representing the Dorset and Kent Protestant causes, who were abolitionists.[126] Some Tory papers too, perhaps reflecting a desire to reach out to a larger daily audience and realizing that that audience held an essentially anti-slavery position, were moderately against

---

[119] Namier and Brooke, III, p. 40.   [120] *Ibid.*
[121] See *The Timers*, for example, June 1, 1804.
[122] *Parl. Deb.*, III (June 24, 1806), pp. 808–9.   [123] Anstey, *Atlantic Slave Trade*, pp. 398–9.
[124] Aspinall, III, pp. 226–7.
[125] *British Critic*, 2 (November 1793), pp. 304, 334; 32 (December 1808), pp. 596–7.
[126] Namier and Brooke, III, p. 129. Sir Hughe Knatchbull-Hugessen, *Kentish Family* (London, 1960), p. 172.

the practice. These included the *Morning Post*[127] and the *New Times*, which panegyrized Wilberforce and favored "Lord Melville's old notion" that all negroes born after 1800 ought to be freed.[128] The only Tory daily, indeed the most ultra and Orange-oriented of all London dailies of the late 1820s, which consistently and vigorously opposed slavery, was the *Standard*.[129] Besides the dailies, the High Church monthly, the *Christian Remembrancer*, reminded its readers in 1828 that Christians must not only oppose slavery but labor for its overthrow[130] and a short-lived anti-Canningite and anti-Catholic Sunday paper, the *Tory*, denounced slavery.[131] In general, however, the right-wing press supported and sustained the West Indian interest and slavery.

The Tory press reaction to complete abolition of slavery in the British empire can be divided into two categories: those who favored abolition but only at some (preferably distant) future time; and those who (often enthusiastically) endorsed slavery as a good for its own sake. The prior category included both major reviews, the *Quarterly* and *Blackwood's*, the former supplementing its anti-abolition policy by prescribing a draconian course of action for both captain and crew of slave trading ships;[132] the latter emphasizing that "slow" was the operative word in any abolition scheme and outlining an intricate plan for education and Christianization of the Blacks before freedom could even be considered.[133] The Rev. George Croly's *Monthly Magazine* in 1826 suggested freedom, perhaps as a goal for the 1850s.[134] The Wellingtonian Tory daily of the 1830s, the *Albion*, also supported abolition at some future date.[135]

The positive pro-slavery argument, whether crude or semi-sophisticated, permeated the publications of the early-nineteenth-century British Right. Some followed Lord Eldon in supporting slavery largely on economic grounds.[136] The *Age*, by 1826 beginning to pass *John Bull* as the leading Sunday newspaper in the United Kingdom, felt that abolition would subvert Britain's West Indian power.[137] Croker's *Guardian* adopted the motto "No Negroes, no colonies."[138]

---

[127] *Morning Post*, May 17, 1823.   [128] *New Times*, April 23 and 24, 1820.
[129] *Standard*, May 1, 1830; October 28, 1830.
[130] *Christian Remembrancer*, 10 (December 1828), p. 770.   [131] *Tory*, June 17, 1827.
[132] *Quarterly Review*, 28 (October 1822), pp. 162, 178.
[133] *Blackwood's Edinburgh Magazine*, 14 (October 1823), p. 455.
[134] *Monthly Magazine*, 1 (January 1826), pp. 1ff.
[135] *Albion*, December 15, 1830.   [136] *Parl. Deb.*, VII (May 16, 1806), p. 231.
[137] *Age*, April 23, 1826.
[138] *Guardian*, January 18, 1824.

Indeed, underlining much of the pro-slavery argument was the realization, as expressed in the House of Lords by Lord Harewood, a West Indian proprietor, that slavery was a necessity in the West Indies as land could not be worked by any other means.[139] The religious motif was sometimes used as well to justify slavery. The *Anti-Jacobin Review*, one of the most consistent of the pro-slavery periodicals, proclaimed that God had sanctioned slavery in Genesis and therefore the question of its morality or lack thereof ought not to arise.[140] The *Monthly Magazine*, too, asserted that God had placed Blacks in the state of slavery and therefore they must be content.[141] The press controlled by John Murray was especially partial to the religious justification. Both the *Quarterly Review* and his daily newspaper, the *Representative*, were fond of the argument that Christ and St. Paul had never condemned slavery.[142]

The themes of admiration for the West Indian planter class and fear for their fate at the hands of newly freed Blacks was sometimes combined with extreme negrophobia to justify the pro-slavery cause.[143] The *Representaive* affected to belive that the planters were the real friends of the slaves and abolition would be a misery for them.[144] *Redhead Yorke's Weekly Political Review*, the *Age*, and the *Anti-Jacobin Review* speculated in most lurid detail regarding mutilated white planters, their throats cut, and their families slaughtered should abolition come about.[145] Such meditations led to further negrophobic and psychosexual attitudes on the part of some of the Tory press. To *Cooper's John Bull*, Blacks were "fat and full-bellied" Niggers.[146] The more successful *Fraser's Magazine* in the 1830s also regarded them as merely "Niggers."[147] *John Bull* thought the "Niggers," slave or free, could never equal the lowliest white.[148] The negrophobia of the *Bull* scarcely knew any bounds. It defended branding as causing "hardly any pain," and pictured a placid West

---

139 *Parl. Deb.*, xii, 3rd ser. (April 19, 1832), p. 598.
140 *Anti-Jacobin Review*, 18 (May 1804), pp. 47–8.
141 *Monthly Magazine*, 1 (January 1826), pp. 1ff.
142 *Representative*, March 8, 1826. *Quarterly Review*, 45 (April, 1831), pp. 222–3.
143 Wordsworth, for example, felt sorry for the planters. Alan G. Hill, ed., *Letters of William and Dorothy Wordsworth* (Oxford, 1979), Wordsworth to Mary Rawson, May 24, 1833, v, pp. 614–15.
144 *Representative*, March 3, 1826.
145 *Redhead Yorke's Weekly Political Review*, January 24, 1807. *Age*, April 23, 1826, p. 396. *Anti-Jacobin Review*, 49 (August 1815), pp. 108–9.
146 *Cooper's John Bull*, January 29, 1826.
147 *Fraser's Magazine*, 2 (December 1830), p. 556.
148 *John Bull*, January 10, 1830, p. 12.

Indian community where "The Negroes are called to work, either
by the blowing of a horn, the crack of a whip (as English sportsmen
are roused to the chase) or by the ringing of a bell, as men are called
to chapel at college."[149] The *Bull* regarded even the possibility of
abolition as a "national evil."[150] Some, even quality periodicals,
followed Charles Ellis, a leader of the West Indian interest in
parliament, in his assertion that some men, in this case Negroes,
simply deserve to be slaves.[151] The *Anti-Jacobin Review* postulated
that Negroes were intellectually and morally inferior to Europeans;
hence they were slaves from the beginning of time and would remain
such for the foreseeable future.[152] *Blackwood's Edinburgh Magazine*,
too, regarded only Europeans as civilized enough to be free of
slavery. Therefore slavery was an evil only in Europe, not amongst
Negroes.[153]

Fear of miscegenation was never far from the surface. Cobbett, in
his "Church and King" period, denounced the Negroes for their
"disregard of decency ... defiance of the dictates of nature; ...
[their] foul ... [their] beastly propensity" and worried that the
"unnatural, and detestable" practice of white women mating with
Negroes would grow, if the latter were allowed free access to the
United Kingdom.[154] The *Anti-Jacobin Review* also found black and
white sexual connections "unnatural."[155]

Such a plethora of pro-slavery and pro-planter argumentation on
the Right points to a discontinuity of humanitarian concerns,
especially as contrasted with a rather level-headed, even perhaps
severe view of (often impecunious) Irish Protestant (and, as we shall
see, even English) landowners. Was the West Indian interest
engaged in extensive subsidization of right-wing politicians and the
press? Both the leading historians of the abolition movement, Roger
Anstey and David Brion Davis, agree that in the 1780s, the interest
was relatively silent in the face of a mounting campaign by Wilberforce and others against the morality and legitimacy of slavery. Only
in the early 1790s did the Society of West Indian Planters and
Merchants spend around £2,000 on newspaper and pamphlet
propaganda to support their cause on general utilitarian rather than

149 *Ibid.*, March 14, 1824, pp. 92–3.   150 *Ibid.*, April 30, 1826, p. 140.
151 *Parl. Deb.*, II (June 13, 1804), p. 652.
152 *Anti-Jacobin Review*, 18 (May 1804), pp. 47–8.
153 *Blackwood's Edinburgh Magazine*, 31 (February 1832), p. 415.
154 *Cobbett's Political Register*, June 16, 1804.
155 *Anti-Jacobin Review*, 49 (August 1815), pp. 116–17.

on moral grounds.[156] Anstey suspects that in the late eighteenth century the hard core of the West Indian connection in the House of Commons was roughly equal to the hard core of the Wilberforceians.[157] By the 1820s, with its opponents in favor of complete abolition gathering steam,[158] the West Indian interest made some attempt to influence the public in its favor. During the general election of 1831, with the Grenville family in financial difficulties, and an expensive general election less than eight months past, the interest paid 2,000 guineas for the expenses of one of its supporters in Buckinghamshire, the ultra Marquess of Chandos.[159] Sir Walter Scott alleged that in 1826, John Wilson Croker and Charles Ellis on behalf of the interest, approached his impecunious son-in-law, the journalist John Gibson Lockhart, with an agreement to pay him £1,500 over three years to write pro-slavery articles for them. They promised secrecy, a point in itself probably indicative of the low public esteem in which the West Indians were held. At first Lockhart declined, though there is some evidence that he later reconsidered.[160] The pro-slavery daily, the *Morning Journal*, may have received some sort of help from the West Indian interest. At least its editor, Robert Alexander, thrown into Newgate for libels against George IV, the Duke of Wellington, and Lord Lyndhurst, wrote a pro-slavery tract from prison.[161]

But in general, especially as compared with its opponents, the West Indian interest was not such as to strike fear in the hearts of its enemies. One of its most active supporters, Theodore Hook's *John Bull*, regretted that in 1828 it had not *one* active member in the House of Commons.[162] Another prominent friend, *Fraser's Magazine*, the year before abolition, bewailed the fact that the interest had "altogether neglected the advocacy of the press, notwithstanding frequent remonstrances ... on our part, and has made no efficient

---

[156] Anstey, *Atlantic Slave Trade*, pp. 95, 292–3. David Brion Davis, *Problem of Slavery in the Age of Revolution, 1770–1823* (Ithaca, 1975), pp. 541–2.

[157] Anstey, *Atlantic Slave Trade*, p. 298.

[158] The well-connected Tory, Charles Arbuthnot, was convinced that the 1830 general election was more concerned with the slave issue than the parliamentary reform one. Arthur Aspinall, ed., *Correspondence of Charles Arbuthnot*, Camden 3rd ser., LXV (London, 1941), p. 181.

[159] John Brooke, Julia Gandy, eds., *Royal Commission on Historical Manuscripts, The Prime Ministers' Papers: Wellington, Political Correspondence I: 1833–November 1834* (London, 1975), p. 46.

[160] *Letters of Sir Walter Scott*, IX: Scott to Mrs. Lockhart, March 7, p. 448; reply, p. 448n.

[161] Robert Alexander, "Fate of the colonies" (London, 1830).

[162] *John Bull*, March 9, 1828, p. 76.

efforts to [influence] the public mind."[163] Nonetheless, the right-wing press in the decades before the final abolition bill of 1833 did evidence on the issue of slavery a substantial break from its general humanitarian tradition. One suspects (and these things are always difficult to trace) that some money was changing hands to produce such a pronounced pro-slavery sentiment. However, it clearly did little good.

III

On issues involving the broad area of political economy the right-wing press continued to exhibit both a Christian humanitarian outlook when confronted with capitalistic arguments and a seeming ability to divorce itself from the charge of being mere organs of landed (or feudal) society. The attitude of that press towards the corn laws of 1815 is a case in point. The landed interest, Whig as well as Tory, in both Houses of parliament was particularly anxious, once the long war ceased, to protect their chief product against foreign competition. The result, in early 1815, was permanent, heavy protective duties placed on foreign grain when there was any question of unfavorable domestic prices.

Such parliamentary bias for the interests of the traditional ruling class, with its resultant higher prices adversely affecting the urban masses, was by no means widely applauded in the right-wing press. Of the leading pro-Liverpool London dailies, only the premier government newspaper, the *Courier*, supported the Corn Law of 1815.[164] The old Pittite *Sun* found it "scandalous" and "oppressive to the great body of the people."[165] The aristocratic-oriented *Morning Post*, which a generation later emerged as *the* great protectionist newspaper of the United Kingdom, accused MPs of being "warped by an unconscious operation of self-interested motives."[166] Three of the leading Tory monthlies, the *Anti-Jacobin Review*, the *British Critic*, and the *New Monthly Magazine*, denounced the Corn Bill.[167] The *British Critic*, especially censorious in its opposition, saw it as bringing "the labouring poor at home into a state infinitely more deplorable than that of the West Indian negroes," and won-

[163] "The press and the Tories" (London, 1833), p. 13.
[164] *Courier*, February 1 and 15, 1815.
[165] *Sun*, February 11, 1815.   [166] *Morning Post*, February 13 and 16, 1815.
[167] *Anti-Jacobin Review*, 50 (May 1816), p. 449. *British Critic*, 2, n.ser (August 1814), pp. 127ff. *New Monthly Magazine*, 3 (April 1, 1815), pp. 275–6; 5 (March 1, 1816), p. 147.

dered whether perhaps "the hunger and nakedness of a numerous family which the father cannot by the utmost labour, either feed or clothe, [are not] compulsion as complete as the discipline of the cart whip?"[168] Before 1832 the *Quarterly Review*, either because the editors or publisher were not especially concerned with the corn laws,[169] or, more probably, because Robert Southey, their leading reviewer on social questions was so opposed to them,[170] had no consistent policy on the corn laws and, depending on their reviewers' bias, went back and forth on the issue.[171]

This near-uniformity against the corn laws could still find echoes in the Tory press of the early 1820s. The Orangeist *True Briton*, the notorious Scottish Tory weekly, *Beacon*, and the Scottish Tory monthly, the *New Edinburgh Review*, all opposed the corn laws.[172] As late as 1825, the very reactionary *British Mercury, John Bull*'s Wednesday newspaper, called for a repeal of the corn laws which would secure "the public from the rapacity of the land-owners."[173] By the 1820s, however, the tide was turning on this issue. The *British Critic* and the *Anti-Jacobin Review*, for example, changed their minds on the undesirability of the corn laws.[174] The *Standard*, whose Christian humanitarianism by no means made its stand on political issues predictable on a racial, class, or economic basis, was typical in its endorsement of the corn laws in 1828 on the twin grounds of their securing greater independence from foreign states and their role as a tax equalizer in the face of the greater poor rates paid by the landed interest.[175] By the 1830s both the ultra and the Wellingtonian press seemed, to varying degrees of enthusiasm, favorable to agricultural

---

[168] *British Critic*, 3, n.ser. (January 1815), pp. 534.

[169] Though Murray's *Representative* supported them. February 6, 1826.

[170] Charles Ramos, ed., *Letters of Robert Southey to John May, 1797 to 1838* (Austin, 1976), p. 143.

[171] See, for example, the differences in tone of two articles – the *Quarterly Review*, 35 (January 1827), pp. 270–1; 36 (October 1827), pp. 393–4. Coleridge too was so opposed to the corn laws that in March 1815, at the market place at Calne, "mounted on the Butcher's Table," he made a "butcherly sort of Speech of an hour long to a very ragged but not very butcherly audience," to persuade them to petition parliament against the corn laws. Earl Leslie Griggs, ed., *Collected Letters of Samuel Taylor Coleridge* (Oxford, 1959), Coleridge to Brabant, March 10, 1815, IV, pp. 549–50. Wordsworth, on the other hand, supported the corn laws, not the only time he adopted a decidedly more reactionary policy than his friends Southey and Coleridge. Ernest de Selincourt, ed., *Letters of William and Dorothy Wordsworth* (Oxford, 1970), Wordsworth to Sara Hutchinson, March 16, 1815, III, p. 219.

[172] *True Briton*, January 31, 1822. *Beacon*, March 17, 1821. *New Edinburgh Review*, April 1822, pp. 364–5, 385.

[173] *British Mercury*, March 30, 1825.

[174] *British Critic*, 16, n.ser. (August 1821), p. 201. *Anti-Jacobin Review*, 57 (October 1819), p. 162.

[175] *Standard*, March 27, 1828.

protection. When the ultra Tory heir presumptive to the throne, the Duke of York, was on his deathbed in 1826, he warned his brother, George IV, against innovations regarding corn or Catholics, "two subjects," said Lord Lansdowne, "which by some secret sympathy had become connected in [his] ... mind as well in that of some others."[176] This conservative identification with the landed interest (most specifically with the corn laws) was unquestionably true by the time of York's death in 1827, and remained in place in an aggravated form through at least the 1840s, if not beyond; it was not, however, necessarily true at the beginning of the long economic debate.

On other issues involving political economy, the right-wing press was generally divided, as was the nation and the government itself, during the years after Waterloo. Between the publication of the *Wealth of Nations* in 1776 and the abolition of the (remaining) Navigation Acts in 1849, a national debate of varying degree of intensity, waxing and waning according to circumstances, took place as to the validity of freer foreign trade versus protection for home agricultural or manufacturing products. This controversy impacted to a greater or lesser degree on issues involving the nature of modern economic forces in general and on the government's role (if any) in poor relief or in the control of the money supply. It was often personalized by vicious reactions to the views of the so-called political economists, especially Adam Smith, the Rev. Thomas Robert Malthus, David Ricardo, and Nassau Senior. The debate (or rather series of debates) was especially important in the years of peace in the 1780s, the years between Waterloo and the Whig assumption of power in 1830 and, of course, the decade following the formation of Sir Robert Peel's second administration in 1841.

It is difficult and unhelpful to discuss a general or consistent right-wing view of sophisticated economic matters. Not for the only time, the Right (and especially the press) appeared to *feel* such matters rather than offer a measured intellectual *analysis* of them. But just as the Right in general seemed to have negative notions of Dissenters or radicals, so an almost ingrained suspicion of foreigners or cosmopolitanism seemed to mediate against much support for freedom of trade or the dismal science and its practitioners. When

---

[176] Arthur Aspinall, ed., *Formation of Canning's Ministry, February to August 1827*, Camden 3rd ser., LIX (London, 1937), pp. 119–20.

the ultra *Standard* asserted that the "Tory party *is the country*,"[177] or John Reeves proclaimed in his notorious high prerogative pamphlet that "I am not a *Citizen of the World* ... I am an Englishman,"[178] a point was being made that could have economic undertones. When Richard Oastler asked to be told "in what age or nation was a capitalist known to be a Patriot?"[179] or the young Southey berated Bonaparte and remembered "Alfred, and the two Bacons, and Hartley, and Milton, and Shakespear, with more patriotic pride than ever,"[180] the pattern for a world view was being laid that would have little patience for invisible hands or iron laws of wages. I have discussed above the difficulty of viewing the Pittites or their press of the 1780s as practitioners of a particularly rightist perspective on the world. In fact, certain sections of the Whig party and press, particularly that associated at least ideologically with Lord North, and most specifically North's old subsidized supporter Henry Bate Dudley's *Morning Herald*, most approximated to such a world view in that somewhat politically confusing decade. Years before the French Revolution, the *Herald* reveled in an extraordinary conspiracy thesis involving a free trade and deistic "French party" seeking and obtaining power, and in the process endangering domestic tranquility in the United States, the Netherlands, Ireland, and Great Britain. This conspiracy used the dissenting ministers, Price and Priestley, as well as Lord Shelburne (the Marquess of Lansdowne) as their English agents.[181] All this, of course, had the prime motivation of stopping Pitt's somewhat Smithian-inspired Anglo-French commercial treaty. Yet, in a larger sense, it also illustrates that Burke's counter-revolutionary opinions of a few years later hardly grew from an intellectual vacuum and in its linking of religion, patriotism, and economics in a conspiratorial web of intrigue, the Northite *Morning Herald* of the 1780s set the pattern for the rhetoric against capitalist and political economist which was characteristic of much of the Tory press in the early nineteenth century.

Although it was largely the Protestant and Orangeist press of the late 1820s that led the most formidable assault upon political economy and not incidentally upon the alleged Wellingtonian toler-

---

177 *Standard*, January 28, 1828.
178 John Reeves, "Thoughts on the English government" (London, 1795), p. 2.
179 Hill, *Toryism*, p. 167.
180 Charles Cuthbert Southey, ed., *Life and Correspondence of Robert Southey* (London, 1850), Southey to Rickman, January 9, 1800, II, p. 46.
181 See, for example, *Morning Herald*, March 20 and 23, 1787.

ance for its nostrums, there was an earlier stream of attacks that long preceded ultraism as a central force in British politics. This happened despite the fact that a number of well-placed loyalist politicians – Burke, the Younger Pitt, Grenville, and Canning – were quite sympathetic to the new political economy. The *Anti-Jacobin Review* in 1800 was denouncing Adam Smith and his free trade notions as well as Edmund Burke's adherence to them in his recently published paper on scarcity.[182] Southey in 1812 in the *Quarterly Review* was commenting on Adam Smith's *Wealth of Nations* as a "tedious and hard-hearted book" and Malthus' theory on population and its relationship to the poor laws as simply "detestable."[183] And, speaking especially of David Ricardo, the *British Critic* in 1819 proposed that "Of all the cants which are canted in this canting age, the cant of political economy, we think, bids fair to be very soon the most tormenting."[184]

By 1827, however, at the time of the union between Bentham's friend, the third Marquess of Lansdowne and his branch of the Whigs with Canning and Huskisson and their branch of the (liberal) Tories, the ultra attack upon free trade became a torrent. The Christian humanitarian *Standard* proclaimed Nassau Senior as humbug and quack and the Bible as the foundation of true political economy.[185] It denounced capitalism as the "golden idol, before whom all in England bow."[186] By 1831, with the Whigs in power and Senior an economic advisor to the government, the *Standard* attacked him, especially for his attempt to deny Ireland a poor law, as belonging to the "effete" school of economics which maintained "the justice and policy of sacrificing human life and human happiness to the accumulation of capital."[187] The daily *Morning Journal* of Robert Alexander, essentially put out of business by Peel and Wellington in 1830, in what was almost the resurrected voice of ancient country Toryism, regarded free trade as "this pernicious system" feeding on an "overgrown capitalist, the large fund-holder, the full-blown sinecurist, the full-fed tax eater ..."[188] *Blackwood's Edinburgh Magazine*, perhaps reflecting Scotland's panic at the banking crisis of 1825, regarded political economists as "in their nature democratic and republican, hostile to aristocracy and

[182] *Anti-Jacobin Review*, 7 (November 1800), pp. 281, 322.
[183] *Quarterly Review*, 8 (December 1812), pp. 226, 337.
[184] *British Critic*, 12, n.ser (December 1819), p. 561.   [185] *Standard*, September 8, 1827.
[186] *Ibid.*, January 4, 1831.   [187] *Ibid.*, August 27, 1831.
[188] *Morning Journal*, November 12, 1828; June 26, 1829.

monarchy."[189] The Rev. George Croly's ultra *Monthly Magazine*, which alone of the Protestant Tory press remained loyal to Grey's ministry *after* the introduction of the 1831 Reform Bill, called for the destruction of machinery which produced unemployment among the workers and described free trade as "that legacy of the Jacobins to the Huskissons."[190] The leading Sunday newspaper in the country, the ultra *Age*, accused the political economists of having discovered that Malthusian infanticide "is a fair measure of State policy – that the poor should not receive Charitable assistance ... that patriotism is nonsense ... "[191]

While the Tory newspapers and journals were in general support-ive of the repeal of Peel's 1819 deflationary cash payments bill as well as, by the 1820s, generally favorable to the retention of the corn laws, and hence more sympathetic to the agricultural than to the industrial interest, they were not in their anti-capitalist – even anti-modernist – rhetoric mere toadies of feudalism. The *Morning Journal* wanted a 5 percent tax on land.[192] *John Bull* was prepared to countenance a 20 percent land tax on an English absentee land-lord.[193] The *British Critic*, the *Anti-Jacobin Review*, and the *Age*, all favored property taxes the main force of which would inevitably fall on the landed classes.[194] More of the Tory press opposed the beloved game laws of the aristocrats than supported them, the *Anti-Jacobin Review* indeed thinking them a "moral evil."[195] But in their stric-tures, especially in the 1820s, against the monopoly of the Bank of England and its extension via branch banks into the provinces, in their espousal of the cause of local banks, in their opposition to the repeal of the traditional usury laws, and in their call for cheap money through the repeal of Peel's 1819 act, these Tory opponents of the underconsumptionist economists followed a path favored by agriculturalists of the eighteenth and nineteenth centuries through-out the Anglo-American world. Two moderate Tory daily news-papers, the *Morning Post* in the 1820s and the *Albion* in the early

189 *Blackwood's Edinburgh Magazine*, 17 (May 1825), p. 543.
190 *Monthly Magazine*, 1 (June 1826), p. 564; 9 (February 1830), p. 119.
191 *Age*, June 1, 1828, p. 176.   192 *Morning Journal*, September 25, 1829.
193 *John Bull*, January 20, 1822, p. 460; March 3, 1822, p. 508.
194 *British Critic*, 7, n.ser. (April 1817), p. 341. *Anti-Jacobin Review*, 59 (February 1821), p. 524
   (though they also wanted to extend it to funded property). *Age*, January 10, 1830, p. 12.
195 *Anti-Jacobin Review*, 50 (February 1816), p. 129. Also opposing the game laws were: *New
   Monthly Magazine*, 5 (February 1, 1816), pp. 64–5; *Quarterly Review*, 15 (April 1816),
   pp. 219–20; *British Critic*, 5, n.ser. (January 1816), p. 81; *Monthly Magazine*, 5 (February
   1828), pp. 125–6.

1830s, did support Peel's 1819 act, but they were unusual.[196] Even
the daily *New Times*, a supporter of Liverpool's ministry, which on
most issues adhered to a liberal Tory line, was quite adamant that
the 1819 act had caused the distress of the 1820s.[197] Hence, in the
1820s, with the above-noted exceptions, the Tory press, both ultra
and Wellingtonian, tended to blame the distress of the period,
especially after mid-decade, on the deflation and under-consump-
tion caused by the return to cash payments in 1819.[198] Parentheti-
cally, this near-unanimity of opinion on the part of the right-wing
press on the so-called "currency question," and the failure of successive Tory governments to pay much if any attention to it, shows as
much as anything the meager power the press had over government
or the little attention government paid in the unreformed parliament to what allegedly represented some level of public opinion.[199]

This effluence of disgust on the Right for what many would term
economic modernity was personalized in the consistent and vicious
attack by those on the Right on the high priest of that modernity,
the Canningite politician and exponent of political economy,
William Huskisson. Born like his mentor Canning in 1770,
Huskisson as a young man spent the early years of the Revolution in
Paris as a secretary at the British embassy.[200] An admirer of both
Huskisson and Canning, William Jerdan, editor of the *Literary
Gazette*, suggested in his memoirs that Huskisson may have assisted in
the destruction of the Bastille, but I know of no evidence to support
this save that he was apparently present at the event.[201] When the
rumors of his youthful Jacobinism were already well established,
Huskisson in 1823 made a speech in Canning's former constituency,
Liverpool, denying that he had ever been a member of the Jacobin

[196] *Morning Post*, May 3, 1823. *Albion*, December 16, 1830.

[197] *New Timers*, May 14, 1821.

[198] Besides the *New Times*, the following right-wing newspapers, journals or magazines
blamed the Peel (1819) committee for the distress of the subsequent era: *Morning Journal*,
September 25, 1829; *Standard*, January 11, 1831; *Watchman*, March 18, 1827; *True Briton*,
January 31, 1822; *John Bull*, April 1826, p. 175; *Anti-Jacobin Review*, 56 (July 1819), p. 433;
Christian Remembrancer, February 1822, p. 126; *Fraser's Magazine*, 2 (December 1830),
p. 574.

[199] On another economic issue, the legality of labor unions, the right-wing press, with one
significant exception, was anti-union. The exception was the Murray press. Both
Murray's daily newspaper, the *Representative*, February 1, 1826, which argued that workers
had as much right to combine as manufacturers, and the *Quarterly Review*, 31 (March
1825), p. 392, which supported Joseph Hume in his successful bid to secure the repeal of
the Combination Acts, championed labor unions.

[200] Burke, *Corr.* vii, p. 434n.

[201] William Jerdan, *Men I Have Known* (London, 1866), p. 269. See "Huskisson" in the *DNB*.

Club but admitting that he had once, in the company of Windham, attended a meeting there out of curiosity. He was a member of a Parisian club, albeit a constitutional monarchist one, the Club of 1789, and he only once took part in their proceedings, giving a speech – appropriately – against paper money.[202] Out of these meager facts grew up one of the most all-encompassing and long-lasting rumors of the nineteenth century, which combined hatred of Jacobinism with a dislike of the new free-trading system, and a mixing up of the two into something profoundly unpatriotic and anti-English.

After Thermidor, if not before, the term "Jacobin" became an epithet devoid of much exact meaning, used by all sorts of individuals on the Right or by the right-wing press to describe some situation or person they particularly disliked. The second Earl of Liverpool, for example, used Jacobin as a synonym for Whig.[203] *John Bull* found Whigs, radicals, and Jacobins "*One* and the *Same* disease."[204] The Orangeist Dublin newspaper, the *Warder*, saw the high Whig *Edinburgh Review* as "the agent of Jacobinism."[205] George III thought Catholic emancipation was Jacobinical.[206] The *Anti-Jacobin Review* suspected Methodism of Jacobin tendencies.[207] The deputy Grand Master of the Orange Order in 1832 accused Grey and his Cabinet of Jacobinism.[208] Even Wilberforce and Burke themselves were accused in print of being Jacobins.[209] None suffered more from this terminological inexactitude than Huskisson. As early as 1793, Burke, unfairly,[210] was discussing Huskisson as writing in favor of the French Revolution.[211] Huskisson served in the last years of the first Pitt ministry as secretary at the Admiralty and retired with Pitt (or more probably Canning) at the time of the Catholic

---

[202] Lewis Melville, ed., *Huskisson Papers* (London, 1931), pp. 4–5.

[203] Second Duke of Wellington, ed., *Civil Correspondence and Memoranda of Field Marshal Arthur Duke of Wellington, K.G.* (London, 1860), Liverpool to Wellington, January 17, 1811, VII, p. 46.

[204] *John Bull*, January 26, 1823, p. 28.   [205] *Warder*, January 4, 1823.

[206] J. Holland, Rose, *William Pitt and the Great War* (London, 1911), p. 436.

[207] *Anti-Jacobin Review*, 13 (December 1802), p. 379.

[208] *Westminster Review*, 30 (January 1836), pp. 494–5.

[209] Davis, *Slavery in Age of Revolution*, p. 364. *Oracle*, July 11, 1797. In the middle of the eighteenth century, Judaism may have played a similar role in this regard to Jacobinism after 1792. At least the author of *The Crisis* thought Judaism another name for the Revolution of 1688 and the Hanoverian legacy. J. C. D. Clark, *Dynamics of Change* (Cambridge, England, 1982), p. 40.

[210] For how very hostile to the French Revolution Huskisson was in 1792, see C. R. Fay, *Huskisson and His Age* (London, 1951).

[211] Burke, *Corr.*, Burke to Elliot, September 22, 1793, VII, pp. 434–5.

crisis. The king for one was happy to see him go as his "style and manner gave disgust to those obliged to confer with him."[212] Three years later, George III justified his reluctance during the second Pitt administration to appoint Huskisson as secretary of the Treasury because he was "secretary to a revolutionary club at Paris."[213] Shortly thereafter, Cobbett – and there could not have been another man in England more naturally inimical to Huskisson – commenced terrible attacks on the secretary as a functioning, not nominal, revolutionary in Paris.[214] Hence began the rumor of Huskisson's Jacobinism, no doubt aggravated by a dislike for Canning and by Huskisson's proven inability to conciliate his governmental colleagues, and on not very subtle attempts to associate the new ideas of free trade and *laissez-faire* with the anti-national cause. The *Age*, in 1828, opined that "that such a party as the Huskissonian should exist any where, is a sad proof of the degradation of the human mind – that it should ever have taken root ... in England, the country of honour, and of freedom, is a misery to be deplored by every patriotic mind ... "[215] In 1827 the *Standard* portrayed Huskisson as "nurtured in Jacobinism" and desirous "to change the nature of all our Institutions, to lower us to the similitude of trans-Atlantic democracy, and then to effect the ruin of all that moves above him, whether with relation to character or to birth."[216] De Quincey in the *Edinburgh Evening Post* in 1828 described Huskisson as "the ci-devant sansculotte member of sansculotte clubs."[217] *Fraser's Magazine* compared him to Dr. François Magendie and his followers who in their quest to promote physiological knowledge and advance science mutilated the arteries, eyes, and entrails of living animals.[218] *Blackwood's Edinburgh Magazine* wondered in 1827 how one of the French Jacobins could become a member of an English Tory ministry.[219] The *Morning Journal* in 1828 and 1829 speculated that Huskisson in his youth failed to imbibe moral lessons from worthy parents regarding the true meaning of a patriotism "untainted with the principles of French Jacobinism." It concluded that he was more

[212] Aspinall, King to Hobart, May 13, 1801, III, p. 536.
[213] Leveson Vernon Harcourt, ed., *Diaries and Correspondence of The Right Hon. George Rose* (London, 1860), II, p. 158.
[214] *Cobbett's Political Register*, December 28, 1805, p. 1014.   [215] *Age*, June 1, 1828, p. 176.
[216] *Standard*, June 18, 1827.
[217] Stuart M. Tave, *New Essays by De Quincey* (Princeton, 1966), p. 277.
[218] *Fraser's Magazine*, 2 (October 1830), p. 255.
[219] *Blackwood's Edinburgh Magazine*, 22 (August 1827), p. 159.

dangerous to Britain than Napoleon Bonaparte had been.[220] And the stories and slurs continued.[221]

In a very real sense, the later critiques of capitalism and *laissez-faire* economics, whether Labor or Marxist, Catholic or Christian Socialist, owe much in inspiration to the vigorous assault fueled by the British Right, and most notably Southey, in the first generation of the Industrial Revolution. The greatest British conservative philosopher of the nineteenth century, Samuel Taylor Coleridge, wrote in 1829, the year of the end of the *ancien régime* in Britain, "On the constitution of the Church and state," in which he meditated at great length upon the problems raised by the new economic system and reached conclusions numbing in their pessimism if even-handed in their condemnation of both agricultural and industrial agents:

> Game Laws, Corn Laws, Cotton Factories, Spitalfields, the tillers of the land paid by poor-rates, and the remainder of the population mechanized into engines for the manufactory of new rich men-yea, the machinery of the wealth of the nation made up of the wretchedness of disease and depravity of those who should constitute the strength of the nation! Disease, I say, and vice, while the wheels are in full motion; but at the first stop the magic wealth-machine is converted into an intolerable weight of pauperism.[222]

While the right-wing press may well have diagnosed the misery of their countrymen, whether Irish, factory workers, or agricultural labourers, better and sometimes more profoundly than their utilitarian and Whiggish enemies, their inability to translate that outrage to their political leadership or to the Conservative party at large, calls into question both their effectiveness and the power of the press to effect meaningful change in what was still a relatively pre-industrial society.

[220] *Morning Journal*, December 6, 1828; June 22, 1829.
[221] See also, for example: *New Anti-Jacobin Review*, May 26, 1827, pp. 2–4; *True Briton*, April 7, 1821; *Beacon*, June 3, 1821. The old ex-revolutionary, Lewis Goldsmith, in the *British Monitor*, February 23, 1823, p. 10157, made the rather back-handed defense of Huskisson from the Jacobin charges that they ought not to matter as we were all revolutionaries in the early 1790s!
[222] "On the constitution of the Church and state" in John Colmer, ed., *Collected Works of Samuel Taylor Coleridge* (Princeton, 1976), II, p. 63.

CHAPTER 8

The Right and Protestantism

The formation and sustaining of a specifically Church of England *mentalité* in the England of the late eighteenth and early nineteenth centuries leads to the same problem of nomenclature which plagues any discussion of the political Right. On the one hand, aided by the intellectual trend towards romanticism and counter-revolutionary political doctrines, the general direction of "Church and King" political factions after 1793 (or even 1776) seems relatively clear. Whether Northite, Burkeite, Pittite, Canningite, Wellingtonian, or ultra, there appears to be a groping towards some vision of a renewed and purified Anglican communion, often of a High Church (however defined) variety. On the other hand, the recognition of the intricate relationships involving "High Church," "non-jurors," "Saints," "evangelicals," "Tractarians," "Catholics," and "Hutchinsonians" makes correct definitions difficult to come by or sort out. Late Georgian Tory England is no more clear on religion than on political nomenclature or doctrine.

THE HIGH CHURCH

The Church of England since its sixteenth-century formation had always accommodated a distinctive, if by no means universally accepted, grouping which placed itself (or was placed by others) in a doctrinal or liturgical setting not nearly as far removed from the medieval religious arena as perhaps the main body of an English establishment influenced more by moderate Genevan Protestantism. The Church doctrine represented by Peter Baro or John Donne with its emphasis upon the *de jure divino* episcopacy or a suspicion of Calvinism[1] gave way around 1700 to a High Church movement

[1] Gordon Rupp, *Religion in England, 1688–1791* (Oxford, 1986), p. 53.

perhaps more concerned with the correct attitude towards the Revolution and the divine right of kings than with any particular slant on the apostolic attitudes towards presbyters and bishops or on theological meditation upon the contending parties at the Synod of Dort. Yet the eighteenth-century High Church movement, seemingly so powerful in the reign of Anne, appeared in general to have foundered by mid-century on the often arid rocks of political posturing and dynastic quarrels. Perhaps the tension between politics and spirituality, always present in an establishment, led to a weakening of the High Church grouping after the failure of Jacobitism, the increasing marginalization of the non-jurors, and the Whig (and sometimes latitudinarian) monopoly after 1714 of all positions of power and authority in the Church. Whatever the case, an aggressive High Church, whether defined liturgically, historically, or politically, followed its Tory twin after 1750 into an increasingly confined position in English life.

Historians have usually recognized the weak position of the post-Anneian High Church. Owen Chadwick writes of an unfulfilled gap between the early-eighteenth-century High Church milieu and that of the Oxford environment after 1833.[2] F. C. Mather, concerned in his scholarship chiefly with the survival of Laudian sacramental and liturgical practices, suspects that the High Church reached its nadir in the late eighteenth century.[3] Nancy Uhlar Murray thought the late-eighteenth-century High Church, such as it was, had little influence over the wider communion. Its Society for the Reformation of Principles attracted little support during its brief existence in the 1790s and she estimates that at the most 100 High Church clergy (as opposed to 500 evangelicals) inhabited the country.[4] Richard Brent even questions whether the High Church had much concrete existence before the 1830s.[5] And Gordon Rupp in his magisterial volume of the *Oxford History of the Christian Church*, covering the years between the Glorious and the French Revolutions, simply ignores any discussion of a High Church party in England after 1750.[6]

2 Owen Chadwick, ed., *Mind of the Oxford Movement* (Stanford, 1967), p. 26.
3 F. C. Mather, "Georgian churchmanship reconsidered," *JEH*, 36 (April 1985), pp. 257–62.
4 Nancy Uhlar Murray, "The influence of the French Revolution on the Church of England and its rivals, 1789–1802," D.Phil. thesis (Oxford University, 1975), pp. 4, 53.
5 Richard Brent, *Liberal Anglican Politics: Whiggery, Religion, and Reform, 1830–1841* (Oxford, 1987), p. 148.
6 Rupp, *Religion in England*. For a viewpoint completely contrary to this prevailing historiography on the importance of a High Church party and movement in pre-Tractarian days,

In some ways this historiographical dismissal of a High Church party is understandable. For example, in 1798, when Charles Daubeny sent a copy of *A Guide to the Church*, certainly the most important single work a High Churchman produced in the three generations before the Oxford movement, to the Primate of All England, the archbishop did not even deign to reply.[7] Yet I would argue that just as a small group within English political and literary society sought to keep certain Tory doctrines and attitudes alive after mid-century, so, often, those same individuals – Samuel Johnson, Bishop Horne, William Stevens, Jones of Nayland, Bishop Horsley, Jonathan Boucher – strove to further a sacramental, Trinitarian, Apostolical, and politically loyalist milieu for High Church traditions.

The early-eighteenth-century High Churchmen, the Johnson and Jones and Horne circles of the later eighteenth century, and the Hackney Phalanx of the early nineteenth century, whether or not they served as valuable mentors to the men of Oxford, certainly fertilized and cross-fertilized each other. In a very real sense, the High Church movement after 1750, slight as it was, owed an impressive intellectual and spiritual debt to the non-juring tradition of those bishops and priests of the established Church who were deprived of their offices under William and Mary for refusing to take the oaths of allegiance to those post-revolutionary sovereigns.

The High Church movement of the early eighteenth century was torn between jurors and non-jurors on a largely political basis; as the century wore on, however, it was largely the spiritual tradition, drawn especially from Charles Leslie and William Law, not the political, which influenced new generations. The non-jurors had anyway largely given up whoring after the false gods of earthly power and authority and emerged into a sort of quietistic spirituality unconcerned with Pretenders or episcopal thrones.[8] Both Sir John Hawkins and Boswell emphasize Johnson's debt to the tradi-

---

see the stimulating study by Peter Benedict Nockles, "Continuity and change in Anglican High Churchmanship in Britain, 1792–1850," D.Phil. thesis (Oxford University, 1982). Nockles argues, quite convincingly, both that the High Church party was of great consequence before 1833 and that it marched to a quite different drummer than the Oxford reformers afterwards.

[7] ESRO, Boucher Papers, Bou/B/5/7a, Daubeny to Boucher, March 18, 1799.

[8] Paul M. Chapman, "Jacobite political argument in England, 1714–1766," Ph.D. dissertation (Cambridge University, 1983), pp. 154–61.

tion, especially from Law's *Serious Call to a Holy Life*.[9] Charles Leslie greatly influenced Horne and Jones of Nayland[10] and indeed Jones suspected during the French Revolution that the Christian loyalty he then felt had grown up from the seeds sown by reading Leslie forty years before.[11] One of the few important results of the Society for the Reformation of Principles, Jones of Nayland's *The Scholar Armed Against the Errors of the Times*, directed against the French Revolution and its English offshoots, republished Leslie's "Short method with the deists" and Law's "Three letters against Bishop Hoadley." Jonathan Boucher in his influential "Views of the causes and consequences of the American Revolution" defends the non-jurors of the 1690s[12] and both he and William Stevens were in touch in the late eighteenth century with the Orthodox Remnant of the Ancient British Church in the person of those episcopal worthies grocer Price of Manchester and apothecary Cartwright of Shrewsbury.[13] The *Anti-Jacobin Review* proudly maintained that had their editors lived after 1689, they would have been non-jurors against William, Mary, and Anne.[14] The Bowdlers, one of the most pre-eminent of the High Church families in England, befriended individual non-jurors and defended the tradition in print.[15]

The High Church movement had familial and social ties which, on a smaller and perhaps less influential scale, were as pronounced as those of their Clapham rivals. The future Bishop Horne and William Stevens were first cousins and attended the same school at Maidstone, Kent.[16] From there Horne went on to University

9   Sir John Hawkins, *Works of Dr. Samuel Johnson Together With His Life and Notes on His Lives of the Poets* (London, 1787), I, pp. 448–51n. James Boswell, *Life of Johnson* (London, 1953), p. 50–1.
10   J. A. W. Gunn, *Beyond Liberty and Property* (Kingston, 1983), p. 164.
11   William Jones, *Works of the Right Reverend George Horne, D.D.* (New York, 1846), I, p. 46.
12   Jonathan Boucher, "View of the causes and consequences of the American Revolution in thirteen discourses" (London, 1797), p. 550n.
13   Anne Y. Zimmer, *Jonathan Boucher: Loyalist in Exile* (Detroit, 1978), p. 235. William Stevens indeed may have been inspired by the non-juring tradition in his suspicion of established churches, one point at least where he clearly prefigured his Oxford successors. [Sir James Park], *Memoirs of William Stevens, Esq.* (London, 1814), Stevens to Skinner, May 1, 1797, pp. 136–7.
14   *Anti-Jacobin Review*, 38 (February 1811), pp. 116–7.
15   [Thomas Bowdler] *Memoirs of the Life of John Bowdler, Esq.* (London, 1824), p. 78. J. C. D. Clark also credits the non-juror devotional and apologetical tradition with playing a large part in what he sees as the intellectual defeat of the English deistic tradition by the middle of the eighteenth century. *English Society, 1688–1832* (Cambridge, England, 1983), p. 148.
16   *Memoirs of Stevens*, pp. 6–7. Evidently, Stevens' mother, Horne's aunt, had married beneath her rank, says Stevens' biographer Judge Park, to a tradesman of inferior status. Park rejoices in a rather unseemly manner that this lower-class father died when William was an

College, Oxford, and a fellowship at Magdalen where Gibbon remembered him as the only fellow who applied himself to scholarship rather than college business and private scandal.[17] Horne, who sometimes signed himself "One of the People called Christians,"[18] ultimately became Dean of Canterbury, Vice Chancellor at Oxford, and Bishop of Norwich. Stevens, the son of a tradesman, was apprenticed to a wholesale hosier and eventually became a printer and Treasurer to Queen Anne's Bounty. It was Stevens, of course, who procured the destitute Anglo-American High Church Tory, Jonathan Boucher, an assistant secretaryship to the Society for the Propagation of the Gospel in Foreign Parts. Jones of Nayland, the Tory Anglican Trinitarian, had known Charles Jenkinson at Charterhouse and Horne at University College. His great patron, besides these two, was Bishop Horsley of Rochester.[19] That generation of High Churchmen found its chief role was as defender of Trinitarian orthodoxy through its tracts and sermons. But it was also active in the establishment of the "Proclamation Society" also known as the Society for the Reformation of Principles,[20] whence emerged the *British Critic* and *The Scholar Armed*, and in an ultimately successful effort to regularize the situation of the clergy and bishops of the Episcopal Church of Scotland. In 1800, William Stevens founded the Club of Nobody's Friends. It served as a virtual Royal Society of the High Church movement, as it included most of the individuals who would lead the party before the dominance of Pusey and Newman.[21]

The circle around the wealthy wine merchant Joshua Watson, known as the Hackney Phalanx, dominated the early-nineteenth-century High Church party. Out of the Phalanx came the National Society in 1811, to promote a Church of England educational system, and the Church Building Commission in 1818, meant to rectify an abiding scandal in English spiritual life. Professor Gash

infant, thus projecting his widow back to her wealthier Horne family circle at Maidstone. Hence, Horne and Stevens grew up in intimacy to the benefit of the Church. *Ibid.*

[17] Georges A. Bonnard, ed., *Memoir of My Life* by Edward Gibbon (New York, 1966), p. 52.

[18] Jones, *Works of Horne*, II, p. 513.

[19] *Short Account of the Life and Writings of the Rev. William Jones* (London, 1801), pp. xli, 3.

[20] For the prospectus of the Proclamation Society, see William Jones, *The Scholar Armed Against the Errors of the Times* (London, 1800), pp. i–iv.

[21] "Biographical list of the members of 'The Club of Nobody's Friends'" (London, 1885). Its members included William Stevens, James Allan Park, John Bowdler, Jonathan Boucher, John Gifford, Joshua Watson, Henry Handley Norris, John Bowles, John Reeves, Lord Kenyon, Bishop Skinner, and Bishop Van Mildert.

indeed suspects that the ultimate reform of the Church of England in the nineteenth century owed more to Hackney than to the more numerous evangelicals.[22] Watson, a friend of Boucher and Stevens since his youth, was married to a niece of Archdeacon Daubeny.[23] His coadjutor, Henry Handley Norris, was Watson's brother's curate at Hackney. Norris, like Jones of Nayland for the first earl, had a tie in to the Liverpool patronage network, made even more important when the second earl became prime minister in 1812, and in fact Norris may have been Liverpool's leading advisor on ecclesiastical patronage.[24]

The Phalanx, or as the Oxford men rather unkindly called them, the "Zs,"[25] included Van Mildert of Durham, of whom Bishop Lloyd thought "orthodoxy oozed out of his pores, and he would talk of it in his dreams";[26] the High Church apologist Archdeacon Daubeny; Bishop Middleton of Calcutta; Hugh James Rose, one of the High Churchmen around the *British Magazine*, established in 1832; successive Bowdlers; Judge Park, William Stevens' biographer and a force in the legalization of the Scottish Episcopal Church; the humanitarian MP Thomas Dyke Acland; Sarah Trimmer, editor of the *Guardian of Education*; John Gifford, editor of the *Anti-Jacobin Review*; John Reeves of the Loyal Association; and John Bowles, the Pittite pamphleteer of the 1790s.[27]

In one aspect of its spiritual propaganda to the British people, its manipulation of the press, the High Church movement was not particularly successful. Nancy Murray thinks that its great accomplishment of the 1790s was the establishment of the *British Critic*, under the aegis of Jones of Nayland and the editorship of the Rev. Robert Nares.[28] But this journal and its editor, at least in the initial series, with its early moderation, and its occasional tolerance for Dr. Priestley and even for Unitarianism, proved an embarrassment for its authors.[29] *The Orthodox Churchman's Magazine*, founded in March

22 Norman Gash, *Aristocracy and People: Britain, 1815–1865* (Cambridge, Mass., 1979), p. 68.

23 Edward Churton, ed., *Memoir of Joshua Watson* (Oxford, 1861), I, pp. 12–17.

24 A. B. Webster, *Joshua Watson: Story of a Layman, 1771–1855* (London, 1954), p. 25.

25 Desmond Bowen, *Idea of the Victorian Church* (Montreal, 1968), pp. 45–50.

26 *Memoir of Watson*, Lloyd to Watson, December 11, 1825, I, p. 282.

27 Webster, *Joshua Watson*, pp. 26–7. Murray, "Influence of French Revolution," pp. 50–7.

28 Murray, "Influence of French Revolution," p. 53.

29 For the *British Critic*'s toleration of Priestley, see 1 (August 1793), pp. 459–60. For its relative tolerance of Unitarianism, see 4 (July 1794), pp. 75–6. By 1801, after one of its reviewers denied the necessity of episcopal ordination, Charles Daubeny thought the *Critic* was "one of those *half & half* publications, which will do more harm than good." ESRO, Boucher Papers, Bou/B/5/20, Daubeny to Boucher, March 3, 1801.

1801, regarded itself as in the tradition of Lancelot Andrews, Bishop Horne of Norwich, and Jones of Nayland.[30] Yet it lasted much less than the decade in which it was founded. Mrs. Sarah Trimmer's *Guardian of Education*, established in 1802, although High Church in its orientation,[31] was not meant to be chiefly a theological publication. There may indeed have been some High Church nonchalance regarding the periodical press after their disappointment in the *British Critic* and their failure with the *Orthodox Churchman's Magazine*. Charles Knight, a coadjutor of Croker's on newspaper matters, says in his memoirs that he was shocked in 1820 to discover that High Church publishers refused to aid his *Plain Englishman*, a monthly, ostensibly geared for the educated working classes, and he was driven into the arms of their Low Church confreres.[32] More successful and long-lasting was the *Christian Remembrancer*, a monthly, established in 1819, coming out of the circle of the Hackney Phalanx and edited by the Rev. Frederick Iremonger.[33]

The preparation of High Church lists such as the membership of the Club of Nobody's Friends or the community of Hackney points to the extreme difficulty of defining exactly what "High Church" meant and of discussing High Church attitudes in both a religious and a political context. On one level a significant section of the right wing (in a secular and a religious sense) were the abiding enemy of English evangelicalism not to speak of Calvinism. From a different perspective, "High Church" and "evangelical" were virtually identical. Too often then the definition of "High Church" in this period collapses before the entangling alliances and belief systems of assorted individuals and groups. When some, like John Wilson Croker, the *Quarterly* reviewer and influential Tory man-of-affairs, a good Irish Protestant, called himself "High Church,"[34] he was probably thinking in largely political terms of "High Church" as a sort of religious equivalent to his "high Toryism" in the state. If he thought of "High Church" in a religious sense, it was probably in line with the firmly *Protestant* High Church party of the reigns of

---

[30] See, for example, *Orthodox Churchman's Magazine*, 8 (January 1805).

[31] It too contained great praise of Bishop Horne and his tradition. *Guardian of Education*, 2 (January 1803), pp. 3–4.

[32] Charles Knight, *Passages of a Working Life During Half a Century* (London, 1864), I, 242–3.

[33] Francis E. Mineka, *Dissidence of Dissent: The Monthly Repository, 1806–1838* (New York, 1972), pp. 58ff.

[34] Louis J. Jennings, ed., *Correspondence and Diaries of John Wilson Croker* (London, 1884), Croker to Bishop of Ferns, March 2, 1825, I, p. 279.

Anne and George I.[35] In any case, he certainly reacted in horror to such eventual nineteenth-century High Church notions as candles or flowers on the communion table or praying to the east.[36] When others, such as Archdeacon Daubeny, discussed "High Church" it was as the vision glorious, with his theory that Timothy and Titus, Ignatius and Polycarp, exercised the same episcopal office as the modern bishops of the Churches of Rome and England, Russia and Sweden.[37] It is doubtful that Croker, for example, held such a view which, before the Oxford movement, at the least, tidied up such matters, makes it difficult to define "High Church" on its own grounds much less in relation to other churchly tendencies.

The relationship between "High Church" and "evangelical" is a case in point of this terminological confusion.[38] F. W. Brown regards Lord Kenyon as the Wilberforce of the High Church movement;[39] Castlereagh and Mrs. Arbuthnot thought him a Saint.[40] The Bowdler family, all of whom were ostensibly High Church, were riven with disagreement over the evangelical and hence, inevitably, dissenting associations, of their younger members.[41] Sir William Dolben, the epitome for decades of High Church, Tory Oxford in the House of Commons, defended, as might be expected, Nowell's Charles I Remembrance sermon in 1772 and (as one of only two votes) Reeves' high prerogative pamphlet in 1795.[42] Less amenable to simple political analysis, he was also a strict Sabbatarian,[43] opposed the American war by 1781,[44] and joined the minority of ninety (and Wilberforce) in 1795 to support Charles Grey's motion in regards to peace with France.[45] Sir Thomas Dyke Acland, a Hackney man and an evangelical, also considered himself

---

[35] Rupp, *Religion in England*, p. 55.   [36] *Quarterly Review*, 72 (May 1843), pp. 232ff.

[37] Charles Daubeny, *Guide to the Church* (New York, 1803), p. 35; *An Appendix to the Guide to the Church* (London, 1830), p. 91.

[38] Part of the problem here, of course, may be the great over-use of "evangelical," a term that has come to define almost everyone in late Hanoverian or early Victorian Britain.

[39] Ford K. Brown, *Fathers of the Victorians: The Age of Wilberforce* (Cambridge, England, 1961), p. 352.

[40] Francis Bamford, Duke of Wellington, eds., *Journal of Mrs. Arbuthnot, 1820–1832* (London, 1950), I, pp. 31–2.

[41] Henry Broxap, *Later Non-Jurors* (Cambridge, England, 1924), p. 306.

[42] W. R. Ward, *Georgian Oxford* (Oxford, 1958), p. 251. *Parl. Hist.*, XXXII (November 26, 1795), p. 650.

[43] John Adolphus, *History of England* (London, 1840), VI, p. 120.

[44] Namier and Brooke, II, pp. 328–9.

[45] *Parl. Hist.*, XXXI (January 26, 1795), p. 1247.

a High Churchman.[46] Sir Robert Harry Inglis, Sidmouth's one-time private secretary, who defeated Peel at Oxford University after the latter's Catholic emancipation apostasy in 1829, was opposed at that election by much of the Wellingtonian press on the declared grounds that he was a Low Churchman of evangelical morality with ties to Bible societies and other dissenting causes.[47] Inglis, on the other hand, thought he was a High Churchman.[48]

The Arminian Methodists, too, had a strangely self-conscious relationship with the High Church. John Wesley, to the end of his long life, called himself a High Churchman[49] – which he presumably meant in a political sense, as he coupled it with his belief in passive obedience and non-resistance, and he had given up any belief in the apostolic succession as early as 1746.[50] Wesley strongly admired Horne, Jones,[51] and Johnson ("that great man")[52] and supported Dr. Nowell at the time of the expulsion of the six predestinarian Oxford students in 1769.[53] In return Johnson approved of Wesley;[54] Jones of Nayland thought him a "wonderful man in his way;"[55] and Bishop Horne as late as 1790 allowed him to preach from a pulpit in his diocese.[56] Despite the overt Anglican–Methodist schism after, if not indeed before, Wesley's death in 1791, and despite the general Tory and High Church excommunication of Methodism thereafter, there was sometimes an interesting relationship between some Methodist-born, lower-class intellectuals and humanitarians and the mother Church in its higher manifestation.

[46] J. S. Reynolds, *Evangelicals at Oxford, 1735–1871* (Oxford, 1953), pp. 3, 157. One common point of departure between evangelicals and High Churchmen may have been the intellectual influence of the non-juror, William Law. Roger Anstey, *Atlantic Slave Trade and British Abolition, 1760–1810* (Atlantic Highlands, N.J., 1975), pp. 164–75.

[47] For example, *Courier*, February 23, 1829.

[48] BL, Bliss Papers, Add. MSS. 34570, Inglis to S. L. Giffard, February 11, 1829, fo. 154. From the other direction, even as firm a Calvinist as the evangelical William Romaine, senior chaplain to the Countess of Huntington, had some political and religious views which smacked of High Church. He was a Hutchinsonian, had vigorously opposed the Jew Bill in the early 1750s – a High Church *cause célèbre* – and in the 1790s presided over weekly communion in the parish of St. Anne, Blackfriars. Rupp, *Religion in England*, p. 473. Mather, "Georgian churchmanship," p. 272.

[49] HMC, 11th Report, Appendix, pt. IV: *Manuscripts of the Earl of Dartmouth* (London, 1887), Wesley to Dartmouth, June 14, 1775, I, pp. 378–9.

[50] Rupp, *Religion in England*, p. 438.

[51] John Telford, ed., *Letters of the Rev. John Wesley* (London, 1931), IV, p. 172n.

[52] Nehemiah Curnock, ed., *Journal of the Rev. John Wesley* (New York, not dated), VI, p. 466.

[53] Ward, *Georgian Oxford*, p. 240.

[54] Frederick A. Pottle, Charles H. Bennett, eds., *Boswell's Journal of a Tour to the Hebrides* (New York, 1936), p. 383.

[55] Jones, *Works of Horne*, I, p. 68.   [56] *Ibid.*, I, p. 66.

There must have been many like Michael Thomas Sadler's mother[57] or J. R. Stephens' father, president of the Methodist Conference in 1827,[58] who always retained a special love for the Church of England, a bridge which enabled their children more easily to make the crossing back in the nineteenth century. And those like Sadler,[59] Mark Robinson,[60] Richard Oastler,[61] or J. R. Stephens[62] who did make the move from Methodist to Anglican usually found themselves attracted to a high Toryism as well.

Numerous so-called High Church men and women were active in Wilberforce's Vice Society, so detested by other Tory figures and by the vast majority of the Tory press. Judge Park, William Stevens' biographer, and Walker King, Burke's literary executor, were vice presidents and the General Committee included John Bowles and the High Church publisher, Charles Rivington. The Bowdlers, Sir William Dolben, Daubeny, Lord Kenyon, John Reeves, Mrs. Trimmer, Van Mildert, and Joshua Watson were all members along with such evangelical luminaries as Zachary Macaulay, the Rev. Charles Simeon, and, of course, Wilberforce himself.[63] Hence we have seen self-defined High Churchmen cooperating and sharing, at some level, spiritual experiences with Calvinist evangelicals and Arminian Methodists. Indeed the High Church Bishop Horsley of Rochester, attacked by his enemies, along with Boucher and Daubeny, as a Laud of the eighteenth century,[64] preached that the Church of England had room for Calvinists and Arminians.[65] And the *British Critic* in 1796 defended Calvin against the strictures of its own founding patron, Jones of Nayland.[66] Therefore, it is no doubt best to take Gordon Rupp's admonition to heart when discussing matters religious in England in this period: "We ought not to think of these men and women as more coherently organized at this stage

---

[57] George Jacob Holyoake, *Life of Joseph Rayner Stephens* (London, 1881), p. 80.

[58] *Ibid.*, p. 19.

[59] [Robert Benton Seeley], *Memoirs of the Life and Writings of Michael Thomas Sadler* (London, 1842), p. 29.

[60] Charles Cuthbert Southey, ed. *Life and Correspondence of Robert Southey* (London, 1850), Robinson to Southey, January 13, 1824, v, p. 163.

[61] Cecil Driver, *Tory Radical: Life of Richard Oastler* (New York, 1946), pp. 25–6.

[62] J. C. Gill, *Ten Hours Parson* (London, 1959), p. 186.

[63] Bishop of Llandaff, "Sermon preached before the Society for the Suppression of Vice, 3rd May 1804" (London, 1804), pp. 39ff.

[64] ESRO, Boucher Papers, Bou/B/5/1, Daubeny to Boucher, May 7, 1798.

[65] *Theological Works* (London, 1845), VI, pp. 124–5.

[66] *British Critic*, 7 (January 1796), pp. 72–3.

than they really were, or that they had some common platform of rigidly defined beliefs."[67]

Hutchinsonianism was not always a banner of High Church union either. Hutchinsonianism, an eighteenth-century reaction against the Newtonian revolution, emphasized an undiluted Trinitarianism, the supremacy of revelation and tradition over nature, a belief in Hebrew as the primeval language formed by God, and a conviction that true science was to be found in the Mosaic Genesis and not the Newtonian *Principia*.[68] Jones of Nayland and Horne became Hutchinsonians while at University College, Oxford. Horne then introduced Stevens to the doctrine.[69] Among other High Church figures who accepted a moderate form of the tenet, which enabled them partially to affirm Newtonian science yet emphasize its underlining spiritual causation, were Daubeny, Van Mildert,[70] and Bishop Skinner[71] of the Scottish Episcopal Church and their organ the *Orthodox Churchman's Magazine*.[72] Two other High Church Oxonians, John Wesley and Samuel Johnson, however, refused to accept the Hutchinsonian dogma.[73] And the *British Critic* accused the Hutchinsonians of "wild opinions."[74]

But the main aspect of the relation between religion and right-wing politics in the Britain of the late eighteenth and early nineteenth centuries must perforce be the attitude of the Right in general and the High Church in particular to its ancient enemies, historic (and not-so-historic) dissent on one side and Roman Catholicism on the other. Out of the tension involved in what was sometimes a three-way interrelationship emerged also a firmer commitment to the Church of England as a unique institution free from the errors of dissent and Rome, Wittenberg and Geneva, able to stand on its feet in the face of any existing Christian communion.

---

[67] Rupp, *Religion in England*, p. 532.   [68] Jones, *Works of Horne*, I, pp. xi–xvii.
[69] *Short Account of Life of Jones*, p. iii. *Memoir of Stevens*, p. 22.
[70] *Memoir of Watson*, I, pp. 40–2.   [71] *Memoir of Stevens*, p. 27.
[72] *Orthodox Churchman's Magazine*, 3 (October 1802), p. 247.
[73] *Journal of Wesley*, IV, pp. 147, 261. W. J. Hardy, ed., HMC, 14th Report, Appendix, pt. IV: *Manuscripts of Lord Kenyon* (London, 1894), pp. 538–40. The Tory *Critical Review* associated the Calvinistic Whitfieldites and the Hutchinsonians as "quacks in divinity" and its editor, Tobias Smollett, considered the Hutchinsonians "fanatics." *Critical Review*, 2 (March 1756), pp. 175–6. T. Smollett, *History of England from the Revolution in 1688, to the Death of George the Second* (London, 1811), VI, p. 277.
[74] *British Critic*, 31 (June 1808), p. 673.

DISSENTERS

The attitude of the Right towards their fellow Protestants in the English dissenting churches was above all an attitude steeped in a peculiar view of history. Among many a Jacobite, neo-Jacobite, Tory, High Churchman, Buteite, and Northite, the Dissenters were engaged in a nefarious conspiracy, hatched in the seventeenth (or even the sixteenth) century to destroy the English monarchy and Church. Thomas Carte, a Jacobite friend of Bishop Atterbury and some of the non-juring clergymen,[75] and author at mid-century of a multi-volume *General History of England,* accused Elizabethan and Stuart Puritans of striving "to subvert the monarchy, as well as the episcopacy, liturgy, and the whole constitution of the Church of England."[76] He also formulated a Barruel-like intrigue of republican-oriented Puritans in 1613 who plotted to see James I's male line extinct and to raise the Palatine elector to the British throne.[77] A quarter century later, Sir John Dalrymple, the Buteite apologist, in his influential *Memoirs of Great Britain and Ireland,* depicted the seventeenth-century Puritans as republican enthusiasts who sought to extend the civil war and commotion which they had occasioned in the German empire, France, and the Low Countries into England and Scotland.[78] Even David Hume, in his generally balanced *History of England,* pictured the Puritans as "secretly lurk[ing] ... in the Church" and as the servants of the "fanatical hypocrite Cromwell."[79]

In Carte and Dalrymple at least there was a not very subtle equation of historical puritanism and treason, an equivalency which in other commentators of the mid and late eighteenth century was either echoed or even transferred to the purported descendants of the Puritans, the Dissenters. Hence, long before the French revolutionary agitation and Burke's famous suggestion that 90 percent of the English Dissenters wanted a republic,[80] a similar insinuation was standard fare in Tory, Northite, and Anglo-American loyalist circles. The future Bishop Horne, then a fellow at Magdalen College, Oxford, in his coronation sermon of 1761, "The Christian

[75] J. Y. T. Greig, ed., *Letters of David Hume* (Oxford, 1932), I, p. 214n.
[76] Thomas Carte, *General History of England* (London, 1752), III, p. 703.
[77] *Ibid.* (London, 1755), IV, pp. 1–2.
[78] Sir John Dalrymple, *Memoirs of Great Britain and Ireland* (London, 1771), I, p. 17.
[79] David Hume, *History of England* (New York, 1879), IV, pp. 374, 470.
[80] Burke, *Corr.* (1967), Burke to Dundas, September 30, 1791, VI, p. 419.

King," fully adopted the notion of a nefarious seventeenth-century Presbyterian and republican conspiracy against Church and state.[81] The Tory John Shebbeare, in his interminable letters to the English people and in other writings of the 1750s, 1760s, and 1770s, presented a negative picture of the Dissenters as "invariable Foes" of the constitution[82] who put self-interest before their country,[83] and who ought to be required by law to wear a green stocking or a yellow cap.[84] A much more important figure than either Horne or Shebbeare, Lord North, as prime minister suggested long before the American question heightened feelings against Dissenters that any weakening of the Thirty-Nine Articles would overthrow the Church as well as return Britain to the days of the Fifth Monarchy Men.[85]

The American Revolution, not surprisingly, introduced such nascent anti-dissenting sentiments to a wider audience. The entire Northite press denounced the Dissenters, both of England and America, as dangerous radicals bent upon the overthrow of the constitution.[86] For example, by 1778, the *Morning Post* was blaming dissenting pulpits on both continents as the chief cause of the rebellion.[87] In subsequent years the *Post* denounced Dissenters as "Vipers in the bosom of the Christian church, who sucked in that poison of asps" in their seminaries[88] and who were largely responsible for the "modern notorious dissemination of obscenity, infidelity, and scepticism."[89] They were addicted to a spirit of persecution derived from the barbarian Calvin who burned Servetus alive.[90] They were the true cause of both the English Revolution of 1641 and the American Revolution of 1776.[91] By 1779, the Bishop of Bristol suggested that all English dissenting ministers be required to take oaths renouncing leveling, Fifth Monarchy, and republican ideals.[92] The Anglo-American Tory loyalists were as firm in their prejudices against Dissenters as the Northite press. Jonathan Boucher in 1776 saw Presbyterian republicans as the *fons et origo* of

---

[81] Jones, *Works of Horne*, II, p. 313.
[82] John Shebbeare, "Sixth letter to the people of England" (London, 1757), p. 15.
[83] John Shebbeare, "First letter to the people of England" (London, 1756), pp. 38–9.
[84] John Shebbeare, ed., *History of the Reign of King Charles the Second, from the Restoration to the End of the Year 1667* by Edward Hyde, first earl of Clarendon (London, 1757?), pp. xxv–xxvi.
[85] *Parl. Hist.*, XVII (February 6, 1772), p. 274.
[86] See, for example, the *General Evening Post*, June 11, 1776, and thereafter.
[87] *Morning Post*, September 29, 1778.   [88] *Ibid.*, March 18 and 23, 1779.
[89] *Ibid.*, March 18, 1779.
[90] *Ibid.*, March 28, 1781.   [91] *Ibid.*, July 24, 1781.
[92] Thomas Newton, *Works* (London, 1787), I, p. 193.

the rebellion,[93] as did Peter Oliver, who in his *Origins and Progress of the American Rebellion* saw the Dissenters in general as forming a "League with the Devil, and a Covenant with Hell."[94]

Hence, long before 1789, the linkage between the non-conformist churches and treason was a firm one in at least certain loyalist circles, despite the attempts, partially successful, of both Chatham and his son, to conciliate the Dissenters. J. E. Cookson has argued that the loyalist, anti-dissenting explosion so evident in British politics in the 1790s actually dated from 1787, when the dissenting attempt to repeal the Test and Corporation Acts gathered steam in earnest.[95] I would suggest that extreme anti-dissenting loyalism was well in place ten years earlier than Cookson locates it.

The Burkeite and Pittite loyalism of the 1790s both agreed in terming Dissenters as traitors to the constitution but in no more vicious a manner than Northite loyalism in the 1770s. *The* (Pittite) *Times*, which had only mildly opposed the repeal of the Test and Corporation Acts in 1789 and 1790,[96] by 1792 was accusing the Presbyterians of twenty years of treason and used "Reformer" as a synonym for "Presbyterians – the descendants of those who murdered *Charles the First*."[97] Besides the Pittite press, the prime minister's other epistolary hacks were equally censorious of the Dissenters. The Rev. John Ireland in "Vindiciae Regiae" compared Jacobins and Puritans and thought the modern French Assembly imbued with "the same spirit which impelled our Long Parliament ... "[98] Cobbett made the further point that the modern Puritans were as bad as those of the seventeenth century.[99] John Bowles accused the Nottingham Dissenters of parading republican standards and the nude goddess of reason during the general election of 1802.[100] Pitt himself, of course, in what was a decisive break with the Chathamite tradition, told George III that he wanted to inaugurate a new test

---

93 *Maryland Historical Magazine*, 8 (1913), Boucher to William Eden, January 7, 1776, pp. 338–43.

94 Douglass Adair, John A. Schutz, eds., *Peter Oliver's Origin and Progress of the American Rebellion: A Tory View* (Stanford, 1961), p. 104.

95 J. E. Cookson, *Friends of Peace* (Cambridge, England, 1982), pp. 2–11.

96 *The Times*, May 25, 1789; March 2, 1790.

97 Rosemary Edith Begemann, "The English press and the French Revolution, 1789–1793," Ph.D. dissertation (Emory University, 1973), p. 246.

98 [Rev. John Ireland], "Vindiciae Regiae" (London, 1797), pp. 69–70.

99 *Cobbett's Political Register*, February 20–27, 1802.

100 [John Bowles], "Postscript to thoughts on the late general election as demonstrative of the progress of Jacobinism" (London, 1803), pp. 125–6.

against Jacobin principles to be administered just to Dissenters.[101] The Burkeite tradition of the 1790s also emphasized, as in Burke's writings and speeches,[102] or in John Reeves' infamous 1795 pamphlet, "Thoughts on the English government,"[103] the equation of modern French and Jacobin principles with historic English puritanism and dissent.[104]

By the early nineteenth century, as the immediate threat from Jacobin precepts seemed to recede both in Britain and in Napoleonic France, this treason–Dissenter equation weakened, with the starkly *political* objections to the Dissenters generally replaced by *religious* objections. Only rarely by the second and third decades of the nineteenth century[105] does one find them denounced as among the greatest of the enemies of the state. So when the High Church Bishop Marsh of Peterborough, a leader of Hackney, expounded in the 1820s on the thesis that if the Calvinists took over the Church of England he himself, noted for his zeal in weeding out their ordinal candidates, would follow Archbishop Laud to the block,[106] he sounded merely ridiculous. It might well be, as Southey said in 1813, that the Dissenters hated the Church of England and wanted to overthrow her,[107] but by that time it was much less certain in rightist circles that they wanted to harm or inaugurate a reign of terror against the state as well.

In this context of slightly thawed relations on the part of the loyalists towards the dissenting churches, one must evaluate the predicament in which a section at least of the Right was placed during the apparent resurgence of radical activity after Waterloo. In some substantial respects the years between 1815 and 1822 saw a regime in crisis far more than the years between 1828 and 1832 did. The culmination of economic hardships, anti-Christian propaganda directed towards the lower classes, scandals in the royal family, the

---

[101] Fifth Earl Stanhope, *Life of the Right Honourable William Pitt* (London, 1861), Pitt to the king, January 31, 1801, III, p. xxv.

[102] Burke, *Works*, IV, p. 324.

[103] John Reeves, "Thoughts on the English government" (London, 1795), pp. 20–22.

[104] Though Sheridan may have exaggerated somewhat when he told the House of Commons that Reeves "represented the Dissenters to be a race not fit to exist, and as worthy of being exterminated as the Caribs of St. Vincent's and the Maroons of Jamaica." *Parl. Hist.*, XXXII (November 26, 1795), p. 629.

[105] As in the obscure right-wing newspaper, *Cooper's John Bull*, April 16, 1826.

[106] "The legality of the questions proposed by ... the Bishop of Peterborough to candidates for holy orders ... considered" (London, 1820), pp. 6–13. "Speech delivered in the House of Lords, on Friday, June 7, 1822" (London, 1822), p. 33.

[107] *Life of Southey*, Southey to Wynn, March 12, 1813, IV, pp. 24–5.

spread of Paineite, Cobbettite, and Carlilean ideas among the masses, certainly caused if not panic at least a feverish concern almost approaching that of the 1790s within sections of the ruling order. Hence, between 1815 and around 1822, there were calls on the Right for conciliatory policies *vis à vis* the Dissenters, calls which indeed look peculiar in the context of the rhetoric of the 1770s and the 1790s.

Yet just as Catholicism seemed less of a threat to Anglicanism after the French Revolution, so dissenting principles caused less perturbation in the 1820s to a Right exposed to the propaganda of Richard and Mary Anne Carlile. Thus much of the government-oriented Tory press, the *Courier*,[108] the *Guardian*,[109] the *New Times*,[110] the *White Dwarf*,[111] and *Blackwood's Edinburgh Magazine*,[112] attempted to lessen the denominational and ideologically charged battles both within and without the national Church. Lord Sidmouth's indirectly subsidized *White Dwarf*, facing the Habeas Corpus crisis of 1817, wanted an anti-radical, anti-infidel Christian union, replacing the old "Church in Danger" cry with the more ecumenical "No King, No Religion, No Ministry, No Order."[113] And the daily *New Times* was almost Burkeian in 1819 when it reminded its readers that the Powers of Darkness could not be fought with the single arm of the Church of England and that neither Catholicism nor nonconformity were now the abiding evil that the anti-Christian propagandists were.[114] Both Wordsworths, the poet and his High Church clerical brother, thought so as well. William informed his patron Lord Lonsdale in 1818 that the Lowther battle cry in Westmorland should now be "King and Constitution" rather than "Church and King."[115] And Christopher feared that the literature of the High Church National Society, with its incessant "members of the Established Church" or "well affected to Church and State" or "friends of the Church" verbiage was needlessly disturbing the relations between the established Church and Dissenters.[116] The biographer of Joshua Watson, the leading

[108] *Courier*, January 8, 1819. [109] *Guardian*, June 10, 1821.
[110] *New Times*, April 8, 1818.
[111] *White Dwarf*, November 29, 1817.
[112] *Blackwood's Edinburgh Magazine*, 7 (August 1820), p. 539.
[113] *White Dwarf*, November 29, 1817. [114] *New Times*, April 28, 1819.
[115] Arthur Aspinall, *Politics and the Press* (London, 1949), p. 356.
[116] *Memoir of Watson*, Christopher Wordsworth to Watson, April 20, 1815, I, pp. 130–1.

Hackney figure, also detects a warmer spirit on his part towards the Dissenters during these years.[117]

When radicalism ceased to be as potent a force in national politics after 1822, any substantial calls for Dissenter–Anglican cooperation also vanished. But little of the heated rhetoric of the earlier period revived. In 1828, although the Tory press (in this sense like both the ultras and the Wellingtonians in parliament) did not in general view the repeal of the Test and Corporation Acts as of the most extraordinary moment, certainly in comparison with its keen interest in Catholic emancipation the following winter, it was virtually united on the subject. Except for the High Church *British Critic*, which, perhaps surprisingly, supported the claims of the Dissenters for a legal license to serve in office,[118] the entire Tory press, whatever its attitude towards Wellington and Peel and whatever its stance in 1829 on Catholic relief, opposed the repeal. The opposition, however, was not terribly bitter; the strongest words against repeal were those of the scabrous *Age* that the bill was "an abortion."[119] In a way, given the centuries of suspicion between Canterbury and its dissenting Protestant critics, it was an anti-climax. However, such was the Right's fixation on the Catholic question during the third decade of the nineteenth century that little energy was (or perhaps could be) expended on what was inevitably seen as a lesser matter.

EVANGELICALS

In some ways and in some circles, replacing the Dissenters as the rightist bogey man was the leader of the "Saints" and the neo-puritan evangelical movement within the established Church, William Wilberforce. Over and above their views on other issues, religious, political, or economic, "puritanism" as a social phenomenon was a divisive subject among loyalists of the early nineteenth century who perhaps disagreed more on the issue than on any other save the correct attitude towards Roman Catholics. Few subjects agitated Cobbett and Windham, for example, more than the puritanical and Wilberforceian assault on the traditional sports of Englishmen such as boxing and bull-baiting. Windham's speeches in

---

[117] Webster, *Joshua Watson*, p. 19.   [118] *British Critic*, 4, 4th ser. (October 1828), p. 304.
[119] *Age*, April 27, 1828, p. 132.

parliament in defense of such practices seem among his most heart-felt[120] and few have doubted that Cobbett's tirades in print against Hannah More and the Vice Society were based upon anything but the most fervent disagreement.[121]

Cobbett's attitude towards More had been quite different during the American days of the 1790s, when French principles were the *only* enemy worth pursuing. Cobbett in fact got much of More published in America. He was indeed writing her admiring letters as late as 1800.[122] Their subsequent most public falling out may well reflect as much as anything the renewal of normal political and religious differences somewhat submerged during the initial stages of an Anglo-Jacobin war. Cobbett and Windham were not alone on the Right in their detestation of More and her puritanism. De Quincey thought her a "horrid bigot" and her works a "disgrace to the nation."[123] And not all visitors to Abbotsford were amused that Walter Scott's daughter, Mrs. John Gibson Lockhart, had named one of her donkeys "Hannah More."[124]

Set most dramatically against Windham and Cobbett were their former ideological confreres such as John Bowles, Cobbett's press coadjutor on the *Porcupine*,[125] and John Bowdler, with his non-juror roots and High Church connections. In their jeremiads against adultery, indecent female dress, and traditional English sports, or in Bowdler's suggestion that female adulteresses be tattooed,[126] they along with other High Church and right-wing figures in the Vice Society could hardly be further away from the vision of England favored by a Windham or a Cobbett. When the historian of the Society for the Suppression of Vice suggests that Bowles fell out with Windham and Cobbett in 1802 not over the war issue – he was as anti-Amiens as they were – but over the puritan one, he was no

---

120 See, for example, BL, Windham Papers, Add. MSS. 37853, Cobbett to Windham, January 17, 1802, fo. 24.
121 See, for example, *Cobbett's Political Register*, February 20–27, 1802, pp. 175–6; January 7–14, 1804, pp. 54–5.
122 University of Illinois at Urbana-Champaign, Cobbett Papers, Cobbett to More, October 20, 1800.
123 John E. Jordan, *De Quincey to Wordsworth: A Biography of a Relationship* (Berkeley, 1963), De Quincey to Mary Wordsworth, September 30, 1809, p. 252.
124 CL, University of Michigan, Croker Papers, Lockhart-Croker Correspondence, Lockhart to Croker, August 3, 1823.
125 BL, Windham Papers, Add. MSS. 37853, Cobbett to Windham, January 20, 1802, fo. 66.
126 See, for example, John Bowles, "Remarks on modern female matters" (London, 1802), pp. 4–8. John Bowdler, "Reform or ruin" (London, 1797), pp. 14–5, 23, 37–8.

doubt correct.[127] And the spirit of Windham and Cobbett and their vision of traditionalism did not die on the Right with Cobbett's defection to radicalism and Windham's return to the Foxites. Many of the vicious and often unprovoked attacks on More, Wilberforce, the Clapham Saints, and the evangelical movement in general – usually without any support from Tory governmental figures or even backbenchers who probably saw little political gain from any sustained attack on the God-fearers – may have had much less to do with pro-slavery views than with loathing of puritanical social mores. This may have been as indigenous an aspect of the Right, or at least large sections of it, as almost any other issue in the early stages of the Industrial Revolution and as much as any other trend pointed towards the subsequent Tory–working class alliance so pronounced in the later nineteenth century.

There is a sense in which an eternal rightist spirit stands against the notion of vice societies to regulate standard and presumably immemorial human behavior as a manifestation of a misplaced enlightenment optimism. The Northite *Morning Post* in the 1770s ridiculed the Society for the Reformation of Manners and its Sabbatarianism.[128] Young Henry Addington in the 1780s, though friendly with Wilberforce, refused to join the Society for the Suppression of Vice because he did not want to set himself up as a "censor castigatorque minorium."[129] Like the hatred for William Huskisson, only more virulent, the distaste for Wilberforce in sections of the Right bordered on pathology and went far beyond any dislike of vice societies or slave emancipation or identification with West Indian planters, though no doubt at some level for some people negrophobia underlined it. For in the Right's attitude toward this one man it was possible to see incarnate a generic disposition towards not only Saints or Calvinistic evangelicals but towards Methodists and Dissenters as well.

One of the few subjects upon which George III and George IV agreed was their attitude toward Wilberforce. Due to his disagreement with Wilberforce over abolition, after 1788 George III's name only twice again graced a reforming institution.[130] The Earl of

---

[127] M. J. D. Roberts, "The Society for the Suppression of Vice and its early critics, 1802–1812," *HJ*, 26 (March 1983), p. 166.

[128] *Morning Post*, January 19, 1778.

[129] George Pellew, *Life and Correspondence of the Right Honourable Henry Addington, First Viscount Sidmouth* (London, 1847), I, p. 51n.

[130] Brown, *Fathers of the Victorians*, p. 85.

Essex, who visited with the king in 1804, found that his detestation of Wilberforce had become violent.[131] George's eldest son called Wilberforce "the little fanatick" and considered him a "republican at heart."[132] Cobbett viewed Wilberforce as the "little Pharisee";[133] Croker wrote that there was no man in public life whom he less respected;[134] De Quincey used terms such as "humbug" and "imbecility" to describe him;[135] Francis Burdett particularly despised him.[136] Lord Eldon found that the more he saw of Wilberforce and his followers, the less he liked them;[137] William Gifford, editor of the *Quarterly Review* saw them as full of "selfish craft."[138]

Significant sections of the right-wing press were equally censorious both of Wilberforce and of the Saints. *John Bull* portrayed Wilberforce as a whining little holy man;[139] *Blackwood's Edinburgh Magazine* as a "pharisaical hypocrite";[140] Goldsmith's *British Monitor* as "a man ... stuffed with religion ... an *ultra-religionist*."[141] George Croly's *Monthly Magazine* betrayed what it called an especial contempt for the conservative Tory Henry Goulburn because he was a Saint.[142] *John Bull* asserted that it supported Robert Peel at the contested and contentious Oxford by-election of 1829 because the more ultra Robert Harry Inglis was a Clapham Saint.[143]

To reduce Wilberforceianism and Methodism to the same level was relatively commonplace on the Right. The *Satirist*, for example, in 1809, ridiculed "the dear people called Methodists" whom it compared with the Wilberforcean Saints.[144] *Common Sense* admitted in its prospectus in 1824 that it disliked "a Wilberforce, or a Negro, a

131 Arthur Aspinall, ed., *Correspondence of George, Prince of Wales, 1770–1812* (New York, 1968), Essex to Lowther, December 25, 1804, v, p. 160n.
132 *Ibid.* (New York, 1964), Prince to York, April 14, 1793, II, pp. 348–9.
133 BL, Windham Papers, Add. MSS. 37853, Cobbett to Windham, October 4, 1802, fo. 55.
134 NLS, Lockhart Papers, Croker to Lockhart, April 26, [1838?], fo. 47.
135 Stuart M. Tave, ed., *New Essays by De Quincey* (Princeton, 1966), pp. 362–3, 366n.
136 M. W. Patterson, *Sir Francis Burdett and His Times (1770–1844)* (London, 1931), I, p. 61.
137 Horace Twiss, *Public and Private Life of Lord Chancellor Eldon* (London, 1844), II, p. 64.
138 Edward J. Stapleton, ed., *Some Official Correspondence of George Canning* (London, 1887), Gifford to Canning, September 8, 1824, I, pp. 224–6. David Brion Davis suggests that one of Roger Anstey's most intriguing arguments regarding abolition of the slave trade is that in 1806, when the major breakthrough took place, the supporters of Wilberforce deliberately suppressed humanitarian arguments. This may have partially reflected a realization of the unpopularity of Wilberforcean principles in certain circles. *Problem of Slavery in the Age of Revolution, 1770–1823* (Ithaca, 1975), p. 348.
139 *John Bull*, February 18, 1821, p. 76; February 25, 1821, p. 85.
140 *Blackwood's Edinburgh Magazine*, 16 (June 1824), p. 679.
141 *British Monitor*, February 18, 1821, p. 8508.
142 *Monthly Magazine*, 7 (April 1829), p. 342.
143 *John Bull*, February 22, 1829, pp. 60–1.   144 *Satirist*, January 1, 1809, pp. 34ff.

Methodist, or a Canter."[145] Despite the obvious doctrinal problem-here – the Methodists were in general the firmest Arminian Prot-estants in the United Kingdom while the religious thrust of the Saints was Calvinistic – on political and devotional issues the two groups were often as one. The great emphasis in Methodism, follow-ing the founder's example, on prison visiting, anti-slavery, Sabbat-arianism, and the avoidance of vice and situations of concupiscence united them, at least in the eyes of the Right, with the main thrust of Wilberforce's group. John Whitaker, a mainstay of both the *British Critic* and the *Anti-Jacobin Review*, found that every sincere Christian, no matter how orthodox, was branded a Methodist. Therefore, he suspected that the opposition to Methodism (and I would add to the Saints as well) came from neither a warmth for Orthodoxy nor the Church "but from a very different principle – from a dislike to the seriousness of spirit, from a hostility to the devoutness of life."[146]

Hence, on the Right, the criticism of the post-Wesley Methodists tended to focus more on their hyperreligiosity (so like the Saints) than on the schismatic aspects of their movement. Cobbett's *Porcu-pine* saw them as "envious and malignant spirits";[147] *Redhead Yorke's Weekly Political Register* as "crazy vagabonds" or "soul-saving maniacs."[148] The *Anti-Jacobin Review* viewed Methodists as indi-viduals of "peculiar physiognomy" and "coarse, hard, and dismal visages" and as *"organs of hypocrisy, idolatry, bigotry, enthusiasm, ambition, despotism, licentiousness, ignorance ..."*[149] Southey in the *Quarterly* thought it the "least attractive and most irrational" of any form of Christianity.[150]

Evangelical Calvinism within the established Church was of course as unpopular to some of the Right as was Methodism without it. Southey, who acquired a loathing of it long before he embraced (if indeed he ever quite did) the formularies of High Church Angli-canism, feared in 1806 that Calvinism was spreading among the lower classes like a pestilence.[151] Mrs. Trimmer, on this point at least

[145] *Common Sense*, August 1, 1824, p. 5.
[146] Rev. R. Polwhele, *Traditions and Recollections* (London, 1825), Whitaker to Polwhele, November 13, 1799, II, p. 505.
[147] *Porcupine*, June 26, 1801.
[148] *Redhead Yorke's Weekly Political Review*, September 26, 1807.
[149] *Anti-Jacobin Review*, 51 (October 1816), p. 201; 30 (February 1808), p. 50.
[150] *Quarterly Review*, 2 (August 1809), p. 54.
[151] John Wood Warter, ed., *Selections From the Letters of Robert Southey* (London, 1856), Southey to Rickman, March 19, 1806, I, p. 371.

earning her title of the High Church's Hannah More,[152] preached against it in her *Guardian of Education*.[153] The *Anti-Jacobin Review* proclaimed it a "doctrina horribilis"[154] and the *British Critic* a "baseless fabric."[155] Of the two leading specifically High Church periodicals of the early nineteenth-century, the *Orthodox Churchman's Magazine* found it more objectionable than Methodism,[156] and the *Christian Remembrancer*, full of "bigotry and rapine."[157] Hackney also threw up Daubeny and Bishop Marsh of Peterborough to combat what the former called the intolerant "spawn of the Scotch covenanters."[158]

Hence, in the early nineteenth-century, the criticism from the Right of both the Arminian Methodists and the Calvinistic Saints tended to focus not, as in the case of the Dissenters in the late eighteenth-century, on their potentially treasonous political connections but rather on their personal puritanism and collective hypocrisy. This resulted in perhaps an even more virulent threat to British institutions than the more overtly anti-Anglican Dissenters presented. One of the most common forms which the accusations of hypocrisy took involved the alleged lack of concern which the Saints presented to home atrocities. No doubt the pro-slavery Right would have vastly enjoyed a diversion of the Saints' efforts towards the plight of the Spitalfield weavers or the boy chimney sweeps as the *Satirist, Common Sense, Morning Journal*, and *Watchman* advocated.[159] That, like the equally successful single-issue pressure group, the Anti-Corn Law League, they did not do so, that they did not split their energies from their chief political cause, anti-slavery, however felicitous for slaves it may have been in the long run, did open them to the charge that they were as *John Bull* termed Exeter Hall, the "temple of hypocrisy."[160]

Notwithstanding such emphasis, there was some equation of Wilberforce and his movement with Jacobinism. As early as 1792, an

---

[152] A name given her in Murray's "Influence of the French revolution," pp. 50–7.
[153] For example, *Guardian of Education*, 2 (January 1803), p. 62.
[154] *Anti-Jacobin Review*, 55 (December 1818), p. 306.
[155] *British Critic*, 15, n.ser. (March 1821), p. 227.
[156] *Orthodox Churchman's Magazine*, April 1801, p. 96.
[157] *Christian Remembrancer*, 10 (March 1829), p. 135.
[158] See, ESRO, Boucher Papers, BOU/B/5/11, Daubeny to Boucher, October 23, 1799. Herbert Marsh, "Inquiry into the consequences of neglecting to give the prayer book with the Bible" (Cambridge, 1812), p. 130.
[159] *Satirist*, August 1, 1808. *Common Sense*, August 15, 1824, p. 21. *Morning Journal*, October 9, 1828. *Watchman*, April 8, 1827.
[160] *John Bull*, June 5, 1831, p. 181.

anonymous pamphlet was accusing him, along with Paine and Clarkson, of constituting the Jacobins of England.[161] And that old Pittite the Earl of Westmorland was convinced that the Slave Importation Restriction Bill had originated among "atheists, enthusiasts, jacobins, and such descriptions of persons."[162] And of course Windham, of whom Wilberforce thought, quite correctly, that no two men could be more different from each other in their ideas than they were,[163] perhaps somewhat playfully suggested that Wilberforce would delight in sending aristocrats to the guillotine.[164] What I suspect much of the Right meant by these common charges was not that Wilberforce (or the Saints or Methodists) intended, like Priestley (and many Dissenters) just might have, to establish a Jacobin republic in England, but rather that by his attempt to take Christianity to what he regarded as its logical conclusion, he meant, in the words of the *Age*, to effect the "subversion of the established order of things."[165]

Gerald Newman in his study of eighteenth-century English nationalism may well be accurate when he discerns the "profoundly subversive" threat, every bit as lethal as the Jacobin one, which the Saints posed to the religious tradition of nominal Christianity, the elitism, the literary culture, the manners, morals, and amusements of Britain's *ancien régime*.[166] And Newman's thesis may well answer the paradox which Gayle Pendleton thought odd and Ford K. Brown thought unbelievable, that the High Church party should attempt to destroy such "conservative pillars" as Hannah More or Wilberforce, given their high views on the subordination of the masses.[167] When Samuel Johnson's High Church protégé, Mrs. Piozzi, maintained that the wicked influence of Wilberforce left "all ranks, all customs, all colours, all religions *jumbled together*,"[168] she was merely reiterating a common criticism of the Saints which entered deep into the intellectual make-up of a certain type of Anglican: Wilberforce and his movement blurred the distinction

[161] Davis, *Problem of Slavery in Age of Revolution*, p. 364.

[162] *Parl. Deb.*, VII (May 16, 1806), p. 230.

[163] Robert Isaac Wilberforce, Samuel Wilberforce, eds., *Correspondence of William Wilberforce* (London, 1840), Wilberforce to More, November 15, 1804, I, p. 340.

[164] Anstey, *Atlantic Slave Trade*, p. 180.   [165] *Age*, July 31, 1825, pp. 92–3.

[166] Gerald Newman, *Rise of English Nationalism* (New York, 1987), pp. 234–5, 237.

[167] Gayle Trusdale Pendleton, "English conservative propaganda during the French Revolution, 1789–1802," Ph.D. dissertation (Emory University, 1976), p. 125n.

[168] Oswald G. Knapp, *Intimate Letters of Hester Piozzi and Penelope Pennington, 1788–1821* (London, 1914), pp. 236, 243–4.

between orthodox Anglicanism and its enemies, whether those foes were formally within or without the established Church. By his strict Calvinist evangelicalism, his seeming adoption of Methodist disciplinary attitudes, his communicating (on occasion) in dissenting chapels,[169] Wilberforce seemed to deny the long-range need for an independent Church of England to minister to the English people.

But to insist that much of the early-nineteenth-century Tory press, and even some notable political figures, loathed Wilberforce, evangelicalism, and its concomitant puritanism, is to retail only half the story. Consistency after all is the virtue of small minds. There is a sense in which Wilberforce and his various causes represented the spirit of the age far more than did William Windham or Theodore Hook and theirs. As can be seen from the composition of the Vice Society, "Church and King" elements were no more immune from that reforming zeal, at least on many issues, than their enemies. Nor were even the most anti-Wilberforceian sections of the press, which after all, had long undertaken crusades against *Whig* infidelity, irreligion, and sexual misconduct, exempt from its own form of prudery. Upper-class society in general, whether Whig or Tory was too full of juicy scandal to allow any inchoate anti-puritanism to get in the way. Part of this prurient assault may have been pornographic, meant as much to sell newspapers or magazines as to register moral outrage. The *Satirist* in 1808[170] and the *Age* in the 1820s[171] printed "Tables of Adultery," listing notorious upper-class examples of the genre that passed through the courts, and in the process no doubt titillating the public. The *Satirist* as well gave monthly accounts of fashionable, noble and anonymous seducers of their country tenants.[172] In the *Porcupine*, Cobbett, the great enemy of vice societies, nonetheless waxed eloquently about "disgraceful" West End London routs and suppers during Passion week and young British ladies who reminded him of Herodias. Yet at the same time he filled his newspaper with sexual double entendres and veiled sexual metaphors along the lines of the "solid advantage" received by the notorious Margravine of Anspach or Godoy's penetration of the favor of the Spanish royal family.[173]

Prominent Tories and servants of Tory governments, if not as

[169] A. D. Harvey, *Britain in the Early Nineteenth Century* (London, 1978), p. 76.
[170] For example, *Satirist*, September 1, 1808, pp. 131–6.
[171] For example, *Age*, July 9, 1826, p. 484.   [172] *Satirist*, August 1, 1808, p. 40 *passim*.
[173] *Porcupine*, April 18, 1801; September 21, 1801; August 28, 1801.

frequent victims of this sort of right-wing denunciation as Whigs, were nonetheless sometimes exposed. The *Satirist* denounced Pitt's Lord Lieutenant of Ireland, the Duke of Rutland, as an adulterer prone to dragging innocent lasses from "their paternal groves to revel in all the dissipations of the Irish court."[174] Both the *Anti-Jacobin Review* and the *Quarterly Review* called for a halt to the cult of Nelson due to his liaison with Emma Hamilton.[175] The *Standard*, which hated him because of his advanced liberal views on political economy, accused Huskisson of association with "unfeminine women of rank ... forgetful of the decencies of morality."[176] After Wellington, as prime minister, and George IV betrayed the ultra Right on Catholic emancipation, their press was full of vicious slurs on Harriet Arbuthnot and Lady Conyngham.[177]

What is noteworthy is the extent to which certain sections of the right-wing press were prepared to inflame the embers of class envy in order to prevail upon the aristocracy, Whig and Tory, to mend its ways. Hence in 1819 the government-subsidized *British Monitor*, after pointing out that the rich increasingly were guilty of adultery, seductions, and gambling, suggested that the chancellor of the exchequer introduce a property tax rather than taxing the tea of the poor.[178] The *White Dwarf* condemned baronets "Gouty and emaciated with London debaucheries" and aristocrats "squandering their property in the gaming-houses of that sink of infamy, Brussels," rather than protecting their powerless agricultural tenants against evil estate agents.[179] A generation before Stephen Blackpool said the same thing in *Hard Times*, the *Standard* admitted that the poor were discriminated against in the current state of the divorce laws which in essence ensured one law for the rich and another for the poor.[180] The *Age* wondered why lower-class drunkards and gamblers were sent to prison but not upper-class ones.[181]

On two concrete issues the right wing and High Church could oppose the dissenting, Methodist, and Wilberforceian Anglican interest altogether, and perhaps attract less odium than a concerted activity against the abolition of slavery: the proliferation of Bible societies, especially the non-denominational British and Foreign

---

[174] *Satirist*, May 1809, p. 471.
[175] *Anti-Jacobin Review*, 22 (December 1805), p. 436. *Quarterly Review*, 11 (April 1814), p. 73.
[176] *Standard*, July 9, 1827.   [177] See, for example, *Morning Journal*, February 5, 1829.
[178] *British Monitor*, December 13, 1819.   [179] *White Dwarf*, December 13, 1817.
[180] *Standard*, March 25, 1830.
[181] *Age*, June 12, 1825, p. 36.

Bible Society, and the question of denominational education in England. Perhaps no organization (save for the University of London) aroused the fire of certain sections of the Right more than the BFBS, founded in 1804, to distribute Bibles to the populations at home and abroad. The ideology behind the organization especially appealed to those areas of the Christian communion most geared toward bibliolatry and least geared toward a liturgical branch of Christianity with its devotion to a prayer book replete with collects and litanies. From a narrow viewpoint, to support the seemingly innocuous and even praiseworthy Bible societies, was to support cooperation with descendants of historic puritanism who had threatened king and Church, and who, in general, denied the necessity of episcopal ordination. The *British Critic* proclaimed the BFBS "evil."[182] The *Anti-Jacobin Review* thought it sinful to cooperate at any level with anti-episcopal Dissenters even in Asia or even if no other medium was available to promote the Christian faith.[183] In the early nineteenth century, the Hackney group and its *Orthodox Churchman's Magazine*[184] shrilly censored the Bible society as did the more vulgar right-wing papers of the 1820s such as *John Bull* and the *Morning Journal*.[185] And few subjects more disoriented and enraged the High Church and orthodox Right, in the press and in Hackney, than the tolerance and indeed support which various ministerial figures gave to the Saints on the issue of the British and Foreign Bible Society.

Nothing more clearly shows the relative weakness and isolation of the Tory and High Church Right, as well as popular support for what later might be termed a Victorian value system, than the way in which leading Tory politicians and the higher-circulation government dailies justified the evangelical position on issues dear to Wilberforce. Both Bishop Marsh of Peterborough[186] and the *Anti-Jacobin Review* were horrified that Spencer Perceval, as prime minister, associated with Bible societies.[187] During the Liverpool administration, Coleridge was disgusted that Viscount Sidmouth, the home secretary, and Nicholas Vansittart, the chancellor of the

[182] *British Critic*, 9, n.ser. (February 1818), p. 204; 2, n.ser. (July 1814), p. 1.
[183] *Anti-Jacobin Review*, 34 (September 1809), pp. 94–6.
[184] *Orthodox Churchman's Magazine*, 9 (July 1805), pp. 56–7.
[185] *John Bull*, September 18, 1825, pp. 301–2. *Morning Journal*, January 22, 1829.
[186] Herbert Marsh, "Letter to the Right Hon. N. Vansittart, M.P." (Cambridge, 1812), p. 410.
[187] *Anti-Jacobin Review*, 39 (May 1811), p. 81.

exchequer, supported national meetings of the British and Foreign Bible Society at the Egyptian Hall in London.[188] In the early 1820s, the *British Critic* criticized the prime minister himself for attending a BFBS meeting on the isle of Thanet;[189] the sort of conduct which led *John Bull* to accuse Liverpool of consorting with puritans, Round-heads, and Quakers.[190] That these views were somewhat eccentric can be seen from the reaction of the greater London press. Croker's *Guardian* defended Wilberforce against Theodore Hook's *John Bull*;[191] as did the Canningite *New Times*.[192] The government-subsidized *Courier*, was as warmly supportive of the Bible Society as was its paymaster Liverpool.[193] The leading ultra-Protestant daily, the *Standard*, viewed the objection of Churchmen to the Bible Society as secondary to the great cause of Christ, and saw the BFBS itself as "an instrument in the hand of God for the diffusion of Christianity throughout the world."[194] The most important monthly periodical in the British Isles, the Tory *Blackwood's Edinburgh Magazine*, perhaps because of its location in the midst of Presbyterian Scotland, was always less oriented towards Anglican causes than most of its sister political publications in Ireland or England. True to form, it consist-ently supported the BFBS throughout the 1820s, even warning the High Churchmen that their attitude towards the Dissenters might plunge the Church into ruin.[195] In general, the closer the relation-ship with the irenic government or the more distant the paper or periodical from the London or Oxford center of High Church Anglicanism, the more tolerant it tended to be towards some level of religious cooperation with Dissenters or the Saints.

The other, related, issue which divided much of the right-wing press and its Hackney allies in the High Church movement from leading Tory politicians and even from the royal family was the cause of denominational education. The latter supported the Lan-castrian schools, where non-sectarian religious training was the norm, while the former cherished the Bellian National Schools

[188] Gabrielle Festing, *John Hookham Frere and His Friends* (London, 1899), Coleridge to Frere, December 19, 1816, pp. 221–2.
[189] *British Critic*, 18, n.ser. (December 1822), p. 562.
[190] *John Bull*, September 18, pp. 301–2.
[191] *Guardian*, June 10, 1821.   [192] *New Times*, October 8, 1821.   .
[193] *Courier*, January 8, 1819.
[194] *Standard*, May 6, 1830.
[195] *Blackwood's Edinburgh Magazine*, 18 (November 1825), pp. 621–35. For a further discussion of the conservative response to the BFBS, see Robert Hole, *Pulpits, Politics and Public Order in England, 1760–1832* (Cambridge, England, 1989), pp. 190–3.

which saw the liturgy and formularies of the Church of England as the medium of instruction. Dissenters, of course, and their evangelical allies were enthusiastic supporters of the Lancastrian experiment.

In this situation, unlike that of the British and Foreign Bible Society, the right-wing press, with only a few exceptions, such as W. Hughes' Percevallian *National Advisor*[196] and, predictably, *Blackwood's Edinburgh Magazine*,[197] supported the Rev. Andrew Bell and his vision of an Anglican national education for the non-elite. Coleridge's paean to "dear Dr. Bell" the "great man"[198] and Southey's laudatory introductory biography of the same dear friend are typical of the shower of praise Bell received from conservative men of literature and journalists. Some, like the reviewer in the *British Critic*,[199] who wished the little children to be frequently reminded of the fate of Korath, Dathan, and Abirham, who took upon themselves the priestly office without ordination, obviously wanted to go farther even than the supremely orthodox Bell. And the vilification by much of the Right of Joseph Lancaster, even before the discovery of his rather unorthodox sexual practices, was on the plane of their similar tirades against Huskisson or Wilberforce. Coleridge proclaimed him privately a "wretched quack" and publicly denounced him as poisoning the poor with paternalistic infidelity.[200] The *Anti-Jacobin Review* doubted Lancaster's Christian credentials[201] and to Archdeacon Daubeny he was a "new Julian the Apostate and an emissary of Satan."[202] Given such views, it made it all the more embarrassing when such luminaries as George III,[203] his prime minister, Spencer Perceval,[204] much of the royal family, some of the Church of England bishops,[205] Pitt's biographer and the permanent secretary to the Pitt Club, John Gifford,[206] and,

---

[196] *National Advisor*, September 7, 1811; January 1, 1812.

[197] *Blackwood's Edinburgh Magazine*, 7 (July 1820), pp. 419–22; 7 (August 1820), pp. 537–8.

[198] Earl Leslie Griggs, ed., *Collected Letters of Samuel Taylor Coleridge* (Oxford, 1959), Coleridge to Bell, April 15, 1808, III, p. 89.

[199] *British Critic*, 2, n.ser. (November 1814), pp. 540–1.

[200] *Letters of Coleridge*, Coleridge to Bell, May 17, 1808, III, p. 105. R. J. White, ed., *Collected Works of Samuel Taylor Coleridge* (Princeton, 1972), VI, pp. 40–1.

[201] *Anti-Jacobin Review*, 29 (January 1808), p. 45.

[202] R. A. Soloway, *Prelates and People: Ecclesiastical Social Thought in England, 1783–1852* (London, 1969), p. 371.

[203] *Anti-Jacobin Review*, 39 (January 1808), p. 45.

[204] Brown, *Fathers of Victorians*, p. 346.

[205] *Anti-Jacobin Review*, 23 (January 1806), pp. 85–6.

[206] Brown, *Fathers of Victorians*, p. 346.

after some hesitation, the Pittite pamphleteer, John Bowles,[207] made clear their support for Lancaster's British and Foreign School Society. The *Anti-Jacobin Review* indeed wondered how the king could reconcile his sponsorship of Lancaster with his much flaunted coronation oath.[208]

In the 1820s, the Tory press was also united in its opposition to the establishment of a University of London devoid of an Anglican religious component. The suppositions of the *British Critic* that it would be a "monster both in politics and morals"[209] or the *Morning Post* that it was meant by "Infidel Politicians" to "advance the progress of infidelity,"[210] are typical views.

With George III supporting Joseph Lancaster, Sidmouth aiding the British and Foreign Bible Society, and Hackney divided in its attitude towards Wilberforceian morality and social justice, it is clear that however strongly certain rightist elements might feel on such matters, no common High Church front could possibly unite Pittite politicians or the Tory press against any perceived threat from evangelicalism. This was especially true after the departure of the Burkeite and Windhamite forces from Pittite ranks weakened those few Pittite politicians who were prepared to stand their ground against it. But the failure of early-nineteenth-century High Church or specifically Tory clerical, political, or journalistic figures to work out some sort of internal agreement on the validity of evangelicalism no doubt left them weakened as well when facing what most of them regarded as an even greater threat to historic Anglicanism than puritanism, a revived and strengthened Church of Rome.

207 John Bowles, "View of the moral state of society, at the close of the eighteenth century. Much enlarged" (London, 1804), pp. 106–7. Brown, *Fathers of Victorians*, p. 346.

208 *Anti-Jacobin Review*, 39 (June 1811), p. 209. There were, of course, those on the Right who combatted any education for the working classes at all. The *Satirist* opposed *any* Sunday schools or system of universal education, March 1, 1812. The *Anti-Jacobin Review* too wondered, along with its horror at Lancaster's non-denominational religious experiments, whether Sunday schools in general might have done more harm than good, 21 (June 1805), p. 156. And the irrepressible *John Bull*, while not tackling the issue of national education as such, in its long crusade against Mechanics' Institutes revealed an anti-intellectual outlook that was by no means unique among its peers. The *Bull* wondered whether a journeyman brick-layer would do better work or achieve happiness or make his family more comfortable by his attendance at Dr. Birkbeck's magnetism discussions or Olinthus Gregory's classes on Hindu poetry, March 19, 1826, 6, p. 93.

209 *British Critic*, 23, n.ser. (April 1825), pp. 347–8.   210 *Morning Post*, March 17, 1828.

CHAPTER 9

The Right and Catholicism

I

Since the birth of modern political and ideological movements, the Church of Rome has always presented a problem to parties and individuals of the non-Catholic Right. (It may also have presented problems to the Catholic Right, but that is another story.) Standing as an oasis of stability in a world seemingly prone to bewildering social, economic, and, after 1789 (or in England, 1641), political change; supremely confident of her self-worth and intellectual rectitude in a sphere where such self-confidence was becoming rarer; presenting her supporters with historical justifications for her authority which impressed even many of her most severe critics; and underlining that authority with an artistic, musical, and liturgical experience that could embody normal simplicity with the occasional baroque grandeur, the Roman Church, especially (though not exclusively) after the French Revolution, exerted a noticeable and understandable fascination upon assorted European non-Catholic men and women. Hence, Johann August Starck, the German Lutheran pastor, sought Lutheran–Catholic solidarity against the principles of 1789;[1] the Lutheran poet Novalis in his highly influential *Die Christenheit oder Europa* prayed for a renewal of faith in the Virgin and the Saints;[2] Friedrich von Gentz, perhaps, after Burke, the greatest of the European counter-revolutionary political theorists, admired Catholicism exceedingly, if from afar;[3] and, of course, Count Leopold Stolberg, Friedrich Schlegal, and Adam Müller adopted a more permanent spiritual relationship with the mother Church.[4]

[1] Klaus Epstein, *Genesis of German Conservatism* (Princeton, 1966), pp. 508–9.
[2] Novalis, *Hymns to the Night and Other Selected Writings* (Indianapolis, 1960), p. 62.
[3] Golo Mann, *Secretary of Europe: Life of Friedrich Gentz, Enemy of Napoleon* (New Haven, 1946), p. 61.
[4] Epstein, *German Conservatism*, p. 674.

217

In England too, which certainly never went as far liturgically or perhaps as far doctrinally from the medieval Church as did the European Lutheran or Calvinist communities, this tug from Rome was felt. The High Church lay leader William Stevens by the 1780s was perfectly willing to countenance praying for the dead,[5] with all the doctrinal baggage which such a practice implied. Archdeacon Daubeny, Stevens' ally in the High Church movement, in his influential *Guide to the Church* (1797), while treating Catholicism with much greater respect than he treats the dissenting churches, developed the branch theory of the Church of Christ, with England, Rome, and Constantinople all separate limbs of that true faith.[6] Cobbett, of course, while full of vicious anti-dissenting prejudices, hankered in a manner of speaking after the medieval orders of monks and nuns who cared for the poor and distressed and repaired the parish churches.[7] In 1819, the *New Times* was prepared to defend, up to a point, the doctrine of transubstantiation.[8] Even more important, the *British Critic*, in a series heavily influenced by the pre-Tractarian High Church movement, acknowledged in the late 1820s the pope as "chief bishop of the Western Church."[9]

Thus, as we shall see, despite an *increase* not a *decrease* in anti-Catholicism on the Right during the early nineteenth century, it is still possible to concur with Marilyn Butler who views the English cultural scene, especially in the 1820s, as partaking in a powerful European religious revival, heavily influenced by High Church or Catholic tendencies.[10] In a way, however, because of the peculiar historical position of the English Church and its somewhat less drastic break than those of the Lutheran and Calvinist communions with the medieval past, it was easier to resurrect or recreate a Catholic *mentalité* in the Church of England than in most of her sister Protestant churches. Hence, much of the spirit which Novalis or Schlegal admired about Catholicism could be transferred in England to the national Church, allowing an admittedly uneasy mixture of Catholic revival and extreme anti-Romanism to coexist

---

5 ESRO, Boucher Papers, BOU/B/3/21, Stevens to Boucher, September 12, 1785.

6 Charles Daubeny, *Guide to the Church* (New York, 1803), p. 131. In his *An Appendix to the Guide to the Church*, Daubeny vigorously defended the Roman Church against charges that it was the whore of Babylon, idolatrous, and no true Church of Christ, (London, 1830), p. 92.

7 John W. Osborne, *William Cobbett: His Thought and His Times* (New Brunswick, NJ, 1966), p. 217. Gertrude Himmelfarb, *Idea of Poverty: England in the Early Industrial Age* (New York, 1985), p. 223.

8 *New Times*, June 11, 1819.   9 *British Critic*, 2, 4th ser. (July 1827), p. 17.

10 Marilyn Butler, *Romantics, Rebels, and Reactionaries* (New York, 1982), p. 174.

in early-nineteenth-century Anglicanism. In the age of Johnson, when the High Church Anglican option was not so prevalent in England, when there was little sense of a High Church press or liturgical expression, it was much easier to take a more benign view of Rome. In part, the level of anti-Romanism rose as the confidence of a renewed High Church Anglicanism waxed.

Even before the Oxford movement of the 1830s, a significant portion of English High Church groupings, however defined, had come to accept the necessity for the apostolic succession. The doubts expressed by both G. I. T. Machin and Desmond Bowen that the doctrine had made much headway, either among the episcopacy or the High Church political class,[11] while accurate in the longer haul may be in error for at least the early nineteenth century. While it had certainly been a common enough belief (though by no means universally held) in the Restoration Church, by the early eighteenth century it may have become more the doctrine of a party rather than of the Church as a whole.[12] There continued to be some support for the apostolic succession in the later eighteenth century. The Jacobite press of the 1750s was still stressing its importance.[13] Samuel Johnson, who of course preferred Catholicism to Presbyterianism largely because of his adherence to the apostolic succession,[14] incorporated it into his very definition of both a Tory and a Jacobite.[15] But, given the paucity of references to the apostolic succession in the century, one wonders if the High Church John Wesley was not in this matter more typical of his communion than his lay admirer, Johnson. For, despite his education by his High Church and Jacobite father in a faith in the apostolic succession, Wesley had come to believe as early as 1746 that bishops and prebyters were of the same order and that both had the ordinal power.[16] F. C. Mather denotes the end of the eighteenth century as the nadir of any observable liturgical High Church movement in

---

[11] G. I. T. Machin, *Politics and the Churches in Great Britain, 1832 to 1868* (Oxford, 1977), pp. 75–6. Desmond Bowen, *Idea of the Victorian Church* (Montreal, 1968), p. 52.

[12] Certainly, in 1702, the Church of England bishops demurred acknowledging the apostolic succession when the lower house of Convocation called for it. Mark Goldie, "The nonjurors, episcopacy, and the origins of the Convocation controversy," in Eveline Cruickshanks, ed., *Ideology and Conspiracy: Aspects of Jacobitism, 1689–1759* (Edinburgh, 1982), p. 28.

[13] See, for example, *True Briton*, 3 (January, 16, 1751), p. 52.

[14] James Boswell, *Life of Johnson* (London, 1953), p. 424.

[15] James Sledd, Gavin Kolb, "Johnson's definitions of Whig and Tory," *PMLA*, 67 (September 1952), p. 882. Boswell, *Life of Johnson*, p. 305.

[16] Gordon Rupp, *Religion in England, 1688–1791* (Oxford, 1986), p. 438.

England in terms of Laudian or Caroline ceremonials such as the sign of the cross, vestments or bowing to the altar.[17] The same period probably saw a similar decline in much effective belief in the apostolic succession.

In 1797, Charles Daubeny's *Guide to the Church* asserted that Timothy, Titus, Ignatius, Polycarp, and Clemens exercised the same episcopal office as modern Church of England bishops.[18] In the *Appendix* (1804) to the *Guide to the Church* Daubeny further expanded upon his classic theory of apostolic succession: the Church included "every Christian society, possessing the characteristic marks of the Church of Christ, [this] I consider to be a separate branch of the Catholic or universal visible Church upon earth." These are "connected together as one body, by the profession of the same fundamental articles of faith, and the same divinely instituted form of government." They included the Churches of England, Ireland, Rome, Denmark, Sweden, Greece, and Russia with the non-national communities of episcopal Churches in Scotland and the United States.[19]

Daubeny's views, or his restatement of traditional if archaic notions, were immediately accepted by the High Church religious press and by some of the secular right-wing press. The *Orthodox Churchman's Magazine* viewed the belief in apostolic succession in 1803 as the *sine qua non* of a true Church[20] and Hackney's *Christian Remembrancer* at its inception in 1819 also described it as the "only qualification" of a Church.[21] Bishop Heber of Calcutta defended the doctrine in the pages of the *Quarterly Review*;[22] the *British Critic* accepted it by the second decade of the nineteenth century;[23] and, more surprisingly, the irreverent Sunday newspaper *John Bull*, perhaps on account of the editor's brother, the High Church Dean of Worcester, made its acceptance one of their consistent causes.[24] The grafting of the full-blown theory of the apostolic succession

---

[17] F. C. Mather, "Georgian churchmanship reconsidered: some variations in Anglican public worship, 1714–1830," *JEH*, 36 (April 1985), pp. 258–60.

[18] Daubeny, *Guide to Church*, p. 35.   [19] Daubeny, *Appendix*, pp. 91–2.

[20] *Orthodox Churchman's Magazine*, 4 (January 1803), p. 47.

[21] *Christian Remembrancer*, August 1819, p. 487.

[22] *Quarterly Review*, 24 (October 1820), p. 2.

[23] *British Critic*, 10, n.ser. (September 1818), p. 313.

[24] *John Bull*, December 14, 1823, p. 396; August 13, 1826, p. 261. When William Wordsworth confessed in 1844 that he was unable to consider episcopal authority one of the great points of Catholic doctrine, he was probably reflecting the prevailing Anglican view of his boyhood. Ernest de Selincourt, ed., *Letters of William and Dorothy Wordsworth: The Later Years* (Oxford, 1939), Wordsworth to Gladstone, March 21, 1844, III, pp. 1199–1200.

upon the already (in some quarters) well-developed view of the Church of England as the purest of earthly Christian communions could produce a captivating ecclesiastical vision. The *Anti-Jacobin Review* in one of its last issues portrayed the English Church as *the* "principal branch of the vine" of Christ's true Church and foresaw her spread throughout southern Africa and Australasia until in the fullness of time and by God's grace English Christianity would pervade the earth.[25]

II

Noticeably absent from Daubeny and the *Anti-Jacobin's* vision glorious was any sympathy with the Reformation. In an age of social and political upheaval remarkably similar in some ways, as Burke discerned in 1791, to the age of the Reformation itself,[26] when the counter-revolutionary virtues of social stability, political orthodoxy, and admiration for tradition were highly prized, it was often difficult to rouse much enthusiasm, even among ostensible Protestants, for past revolts against pontifical or regal authority. Certainly parallels between reformers of the sixteenth and eighteenth centuries were not lost on Catholic Europe. A generation before 1789, Fernando de Zevallos, a Spanish Hieronymite monk, was arguing that the *philosophes* were the offspring of the Protestant reformers.[27] Abbé Barruel, in one of his first noteworthy publications, identified the French revolutionaries of 1791 with rebellious Hussites, Lutherans, and Calvinists and predicted that as the ancient Reformation led to religious anarchy so would the modern one lead to political disorder.[28] And the two leading counter-revolutionary political theorists, de Maistre and de Bonald, viewed the edict of Nantes as, in the latter's words, the fountainhead of the French Revolution.[29] Even in Protestant Europe, Novalis viewed Pastor Martin's dividing of the

---

25 *Anti-Jacobin Review*, 59 (September 1820), appendix, p. 2. Peter Benedict Nockles, too, sees the belief in the apostolic succession quite widespread in High Church circles after 1800. "Continuity and change in Anglican High Churchmanship in Britain, 1792–1850," D.Phil. thesis (Oxford University, 1982), pp. 165ff.

26 Burke, *Works*, IV, pp. 318–9.

27 Richard Herr, *Eighteenth-Century Revolution in Spain* (Princeton, 1958), p. 215.

28 Paul H. Beik, *French Revolution Seen From the Right: Social Theories in Motion, 1789–1799* in *Transactions of the American Philosophical Society* (Philadelphia, 1956), p. 48.

29 Jacques Godechot, *Counter-Revolution: Doctrine and Action, 1789–1804*, (London, 1972), pp. 94, 97.

universal Christian community as leading Europe to "religious anarchy."[30]

Such opinions, both Catholic and Protestant, both preceding and following the French Revolution, found echoes on the Right in Protestant England. The political struggles of the seventeenth century between Puritanism and Cavalier Anglicanism had, of course, left a residue of historical and religious bitterness that still aggravated English Christianity in the eighteenth and nineteenth centuries. But over and above that was (for the English Right) the problem of the Reformation itself. The Tory John Shebbeare in his unpublished "Introduction" to Clarendon's *History of the Reign of Charles II* came close to questioning the necessity for the Reformation.[31] John Reeves remarked somewhat injudiciously in his notorious high prerogative pamphlet, "Thoughts on the English government," that "most of the errors and misconceptions relative to the nature of our Government, have taken their rise from those two great events, *The Reformation* and what is called *The Revolution*."[32] Charles Daubeny, the leading theorist of the High Church movement, was equally censorious of the Reformation. In his *Guide to the Church* he made it clear that his faith derived not from Luther or Calvin but from the Bible[33] and in his *Appendix* stressed that all the reformers were men more of zeal than of judgment.[34] Daubeny was always careful to argue, in light of his views on the Church of England's enjoying a pure apostolic succession from the medieval Church, that the Reformation was caused by the corruption, not doctrinal error, of the Roman Church.[35] Thus, when the usually satirical *John Bull* apostrophized in 1826 that they were *"Catholic"* with the apostolic succession and as such disregarded Martin

---

[30] Novalis, *Hymns to Night*, p. 49.

[31] John Shebbeare, ed., *History of the Reign of King Charles the Second, from the Restoration to the End of the Year 1667* by Edward Hyde, first Earl of Clarendon (London, 1757?), p. iv.

[32] John Reeves, "Thoughts on the English government" (London, 1795), p. 25. Such language allowed R. B. Sheridan to decimate Reeves in the House of Commons. *Parl. Hist.*, xxxii (November 26, 1795), pp. 628–9.

[33] Daubeny, *Guide to Church*, p. 83.   [34] Daubeny, *Appendix*, p. 161.

[35] Nancy Uhlar Murray, "Influence of the French Revolution on the Church of England and its rivals, 1789–1802," D.Phil. thesis (Oxford University, 1975), p. 68. Owen Chadwick suspects that this High Church repudiation of Lutheranism and Calvinism – a repudiation more serious than at any time since the Reformation – was due to the spread of rationalism in continental Protestantism. This, of course, assumes that Shebbeare, Daubeny, Reeves and others paid much attention to such intellectual ferment. I have seen little evidence that they did. I would suspect that this anti-Reformation feeling was more deeply rooted in English history and merely aggravated after 1789. *Mind of the Oxford Movement* (Stanford, 1967), p. 23.

Luther, John Calvin, and the Synod of Dort as they did popery,[36] or when Hurrell Froude, the *fons et origo* of the Oxford movement, wrote of "odious Protestantism stick[ing] ... in people's gizzard,"[37] they were reflecting a persistent – if by no means dominant – repudiation of the continental reforming tradition on the part of the English Right.

Going along with this questioning attitude towards the reformers was an attempt, at least in the first generation of the revived High Church movement, to deny the ancient Protestant notion, based on the prophetic books of *Daniel* and *Revelation*, that papal Rome was Anti-Christ. Indeed, no one issue so separated the pre-1800 and post-1800 High Church movement as much as the former's assertion that Anti-Christ did not reside in Rome and the latter's suspicion (at the least) that he did. Both Bishop Horsley of Rochester and the Rev. James Kirby, two leaders of the High Church movement in the 1790s, denied that the pope was Anti-Christ.[38] Jones of Nayland in fact explicitly identified French principles (in a generic way) not the Bishop of Rome, as the Man of Sin.[39]

The favorable view of some High Church elements towards Roman Catholicism points towards an eighteenth-century phenomenon, existing before as well as immediately after the French Revolution, and standing in stark contrast to the general High Church attitude in the early nineteenth century. Part of this pro-Catholic theme may be a residue of Jacobite or even Tory prejudices alive long after the demise of Jacobitism and the turn of the term "Tory" from the name of an important political party to at best a description of a tendency. But that a pro-Catholic attitude was wider than Jacobitism or Toryism can be seen from, for example, the Northite press of the age of the American Revolution, in itself neither Jacobite nor Tory. Part of this phenomenon may arise from an ideological grouping of orthodox Trinitarian sympathizers, Roman Catholics and Anglicans, united in the face of the increasing rationalistic unitarianism of the dissenting churches (a threat largely deflected by the early nineteenth century) not to speak of the Voltaireian

---

36 *John Bull*, August 13, 1826, p. 261.
37 Machin, *Politics and Churches*, p. 81. Nockles seems to regard this anti-Reformation tradition of the Oxford movement as somehow unique to them. "Continuity and change," p. 317. I think, however, that it was very much present in the older, High Church tradition.
38 Murray, "Influence of French Revolution," p. 67.
39 *Anti-Jacobin Review*, 5 (March 1800), p. 472.

menace. Then too, the obvious weakness of the Roman Church in the eighteenth (as opposed to the succeeding) century may have caused its normal Anglican critics to sheathe their swords a bit. Whatever the cause, the general attitude of what can loosely be called the eighteenth-century English "Right" towards Roman Catholicism calls somewhat into question J. C. D. Clark's contention that only in the unusual circumstances of the 1790s was English Trinitarian Protestantism not largely anti-papist.[40]

Paul K. Monod has offered the insight that the early-eighteenth-century and mid-eighteenth-century Jacobite press consistently held Presbyterianism and republicanism to be far worse forms of slavery than Roman Catholicism or monarchy.[41] And as the Jacobite press of the Walpoleian period slid, sometimes imperceptibly, into the Tory press of the post-Culloden age, the same general tolerance for Catholicism can be observed. For example, *Felix Farley's Bristol Journal* in the 1750s, both Methodist–Anglican and Tory-oriented, preached the line that atheism and immorality were now the great dangers to England rather than popery.[42] More important than a relatively obscure West Country newspaper, one of the two great mid-eighteenth-century literary monthlies, the Tory *Critical Review*, exhibited even more consistent and more pointed pro-Catholic sentiments. At various times in 1761, for example, reviewers were describing Catholicism as "cruelly persecuted and basely misrepresented" and urging religious writers to cease their attacks upon Romanists since "the days of ignorance, on which the dangerous structure of superstitious zeal was raised, are now happily elapsed."[43] This line continued until 1791 or for as long as the *Critical* remained in a loyalist series, as for example in 1781 when the review proclaimed that "in this enlightened age, popery assumes a new form; and sensible people are no longer alarmed at the phantoms of superstition . . ."[44]

Other relics of pre-1760 Toryism espoused similar viewpoints.

---

[40] J. C. D. Clark, *English Society, 1688–1832* (Cambridge, England, 1985), p. 390. Coliss Mark Haydon, too, in his excellent thesis on anti-Catholicism may overplay the importance of the 1790s in the acceptance by the elite of Roman Catholics and demonizing of Dissenters. "Anti-Catholicism in eighteenth-century England, *c.* 1714–*c.* 1780," D.Phil. thesis (Oxford University, 1985), pp. 295ff.

[41] Paul K. Monod, "For the king to come into his own again: Jacobite political culture in England, 1688–1788," Ph.D. dissertation (Yale University, 1985), p. 56.

[42] *Felix Farley's Bristol Journal*, January 18, 1755.

[43] *Critical Review*, 11 (January 1761), pp. 44–5; 11 (February 1761), p. 116.

[44] *Ibid.*, 51 (January 1781), p. 51.

William King, the guiding spirit of Oxford Toryism, maintained in his memoirs a cordial disposition towards Catholicism.[45] Boswell's Johnson preferred Roman Catholicism to Protestant Presbyterianism on account of the apostolic succession[46] and Piozzi's Johnson mourned the dissolution of the Society of Jesus itself in 1773.[47] John Shebbeare, the Tory apologist of the 1750s and 1760s, not surprisingly also viewed a Presbyterian as worse than a Romanist on the grounds that just in one century, the seventeenth, the former shed more blood than the latter had done throughout history.[48] Perhaps more remarkably in the 1770s when his extreme Toryism had shaded into pensioned Northite loyalism, Shebbeare defended the Roman Catholic martyrs under Elizabeth as merely "preaching their doctrines, like Augustin, who first promulgated the same Christian faith, and established that religion, for which they died, among our ancestors." Shebbeare condemned the Puritan advisors of Elizabeth and James for persecuting the Catholic martyrs and even for (possibly) contriving the Gunpowder Plot. He also called for the revocation of the anti-Catholic penal laws as a "disgrace to government and to the liberal spirit of our church and constitution . . ."[49]

The two most visible members of an Anglo-American "Tory" tradition which emerged out of the struggle against (largely) Presbyterian and Congregational interests in the colonies were also more tolerant of Catholicism than most opponents of the Quebec Act on either continent. Governor Hutchinson of Massachusetts had by the 1770s, as his most recent biographer has emphasized, moved beyond his New England contemporaries in his moderately pro-Catholic views.[50] Jonathan Boucher, though situated in the Anglican southern colonies, at least claimed a generation later to have delivered sermons before the first shot of the American rebellion was fired calling for toleration for Catholics, describing Anglican anti-Catholicism as a "groundless grudge," and reminding his fellow

45 William King, *Political and Literary Anecdotes of His Own Time* (London, 1818) p. 14.
46 Boswell, *Life of Johnson*, p. 424.
47 S. C. Roberts, ed., *Anecdotes of Samuel Johnson* by Hester Lynch Piozzi (Freeport, New York, 1969), pp. 66–9.
48 John Shebbeare, "Letters on the English nation" (London, 1755), I, pp. 83–4.
49 John Shebbeare, "An answer to the queries" (London, 1775), pp. 142–5. Lord Mansfield, of course, in the famous case of James Webb, in 1768, also decried the necessity of enforcing the anti-Catholic penal laws on the grounds that neither popes nor Jesuits were any longer powers to be feared. John Halliday, *Life of Mansfield* (London, 1797), p. 170ff.
50 William Pencak, *America's Burke: Mind of Thomas Hutchinson* (Washington, 1982), p. 91.

colonials that Magna Carta was obtained from Romanists.[51] When he came to father a large family at an advanced age after the American war, Boucher wished for a newborn son in a sort of baptismal blessing that he would be further removed from presbyterianism than from popery.[52]

The fledgling High Church movement too, in opposition to its extreme anti-Catholic stand in the nineteenth century, maintained a moderately respectful attitude towards the Roman Church. William Stevens, the High Church Treasurer of Queen Anne's Bounty, certainly viewed historical and contemporary presbyterianism as equal in its persecuting zeal to Roman Catholicism.[53] Archdeacon Daubeny, besides restating the essential catholicity of the Church of England, had a more favorable opinion of the purity of Roman Catholic doctrine than of some non-Anglican Protestant theology.[54]

The Northite press of the 1770s and 1780s was pro-Catholic, including the *General Evening Post*, and (especially) Henry Bate Dudley's *Morning Post* and *Morning Herald*. All three papers emphasized the by now familiar refrain that the Presbyterians were doctrinally and politically more dangerous than the Roman Catholics.[55] The *Post* favored, as did its patron Lord North, a relaxation of the Irish penal laws directed against Roman Catholics, but it also suggested that "the film of bigotry and superstition, is now entirely washed from their [Irish Catholic] eyes," and so, unlike the north Irish Protestant Dissenters, they were now good subjects of George III.[56] The *Herald* in 1781 favored not only relaxing the penal laws against Catholics, but enforcing them in the strictest possible manner against Presbyterians.[57] The leading daily newspaper of

[51] Jonathan Boucher, "View of the causes and consequences of the American revolution in thirteen discourses" (London, 1797), pp. 244–5, 270–1, 277, 286–9.

[52] Anne Y. Zimmer, *Jonathan Boucher: Loyalist in Exile* (Detroit, 1978), p. 245.

[53] [William Stevens], "The revolution vindicated and constitutional liberty asserted" (London, 1777), p. 56.

[54] Daubeny, *Appendix*, p. 393.

[55] See, for example, *General Evening Post*, June 11–13, 1776. *Morning Post*, August 30, 1779. *Morning Herald*, March 24, 1781. The elder Pitt, bred in a purer and more old-fashioned Protestantism, was appalled by analogies favoring Catholics over Dissenters. He wondered how the Bishop of Gloucester could equate the errors of Dissenters, which involved church government or ceremonial, with those of popery's "rank idolatry" and "subversion of all civil as well as religious liberty." William Stanhope Taylor, John Henry Pringle, eds., *Correspondence of William Pitt, Earl of Chatham* (London, 1838), Pitt to Gloucester, October 1762, II, pp. 187–9.

[56] *Morning Post*, April 10, 1778.   [57] *Morning Herald*, March 24, 1781; September 8, 1781.

George III and Lord North also suggested exiling all the Irish and English Dissenters to Scotland and forbidding their public meetings[58] – points to remember in the ever-abiding debate over George III's politics.

Burke, of course, despite his devout Anglicanism and his background in a party which shared the traditional Whig antipathy towards Rome – most obvious at the period of the Quebec Act – was always sympathetic to the religion and the people whence his family had sprung. As he told his son Richard in 1792, besides seeing little difference between the Thirty-Nine Articles and Roman Catholic doctrine, he would far rather see Ireland a happy Catholic land, free of Protestants, than as "an enslaved ... degraded Catholick country as it is ..."[59]

The 1790s were the *anni mirabili* of such pro-Catholic and for that matter pro-Irish sentiments on the Right, as these opinions reached into political circles and highways and byways where they would not, perhaps, normally have entered. Certainly the main cause was the French Revolution and its persecution of the Roman Church, fostering sentiments similar to those of Burke's remark to Catherine II that the cause of French Catholicism was the cause of all churches.[60] And the ancient charge that Dissenters were more dangerous to the Church establishment than Roman Catholics was only strengthened during the initial stages of the French revolutionary period. The circle around Burke constantly used the comparison.[61] Canning practically built his political ideology upon it.[62] Even John Reeves of the Association movement, who defended George III's position that his coronation oath debarred Roman Catholics from parliament and who supported the king's dismissal of Pitt in 1801,[63] was adamant that the greatest danger to Church and state came from presbyterianism not from popery.[64] Pitt's intimate friend, Lord Mulgrave, like his master, supported *Catholic* emancipation in 1801 but had qualms about extending the same tolerance to

---

[58] *Ibid.*, September 8 and 11, 1781.
[59] Burke, *Corr.*, Burke to Richard Burke, March 23, 1792, VII, p. 118.
[60] Burke, *Works*, VI, p. 116.
[61] See, for example, BL, Windham Papers, Add. MSS. 37849. Windham to Hippisley, July 6, 1805, fo. 277.
[62] See, for example, *Parl. Deb.*, XIII, n.ser. (April 21, 1825), p. 90.
[63] John Reeves, "Considerations on the coronation oath" (London, 1801), pp. 40–1. BL Hardwicke Papers, Add. MSS. 45038, Reeves to Yorke, December 29, 1804, fos. 71–2.
[64] Reeves, "Thoughts on government," pp. 32–3.

Dissenters.[65] Indeed, if George III was surprised in 1801 at the pro-Catholic stance of his prime minister and much of his Cabinet, he took few political soundings or read few Pittite or High Church newspapers or journals.

All sorts of people and parties and newspapers embraced or at least countenanced the cause of Irish or English Catholics (even to the point of political emancipation) who were probably ashamed of their progressive stand a generation or so later. Spencer Perceval's grandson and biographer, Spencer Walpole, reported that his grandfather's papers for the spring of 1799 contained a draft of a speech, only briefly reported in *Hansard*, where the queen's then solicitor general wrote that the projected Union would diminish "perhaps, the necessity for keeping alive the political distinction between the Catholics and Protestants, ... thus giving to them all the full blessing of the English constitution, which they at present imperfectly enjoy."[66] Lord Glenbervie asserted in his diary for 1801 that Lord Liverpool told him that his son Hawkesbury, later the anti-Catholic premier of 1812–1827, thought that Catholic emancipation "might be right under certain modifications and to a degree."[67] Lord Malmesbury maintained in 1801 that the Duke of Portland (who was after all a Burkeian) thought Catholic emancipation was then necessary even though he was later the anti-Catholic prime minister who presided over the notorious "Church in Danger" general election of 1807.[68] Even Henry Addington, George III's choice to succeed Pitt as prime minister in 1801, and whose very name became virtually synonymous with the most aggressive official anti-Catholicism, if the *British Critic* report on his 1799 parliamentary speech is to be credited, coupled an ultimate acceptance of emancipation only with the event of the Union.[69]

Another chief actor in the struggle against Catholic emancipation after 1812, who adopted a much more equivocal stance earlier, was the future George IV. The young George's political route through British politics between 1781 and 1812 was tortuous in regard to both principles and personnel under any circumstances. But with

[65] Edmund Phipps, *Memoirs of the Political and Literary Life of Robert Plumer Ward, Esq.* (London, 1850), Mulgrave to Phipps, February 9, 1801, I, pp. 44–5.
[66] Spencer Walpole, *Life of the Rt. Hon. Spencer Perceval* (London, 1874), I, p. 81.
[67] Francis Bickley, ed., *Diaries of Sylvester Douglas, Lord Glenbervie* (London, 1928), I, p. 157.
[68] Third Earl of Malmesbury, ed., *Diaries and Correspondence of James Harris, First Earl of Malmesbury* (London, 1844), IV, p. 20.
[69] *British Critic*, 13 (May 1799), p. 528.

the Catholic issue factored in the record is muddled even for George, and his real views (assuming he had any) are difficult to gauge. Lord Kenyon claimed in a published pamphlet in 1812 that the regent had come to oppose further Catholic concessions as early as 1794–1795, during the controversial Fitzwilliam viceroyalty.[70] This is certainly incorrect, for in 1797 the Prince of Wales sent a memorial to the prime minister calling for Catholic emancipation.[71] Creevey remembered, during William IV's reign, about an opposition dinner which he had attended at Carlton House in 1805, at which the prince "made a long harangue in favour of the Catholics."[72] George assured Lord Holland at a personal interview in 1808 that emancipation was his ultimate goal.[73] On the other hand, in 1810, he told J. W. Croker that he was as good a "Brunswicker" as his father.[74] Then as late as January and February 1812, the regent informed Perceval that his own sentiments on Catholic relief were the same as Canning's and while "It was understood that the Catholic claims were to be postponed during the King's life," afterwards the matter of adequate securities for Church and state would come into play.[75] But however the question was framed, the preponderant evidence before 1812 was that the regent had no particularly hard line on the Catholic question in any way comparable with his later position. And rather than (or in addition to) seeing George as a trimmer on the issue, his position was possibly typical of that of his right-wing supporters in that, accompanied by all sorts of doubts and hesitations, he passed from a generally pro-Catholic position in the 1790s to a decidedly anti-Catholic stance sometime after 1812. The national right-wing press certainly made a similar transit.

In general, the Pittite or Tory or Burkeite English press of the 1790s was pro-Catholic. The Pittite *Sun*, for example, during both the prelude to Fitzwilliam's viceroyalty in 1794 and during the Union debates at the end of the decade clearly approved of Catholic

---

[70] Lord Kenyon, "Observations on the Roman Catholic question" (London, 1812), p. 110.

[71] Duke of Wellington, ed., *Despatches, Correspondence and Memoranda of Field Marshal Arthur Duke of Wellington, K.G.* (London, 1873), Prince of Wales to Pitt, February 8,m 1797, v, pp. 402–3.

[72] Sir Herbert Maxwell, ed., *Creevey Papers* (New York, 1904), p. 47.

[73] Arthur Aspinall, ed., *Correspondence of George, Prince of Wales, 1770–1812* (New York, 1969), vi, p. 216.

[74] Louis J. Jennings, ed., *Correspondence and Diaries of John Wilson Croker* (London, 1884), ii, p. 15.

[75] *Correspondence of Prince of Wales*, viii, pp. 306, 316.

emancipation.[76] The Burkeian *Revolutionary Magazine* adopted an extremely pro-Catholic viewpoint, going so far as to maintain that any change in Ireland (presumably even towards Jacobinism) would be preferable to the hideous status quo for Irish Catholics and admitting that among the severest grievances of Irishmen were their established Church and the tithe system.[77] The *British Critic* took a quite tolerant position from its inception on both Catholicism in general and Irish Catholics in particular.[78] During the Union debates of 1800 and the Catholic emancipation political crisis of 1801, the *British Critic* failed indeed to support emancipation, but it did suggest that *only* the coronation oath stood in its way, which seemed to imply that before the next coronation parliament might have to take legislative action to remedy the defect.[79]

After 1801 the right-wing press, especially in the specialized religious and political weeklies and magazines, began the process, completed only in the 1820s, of making anti-Catholicism the defining characteristic of the British Right. It took some of the press and even some politicians, like their regent and king, a certain time to adjust to changing circumstances. Even as late as the Perceval administration, presided over by a notorious anti-Catholic, much of the government-oriented press remained relatively pro-Catholic. The *National Advisor*, a bi-weekly whose publisher and printer, William Hughes, maintained particularly close relations with the Perceval wing of the administration,[80] proclaimed that the Irish Catholics "appear to have a right to hope for, and expect that in an enlightened age, they may be received as kindred brethren of an enlightened nation."[81] The subsidized *Courier* in 1810 advocated giving English Roman Catholics the vote, access to corporations, and high rank in the armed forces.[82] In 1812 it endorsed eventual and full emancipation.[83] Two other Tory daily newspapers sup-

---

[76] *Sun*, September 20, 1794; January 25 and 31, 1799. The *London Chronicle*, a not very ideological but general supporter of the Pitt ministry, also often praised Irish Catholics in the 1790s, January 12–14, 1797.

[77] *Revolutionary Magazine* (1795), pp. 189–90.

[78] *British Critic*, 2 (September 1793), p. 100; 4 (December 1794), p. 606.

[79] *Ibid.*, 16 (October 1800), p. 430; 17 (March 1801), p. 287. J. C. D. Clark apparently agrees even in retrospect that the coronation oath did indeed stand as a legitimate barrier against Catholics sitting in parliament. *Sunday Times*, April 17, 1988, p. 68.

[80] Denis Gray, *Spencer Perceval* (Manchester, 1963), p. 134.

[81] *National Advisor*, October 19, 1811.

[82] *Courier*, February 23, 1810.   [83] *Ibid.*, February 3, 1812.

ported Catholic emancipation in 1812, the *Morning Post* (on the condition that safeguards could be discovered)[84] and the *Pilot*.[85]

Neither of the two great Tory journals, the *Quarterly Review*, founded in 1809, nor *Blackwood's Edinburgh Magazine*, founded in 1817, was at all prepared, the former from its Canningite origins, the latter from perhaps less factional motives, to agitate against Catholic emancipation until well into the 1820s. *Blackwood's*, indeed, while not explicitly endorsing emancipation, published in its early years articles quite sympathetic towards Catholicism, as in 1820, "On the education of the poor of Ireland," where the Catholic clergy were extolled for their "touching ... simplicity," "guileless disposition," "Courteous manners," and "primitive innocence of life."[86]

In April 1812, the second Earl of Liverpool, within two months to embark upon his long premiership, was still hedging his bets on emancipation. While not in favor of immediate relief, he was still able to tell the House of Lords that "I do not shut out the hope that some serious and essential changes may take place. If they do the question may come, under new circumstances, before Parliament. Then will be the proper time to entertain the consideration of the question."[87]

So, as late as 1812, the future king and future prime minister alike, as well as a substantial portion of the Tory press, were still able to discuss emancipation as something if not imminent then at least theoretically possible. Indeed, in the much more highly ideological atmosphere of 1825, when increasingly the Catholic question was coming (to the disgust of many politicians) to define political principle, Canning somewhat wistfully looked back to 1812 as "the halcyon days of the Catholic question, and happy should I be if there were any near prospect of the like again!"[88]

But if it was still respectable in 1812 for press and politicians on the Right to retain some semblance of a Pittite and Burkeian

---

[84] *Morning Post*, May 23, 1812.   [85] *Pilot*, January 8, 1812.

[86] *Blackwood's Edinburgh Magazine*, 7 (August 1820), pp. 538–9. William Maginn, one of Blackwood's stable of witty writers, himself an Irish Protestant, and later editor of the ferociously anti-Catholic *Fraser's Magazine*, warned William Blackwood in 1821 that he was wrongly espousing pro-Catholic attitudes: "It obliges none of your friends, and disobliges us. The question in fact ought to be avoided altogether." NLS, Blackwood Papers, 4007, Maginn to Blackwood, May 9, 1821, fo. 102. The fact that Maginn in 1821 still thought it possible for a Tory journal to avoid altogether the Catholic issue shows how much farther the Protestant cause came by just the mid-1820s.

[87] *Parl. Deb.*, XXII, (April 21, 1812), p. 639.

[88] *Ibid.*, XII, n.ser. (February 15, 1825), pp. 490–1.

support for Catholic emancipation, an attitude virtually (if not quite) ubiquitous before 1800, the trend long before 1812 had been in the opposite direction. In particular, following George III's decision to accept Pitt's resignation on the issue of Catholic relief in February 1801, if not in a few cases slightly before, the Pittite and Burkeian (as well as the older Tory) traditions on this matter were effectively and vigorously shelved. The two new High Church publications, the *Orthodox Churchman's Magazine*, founded in March 1801, and Sarah Trimmer's *Guardian of Education*, founded in January 1802, were both solidly anti-Catholic in a manner quite distinct from any High Church or orthodox Trinitarian publication of the mid to late eighteenth century. The *Orthodox Churchman's Magazine* first appeared coterminously with Pitt's resignation and, not surprisingly, announced its determination to oppose Catholic emancipation as well as Dissenters and Deists.[89] By 1808, at its conclusion as a publication, it had become progressively more anti-Catholic. This may not have been the original intent of its founders in the late 1790s. The idea for the magazine may have come from John Gifford, editor of the *Anti-Jacobin Review*, who envisioned establishing a *Church of England Magazine* to support the establishment, not against Roman Catholics, but "against the multitude of sectaries and sectarian publications with which the country now swarms ... "[90] The *Guardian of Education*, in 1804, revived equation of the pope with Anti-Christ and by 1806 suspected that Catholicism in general was the harlot of the *Book of Revelation*.[91] Upon Pitt's departure from Downing Street, a number of his literary hacks such as the Rev. John Ireland, who in 1801 described the Protestant cause as "the *sensorium* of our country,"[92] and John Bowles,[93] almost immediately adopted vigorously anti-Catholic literary personae.[94] The two major rightwing journals of the 1790s, the *British Critic* and the *Anti-Jacobin Review*, both vaguely tolerant of Catholicism in that decade,[95] made

[89] *Orthodox Churchman's Magazine*, 1 (March 1801), p. 1.
[90] R. Polwhele, *Traditions and Recollections* (London, 1826), Gifford to Polwhele, August 9, 1799, II, p. 511.
[91] *Guardian of Education*, 3 (January 1804), p. 81; 5 (March 1806), p. 122.
[92] [John Ireland], "Letters of Fabius to the Right Hon. William Pitt on his proposed abolition of the test" (London, 1801), p. 61.
[93] John Bowles, "Reflections political and moral at the conclusion of the war" (London, 1802), pp. 86–7.
[94] Privately, Pitt's old tutor, the Bishop of Lincoln, also decided that he was anti-Catholic. BL, Rose Papers, Add. MSS. 42773, Lincoln to Rose, January 15, 1802, fo. 10.
[95] *Anti-Jacobin Review*, 5 (March 1800), p. 472.

absolutely clear their general anti-Catholicism after 1801. A reviewer for the *British Critic* now toyed with the notion that the pope indeed might be Anti-Christ[96] and the *Anti-Jacobin Review* was well on its way to seeing Catholicism as an "idolatrous religion" with the Bishops of Rome as "vicars of the devils."[97]

As with the religiously oriented High Church journals or magazines founded during the first decade of the nineteenth century, so the more secularly oriented rightist journals (with the significant exception of the *Quarterly Review*) were also vigorously anti-Catholic. The Tory publicist F. W. Blagdon controlled two anti-Catholic publications: the *Weekly Political Register*, which regarded emancipation as a "detestable abortion,"[98] and the *Phoenix*.[99] Henry Redhead Yorke's *Weekly Political Review* was equally censorious of Rome.[100] The Orange-oriented *Protestant Advocate*, a sort of digest of anti-Catholic propaganda taken from various places throughout the three kingdoms and throughout history, was founded in 1812 specifically to foment a more aggressive Protestant stance against emancipation.[101] In October 1816, it merged with the *Anti-Jacobin Review* which increased the ideological content of the latter, giving it even a slightly unbalanced tone in what became an orgy of recrimination and violence against every aspect of Romanism, past and present.[102] In Scotland, the *Edinburgh Annual Register*, founded in 1810 by Walter Scott, to which Robert Southey was a leading contributor, likewise took a vigorously anti-Catholic stance.[103] It seems that after 1801, the right-wing weeklies, monthlies, or registers tended to embrace anti-Catholicism much more aggressively than did the daily rightist press, which, perhaps because it sought a wider audience, remained a decade or more behind the more specialized journals of opinion.

The High Church movement too, perhaps partially due in its Hackney phase to a growth in self-confidence, and in an age in which it seemed to midwife journals and educational societies, and to secure an increasing proportion of the higher clergy to its ranks, ceased viewing the Roman Church in a sympathetic light at any

---

96 *British Critic*, 23 (March 1804), p. 247.
97 *Anti-Jacobin Review*, 29 (December 1807), p. xi; 59 (September 1820), p. 78.
98 *Blagdon's Weekly Political Register*, January 24, 1810.   99 *Phoenix*, April 17, 1808.
100 *Redhead Yorke's Weekly Political Review*, March 7, 1807.
101 *Protestant Advocate*, October 1812, pp. 1–7.
102 See, for example, *Anti-Jacobin Review*, 54 (March 1818), p. 81.
103 See, for example, *Edinburgh Annual Register* (Edinburgh, 1810), pp. 7–9.

level. William Van Mildert, founder of the *Christian Remembrancer* and a future High Church Bishop of Durham, in his Boyle lectures early in the century, identified the pope as Anti-Christ and Catholicism as a "monstrous system" and a great anti-Christian movement.[104] The Rev. Robert Nares, whom Jones of Nayland had chosen to edit the *British Critic* in 1793,[105] and who, as editor, had adopted a relatively pro-Catholic line during the 1790s, by 1810, as Archdeacon of Stafford, opposed emancipation which, he wrote, would "subvert the established Protestant Constitution."[106]

Herbert Marsh, the Margaret Professor of Divinity at Cambridge and High Church Bishop of Peterborough, soundly reversed the old rightist slogan that Presbyterians were more dangerous than Romanists on the grounds that while both Catholics and Dissenters were averse to the Anglican episcopal establishment, the former's allegiance to a foreign power precluded any political role in the state.[107] In his *Comparative View of the Churches of England and Rome*, published in 1814, Marsh argued, very much in opposition to the spirit of Daubeny's ecumenical stance of a decade earlier, the doctrinal distinctiveness of both Churches and minutely accentuated all possible points of difference between the two communions. He concluded that the Church of England was a "system of *religious liberty*," while that of Rome resembled a system of "*religious slavery*."[108] Daubeny himself, however, had by the second and third decades of the nineteenth century moved far away from his tolerant and even (at times) fraternal embrace of Catholicism between 1797 and 1804. In his 1818 pamphlet, "On the nature, progress, and consequences of schism," and in his 1824 book *The Protestant's Companion*, Daubeny, like Marsh, found popery the "greatest enemy of our Protestant Church" and talked of the "insidious acts and imposing fallacies of the Romish priesthood." And indeed, Rome was "of all the Churches in Christendom, the most heretical one

---

104 William Van Mildert, *An Historical View of the Rise and Progress of Infidelity* (London, 1808), I, pp. 233–4, 243, 451–2. In 1831, the last year of his life, Van Mildert, then Bishop of Durham, in his "Charge" to his clergy, still finds popery, along with atheism, infidelity, and dissent, an open enemy to the national Church. It would have been rare to find such an analogy used between the American Revolution and 1801. (Oxford, 1831), p. 11.
105 An appointment which Jones later came to regret. John Freeman, *Life of the Rev. William Kirby, M.A.* (London, 1852), Jones to Kirby, n.d. pp. 42–3.
106 Robert Nares, "Protestantism the blessing of Britain" (London, 1810), p. 17n.
107 Herbert Marsh, "Letter to Reverend Peter Gandolphy" (Cambridge, 1813), pp. 88–9.
108 Herbert Marsh, *Comparative View of the Churches of England and Rome* (London, 1841), pp. 2–3, 216, 234–8.

..."[109] The High Church Bishop Blomfield of London had at one time favored Catholic emancipation but changed his mind by 1828.[110] The fathers of Hackney – Joshua Watson, H. H. Norris, and Christopher Wordsworth – also had little time for Rome. Watson's memoirist says that his subject opposed Catholic emancipation on both political and religious grounds.[111] Norris wrote an extraordinarily negative book on the Jesuit order.[112] And the Dean of Bocking, who maintained a friendly view of the Dissenters, preached a sermon at Chichester before the National Society, proclaiming Rome a far more fatal enemy to the gospel than Julian the Apostate. Rome, wrote Wordsworth, was "possessed by a carnal and anti-Christian spirit" which sought only "the enlargement of the dominion of slavery, superstition, fanaticism, falsehood ..."[113]

The Rev. John Ireland may or may not have been correct in 1801, during the Catholic emancipation crisis, when he wrote that the Protestant cause was "the *sensorium* of our country."[114] But certainly by the 1820s it was the sensorium of the Right. It increasingly became difficult for Tory or High Church individuals much less those newspapers or journals which had been traditionally pro-Catholic or even neutral on the Catholic issue to sustain their viewpoints. Even as loyal a Burkeite as French Laurence, whom his failing (perhaps in mind as well as body) master during his last days at Beaconsfield had anointed as his successor,[115] wrote shortly before his own death in 1809 a short dissertation on the *Book of Revelation* in which he asserted, in line with the old Protestant interpretation, that the pope was Anti-Christ.[116] In 1817, after several years of attempted compromise at the London Pitt Club, and some solicitude for the feelings of Canning and Castlereagh, the Protestant Ascendancy toast was revived, which led to the withdrawal of the Canningites from the organization.[117]

The press followed the clerics and politicians. Dr. Stoddard's

---

[109] Charles Daubeny, "On the nature, progress, and consequences of schism" (London, 1818), pp. 156–7. Charles Daubeny, *Protestant's Companion* (London, 1824), pp. 277–8, 330.

[110] Olive J. Brose, *Church and Parliament* (Stanford, 1969), p. 73.

[111] Edward Churton, ed., *Memoir of Joshua Watson* (Oxford, 1861), I, p. 301.

[112] [H. H. Norris], *Principles of the Jesuits* (London, 1839).

[113] Christopher Wordsworth, *Sermons* (London, 1814), II, pp. 226–8.

[114] See footnote no. 92.

[115] Burke, *Corr.*, Burke to Laurence, December 23, 1796, IX, pp. 196–7.

[116] *British Critic*, 41 (February 1813), pp. 147–52.

[117] James J. Sack, "Memory of Burke and the memory of Pitt," *HJ*, 30 (September 1987), pp. 636–7.

daily *New Times* since its inception in 1817 had supported Catholic emancipation, and indeed it continued to do so as late as 1825.[118] By 1827, however, it had completely changed its position.[119] More important than the *New Times* were the two Tory dailies, the *Morning Post* and the *Courier*. Both had supported emancipation as late as 1812, albeit with some reservations;[120] both opposed the idea completely by 1825.[121] *Blackwood's Edinburgh Magazine*, pro-Catholic in the early 1820s,[122] switched in the mid-1820s.[123] The even more prominent *Quarterly Review* had traditionally (like the Liverpool Cabinet taken as a whole) expressed no opinion on emancipation.[124] Or as Southey put it in 1812: "Canning has smitten the *Quarterly* with a dead policy upon the Catholic Question."[125] But by 1828, with Canning dead and Southey in the ascendant on the review, the *Quarterly* dutifully joined its Tory confreres in strict opposition to any Catholic relief.[126] The premier Pittite daily newspaper, the *Sun*, although it passed from strict ministerial control at the time of the Caroline case, while still giving the Liverpool ministry general support, revoked its former opinion in favor of the Catholics.[127] The *Monthly Magazine*, formerly Unitarian and radical in its politics, but since 1826, in a new Tory series, under the editorship of the Rev. George Croly, remained in favor of Catholic emancipation until the end of 1828, when it made a not very graceful exodus to the opposite camp. The *Monthly* subsequently became the most furious anti-Catholic magazine in Britain.[128]

But not only did the right-wing press swing from supporting to opposing Catholic relief in the period from the Pitt to the Wellington administrations, there is also circumstantial evidence that by the 1820s any newspaper, journal, or magazine addressed primarily to a

---

[118] *New Times*, April 28, 1825.   [119] *Ibid.*, February 15, 1827.

[120] See footnotes nos. 83 and 84.

[121] *Morning Post*, May 10, 1825. *Courier*, April 9, 1825.

[122] See footnote no. 86. When George IV visited Ireland in 1821, in what sounded like official editorial policy, the magazine opined on Catholic emancipation that "whenever the measure can be carried without danger, we wish it carried ... we may hope that such a time will speedily arrive." *Blackwood's Edinburgh Magazine*, 10 (September 1821), p. 227.

[123] *Ibid.*, 15 (March 1824), p. 287.

[124] As early as 1810, it was very moderate and neutral on emancipation. *Quarterly Review*, 3 (February 1810), pp. 114ff.

[125] Charles Cuthbert Southey, ed., *Life and Correspondence of Robert Southey* (London, 1850), Southey to Bedford, January 4, 1812, III, p. 325.

[126] *Quarterly Review*, 38 (October 1828), p. 557.   [127] *Sun*, November 1 and 20, 1819.

[128] *Monthly Magazine*, 2 (July 1826), pp. 10–11; 5 (February 1828), p. 74; 6 (December 1828), pp. 561ff.

Tory audience which did not excoriate Catholicism could not survive. The *Guardian*, a Sunday newspaper established in late 1819, had talented and well-connected backers and writers, including John Wilson Croker, its founder, the Rev. George Croly and Charles Knight, its editors, John Murray, the publisher, as a part proprietor, and John Gibson Lockhart, Walter Scott,[129] and William Wordsworth[130] as occasional contributors. Like Croker himself, the paper supported Catholic emancipation.[131] It was spectacularly unsuccessful and, after numerous changes of editor and proprietor, was put to sleep in 1824. Three Tory reviews were started in the 1819–1823 period – the *Edinburgh Monthly Review*,[132] the *New Edinburgh Review*,[133] the *Monthly Censor or General Review of Domestic and Foreign Literature*[134] – and all tried to remain either neutral on Catholic relief or supportive of it: all three failed in relatively short order.

In no way do I mean to suggest that espousal, whether enthusiastic or resigned, of Catholic relief was the chief reason for the failure of much of the pro-Catholic right-wing press – Croker, for example, was well aware that in the *Guardian*, he was overseeing a "worse than mediocre" newspaper[135] – but I do suspect that by the 1820s the Tory reading public's tolerance of much deviance from an anti-Catholic line was limited. There may, of course, have been a subtle financial angle in the mass conversion of the Tory press to anti-Catholicism: a financial angle not in the sense that the Liverpool or Wellington governments rewarded such change by direct or indirect subsidies – there is no evidence of this – but rather the financial pressure of readers who refused to buy pro-Catholic Tory periodicals or newspapers. The circulation of the waffling *Quarterly Review* had fallen off by around 50 percent by the end of the Liverpool administration from its lucrative situation of a decade before. And A. A. Watts, for one, suggested that the *Manchester Courier*'s conversion in 1825 to the anti-Catholic stand had increased circulation enormously.[136]

[129] NLS, Walter Scott Papers, 3890, Croker to Scott, November 29, 1819, fo. 228.
[130] Pierpont Morgan Library, Southey-Croker Papers, Southey to Croker, January 9, 1820.
[131] *Guardian*, April 1, 1821; January 19, 1823.
[132] *Edinburgh Monthly Review*, 2 (August 1819), p. 210.
[133] *New Edinburgh Review*, April 1823, p. 470. [134] *Monthly Censor*, March 1823, p. 270.
[135] CL, University of Michigan, Croker Papers, "Private letter book," Croker to Croly, January 10, 1820.
[136] The editor in 1816 claimed that the *Quarterly* sold 8,000 per number. West Yorkshire Archives, Leeds, Harewood Papers, Gifford to Canning, July 16, 1816. Ten years later, it was facing severe circulation problems. NLS, Blackwood Papers, 4016, T. C. Croker to

Whatever the reason may have been, by 1828, and in most cases several years before, in the entire scope of the national Tory press, in the newspapers, magazines, and journals emanating from London and probably from Dublin and Edinburgh, there appears not to have been any support for the Catholic cause. Such had been the success of Tory anti-Catholic clubs, sermons, and other propaganda that the Catholic" element in the "Tory party", once arguably coequal if not predominant, was virtually unrepresented in written opinion. Such unanimity may help explain the rancid atmosphere of Tory politics after the apostasy of 1829.

III

The reasons behind such a sea-change of opinion between 1801 and the mid-1820s on the most controversial issue in Tory politics were numerous. The anti-Catholicism engendered during these years of debate also varied in intensity and depth of commitment as well, of course, as in quality of argument. There were possibly objective causes for this shift involving matters outside the British isles. The seemingly weak rule of a Clement XIV or Pius VI who dissolved the Society of Jesus and appeared impotent before the anti-clericalism of the Enlightenment and the anti-papalism of the French Revolution was succeeded by the more aggressive regime of Pius VII and Cardinal Consalvi. This situation was mirrored in England by the change from a feeble Cis-Alpine church of the famous (or infamous) Protesting Catholic dissenters of the 1780s to the proselytizing, self-confident communion of Bishop Milner of the 1820s. Then the rapprochement between the Roman Catholic Church and the French Republic and Empire, as illustrated by the 1801 Concordat and the 1804 coronation, neatly coincided with the anti-Catholic crisis in English politics lasting from Pitt's resignation in the winter of 1801 to the formal rejection of the Catholic Emancipation Bill by parliament in the spring of 1805. Pius VII's description of Britain's leading enemy as "Our good and well-beloved son"[137] did not go unnoticed in the beleaguered islands and Lord Kenyon, trained by High Churchmen in the eighteenth century and an Orange and

Blackwood, February 3, 1826, fo. 185. For the *Manchester Courier*, see, Estus Cantrell Polk, *Letters of Alaric Alexander Watts From the Blackwood Papers in the National Library of Scotland* (Lubbock, 1952), Watts to Blackwood, June 9, 1825, p. 317.
[137] Andre Maurois, *Chateaubriand* (New York, 1969), p. 138.

ultra leader in the nineteenth, was not alone in his public denunciation of an impious coronation.[138] Lord Hawkesbury, the future prime minister, for example, used this quasi-alliance between Rome and Bonaparte in 1805 to justify in parliament his own change of mind on Catholic relief.[139]

Yet even before the Concordat, the *Anti-Jacobin Review* was warning about the "prodigious" number of émigré priests in England.[140] Indeed, upon Pitt's resignation in February 1801, Lord Glenbervie reported that nearly all the London clergy in their pulpits "seem to have sounded the alarm for the Church."[141] Hence, anger at Pius VII's actions may have been as much an excuse as a cause for the change in opinion so observable during and after 1801. It is possible, of course, that the sudden recognition that after the Union the Catholic portion of the United Kingdom's population would approach one-third concentrated the collective minds of the clergy and the right wing in general. However, this sounds like *ex post facto* reasoning. Certainly the *initial* burst of anti-Catholicism after 1801 came from High Church publications, heavily dependent upon clerical contributors – the secular right-wing press was in general a bit later in fully integrating the anti-Catholic ethos into its world view. Post-1801 clerical anti-Catholicism was probably nothing new. It had no doubt incubated in the Church for years, merely waiting for an opportune moment to emerge. When the Pittite-subsidized *Times* rather indelicately (and unusually for the period) rejoiced in the early 1790s over the apparent destruction of the whore of Babylon,[142] there may have been many a country clergyman edified by such sentiments. But with the three chief leaders of conservative opinion in the 1790s – Burke, Pitt, and George III – either strongly pro-Catholic or silent on the matter, with the clerically oriented press and the government-sponsored press extremely tolerant of Catholics, it would hardly have seemed an auspicious time to beat with any traditional cudgels in the opposing direction. But by 1801, with Burke dead, Pitt out of office and the king – that fountain of honor and patronage – showing his true colors, there was nothing to stop the clergy and their supporters from addressing their own genuine opinions.

---

[138] Kenyon, "Observations," p. 48.   [139] *Parl. Deb.*, iv, (May, 10, 1805), p. 682.

[140] *Anti-Jacobin Review*, 10 (October 1801), p. 205.

[141] *Diaries of Glenbervie*, i, p. 157.

[142] Gayle Trusdale Pendleton, "English conservative propaganda during the French Revolution, 1789–1802," Ph.D. dissertation (Emory University, 1976), p. 336.

It is also possible that clerical and High Church circles, eager for patronage and preferment, were merely following the lead of the Defender of their Faith now that he had made it abundantly clear that no further concessions to Catholic (or Irish majority) opinion would be allowed. Indeed, the last important political role which the British monarchy may have played in its long involvement in the national life may have been the skill with which its leading members, Georges III and IV, and the Dukes of York and Cumberland, managed to defer the triumph of Catholic emancipation for nearly a third of a century after the Irish rebellion – at a political cost to the newly United Kingdom which proved ultimately fatal. The leading historian of early-nineteenth-century Orangeism suggests the importance of an Orange circle during the early regency period centered on the Duke of York and Lord Yarmouth, the son of the regent's mistress, which may have helped influence the susceptible George against emancipation.[143] And Lord Palmerston in his memoirs wonders how many British politicians were anti-Catholic after 1812 in hopes of currying favor with the Duke of York, a potential Frederick I, ever closer to the throne.[144] But while leading clerics and politicians on the Right may have been and no doubt were under some royal influence in their increasing nineteenth-century anti-Catholicism, at least as crucial may have been the stark fact of the Irish rebellion and its literary aftermath in the extraordinary importance of the two works by Sir Richard Musgrave,[145] MP for Lismore in the Irish parliament from 1778 to 1800. The first was a short pamphlet, published in Dublin in 1799, and going through three editions: "A concise account of the material events and atrocities which occurred in the present rebellion ... "; the second, a more substantial two-volume work published in 1801, the year of the national emancipation crisis, *Memoirs of the Different Rebellions in Ireland from the Arrival of the English, Also, A Particular Detail of That Which Broke Out the 23rd of May, 1798, With the History of the Conspiracy Which Preceded It.*

If every great political movement has its book, Musgrave's accounts of the 1798 Irish rebellion served as the catalyst for nineteenth-century British anti-Catholicism and to a lesser extent, of

---

[143] Hereward Senior, *Orangeism in Ireland and Britain, 1795–1836* (London, 1966), p. 165.

[144] Sir Henry Bulwer Lytton, *Life of Henry John Temple, Viscount Palmerston: With Selections From His Diaries and Correspondence* (London, 1870), I, p. 372.

[145] *The DNB* asserts that while high sheriff of Waterford, Musgrave flogged a Whiteboy with his own hands as no one else could be found to execute the sentence.

British conservatism. In fact, odd as it may seem, a case might be made that Musgrave's "Concise account" and *Memoirs* far more than Burke's "Reflections" or "Regicide peace" defined the pre-Disraelian British Right. Both volumes of the more mature effort are replete with horrors of almost pornographic quality practiced against the Protestant population of Ireland: Catholic oaths for their wholesale extirpation; poisoning of their soldiers' bread and milk; their torture and murder with sharpened pikes; their grisly butchering at Wexford; their deaths en masse in suffocating flames while locked up in rural barns.[146] Musgrave's work shook the *Anti-Jacobin Review* from its considered opinion that the Irish rebellion was not a religious insurrection.[147] The *British Critic*, upon reviewing Musgrave, agreed with the *Anti-Jacobin* and in addition deduced that the popery of 1798 had proved itself as one with the popery of the massacre of St. Bartholomew.[148] Thereafter, the memory of the 1798 rebellion as filtered through Musgrave's lens was a staple of the anti-Catholic Right. Lord Kenyon proclaimed to the world his reverence for Musgrave;[149] Southey dwelt with approbation on the baronet's equally partisan account of the massacres of the 1640s;[150] the regular correspondent for *Blagdon's Weekly Political Register* suggested that all the Jacobin cruelties of the 1790s were petty compared with what Musgrave described in Ireland in just one year.[151]

The notion that Musgrave popularized of a potential Catholic extermination of the Irish Protestant population became one of the abiding themes of the Protestant Right after 1801. Before Musgrave, however haltingly, Enlightenment England of whatever political persuasion had tended to view the Roman Catholic majority as the victims of Irish history. After Musgrave, at least on the Right, this equation was neatly reversed, with the Protestants now clearly the martyrs, actual or potential, of vengeful and bloodthirsty Papists. Henry Redhead Yorke suspected that Irish Catholics had a bloody scroll prepared of their Protestant victims.[152] The appearance in Ireland in 1822 of the "healer" Dean of Bamberg, Prince Hohen-

---

[146] Sir Richard Musgrave, *Memoirs of the Different Rebellions in Ireland* (Dublin, 1802), I, pp. 347, 528ff; II, pp. 17, 77.
[147] *Anti-Jacobin Review*, 4 (September 1799), pp. 82–3.
[148] *British Critic*, 18 (October 1801), pp. 384–5.
[149] Kenyon, "Observations," p. 62.   [150] *Edinburgh Annual Register* (1810), pp. 7–9.
[151] *Blagdon's Weekly Political Register*, January 17, 1810, pp. 527ff.
[152] *Redhead Yorke's Weekly Political Review*, March 7, 1807.

lohe, the spread of the folk version of the obscure prophecies of Pastorini, which seemed to foresee the total extermination of Protestants in 1825, and, above all, the flourishing of Daniel O'Connell's Catholic Association after 1823 merely reinforced the forebodings engendered by Musgrave's work. The Orange press in Dublin, such as the *Warder*, openly discussed the intention of the Catholic Association to extirpate Irish Protestants.[153] Perhaps more surprisingly, in 1824 *Blackwood's Edinburgh Magazine*, in the midst of its change of mind concerning Catholic relief, also emphasized the association's desire to "exterminate" all Irish Protestants.[154] And the formerly pro-Catholic theologian, Archdeacon Daubeny, in the midst of an 1824 panegyric to Musgrave, accused Pius VII personally of sanctioning Pastorini's prophecy and viewing the mass extermination of Protestants as doing "God special service."[155] In the House of Commons in 1829, E. W. Pendarves informed his colleagues that at Truro, when the signing of the anti-Catholic petitions took place during the final emancipation crisis, tables were covered with inflammatory pictures of Irish Catholics burning Protestants at the stake.[156]

Yet it was not only the vagaries of Irish history and contemporary politics that incensed the British Right. They were equally conscious of both English and continental examples of popery's sins. Musgrave himself warned that English Roman Catholics would explode into rebellion too if they increased in numbers.[157] In the House of Lords, Viscount Sidmouth and the Duke of Cumberland, who possessed little of the Jacobite nostalgia which permeated his eldest brother and his niece, regularly denounced such English worthies as Mary I or James II,[158] and Sidmouth as well clearly enjoyed frequent discussion of the massacre of St. Bartholomew's Day.[159] *John Bull*, usually a satirical weekly, unearthed the decretals of the Fourth Lateran Council on the extirpation of heretics and of Constance against keeping faith with schismatics to prove the papacy the "most cruel spiritual tyranny that ever disgraced a Church."[160] And long before he entered parliament as the ultra hope, Michael Thomas

[153] *Warder*, May 17, 1823.   [154] *Blackwood's Edinburgh Magazine*, 15 (May 1824), p. 506.
[155] Daubeny, *Protestant's Companion*, pp. 277–8, 346.
[156] *Parl. Deb.*, xx, n.ser. (February 24, 1829), p. 526.
[157] Musgrave, *Memoirs*, pp. xiv–xv.   [158] *Parl. Deb.*, iv (May 10, 1805), pp. 692–3.
[159] *Ibid.*, pp. 696–7.   [160] *John Bull*, May 5, 1822, p. 580.

Sadler was wont to give speeches to his Leeds fellow-townsmen on the Marian martyrs writhing in agony in the torturing flames.[161]

The myriad of accusations against Roman Catholics developed from Irish, English and continental and historical antecedents to encompass charges of popery as a totally foreign entity, as Jacobin, as Anti-Christ. The issue of that allegiance which Roman Catholics unquestionably owed to a foreign power, the ruler of central Italy as well as vicar of Christ on earth, had of course energized Protestant princes since the sixteenth century (and for that matter Roman Catholic princes both before and after the Reformation). The poet Wordsworth[162] and the High Church Bishop of Peterborough used the argument of foreign allegiance to justify their qualms regarding Catholic political relief, though Bishop Marsh admitted Roman Catholics could be good citizens, simply not parliamentarians.[163] Others were less charitable or more vulgar. The *Anti-Jacobin Review* in 1807, finding Catholicism an "idolatrous religion" decided a Roman Catholic could not be a faithful subject to a Protestant prince;[164] *Common Sense* in 1825 found it a "diabolical religion" and reached the same conclusion.[165] John Murray's *Representative* wondered in 1826 whether the papal power over English Catholics, in or out of parliament, would go as far as it did in Portugal, where the Bishop of Rome regularly issued dispensations to the house of Braganza allowing (by English law) incestuous niece–uncle marriages.[166]

This problem of overlapping jurisdictions led some Tory publications to flirt close to something resembling treason. W. F. Blagdon's *Phoenix* doubted in 1808 whether even the omnicompetent parliament had the power to alter the religious regulations of England, Scotland, or Ireland.[167] The *Morning Journal*, in 1829, illustrating the sort of logic which enabled Wellington to haul it before the courts for seditious libel, suggested, in case of emancipation, that the people exercise their right of resistance under the terms of the Act of Settlement.[168] And such was the political danger

---

[161] [Robert Benton Seeley], *Memoirs of the Life and Writings of Michael Thomas Sadler* (London, 1842), pp. 22–3. Sadler expostulated on the "myriads of human victims, more numbers than those of Moloch who fell prey to the bestialities of popery."

[162] *Letters of Wordsworth*, Wordsworth to the Bishop of London, March 3, 1829, v, pp. 37–8.

[163] Marsh, "Letter to Gandolphy," pp. 88–9.

[164] *Anti-Jacobin Review*, 29 (December 1807), p. xi.

[165] *Common Sense*, January 9, 1825, p. 12.   [166] *Representative*, June 27, 1826, p. 526.

[167] *Phoenix*, April 17, 1808.   [168] *Morning Journal*, April 2, 1829.

entailed upon Britain by the double allegiance question that both the *Representative* and the *Age* had concluded by the late 1820s that the penal laws ought never to have been abolished in England or Ireland in the eighteenth century.[169]

Even Jacobinism became confounded with its greatest enemy, Catholicism, in the minds of some on the English Right. The Pittite pamphleteer John Bowles, arguably second only to Burke himself in his impact on the formation of right-wing ideological opinion in the 1790s, suggested (with some justification) that Jacobin notions of government deriving from the people originated in popish schoolmen.[170] Both John Murray's *Representative* and Theodore Hook's *British Mercury* found Catholicism and Jacobinism equally pernicious[171] and F. W. Blagdon's *Weekly Political Register* found Catholicism much worse.[172]

A more virulent charge against the papacy than comparison to or collusion with Jacobinism was the resurrection on the Right of the ancient Protestant accusation, generally dormant in the later eighteenth century, of connivance with an altogether more sinister force than Robespierre or Bonaparte: Lucifer himself. Spencer Perceval was not the only Tory ideologue in the early nineteenth century who became enamored with viewing the fulfillment of biblical prophecy in the events of his own time.[173] William Van Mildert, future High Church Bishop of Durham, in his Boyle lectures,[174] Mrs. Trimmer's *Guardian of Education*,[175] the series of the *British Critic* in the early nineteenth century,[176] Coleridge in "On the constitution of Church and state,"[177] the Rev. George Croly, editor of the *Monthly Magazine*,[178] all countenanced the notion that the

---

[169] *Representative*, January 26, 1826. *Age*, November 16, 1828, p. 364. Southey too in the *Quarterly*, along a similar line of reasoning, continued his long-held anti-Pitt views by contending that Pitt's Catholic policies led to greater evils for Britain than did his woeful management of the revolutionary and Napoleonic wars. 38 (October 1828), p. 557.

[170] BL, Windham Papers, Add. MSS. 37881, Bowles to Windham, December 20, 1802, fo. 38. Taken from Bowles' "Thoughts on the late general election."

[171] *British Mercury*, September 15, 1824.

[172] *Blagdon's Weekly Political Register*, January 17, 1810.

[173] Through his study of biblical prophecy, Perceval thought that the world would end in 1926 and that the French Revolution was divinely ordained for the downfall of Catholicism. Thorne, IV, p. 766.

[174] Van Mildert, *Historical View*, I, p. 233.

[175] *Guardian of Education*, 3 (January 1804), p. 81.

[176] *British Critic*, 23 (March 1804), p. 247; 23 (May 1804), p. 542.

[177] "On the constitution of the Church and State" in John Colmer, ed., *Collected Works of Samuel Taylor Coleridge* (Princeton, 1976), II, pp. 131–3.

[178] George Croly, "Englishman's polar star" (Preston, 1828), pp. 47–8.

Bishop of Rome was indeed *the* (or an integral part of) Anti-Christ. The *Anti-Jacobin Review*, in its last series between 1816 and 1821, when the Orange-oriented *Protestant Advocate* joined it, was especially prone to this dark and brooding environment. In 1817 and 1818, in passages that stand out for their zealotry even in an age accustomed to press exaggerations, the *Anti-Jacobin* saw the Church of Rome as so "drunk with blood, that to her must be applied the prophecy of the woman sitting on the seven-headed beast clothed in scarlet ... " and as an "idolatrous church ... *Babylon the Great, the mother of Harlots, and of the Abominations of the Earth, drunk with the blood of the Saints*" with the number 666 applied to popedom.[179]

An entirely different plane of Tory anti-Catholic argumentation came from a libertarian perspective, transporting into a nineteenth-century setting a traditional seventeenth-century Whiggish critique of Catholicism as oriented towards absolutism and inimical to freedom and modernity. It was to this tradition, for example, that Pitt's literary hack of the 1790s, the Rev. John Ireland, appealed in 1801 in his "Letters of Fabius," when he reminded the late premier of the dangers of Catholicism and of Pitt's own "true Whig proclivities."[180] The Roman Catholic propensity to deny religious toleration to those within its own purview no doubt did sincerely bother some Tories. Southey, for example, at one stage in his career, was prepared to countenance the abolition of the Test for all Protestants and even for Jews but favored denying parliament to Roman Catholics just because of this failure to grant mutual recognition to other religious groups.[181] Unlike some of its coadjutors, the *Morning Post* refused to attack the religious aspects of Catholicism, such as the Real Presence or the honor paid to the Virgin Mary, but did denounce its despotic and intolerant character.[182] The *British Critic*, in a series in the 1820s more tolerant than those earlier in the century, pronounced itself hostile to Catholic emancipation *only* because of this papal narrowness.[183] *Blackwood's Edinburgh Magazine*, after nearly a half decade of general neutrality verging at time on pro-Catholic sentiment, tended, when it dramatically switched to an anti-Catholic line in the mid-1820s, to emphasize libertarian aspects of such opposition. Like the *Morning Post, Blackwood's*

---

[179] *Anti-Jacobin Review*, 54 (March 1818), p. 81; 55 (September 1818), p. 69.
[180] "Letters of Fabius," p. 26.
[181] *Life of Southey*, Southey to Wynn, April 1807, III, p. 75.
[182] *Morning Post*, June 24, 1812.
[183] *British Critic*, 19, n.ser. (January 1823), p. 108.

renounced any particular quarrel with Catholic doctrine and asserted indeed that it would accept emancipation if the *Index Librorum Prohibitorum*[184] were eliminated, freedom of inquiry allowed, and the Roman marriage and excommunicatory laws overhauled.[185]

The ultras also took their cue from a generally libertarian analysis of English and European society. In fact, anti-Catholicism led them into strange and uncharted highways and byways. After 1827, the leading ultra publication in the United Kingdom was the daily *Standard* newspaper. In its opposition to St. Dominic, the council of Constance, Mary I, Bartholomew's Day, 1641 and the Irish massacres, the Inquisition, and, in general, "a history which, for a collection of horrors, blasphemy, lewdness, perjury, plunder, and massacre, is unequalled in the records of guilt," the *Standard* called upon the spirit of Benjamin Constant and the "*liberaux* of the Continent" and "all the educated and enlightened classes of France, Italy, and Germany."[186] In the House of Commons, for example, the ultra George Bankes, the son of "Protestant Bankes" himself, was greeted with loud cheers when in 1827, he denounced the clerical government of Charles X as threatening the freedom of the press, "that root and fountain of liberty," and suggested that France "retrograded in liberty in proportion as her priests have regained their influence . . ."[187]

The French revolution of 1830 also enrolled the ultras on the liberal side. In the most famous of Victorian autobiographies, John Henry Newman discusses the almost physical disgust he felt upon docking in Algiers in 1833 and seeing the newly legitimized tricolor flying over a French ship.[188] Let no one, however, suspect that Newman's views were typical expressions of ultra or conservative sympathies. Ultra opinion was usually condemnatory of Charles X and sympathetic to his Orléanist successor, Louis Philippe. This was occasioned by both the obvious anti-Catholic motif as well as by the chance to embarrass the Wellington administration, which had

---

[184] Which *Blackwood's Edinburgh Magazine* reminded its readers contained Locke, Bacon, Milton, Copernicus, Kepler, and Descartes. 24 (December 1828), p. 813. The *Index* was also taken note of during debates on Catholic relief in the House of Commons. In 1825, Inglis read it to the House. *Parl. Deb.*, XIII, n.ser. (April 21, 1825), p. 490.

[185] *Blackwood's Edinburgh Magazine*, 15 (March 1824), p. 282.

[186] *Standard*, September 15, 1828.

[187] *Parl. Deb.*, XVI, n.ser. (March 5, 1827), p. 885.

[188] John Henry Newman, *Apologia Pro Vita Sua* (New York, 1968), p. 39.

maintained cordial if not effusive relations with the Bourbon regime and which was bothered by its violent overthrow. The *Morning Journal*, in April 1830, in one of the last issues before its libel sins and the Wellington prosecution killed it, looked forward hopefully to another revolution in France, heralding a death blow to popery.[189] The weekly *Age* described Charles X as a "drivelling, mass-going, confessing, self-flagellating old idiot" as well as a "blind besotted ... old woman" who deserved exposure to the pillory.[190] The *Standard* accused him of introducing "Asiatic slavery" into his kingdom.[191] After the revolution, *Fraser's Magazine*, while it blamed Charles X for having led an "insufferable despotism," found the new king of the French presiding over a "liberal and beneficial government."[192] George Croly's *Monthly Magazine* depicted Charles X's hands as vampirishly dripping with blood of his unfortunate subjects.[193]

For the ultras, the denunciation of the pro-Catholic wing of the Tory party and concern for the Protestant position of the United Kingdom as a whole under the Constitution of 1688–1689 (or as near a facsimile to it as possible) was more important than virtually *anything* transpiring on the continent. This situation produced a paradox. The further politicians like Sir Richard Vyvyan or newspaper editors like S. L. Giffard of the *Standard* were to the Right of the English political spectrum, the more liberal a policy they would advocate in Europe. Strange bedfellows were not a characteristic of only European rightist ideologists of the twentieth century. Hence, Wellington suspected that the *Standard* really took Isabella II's side in the Spanish civil war of the 1830s because Carlos was more of a Roman Catholic.[194] Indeed, the ultra-Tory Protestants of the 1820s and 1830s lived in a perfervid atmosphere of suspicion and recrimination exemplified by anti-Apostolicism. Vyvyan told the House of Commons during the emancipation debates in 1829 that there was a "great conspiracy ... now on foot and in progress in Europe," formed by

certain despots abroad ... planned by the Congress of Vienna, afterwards recognized at Verona; and finally, in the very capital of France ... The

---

[189] *Morning Journal*, April 10, 1830.
[190] *Age*, October 30, 1830, p. 316; August 8, 1830, p. 252.
[191] *Standard*, July 31, 1830.   [192] *Fraser's Magazine*, 2 (September 1830), p. 233.
[193] *Monthly Magazine*, 10 (September 1830), p. 240.
[194] John Brooke, Julia Gandy, eds., *Royal Commission on Historical Manuscripts, The Prime Minister's Papers: Wellington, Political Correspondence I: 1833–November 1834* (London, 1975), Wellington to Mahon, November 29, 1833, p. 364.

head of this conspiracy was the conclave at Rome, and the servants who were to carry the plan into effect were the Jesuits . . . assisted by the monarchs of Europe.[195]

He told his electors in Cornwall during his successful election campaign in 1830 that the Catholic question concerned not only Britain but "was connected with the general struggle going on in all Europe between liberalism and tyranny." Vyvyan saw the Holy Alliance as an integral part of the conspiracy, especially in its attack upon the liberal constitutions in Spain, Naples, and Portugal, and in the French attack upon Spain in 1823.[196] Variants of this Apostolical conspiracy were taken up between 1825 and 1832 by the entire ultra Tory press.[197] Hence, as on the issues of parliamentary reform, what Disraeli and Carlyle would later term the "condition of England question," and even the oppressive rule of the Irish Protestant landlord class, a certain section of the ultra body politic and propaganda machine was quite prepared, so overwhelming was its hatred for Catholicism, to embrace progressive positions and principles at general variance to that of the normal image of a "Tory world view," if by so doing its greatest enemy might be, if only rhetorically, weakened.

After the mid-1820s, the defense of the Johnsonian, Burkeian, and even Pittite world view concerning Catholics and Dissenters, emancipation and relief, what with anti-Catholicism more and more the glue which held together significant elements of the Tory party and press, was more and more restricted to the person of George Canning and a few of his immediate associates. The sense in which the Tory press was closed to Canning and even, to a much lesser extent after 1828, to the Duke of Wellington and Peel, is best illustrated by their reliance on more or less liberal mouthpieces to present their views to the British public: in Canning's case, the *Star*;[198] in Wellington and Peel's, *The Times*.[199] The best that could be expected from the Tory press on the Catholic question by the mid

---

[195] *Parl. Deb.*, xx, n.ser. (February 24, 1829), p. 522.   [196] *Standard*, August 9, 1830.
[197] *Ibid.*, January 17, 1829.
[198] George Spencer Beasley, *Letters of John Galt From the Blackwood Papers in the National Library of Scotland* (Lubbock, 1951), Galt to Blackwood, March 3, 1823, pp. 123–4.
[199] Arthur Aspinall, *Politics and the Press* (London, 1949), pp. 314–5. As I have noted elsewhere, a number of the non-ultra Tory newspapers and journals remained loyal to Wellington after the traumatic events of 1829, for example, *John Bull*, the *British Critic*, the *Quarterly Review*, the *Morning Post*, and the *Courier*. But is was a dutiful and unenthusiastic loyalty. James J. Sack, "Wellington and the Tory Press, 1828–1830," in Norman Gash, ed., *Wellington* (Manchester, 1990), pp. 161–3.

to late 1820s was the studied understanding of the *Courier* to those who disagreed with them[200] or the occasional ridicule by a moderately anti-Catholic journal, the *British Critic*, of the notion that the much discussed biblical "Beast" was the papal power.[201] To be sure, the defense of Catholic emancipation on the Canningite Right sometimes seemed to involve a form of social snobbery. If Lockhart's vision of his father-in-law is to be credited[202] or Huskisson's opposition to the repeal of the Test and Corporation Acts not be misconstrued, their preference for Roman Catholics, who after all contained kings and nobles in their communion, as over and above the lower-class Dissenters, was somewhat class based.[203]

The most aggressive public defense of the Burkeite and Pittite cause on Catholic relief came from George Canning, who from Castlereagh's death to his own (and indeed beyond) seemed uniquely capable, like Fox in his day, of dividing the political nation into his friends and his enemies. As the aged Gladstone reminisced to A. C. Benson of Eton in the 1820s: "We were not liberal or tories in those days . . . We were Canning or non-Canning."[204] As some of the press realized at the time,[205] Canning, in his spiritual and foreign policy views of the interest of England, had gone beyond party or connection, as Edmund Burke had done in his Irish, Indian or Catholic designs of over a generation before. Their critics from the extreme Right saw the same dangers and tendencies in both men, even to the point of Jacobinism.[206] And Canning was one of the few Tories still to espouse Burke's opinions in the Commons in the 1820s,[207] as he still espoused those of the non-sanitized Pitt.[208]

---

[200] *Courier*, April 1825.

[201] *British Critic*, 23, n.ser. (March 1825), p. 249. In 1828, newly united with the equally moderate *Quarterly Theological Review and Ecclesiastical Record*, the *British Critic* proclaimed predestination a "more appalling dogma" even than the Roman Catholic teaching of "no salvation outside the Church." Whatever the private views of their editors, few other anti-Catholic Tory publications would have admitted as much as the great crisis of emancipation approached. 3, 4th ser. (April 1828), p. 358.

[202] A. L. Strout, "Some unpublished letters of John Gibson Lockhart to John Wilson Croker," *Notes and Queries*, (August 25, 1945), Lockhart to Croker, May 26, 1845, 189, p. 83.

[203] *Parl. Deb.*, xviii, n.ser. (February 26, 1828), p. 734.

[204] David Newsome, *On the Edge of Paradise, A. C. Benson: the Diarist* (Chicago, 1980), p. 96.

[205] *Fraser's Magazine*, 1 (February 3, 1830), p. 3.

[206] Chateaubriand, of course, called Canning the first Jacobin of Europe. *Blackwood's Edinburgh Magazine*, 26 (October 1829), p. 696. The right-wing *Oracle* thought Burke a Jacobin of sorts too. July 11, 1797.

[207] Sack, "Memory of Burke," p. 626n.

[208] *Parl. Deb.*, xvi, n.ser. (March 6, 1827), p. 1006.

Canning indeed bid fair in his person, even if lacking the generosity of Burke or the studied simplicity of Pitt, to reconcile the two traditions of Burke and Pitt insofar as such a task was ever possible.[209]

Far more than, for example, the dutiful "Catholic" Castlereagh, Canning attacked the historical, doctrinal, and dual allegiance arguments against Catholic relief, and often in a way that betrayed his very Burkeian mistrust of Dissenters. Hence he wondered in the House of Commons what the public had to do with Charles IX or Admiral Coligny or who cared if "the Guises sprinkled themselves with the blood of their unfortunate victims or that the duke d'Angoulême viewed his [Coligny's] butchered corpse with emotions of delight?" Canning, no more prepared than Burke had been to allow the appeal to history to become an appeal to the common criminality of mankind, wondered, "What good can it do to recall the memory of them?"[210] In his famous *Sursum Corda* speech, Canning, not for the last time, came close to a defense of transubstantiation, and emphasized "the great fundamental doctrines" which as a "Church-of-England man" he shared with Romanism, as opposed to his essential differences with many of the Dissenters.[211] Canning implicitly denied that a papist could not bear true allegiance to the king, reminding his colleagues in the House of Commons that it was not Catholicism which brought Charles I to the block or stripped Laud and his fellow bishops of their miters and peerages.[212]

In 1829, during the final Catholic emancipation debates, the most Burkeian and Canningite argumentation in favor of relief came from Bishop Copleston of Llandaff, a High Churchman and a "tory of the school of Canning."[213] Copleston wondered how Lord Eldon as well as some of the Irish bishops could describe Catholicism as idolatrous.

Can a minister of the church of England dare to utter such a sentiment? Does he not know that we have always regarded the Church of Rome as a branch of the universal Church of Christ? Does he not know that we admit her baptism to be valid, her ordinations to be valid, and that she holds all

---

[209] The hatred in which Canning was held by ultra newspapers and politicians is illustrated in their comments after his untimely death. The *Standard* accused him of atheism. *Courier*, August 11, 1827. And some within the Duke of Newcastle's circle rejoiced that "Providence has once more befriended old England." University of Nottingham, Newcastle Papers, NeC5340, Combermere to Newcastle, December 31, 1827. I owe this last reference to Douglas M. Peers.

[210] *Parl. Deb.*, xxiii (June 22, 1812), pp. 653–4.

[211] *Ibid.*, vi, n.ser. (April 2, 1821), p. 1547.

[212] *Ibid.*, xiii, n.ser. (April 21, 1825), p. 90.   [213] See the *DNB* under "Copleston."

the essential doctrines of Christianity ... We ... derive all our spiritual authority, our very existence as a church transmitted to us through that channel ...[214]

Yet emancipation, when it came two years after Canning's death, to the horror of all ultras and, perhaps, most Tories, arrived in a fashion which in general eschewed ideological considerations, much less Burke's memory, and laid the foundation upon good old practical English common sense and even utilitarianism.[215] Perhaps this was in the long run all for the best in the Conservative party. Had their leaders, Wellington, Peel, and the rest, waged a near ideological campaign in favor of emancipation – as Canning might have done – and then won a crushing victory, it might have been harder for the Tories to rise and fight another day.

[214] *Parl. Deb.*, xxi, n.ser. (April 17, 1829), p. 489.
[215] Which perhaps explains Bentham's regard for Wellington's safety. Elizabeth Longford, *Wellington: Pillar of State* (New York, 1972), p. 189.

Conclusion

Long before the commencement of the final struggle for Catholic emancipation in 1829 or for parliamentary reform in 1831, and despite the victory of ostensibly progressive forces in both battles, there was certainly an important right-wing expression bubbling over in British society which added immeasurably to these and other political, religious, and economic debates. As the preceding chapters indicate, however, any exact definition of the "Right," presents many conundrums. As is usually the case when discussing any political party or philosophical susceptibility, on the one hand, the historian can define his quarry in negative terms, in this instance, a rightist viewpoint in British politics which stood over and against an emerging leftist world view which emphasized the rights of Dissenters, a rather cool view of the English and Irish national Church, an enthusiasm for European liberalism, a tolerance (at the least) for a libertarian personal morality, a Smithian and Ricardian economic dispensation, and a more open attitude towards the empowerment of the middle class and (some) artisans.

Not surprisingly perhaps, it is more difficult to discuss a rightist perspective in positive terms. Just as historians experience obstacles in coming to grips with the exact meaning of English Protestantism in the 1530s or of Italian Fascism in the 1920s, so to discuss an English rightist – much less a conservative – world view in the 1790s or 1820s, before either word was widely used in Britain, involves so many compromises, codicils, or exceptional clauses as to render it philosophically if not linguistically suspect. Can figures as diverse in their political and social ideas as Burke and Addington, Johnson and Kenyon, Henry Bate Dudley and S. L. Giffard be wrapped up in the same cocoon, broadly labelled right-wing or conservative? Certainly if a similar response to concrete national issues is the sole test of the matter, the answer is negative. Yet what Burke called "the

252

Babbles"[1] of the moment, the transitory war, the quarrel over ministerial appointments, even disagreement over highly charged Irish legislation, may not be the most salient points here. If a deep and abiding commitment to an Anglican spiritual basis for the national life is factored into the equation, a common right-wing or conservative philosophy, however, difficult to define, becomes more apparent.

It may also be that disposition is as important in a right-wing political commitment as specific actions or beliefs. Here exact definitions recede in importance compared to more intangible qualities. Thus in terms applicable to the early Protestant or Fascist as well as to the right-winger of the age of North or Liverpool, as James Boswell understood, one knows one when one sees one. Hence a rightist perspective might well be identified more by a certain edge or inflection in the argument, a certain way of emphasizing the word "king" or "Cromwell," "Jew" or "Pope," "bishop" or "swinish multitude," than by a more positivistic determination or critique.

Whether this right-wing perspective should be viewed as in any significant way co-determinant with or grafted upon a "Tory party" is problematic. To refer before 1831 or 1832 to a Tory party in parliament, much less a conservative one, and by that to mean a group of men self-consciously acting upon a set of more or less agreed-upon principles, is probably misplaced chronologically, even if at times understandable for the sake of content or to avoid confusion. The fluctuating "Church and King" factions and groups, Buteite, Northite, Pittite, Canningite, Wellingtonian or what have you, which made up the chief governing party of England during the reigns of George III and George IV, while they were collectively or individually sometimes termed "Tory," are probably best divested of too formal a party nomenclature until the coming of "conservative" after 1830 allowed politicians gracefully to adopt the shorter terminology, "Tory," as a nickname for the philosophically descriptive if more cumbersome word, "conservative."

It would also be difficult to prove that the persistence of a right-wing perspective, important though it might prove in the long haul, had a resonance of the greatest importance in parliament before the substantial fragmentation of the royal role in ministerial formation after 1830. Only after the appeal to the wider electorate

---

[1] Burke, *Corr.*, II, p. 282.

after 1832 by something resembling modern political parties did the parliamentary leadership come to greatly value, if not always follow, the sort of out-of-doors and non-elite opinion associated with highly ideologized Tory or conservative newspapers, journals, clubs, and pressure groups. The alacrity with which, for example, provincial Tory newspapers were founded after 1831[2] and the nonchalance which loyalist governments with their incessant stamp duties had exhibited towards the press beforehand,[3] illustrates the new importance some Tories then placed upon an appeal to public opinion as opposed to a reliance upon the sovereign for the achievement of political power.

There is much more to be said on this subject but I suspect that the rightist perspective (or its reflection in the press in particular) from Johnson to Burke, from Henry Bate Dudley to S. L. Giffard was not especially welcomed by successive ministries or by the parliamentary classes in general. From the perspective of North, Pitt, Perceval, or Liverpool it may have been less of a positive or sustaining influence which they saluted or embraced and more of an albatross about their necks, albeit to be treated gingerly, or even (in the case of the press) sometimes grudgingly subsidized. One sometimes gets the sense that rightist opinion was more of a combustible pressure group outside of the governing coalition, rarely invited inside, and mistrusted by those in the charmed circle, rather than a valued and cooperative force harnessed to aid and sustain those Northite, Pittite, and Wellingtonian coalitions in power. A more sustaining role may have come after 1832. Since, as a body of opinion called into existence by successive religious and political events, it was not about to go away, perhaps the later generations of Disraeli and then Salisbury (and even the mature Peel) dealt with ideas in a more creative fashion than did the generation of Pitt or Liverpool. Anyway, to speak of the Right or conservatism or even Toryism in 1846 or 1869 or 1902 is much easier and more meaningful than to use the same terms when discussing 1776, 1793, 1801 or 1830, when the language appears mildly unfocused and anachronistic.

Hence rightist opinion from the 1750s to 1832 was eclectic and

---

[2] See, for example, BL, Peel Papers, Add. MSS. 40524, Watts to Peel, February 1, 1843, fos. 118–20.

[3] See the scolding of the Liverpool government on these grounds by the organ of the Pitt Club, the *New Monthly Magazine*, July 1, 1815, p. 575.

difficult to define. A highly ideologized argumentative style and set of opinions emerged out of a Jacobite or Tory world view and were here and there present in the press, in pamphlet literature, in sermons, sometimes (though less frequently) in parliamentary speeches, sometimes sponsored by the government or factions within a ministry, often seemingly appearing without any particular ministerial sanction or even approval. Yet, while weaker in the beginning of the period, these attitudes or opinions generally strengthened after 1776 and 1792, until sponsored by poets, novelists, newspaper editors, journalists, parliamentarians, and clerical figures, a substantial body of thought was created which a widening political nation could dip into as desired to hone or heat up arguments, to provide historical and religious parallels, or to affect changes in a government program.

The Right was made up of half-remembered echoes of seventeenth-century battles long won or lost, of an often skewed recollection of great eighteenth-century political or moral figures such as George III, Johnson, Burke, or the Younger Pitt, of an ancient and abiding Christian humanitarianism, and of the fears and hatreds, both before and after 1789, engendered from revolutionary and radical occurrences. Most importantly, as J. C. D. Clark has suspected, the English Right, both Wellingtonian and ultra, as the sides divided during the climacteric struggle for emancipation, manifested a renewed commitment, striking in its intensity after the cool and rationalistic eighteenth-century religious environment, to the Church of England (often in its higher revelation). Whatever may have been the case in 1760 or 1780, insofar as any one institution or idea served as the *ne plus ultra* of what it meant to be attached to the Right in politics in 1830, it was extreme adherence not to the monarchy or even to a particular vision of an ideal class or political structure, but to "thy holy church universal in the right way."

That such a captivating vision was seductive even beyond the confines of the Right perhaps explains as much as anything Richard Brent's identification of the keen Anglican religiosity, albeit of a more liberal hue, evolving in the 1820s and 1830s in the younger scions of the older and often skeptical Whig families.[4]

This is not to suggest that all the individuals discussed in this volume, or their political and patronage networks, or the press they

---

[4] Richard Brent, *Liberal Anglican Politics: Whiggery, Religion, and Reform, 1830–1841* (Oxford, 1987).

founded and worked for, can be easily lumped together as examples of extreme religiosity. There were always important "Tories" who on a personal level were less than enthusiastic about religious practices or even belief. Not only William Pitt but also those two fraternal and stalwart defenders of the Anglican constitution, Lords Eldon and Stowell, were notoriously neglectful of their churchly duties.[5] Disraeli, himself hardly a paragon of Anglican punctiliousness, doubted that Lord Lyndhurst was a believer.[6] The chief of the ultra Protestants, HRH the Duke of Cumberland told the Primate of All England that he went to church largely for the sake of example.[7]

The attitude of a number of significant Buteist and (later) Tory journalists suggest a similar cast of mind to that which Jeremy Popkin discovered among French right-wing journalists of the 1790s: they viewed Christianity more from a utilitarian than from a revelatory basis.[8] Hence, Arthur Murphy[9] of the *Auditor*, John Campbell,[10] Bute's chief pensioned writer, Tobias Smollett[11] of the *Critical Review*, and John Gibson Lockhart of the *Quarterly Review*,[12] and no doubt others, seldom darkened churches by their presence.

Nonetheless, by the early nineteenth century, the pull of religion for the party associated with "Church and King" is probably quantifiable. As compared with some of George III's earlier ministerial choices such as the Duke of Grafton, Lord Shelburne, or the Younger Pitt, a public religiosity became almost a *sine qua non* for politicians interested in the highest office, if one considers the cases of Addington, Portland, Perceval, Liverpool, or Goderich. Wellington, despite a somewhat irregular family life, probably felt the same motivation as his enemy Cumberland in relation to church-going.[13] In 1758, would anyone have cared if the elder Pitt went to church? By 1810, partially due to the growth of right-wing advocatory journalism, such questions were lovingly mulled over in the press. Canning's life and death is a case in point. Despite Lady Holland's

[5] Horace Twiss, *Public and Private Life of Lord Chancellor Eldon* (London, 1844), III, p. 488.
William Edward Surtees, *Sketch of the Lives of Lords Stowell and Eldon* (London, 1846), p. 143.
[6] Helen M. Swartz, Marvin Swartz, *Disraeli's Reminiscences* (New York, 1976), p. 95.
[7] Aspinall, III, p. 527n.
[8] Jeremy D. Popkin, *Right-Wing Press in France, 1792–1800* (Chapel Hill, 1980), pp. 116, 164.
[9] John Pike Emery, *Arthur Murphy* (Philadelphia, 1946), p. 144.
[10] See *DNB* under "Campbell, John."
[11] Lewis Mansfield Knapp, *Tobias Smollett* (Princeton, 1949), p. 307. In "Adventures of an Atom," Smollett certainly ridicules the doctrine and creed of the Church of England. James P. Browne, ed., *Works of Tobias Smollett* (London, 1872), pp. 341–2.
[12] Andrew Lang, *Life and Letters of John Gibson Lockhart* (New York, 1970), II, p. 397.
[13] Elizabeth Longford, *Wellington: Pillar of State* (New York, 1972), p. 88.

accusations, recorded by Tom Moore, that he was frequently unfaithful to his wife,[14] the ultra *Standard* was excessive in declaring in 1827 that Canning as prime minister died an atheist.[15] His cousin, William Canning, evidently motivated by the wider family circle, admitted that as a young man Canning was not attentive to religious duties,[16] but that after his marriage in 1800 he was as regular in church attendance as possible.[17] The pro-Canningite *Courier*, adding to the debate, asserted, again probably on familial authority, that when for one reason or another he was unable to attend Sunday church, Canning assembled his entire family, including the servants, to read the Liturgy.[18] While a Whiggish Melbourne in the 1830s might yet get away with an obvious religious nonchalance it is doubtful if his counterparts on the Right could have.

Hence increasingly as the period of the high Enlightenment advanced and the French and Industrial Revolutions took place, the English right wing (whether sincere or not) defined itself very largely with confessional and spiritual vocabularies. It committed itself to at least a public defense and formal adherence to the commandments and formularies of orthodox Christianity. This was the Right's strength and its shield. The fact that its opponents, whether Whig or radical, were never quite able to duplicate such allegiance or commitment (and in some cases repudiated it altogether) was a source of their weakness and marginalization. Only when an extension of the electorate after 1832 – sometimes in a dissenting direction – somewhat leveled the playing field and the effective role of the Anglican sovereign in choosing ministers was lessened, did religion cease to absorb the energies and attention of much of the propaganda effort of the party of Order.

The later destruction of that Anglican–Tory consensus of 1830 has been traced, at least on the high philosophical level, in the work of Maurice Cowling.[19] Yet despite Catholic emancipation and the fissures and sorrows it caused the Right in 1829 and 1830, few signs were then exhibited of the change in nuance towards greater secularization or even rationalism, towards a preoccupation with

---

[14] Wilfred S. Dowden, ed., *Journal of Thomas Moore* (Newark, 1983), II, p. 462.
[15] *Courier*, August 11, 1827.
[16] When, among other things, he was most under Pitt's influence.
[17] *Standard*, August 20, 1827.
[18] *Courier*, August 11, 1827.
[19] Maurice J. Cowling, *Religion and Public Doctrine in Modern England* (Cambridge, England, 1980).

economics or the social question, with foreign policy or defense or imperial matters, which British conservatism would emphasize in succeeding generations. Religion, and specifically the place of the Church of England in the national life, was still the overwhelming conservative concern on the eve of the Whig reform triumph.

Select Bibliography

PRIMARY SOURCES

UNPUBLISHED MANUSCRIPT SOURCES

The Bodleian Library, Oxford

S. L. Giffard Letters

British Library, Department of Manuscripts, London

i. Add[itional] M[anu]S[cript]S
   Aberdeen Papers
   Berkeley Papers
   Bliss Papers
   Dropmore (Grenville) Papers
   Ellis Papers
   Halsbury Papers
   Hardwicke Papers
   Herries Papers
   Liverpool Papers
   Newcastle Papers
   Sir R. Owens Papers
   Peel Papers
   Rose Papers
   Whiteford Papers
   Windham Papers
ii. Eg[erton] M[anu]S[cript]S
   Strange Papers

Clements Library, University of Michigan, Ann Arbor

Croker Papers

East Sussex Record Office, Lewes

Boucher Papers

National Library of Scotland, Edinburgh

Blackwood Papers
Gleig Papers
Lockhart Papers
Walter Scott Papers

Pierpont Morgan Library, New York (seen in transcript)

Southey-Croker Papers

Public Record Office, London

Chatham Papers
Foreign Office Papers
Home Office Papers

Regenstein Library, University of Chicago, Chicago

Hook Papers

Sheffield City Libraries, Sheffield (seen in transcript)

Burke Papers

University of Illinois at Urbana-Champaign

Cobbett Papers

West Yorkshire Archives, Leeds

Harewood (Canning) Papers

NEWSPAPERS AND PERIODICALS

Age
Albion
Anti-Gallican Monitor
Anti-Jacobin
Anti-Jacobin Review
Auditor

Beacon
Blackwood's Edinburgh Magazine
Blagdon's Weekly Political Register
British Critic
British Magazine
British Mercury
British Monitor
Briton
Brunswick or True Blue
Bull Dog
Busy Body
Christian Magazine
Christian Remembrancer
Cobbett's Political Register
Common Sense
Con-Test
Cooper's John Bull
Courier
Court Magazine
Court Miscellany
Crab-Tree
Critical Review
Day
Dublin University Magazine
Edinburgh Annual Register
Edinburgh Monthly Review
Edinburgh Review
Felix Farley's Bristol Journal
Fraser's Magazine
General Evening Post
Gentleman's Magazine
Guardian
Guardian of Education
Jackson's Oxford Journal
John Bull
Literary Gazette
Literary Magazine
Lloyd's Evening Post
London Chronicle
London Evening Post
London Magazine
Monitor
Monthly Censor
Monthly Magazine
Monthly Review

Morning Chronicle
Morning Herald
Morning Journal
Morning Post
National Adviser
New Anti-Jacobin Review
New Edinburgh Review
New European Magazine
New Monthly Magazine
New Times
North Briton
Oracle
Orthodox Churchman's Magazine
Phoenix
Pilot
Plain Englishman
Porcupine
Protestant Advocate
Public Advertiser
Public Ledger
Quarterly Review
Quarterly Theological Review and Ecclesiastical Record
Redhead Yorke's Weekly Political Review
Representative
Revolutionary Magazine
Satirist
St. James's Chronicle
Standard
Star of Brunswick
Sun
Tait's Edinburgh Magazine
The Times
Tomahawk! or Censor General
Tory
True Briton
Warder
Watchman
Westminster Review
White Dwarf
Whitehall Evening Post
York Courant

PRINTED PRIMARY WORKS: ARTICLES, BOOKS, DIARIES, LETTERS,
BIOGRAPHIES OF THE EIGHTEENTH AND NINETEENTH CENTURIES,
PAMPHLETS, SERMONS, AND TRACTS

Adair, D., Schutz, J. A., eds., *Peter Oliver's Origin and Progress of the American Rebellion: A Tory View* (Stanford, 1961)

Adolphus, J., *History of England* (London, 1840), I, VI

Agutter, W., "Abolition of the slave trade considered" (London, 1788)

Albemarle, G. T., Earl of, *Memoirs of the Marquis of Rockingham* (London, 1852), I

Alexander, R., "Fate of the colonies" (London, 1830)

Anson, Sir W. R., ed., *Autobiography and Political Correspondence of Augustus Henry Third Duke of Grafton, K. G.* (London, 1898)

Ashe, T., ed., *Table Talk and Omniana of Samuel Taylor Coleridge* (London, 1909)

Aspinall, A., ed., *Correspondence of Charles Arbuthnot*, Camden, 3rd ser., LXV (London, 1941)

Correspondence of George, Prince of Wales, 1770–1812 (8 vols., New York, 1963–1971)

Formation of Canning's Ministry February to August 1827, Camden, 3rd ser., LIX (London, 1937)

Later Correspondence of George III (5 vols., Cambridge, England, 1962–1970)

Letters of George IV (1812–1830) (3 vols., Cambridge, England, 1938)

Three Early Nineteenth Century Diaries (London, 1952)

"An authentic account of the trials at large of George Robert Fitzgerald, esq., Timothy Brecknock ... " (London, 1786)

Bagot, J., ed., *George Canning and his Friends* (2 vols., London, 1909)

Balderston, K. C., ed., *Thraliana: Diary of Mrs. Hester Lynch Thrale (Later Mrs. Piozzi), 1776–1809* (2 vols., Oxford, 1951)

Bamford, F., Wellington, Duke of, eds., *Journal of Mrs. Arbuthnot, 1820–1832* (2 vols., London, 1950)

Baring, Mrs. H., ed., *Diary of the Right Hon. William Windham, 1784–1810* (London, 1866)

Barker, G. F. R., ed., *Memoirs of the Reign of King George III by Horace Walpole* (4 vols., London, 1894)

Bates, W., ed., *A Gallery of Illustrious Literary Characters (1830–1838)* (London, 1873)

Bath and Wells, Bishop of, ed., *Journal and Correspondence of William, Lord Auckland* (4 vols., London, 1861)

Beasley, G. S., *Letters of John Galt from the Blackwood Papers in the National Library of Scotland* (Lubbock, 1951)

Bickley, F., ed., *Diaries of Sylvester Douglas, Lord Glenbervie* (2 vols., London, 1928)

"Biographical list of the members of 'The Club of Nobody's Friends'" (London, 1885)

Bisset, R., *History of the Reign of George III* (5 vols., London, 1803)
Blackstone, Sir W., *Commentaries on the Laws of England* (Philadelphia, 1862), 1
Bonnard, G. A., ed., *Memoirs of My Life* by Edward Gibbon (New York, 1966)
Boswell, J., *Life of Johnson* (London, 1953)
Boucher, J., "Letters," *Maryland Historical Magazine*, 8–10 (June 1913– June 1915)
"View of the causes and consequences of the American Revolution in thirteen discourses" (London, 1797)
Bouchier, J., ed., *Reminiscences of an American Loyalist, 1738–1789* (Boston, 1925)
Bourne, K., ed., *Letters of the Third Viscount Palmerston to Lawrence and Elizabeth Sulivan, 1804–1863*, Camden, 4th ser., xxiii (London, 1979)
Bowdler, J., "Reform or ruin" (London, 1797)
[Bowdler, T.], *Memoirs of the Life of John Bowdler, Esq.* (London, 1824)
Bowles, J., "French aggression praised from Mr. Erskine's 'View of the causes of the war'" (London, 1797)
[Bowles, J.], "Postscript to thoughts on the late general election as demonstrative of the progress of Jacobinism" (London, 1803)
[Bowles, J.], "A protest against T. Paine's 'Rights of man'" (Edinburgh, 1792)
Bowles, J., "Reflections political and moral at the conclusion of the war" (London, 1802)
Bowles, J., "Remarks on modern female matters" (London, 1802)
Bowles, J., "View of the moral state of society at the close of the eighteenth century. Much enlarged." (London, 1804)
Brady, F., Pottle, F. A., eds., *Boswell on the Grand Tour, Italy, Corsica, and France, 1765–1766* (New York, 1955)
[Brecknock, T.], *"Droit le Roy"* (London, 1764)
Brooke, J., ed., *Memoirs of King George II* by Horace Walpole (New Haven, 1985)
Brooke, J., Gandy, J., eds., *Royal Commission on Historical Manuscripts, The Prime Ministers' Papers: Wellington, Political Correspondence I: 1833– November 1834* (London, 1975)
Brougham, H., Lord, *Historical Sketches of Statesmen Who Flourished in the Time of George III* (2 vols., London, 1839)
Brown, P. D., Schweizer, K. W., eds., *Devonshire Diary*, Camden, 4th ser., xxvii (London, 1982)
Browne, J. P., ed., *Works of Tobias Smollett* (London, 1872)
Bulwer, Sir H. L., *Life of Henry John Temple, Viscount Palmerston: with Selections from his Diaries and Correspondence* (London, 1870), 1
Burke, E., *Works of the Right Honourable Edmund Burke* (12 vols., London, 1887)
Butler, C., *Philological and Biographical Works* (London, 1817), ii

[Butler, J.], "Address to Cocoa-Tree from a Whig" (London, 1763)

Cannon, J., ed., *Letters of Junius* (Oxford, 1978)

Carlisle, Bishop of, "Sermon preached before the Lords ... on ... January 30, 1765" (London, 1765)

Carswell, J., Dralle, L. A., eds., *Political Journal of George Bubb Dodington* (Oxford, 1965)

Carte, T., *General History of England* (4 vols., London, 1747–1755)

Churton, E., ed., *Memoir of Joshua Watson* (2 vols., Oxford, 1861)

Clark, J. C. D., ed., *Memoirs and Speeches of James 2nd Earl Waldegrave 1742–1763* (Cambridge, England, 1988)

Cobbett, W., ed., *Parliamentary History of England, from the Earliest Period to the Year 1803* (36 vols., London, 1806–1820)

Colchester, C., Lord, ed., *Diary and Correspondence of Charles Abbot Lord Colchester* (3 vols., London, 1861)

Colchester, C., Lord, ed., *A Political Diary, 1828–1830* by Edward Law Lord Ellenborough (2 vols., London, 1881)

"Collection of letters on the thirtieth of January and twenty-ninth of May" (London, 1784)

Colmer, J., *et al*, eds., *Collected Works of Samuel Taylor Coleridge* (Princeton, 1976–1988), II–III

Cooper, M., "A sermon preached before the university of Oxford ... Dec. 13, 1776" (Oxford, 1777)

Copeland, T. W., *et al*, eds., *Correspondence of Edmund Burke* (10 vols., Cambridge, England, 1958–1978)

"The Crewe Papers," *Miscellanies of the Philobiblon Society*, 9 (London, 1865–1866)

Croly, G., "Englishman's polar star" (Preston, 1828)

Historical Sketches, Speeches, and Characters (London, 1842)

Life and Times of his late Majesty George the Fourth (London, 1830)

Curnock, N., ed., *Journal of the Rev. John Wesley* (New York, n.d.), VI

Dalrymple, Sir J., "Appeal of reason to the people of England on the present state of parties in the nation" (London, 1763)

"Appeal to the facts" (London, 1763)

Memoirs of Great Britain and Ireland (London, 1771), I

Daubeny, C., *An Appendix to the Guide to the Church* (London, 1830)

Guide to the Church (New York, 1803)

"On the nature, progress, and consequences of schism" (London, 1818)

Protestant's Companion (London, 1824)

DeLancey, E. F., ed., *History of New York During the Revolutionary War* by Thomas Jones (New York, 1879), I

Dowden, W. S., ed., *Journal of Thomas Moore* (Newark, 1983–1986), II, III

Eden, Sir F. M., "Eight letters on the peace" (London, 1802)

Engell, J., Bate, W. J., eds., *Collected Works of Samuel Taylor Coleridge; Biographia Literaria* (Princeton, 1983), VII

Extraordinary Red Book (London, 1817)

Festing, G., *John Hookham Frere and his Friends* (London, 1899)
Fifer, C. N., ed., *Correspondence of James Boswell with Certain Members of The Club* (New York, 1976)
Fletcher, J., "American patriotism" (London, 1776)
"A Vindication of the Rev. Mr. Wesley's 'Calm address to our American colonies'" (London, 1776)
Fortescue, Sir J., ed., *Correspondence of King George III from 1760 to December 1783* (6 vols., London, 1927–1928)
Freeman, J., *Life of the Rev. William Kirby, M. A.* (London, 1852)
Friedman, A., ed., *Collected Works of Oliver Goldsmith* (5 vols., Oxford, 1966)
Galt, J., *Autobiography* (London, 1833), II
Gifford, J., "A letter to the Earl of Lauderdale." (London, 1800)
Grant, J., *Great Metropolis* (2 vols., London, 1836)
The Newspaper Press: Its Origins – Progress – and Present Position (2 vols., London, 1871)
Green, T. H., Grose, T. H., eds., *Essays, Moral, Political and Literary* by David Hume (London, 1875), I
Greene, D. J., ed., *Yale Edition of the Works of Samuel Johnson, Political Writings* (New Haven, 1977), X
Greig, J. Y. T., ed., *Letters of David Hume* (2 vols., Oxford, 1932)
Grenville, Lord, ed., "Letters written by the late Earl of Chatham to his nephew Thomas Pitt ..." (London, 1821)
Grierson, H. J. C., ed., *Letters of Sir Walter Scott* (12 vols., London, 1971)
Griggs, E. L., ed., *Collected Letters of Samuel Taylor Coleridge* (6 vols., Oxford, 1956–1971)
Gunn, J. A. W., *et al.*, eds., *Benjamin Disraeli Letters, 1815–1847* (4 vols., Toronto, 1982–1989)
Halliday, J., *Life of Mansfield* (London, 1797)
Hansard, T. C., ed., *Parliamentary Debates from the Year 1803 to the Present Time* (London, 1812–)
Harcourt, L. V., ed., *Diaries and Correspondence of the Right Hon. George Rose* (2 vols., London, 1860)
Hardy, F., *Memoirs of the Political and Private Life of Charlemont* (London, 1810)
Hardy, W. J., ed., Historical Manuscripts Commission, 14th report, Appendix, pt. IV, *Manuscripts of Lord Kenyon* (London, 1894)
Hawkins, Sir J., *Works of Samuel Johnson* (London, 1787), I
Hazlitt, W., *Political Essays* (London, 1819)
Historical Manuscripts Commission [11th report, Appendix, pt. IV]: *Manuscripts of the Earl of Dartmouth* (London, 1887), I
Historical Manuscripts Commission: *Manuscripts of J. B. Fortescue ... preserved at Dropmore* (London, 1905), IV
"History of the late minority" (London, 1765)
Holland, H. E., Lord, ed., *Memoirs of the Whig Party During My Time* by Henry Richard Lord Holland (2 vols., London, 1859)

Holyoake, C. J., *Life of Joseph Raynes Stephens* (London, 1881)
"Honest grief of a Tory" (London, 1759)
Horsley, S., bishop of St. Asaph, *Theological works* (London, 1845), VI
Houtchens, L. H. and C. W., eds., *Political and Occasional Essays* by Leigh Hunt (New York, 1962)
Howe, P. P., ed., *Complete Works of William Hazlitt* (New York, 1967), VIII
Hume, D., *History of England* (New York, 1879), IV–VI
Hutchinson, P. O., *Diary and Letters of ... Thomas Hutchinson* (2 vols., London, 1883–1886)
Hutton, J., ed., *Selections from the Letters and Correspondence of Sir James Bland Burges, Bart.* (London, 1885)
Ilchester, Earl of, ed., *Journal of the Hon. Henry Edward Fox, 1818–1830* (London, 1923)
[Ireland, Rev. J.], "Letters of Fabius to the Right Hon. William Pitt on his proposed abolition of the test" (London, 1801)
"Vindiciae Regiae" (London, 1797)
Irish University Press Series of British Parliamentary Papers: Newspapers, 2 (Shannon, Ireland, 1971)
Jennings, L. J., ed., *Correspondence and Diaries of John Wilson Croker* (3 vols., London, 1884)
Jerdan, W., *Autobiography* (2 vols., London, 1852)
Men I Have Known (London, 1866)
Jones, W., *The Scholar Armed Against the Errors of the Times* (London, 1800)
Works of the Right Reverend George Horne, D. D. (2 vols., New York, 1846)
Jucker, N. S., ed., *Jenkinson Papers, 1760–1766* (London, 1949)
Kenyon, Lord, "Observations on the Roman Catholic question" (London, 1812)
King, W., *Political and Literary Anecdotes of his own Times* (London, 1818)
Klibansky, R., Mossner, E. C., eds., *New Letters of David Hume* (Oxford, 1954)
Knapp, O. G., *Intimate Letters of Hester Piozzi and Penelope Pennington, 1778–1821* (London, 1914)
Knight, C., *Passages of a Working Life During Half a Century* (2 vols., London, 1864)
Lane-Poole, S., *Life of the Right Honourable Stratford Canning* (2 vols., London, 1888)
Lang, A., *Life and Letters of John Gibson Lockhart* (New York, 1970)
Laws and Ordinances of the Orange Institution (London, 1822)
"The legality of the questions proposed by ... the Bishop of ... Peterborough to candidates for holy orders considered" (London, 1820)
Lincoln, Bishop of, "Sermon preached before the Lords ... on ... January 31, 1763" (London, 1763)
"A sermon preached before the Lords ... on ... January 30, 1789" (London, 1789)
Lively, J., ed., *Works of Joseph de Maistre* (New York, 1971)

Llandaff, Bishop of, "Sermon preached before the Lords . . . on . . . January 30, 1772" (London, 1772)
"Sermon preached before the Lords . . . on . . . January 30, 1784" (London, 1784)
"Sermon preached before the Society for the Suppression of Vice, 3rd May 1804" (London, 1804)
Low, D. M., ed., *Gibbon's Journal to January 28th 1763* (London, 1929)
Lustig, I. S., Pottle, F. A., eds., *Boswell: Applause of the Jury, 1782–1785* (New York, 1981)
Macaulay, T. B., *Critical, Historical, and Miscellaneous Essays* (New York, 1860) VI, VIII
Mackintosh, R. J., ed., *Memoirs of the Life of the Right Honourable Sir James Mackintosh* (2 vols., London, 1836)
Mallet, D., *Poetical Works* (Edinburgh, 1780)
Malmesbury, third Earl of, ed., *Diaries and Correspondence of James Harris, First Earl of Malmesbury* (4 vols., London, 1844)
Series of Letters of the first Earl of Malmesbury, His Family and Friends from 1745 to 1820 (2 vols., London, 1870)
Markham, Sir C., *Memoir of Archbishop Markham (1719–1807)* (Oxford, 1906)
Markham, W., "Sermon preached before the Society for the Propagation of the Gospel in Foreign Parts, February 2, 1777" (London, 1777)
Marsh, H., *Comparative View of the Churches of England and Rome* (London, 1841)
"Inquiry into the consequences of neglecting to give the prayer book with the Bible" (Cambridge, 1812)
"Letter to Reverend Peter Gandolphy" (Cambridge, 1813)
"Letter to the Right Hon. N. Vansittart, MP" (Cambridge, 1812)
Maxwell, Sir H., ed., *Creevey Papers* (New York, 1904)
Melville, L., ed., *Huskisson Papers* (London, 1931)
Memoirs of the Public Life of Sir Walter Blackett (Newcastle, 1819)
Minto, Countess of, ed., *Life and Letters of Sir Gilbert Elliot First Earl of Minto from 1751 to 1806* (3 vols., London, 1874)
Montagu, R. W., ed., *Miscellanies: Prose and Verses by William Maginn* (2 vols., London, 1885)
Musgrave, Sir R., *Memoirs of the Different Rebellions in Ireland* (2 vols., Dublin, 1802)
Nares, R., "Principles of government" (London, 1792)
"Protestantism the blessing of Britain" (London, 1810)
Newman, J. H., *Apologia Pro Vita Sua* (New York, 1968)
Newton, T. (Bishop of Bristol), *Works* (London, 1787), I
[Norris, H. H.], *Principles of the Jesuits* (London, 1839)
Norton, J. E., ed., *Letters of Edward Gibbon* (3 vols., London, 1956)
Novalis, *Hymns to the Night and Other Selected Writings* (Indianapolis, 1960)
Nowell, T., "Sermon preached before the . . . House of Commons . . . on . . . January 30, 1772" (London, 1772)

Orange Institution: A Slight Sketch (London, 1813)
"A Parallel; drawn between the administration in the four last years of
    Queen Anne, and the four first of George the Third" (London, 1766)
[Park, Sir J.], *Memoirs of William Stevens, Esq.* (London, 1814)
Parker, C. S., ed., *Sir Robert Peel from his Private Papers* (3 vols., London,
    1891–1899)
Pearce, R. R., *Memoirs and Correspondence of the Most Noble Richard Marquess
    Wellesley* (2 vols., London, 1846)
Pellew, G., *Life and Correspondence of the Right Honourable Henry Addington First
    Viscount Sidmouth* (3 vols., London, 1847)
Peterborough, Bishop of, "Sermon preached before the House of Lords . . .
    on . . . January 30, 1758" (London, 1758)
"Speech delivered in the House of Lords, on Friday, June 7, 1822"
    (London, 1822)
Phipps, E., *Memoirs of the Political and Literary Life of Robert Plumer Ward* (2
    vols., London, 1850)
Playfair, W., *Political Portraits in This New Area* (London, 1813)
Polk, E. C., ed., *Letters of Alaric Alexander Watts from the Blackwood Papers in
    the National Library of Scotland* (Lubbock, 1952)
Polwhele, Rev. R., *Traditions and Recollections* (London, 1826), II
Pottle, F. A., ed., *Boswell in Holland, 1763–1764* (New York, 1952)
    Boswell on the Grand Tour, Germany and Switzerland, 1764 (New York,
    1953)
Pottle, F. A., Bennett, C. H., eds., *Boswell's Journal of a Tour to the Hebrides*
    (New York, 1936)
"The press and the Tories" (London, 1833)
Ramos, C., ed., *Letters of Robert Southey to John May, 1797 to 1838* (Austin,
    1976)
Reed, J. W., ed., *Boswell, Laird of Auchinleck, 1778–1782* (New York, 1977)
Reeves, J., "Considerations on the coronation oath" (London, 1801)
"Thoughts on the English government" (London, 1795)
Richardson, W., "Sermon preached before the . . . House of Commons . . .
    on . . . January 30, 1764" (London, 1764)
Roberts, S. C., ed., *Anecdotes of Samuel Johnson* by Hesther Lynch Piozzi
    (Freeport, New York, 1969)
Robison, J., *Proofs of a Conspiracy against all the Religions and Governments of
    Europe* (Edinburgh, 1797)
Roche, E., *London in A Thousand Years; with Other Poems* (London, 1830)
[Rosebery, Earl of], *Wellesley Papers* (2 vols., London, 1914)
Rosebery, Earl of, ed., *Windham Papers* (2 vols., Boston, 1913)
Russell, Lord J., ed., *Correspondence of John, Fourth Duke of Bedford* (London,
    1843), II
Ryskamp, C., ed., *Boswell: Ominous Years, 1774–1776* (New York, 1963)
Sadler, T., ed., *Diary, Reminiscences, and Correspondence of Henry Crabb Robin-
    son* (2 vols., London, 1869)

St. David's Bishop of, "Sermon preached before the Lords ... on ... January 30, 1762" (London, 1762)

Saunders, B., *Life and Letters of James Macpherson* (London, 1894)

Savage, J., "Account of the London daily newspapers" (London, 1811)

Scott, G., Pottle, F. A., eds., *Private Papers of James Boswell from Malahide Castle in the Collection of Lt. Colonel Ralph Heyward Isham* (privately printed, 1932)

"Second letter from Wiltshire to the *Monitor*" (London, 1759)

Sedgwick, R., ed., *Letters from George III to Lord Bute, 1756–1766* (Westport, Conn., 1981)

[Seeley, R. B.], *Memoirs of the Life and Writings of Michael Thomas Sadler* (London, 1842)

de Selincourt, E., *et al*, eds., *Letters of William and Dorothy Wordsworth* (Oxford, 1967–1979), I–V

Shebbeare, J., "An answer to the queries" (London, 1775)

"Fifth letter to the people of England on the subversion of the *constitution*" (London, 1757)

"First letter to the people of England" (London, 1756)

History of the Sumatrans (2 vols., London, 1763)

"Letters on the English nation" (London, 1755)

Marriage Act: A Novel (London, 1754), II

"Second letter to the people of England" (London, 1755)

"Seventh letter to the people of England" (London, 1758)

"Sixth letter to the people of England on the progress of national ruin" (London, 1757)

Shebbeare, J., ed., *History of the Reign of King Charles the Second from the Revolution to the End of the Year 1667* by Edward Hyde first Earl of Clarendon (London, 1757?), I

Short Account of the Life and Writings of the Rev. William Jones (London, 1801)

Skinner, J., *Annals of Scottish Episcopacy* (Edinburgh, 1818)

Smiles, S., *A Publisher and his Friends: Memoir and Correspondence of the late John Murray* (2 vols., London, 1891)

Smith, W. J., ed., *Grenville Papers* (4 vols., London, 1852–1853)

Smollett, T., *Complete History of England to the ... Treaty of Aix La Chapelle* (London, 1757), III–IV

History of England ... to the Death of George the Second (London, 1811), VI

Southey, C. C., ed., *Life and Correspondence of Robert Southey* (6 vols., London, 1849–1850)

Southey, R., *Essays, Moral and Political* (Shannon, 1971)

Life of Wesley and the Rise and Progress of Methodism (London, 1820), I

Speeches in Parliament of Samuel Horsley, late Bishop of St. Asaph (Dundee, 1813)

Stanhope, Earl, *Life of the Right Honourable William Pitt* (London, 1861), II, III

Stapleton, A. G., *George Canning and his Times* (London, 1859)

Stapleton, E. J., ed., *Some Official Correspondence of George Canning* (2 vols., London, 1887)

Stavordale, Lord, ed., *Further Memoirs of the Whig Party, 1807–1821* by Henry Richard Vassall, third Lord Holland (New York, 1905)

Steuart, A. F., *Last Journals of Horace Walpole* (2 vols., London, 1910)

[Stevens, W.]. "A discourse on the English constitution" (London, 1776) "The revolution vindicated and constitutional liberty asserted ..." (London, 1777)

Strachey, L., Fulford, R., eds., *Greville Memoirs, 1814–1860* (8 vols., London, 1938)

Strout, A. L., "Some unpublished letters of John Gibson Lockhart to John Wilson Crocker," *Notes and Queries*, 189 (25 August 1945)

Surtees, W. W., *Sketch of the Lives of Lords Stowell and Eldon* (London, 1846)

Swartz, H. M. and M., *Disraeli's Reminiscences* (New York, 1976)

Tave, S. M., ed., *New Essays by De Quincey* (Princeton, 1966)

Taylor, J., *Records of My Life* (2 vols., London, 1832)

Taylor, W. S., Pringle, J. H., eds., *Correspondence of William Pitt, Earl of Chatham* (4 vols., London, 1838–1840)

Telford, J., ed., *Letters of the Rev. John Wesley A.M.* (London, 1931), IV–VII

Tomlinson, J. R. G., ed., *Additional Grenville Papers* (Manchester, 1962)

"True Whig displaced" (London, 1762)

Tucker, J., "Four letters on important national subjects addressed to ... Shelburne" (London, 1783)

Twiss, H., *Public and Private Life of Lord Chancellor Eldon* (3 vols., London, 1844)

Van Mildert, W., "Charge" (Oxford, 1831)

An Historical View of the Rise and Progress of Infidelity (London, 1808), I

[Wade, J.], *Extraordinary Black Book* (London, 1832)

Black Book (London, 1820)

Walpole, S., *Life of the Rt. Hon. Spencer Perceval* (London, 1874), I

Warter, J. W., ed., *Selections from the Letters of Robert Southey* (4 vols., London, 1856)

Watts, A. A., *Alaric Watts: A Narrative of his Life* (2 vols., London, 1884)

Weis, C.McC., Pottle, F. A., eds., *Boswell in Extremes, 1776–1778* (New York, 1970)

Wellington, second Duke of, ed., *Civil Correspondence and Memoranda of Field Marshal Arthur Duke of Wellington, K.G.* (15 vols., London, 1858–1872)

Despatches, Correspondence, and Memoranda of Field Marshal Arthur Duke of Wellington (8 vols., London, 1867–1880)

Wellington, seventh Duke of, ed., *Wellington and his Friends* (London, 1965)

Wilberforce, R. I. and S., eds., *Correspondence of William Wilberforce* (2 vols., London, 1840)

Wimsatt, W., *et al*, eds., *Boswell for the Defense, 1769–1774* (New York, 1959)

Wordsworth, C., *Sermons* (London, 1814), II

Wortley, Mrs. E. S., ed., *A Prime Minister and his Son* (London, 1925)

Wraxall, Sir N. W., *Historical Memoirs of My Own Time* (Philadelphia, 1837)

Posthumous Memoirs of His Own Time (Philadelphia, 1845)

SECONDARY SOURCES

PRINTED SECONDARY WORKS

Anstey, R., *Atlantic Slave Trade and British Abolition, 1760–1810* (Atlantic Highlands, N. J., 1975)

Arnstein, W. L., *Protestant versus Catholic in Mid-Victorian England* (Columbia, Mo., 1982)

Aspinall, A., *Politics and the Press* (London, 1949)

Avery, M. E., "Toryism in the age of the American Revolution: John Lind and John Shebbeare," *Historical Studies: Australia and New Zealand*, 18 (April 1978)

Bataille, R. R., "Hugh Kelly's journalism: facts and conjecture," *Journal of Newspaper and Periodical History*, 1, no. 3 (1985)

Bate, W. J., *Samuel Johnson* (New York, 1975)

Beik, P. H., *The French Revolution Seen from the Right, Transactions of the American Philosophical Society*, (Philadelphia, 1956)

Berman, D., "The Irish counter-Enlightenment," in R. Kearney, ed., *The Irish Mind* (Dublin, 1985)

Bird, A., *Damnable Duke of Cumberland* (London, 1966)

Black, E. C., *The Association* (Cambridge, Mass., 1963)

Black, J., *English Press in the Eighteenth Century* (London, 1987)

Blake, R., *Conservative Party from Peel to Churchill* (New York, 1970)

Bowen, D., *Idea of the Victorian Church* (Montreal, 1968)

Bradfield, B. T., "Sir Richard Vyvyan and the fall of Wellington's government," *University of Birmingham Historical Journal*, 11, no. 2 (1968)

Bradford, S., *Disraeli* (New York, 1983)

Bradley, J. E., *Popular Politics and the American Revolution in England* (Macon, 1986)

Brent, R., *Liberal Anglican Politics: Whiggery, Religion, and Reform, 1830–1841* (Oxford, 1987)

Brewer, J., "English radicalism in the age of George III," in J. G. A. Pocock, ed., *Three British Revolutions: 1641, 1688, 1776* (Princeton, 1980)
  "The Misfortunes of Lord Bute," *Historical Journal*, 16 (1973)
  Party Ideology and Popular Politics at the Accession of George III (Cambridge, England, 1976)

Briggs, A., *Making of Modern England, 1784–1867* (New York, 1959)

Brightfield, M. F., *John Wilson Croker* (London, 1940)

Brock, M., *Great Reform Act* (London, 1973)

Bronson, B. J., *Johnson Agonistes and Other Essays* (Cambridge, England, 1946)

Brooke, J., *Chatham Administration, 1776–1768* (London, 1956)

Brose, O. J., *Church and Parliament* (Stanford, 1969)

Brown, F. K., *Fathers of the Victorians: The Age of Wilberforce* (Cambridge, England, 1961)

Browning, R., *Political and Constitutional Ideas of Court Whigs* (Baton Rouge, 1982)

Broxap, H., *Later Non-Jurors* (Cambridge, England, 1924)

Butler, M., *Romantics, Rebels, and Reactionaries* (Oxford, 1981)

Butler, P., *Gladstone: Church, State, and Tractarians* (Oxford, 1982)

Butterfield, H., *George III and the Historians* (New York, 1959)

Cannon, J., *Parliamentary Reform, 1640–1832* (Cambridge, England, 1985)

Carnall, G., *Robert Southey and his Age: The Development of a Conservative Mind* (Oxford, 1960)

Chadwick, O., ed., *Mind of the Oxford Movement* (Stanford, 1967)

Christie, I. R., "The anatomy of the opposition in the parliament of 1784," *Parliamentary History*, 9, pt. 1 (1990)

Crisis of Empire (New York, 1966)

Myth and Reality in Late-Eighteenth-Century British Politics and other Essays (London, 1970)

"Party in politics in the age of Lord North's administration," *Parliamentary History*, 6, pt. 1 (1987)

Stress and Stability in Late Eighteenth-Century Britain (Oxford, 1984)

"The Tory party, Jacobitism and the 'Forty-five: a note," *Historical Journal*, 30 (December 1987)

Claeys, G. *Machinery, Money and the Millenium* (Princeton, 1987)

Clark, J. C. D., "Decline of party, 1740–1760," *English Historical Review*, 93 (July 1978)

Dynamics of Change (Cambridge, England, 1982)

"Eighteenth-century social history," *Historical Journal*, 27 (September 1984)

English Society, 1688–1832 (Cambridge, England, 1985)

"A general theory of party, opposition and government, 1688–1832" *Historical Journal*, 23 (June 1980)

Coleman, B., *Conservatism and the Conservative Party in Nineteenth-Century Britain* (London, 1988)

Colley, L., "Apotheosis of George III," *Past and Present*, 102 (1984)

In Defiance of Oligarchy (Cambridge, England, 1982)

"Eighteenth-century English radicalism before Wilkes," *Transactions of the Royal Historical Society*, 31, 5th ser. (1981)

Cookson, J. E., *Friends of Peace* (Cambridge, England, 1982)

Lord Liverpool's Administration, 1815–1822 (Hamden, Conn., 1975)

Cowling, M. J., *Religion and Public Doctrine in Modern England* (Cambridge, England, 1980)

Cranfield, G. A., *Development of the Provincial Newspaper, 1700–1760* (Oxford, 1962)

Crosby, T. L., *English Farmers and the Politics of Protection, 1815–1852* (Hassocks, Sussex, England, 1977)

Cruickshanks, E., *Political Untouchables: The Tories and the '45* (New York, 1979)

Davis, D. B., *Problem of Slavery in the Age of Revolution, 1770–1823* (Ithaca, 1975)
  Problem of Slavery in Western Culture (Ithaca, 1966)
Deane, S., *French Revolution and Enlightenment in England, 1789–1832* (Cambridge, Mass., 1988)
Ditchfield, G. M., "Subscription issue in British parliamentary politics, 1772–9," *Parliamentary History*, 7, pt. 1 (1988)
Dozier, R. R., *For King, Constitution, and Country* (Lexington, 1983)
Driver, C., *Tory Radical* (New York, 1946)
Ehrman, J., *The Younger Pitt: The Years of Acclaim* (New York, 1969)
Ellis, K., *The Post Office in the Eighteenth Century* (London, 1958)
Emery, J. P., *Arthur Murphy* (Philadelphia, 1946)
Epstein, K., *Genesis of German Conservatism* (Princeton, 1966)
Epstein, W. H., *John Cleland* (New York, 1974)
Erskine-Hill, H., "Literature and the Jacobite Cause," in Eveline Cruickshanks, ed., *Ideology and Conspiracy* (Edinburgh, 1982)
Fay, C. R., *Huskisson and His Age* (London, 1951)
Feiling, K., *Sketches in Nineteenth Century Biography* (London, 1930)
Fitzmaurice, Lord, *Life of William Earl of Shelburne* (London, 1912).
Flick, C., *Birmingham Political Union and the Movement for Reform in Britain, 1830–1839* (Hamden, Conn., 1978)
Fontana, B., *Rethinking the Politics of Commercial Society: the Edinburgh Review, 1802–1832* (Cambridge, England, 1985)
Ford, P. L., *Josiah Tucker and his Writings* (Chicago, n.d.)
Foster, J. R., "Smollett's pamphleteering foe Shebbeare," *PMLA*, 157, no. 4, pt. 1 (December 1942)
Gash, N., *Aristocracy and People* (Cambridge, Mass., 1979)
  Pillars of Government and Other Essays on State and Society, c. 1770–c. 1880 (London, 1986)
  Reaction and Reconstruction in English Politics, 1832–1852 (Oxford, 1965)
Gill, J. C., *Ten Hours Parson* (London, 1959)
Ginter, D. E., "Loyalist Association movement of 1792–3 and British public opinion," *Historical Journal*, 9 (1966)
Godechot, J., *Counter-revolution: Doctrine and Action, 1789–1804* (London, 1972)
Goldie, M., "The non-jurors, episcopacy, and the origins of the Convocation controversy," in E. Cruickshanks, ed., *Ideology and Conspiracy* (Edinburgh, 1982)
Gordon, B., *Economic Doctrine and Tory Liberalism, 1824–1830* (London, 1979)
Graham, W., *English Literary Periodicals* (New York, 1966)
Gray, D., *Spencer Perceval* (Manchester, 1963)
Greene, D. J., *Politics of Samuel Johnson* (New Haven, 1960)
Greenwood, D., *William King, Tory and Jacobite* (Oxford, 1969)
Gunn, J. A. W., *Beyond Liberty and Property* (Kingston, 1983)
Guttridge, G. H., *English Whiggism and the American Revolution* (Berkeley, 1966)

Halévy, E., *Triumph of Reform, 1830–1841* (London, 1950)
Harris, M., *London Newspapers in the Age of Walpole* (Rutherford, N. J., 1987).
Harvey, A. D., *Britain in the Early Nineteenth Century* (London, 1978)
Hill, B. W., *British Parliamentary Parties, 1742–1832* (London, 1985)
Hill, R. L., *Toryism and the People, 1832–1846* (London, 1929)
Himmelfarb, G., *Idea of Poverty* (New York, 1985)
Hindle, W., *Morning Post, 1772–1937* (London, 1937)
History of The Times: "The Thunderer" in the Making, 1785–1841 (New York, 1935)
Hole, R., *Pulpits, Politics and Public Order in England, 1760–1832* (Cambridge, England, 1989)
Jenkins, J. P., "Jacobites and Freemasons in eighteenth-century Wales," *Welsh History Review*, 9 (December 1979)
Jones, C. E., *Smollett Studies* (Berkeley, 1942)
Jones, F., "Society of Sea Serjeants," *Transactions of the Honourable Society of Cymmrodorion* (1967)
Jordan, J. E., *De Quincey to Wordsworth: A Biography of a Relationship* (Berkeley, 1963)
Knapp, L. M., *Tobias Smollett* (Princeton, 1949)
Knatchbull-Hugessen, Sir H., *Kentish Family* (London, 1960)
Kramnick, I., *Rage of Edmund Burke* (New York, 1977)
Langford, P., *First Rockingham Administration* (Oxford, 1973)
   "Old Whigs, old Tories, and the American Revolution," *Journal of Imperial and Commonwealth History* (January 1980)
Lawson, P., "Anatomy of a civil war," *Parliamentary History*, 8 (1989)
Lees-Milne, J., *Last Stuarts* (New York, 1983)
Lenman, B., *Jacobite Risings in Britain, 1689–1746* (London, 1980)
Livermore, H. V., *New History of Portugal* (Cambridge, 1961)
Lockmiller, D. A., *Sir William Blackstone* (Chapel Hill, 1938)
Longford, E., *Wellington: Pillar of State* (New York, 1972)
Lutnick, S., *The American Revolution and the British Press, 1775–1783* (Columbia, Mo., 1967)
McDowell, R. B., *Ireland in the Age of Imperialism and Revolution, 1760–1801* (Oxford, 1979)
Machin, G. I. T., *Catholic Question in English Politics, 1820 to 1830* (Oxford, 1964)
   Politics and the Churches in Great Britain, 1832 to 1868 (Oxford, 1977)
Mann, G., *Secretary of Europe: Life of Friedrich Gentz* (New Haven, 1946)
Mannheim, K., *Essays on Sociology and Social Psychology* (London, 1953)
Mather, F. C., "Georgian churchmanship reconsidered: some variations in Anglican public worship, 1714–1830," *Journal of Ecclesiastical History*, 36 (April 1985)
Maurois, A., *Chateaubriand* (New York, 1969)
Mineka, F. E., *Dissidence of Dissent: The Monthly Repository, 1806–1838* (New York, 1972)

Mitchell, A., "The Association movement of 1792–3," *Historical Journal*, 4 (1961)
Mitchell, L., *Holland House* (London, 1980)
Monod, P. K., *Jacobitism and the English People, 1688–1788* (Cambridge, England, 1989)
de Montluzin, E. L., *The Anti-Jacobin, 1798–1800* (London, 1988)
Moore, D. C., "The Other Face of Reform," *Victorian Studies*, 5, pt. 1 (1961)
Mossner, E. C., *Forgotten Hume: Le Bon David* (New York, 1943)
Namier, Sir L. B., *England in the Age of the American Revolution* (London, 1961)
  Personalities and Powers (New York, 1955)
Namier, Sir L. B., Brooke, J., eds., *History of Parliament: House of Commons, 1754–1790* (3 vols., New York, 1964)
Newman, G., *Rise of English Nationalism* (New York, 1987)
O'Gorman, F., *Emergence of the British Two-Party System, 1760–1832* (London, 1982)
  The Rise of Party in England: Rockingham Whigs, 1760–1782 (London, 1975)
  Voters, Patrons, and Parties: The Unreformed Electoral System of Hanoverian England, 1743–1832 (Oxford, 1989)
Osborne, J. W., *William Cobbett: His Thought and His Times* (New Brunswick, N. J., 1966)
Owen, J. B., "Survival of country attitudes in the eighteenth-century House of Commons," in Bromley, J. S., Kossmann, E. H., eds., *Britain and the Netherlands: Metropolis, Dominion and Province* (The Hague, 1971), IV
Patterson, M. W., *Sir Francis Burdett and his Times (1770–1841)* (London, 1931)
Pencak, W., *America's Burke: The Mind of Thomas Hutchinson* (Washington, 1982)
Perkin, H., *Origins of Modern English Society, 1780–1880* (London, 1969)
Perry, T. W., *Public Opinion, Propaganda, and Politics in Eighteenth-Century England* (Cambridge, Mass., 1962)
Peters, M., "Names and cant," *Parliamentary History*, 3 (1984)
  Pitt and Popularity (Oxford, 1980)
Phillips, J. A., *Electoral Behavior in Unreformed England* (Princeton, 1982)
  "From municipal matters to parliamentary principles," *Journal of British Studies*, 27 (October 1988)
Phillips, W., "William Cartwright, non-juror, and his chronological history of Shrewsbury," *Transactions of the Shropshire Archaeological and Natural History Society*, 4, 4th ser. (1914)
Pocock, J. G. A., *Virtue, Commerce, and History* (Cambridge, England, 1985)
Popkin, J., *Right-wing Press in France, 1792–1800* (Chapel Hill, 1980)
Quinton, A., *The Politics of Imperfection* (London, 1978)
Randall, H. W., "Rise and fall of a martyrology: sermons on Charles I," *Huntington Library Quarterly*, 10 (February 1947)

Rea, R. R., *English Press in Politics, 1760–1774* (Lincoln, 1963)
Rémond, R., *The Right Wing in France* (Philadelphia, 1966)
Reynolds, J. S., *Evangelicals at Oxford, 1735–1871* (Oxford, 1953)
Ritcheson, C. R., *British Politics and the American Revolution* (Norman, 1954)
Roberts, J. D., "The Society for the Suppression of Vice and its early critics, 1802–1812," *Historical Journal*, 26 (March 1983)
Roberts, J. M., "The French origins of the right," *Transactions of the Royal Historical Society*, 23, 5th ser. (1973)
  Mythology of Secret Societies (London, 1972)
Rose, J. H., *William Pitt and the Great War* (London, 1911)
Rose, R. B., "The Priestley riots of 1791," *Past and Present* 18 (November 1960)
Rupp, G., *Religion in England, 1688–1791* (Oxford, 1986)
Sack, J. J., "The memory of Burke and the memory of Pitt," *Historical Journal*, 30 (September 1987)
  "Wellington and the Tory press, 1828–1830," in N. Gash, ed., *Wellington* (Manchester, 1990)
Sadleir, M., *Bulwer: A Panorama* (London, 1931)
de Sauvigny, G. de B., *Bourbon Restoration* (Philadelphia, 1966)
Schweizer, K., Klein, R., "The French revolution and developments in the London daily press to 1793," *Publishing History*, 18 (1985)
Sedgwick, R., *History of Parliament: House of Commons, 1715–1754* (New York, 1970)
Senior, H., *Orangeism in Ireland and Britain, 1795–1836* (London, 1966)
Shine, H. and H. C., *The Quarterly Review under Gifford* (Chapel Hill, 1949)
Sledd, J., Kalb, G., "Johnson's definitions of Whig and Tory," *PMLA*, 67 (September 1952)
Soloway, R. A., *Prelates and People* (London, 1969)
Spalding, P., *Oglethorpe: A Brief Biography* (Macon, 1984)
Spector, R. D., *English Literary Periodicals and the Climate of Opinion During the Seven Years' War* (The Hague, 1966)
Stewart, R., *Foundation of the Conservative Party, 1830–1867* (London, 1978)
Sullivan, A., ed., *British Literary Magazines: Augustan Age and the Age of Johnson* (Westport, Conn., 1983)
  British Literary Magazines: The Romantic Age (1789–1836) (Westport, Conn., 1983)
Sutherland, L. S., Mitchell, L. G., eds., *History of the University of Oxford* v: *Eighteenth Century* (Oxford, 1986)
Taylor, S., "Sir Robert Walpole, the Church of England, and the Quaker tithe bill of 1736," *Historical Journal*, 28 (March 1985)
Temperley, H., *Foreign Policy of Canning, 1822–1827* (London, 1925)
Thomas, P. D. G., "Sir Roger Newdigate's essays on party, c. 1760," *English Historical Review*, 102 (April 1987)
Thomas, W., *Philosophical Radicals* (Oxford, 1979)
Thompson, E. P., *Making of the English Working Class* (New York, 1966)

"Moral economy of the English crowd in the eighteenth century," *Past and Present* (1971)

Whigs and Hunters (New York, 1975)

Thorne, R. G., *History of Parliament: House of Commons, 1790–1820* (5 vols., London, 1986)

Thrall, M. M. H., *Rebellious Fraser's* (New York, 1934)

Valentine, A., *Lord North* (Norman, 1967)

Wain, J., *Samuel Johnson* (New York, 1974)

Walcott, R., *English Politics in the Early Eighteenth Century* (Cambridge, Mass., 1956)

Ward, J. T., *Factory Movement, 1830–1855* (London, 1962)

Ward, W. R., *Georgian Oxford* (Oxford, 1958)

Waterman, A. M. C., *Revolution, Economics and Religion: Christian Political Economy, 1798–1833* (Cambridge, England, 1991)

Webster, A. B., *Joshua Watson: Story of a Layman, 1771–1855* (London, 1954)

Werkmeister, L., *The London Daily Press, 1772–1792* (Lincoln, 1963)

A Newspaper History of England, 1792–1793 (Lincoln, 1967)

Western, J. R., "The Volunteer movement as an anti-revolutionary force, 1793–1801," *English Historical Review*, 71 (October 1956)

Wood, G., "Conspiracy and the paranoid style," *William and Mary Quarterly*, 39 (July 1982)

Zimmer, A. Y., *Jonathan Boucher: Loyalist in Exile* (Detroit, 1978)

Zimmer, A. Y., Kelly, A. H., "Jonathan Boucher: Constitutional conservative," *Journal of American History*, 58 (March 1972)

UNPUBLISHED THESES

Begemann, R. E., "English press and the French Revolution, 1789–1793," Ph.D. dissertation (Emory University, 1973)

Bradford, B. T., "Sir Richard Vyvyan and Tory politics with special reference to the period 1825–46," Ph.D. dissertation (University of London, 1965)

Chapman, P. M., "Jacobite political argument in England, 1714–1766," Ph.D. dissertation (Cambridge University, 1983)

Haydon, C. M., "Anti-Catholicism in eighteenth-century England, c. 1714–c. 1780," D.Phil. thesis (Oxford University, 1985)

Monod, P. K., "For the king to come into his own again: Jacobite political culture in England, 1688–1788," Ph.D. dissertation (Yale University, 1985)

Murray, N. U., "The influence of the French Revolution on the Church of England and its rivals, 1789–1802," D.Phil. thesis (Oxford University, 1975).

Nockles, P. B., "Continuity and change in Anglican High Churchmanship in Britain, 1792–1850," D.Phil. thesis (Oxford University, 1982)

Pendleton, G. T., "English conservative propaganda during the French Revolution, 1789–1802," Ph.D. dissertation (Emory University, 1976)

Simes, D. G. S., "Ultra Tories in British politics, 1824–1834," D.Phil. thesis (Oxford University, 1974)

Index